Called by the Gospel

Called By The Gospel
Introductions to Christian History and Thought
From a Distinctly Lutheran Perspective

Volume 1
Called to Be God's People: An Introduction to the Old Testament
Andrew E. Steinmann, editor

Called to Be God's People, Abridged Edition:
An Introduction to the Old Testament
Michael Eschelbach, Editor

Volume 2
Called by the Gospel: An Introduction to the New Testament
Michael P. Middendorf and Mark Schuler

Volume 3
Called to Believe, Teach and Confess: An Introduction to Doctrinal Theology
Stephen P. Mueller, editor

Called to Believe
(Abridged Edition)
Stephen P. Mueller, editor

Called To Be God's People
Abridged Edition

An Introduction to the Old Testament

Andrew E. Steinmann
Michael Eschelbach
Curtis Giese
Paul Puffe

WIPF & STOCK · Eugene, Oregon

CALLED TO BE GOD'S PEOPLE, ABRIDGED EDITION

Wipf & Stock
An imprint of Wipf and Stock Publishers
199 W. 8th Avenue, Suite 3
Eugene OR, 97401
www.wipfandstock.com

ISBN : 978-1-4982-2908-1

Manufactured in the U.S.A.

Table of Contents

Section 5: The Prophets

Section 6: Beyond the Old Testament

Foreword

For Christians the study of the Old Testament is not simply a historical exercise or a prelude to the study of the New Testament. Instead, it is part-and-parcel of the entire message of God about the redemption of sinful humans through the promised Messiah, a promise fulfilled in Christ Jesus. The Old Testament anticipates the New, and without it the New Testament cannot be fully understood.

This textbook was written by authors who "accept without reservation...the Scriptures of the Old and the New Testament as the written Word of God and the only rule and norm of faith and of practice..." and who also accept "...all the Symbolical Books of the Evangelical Lutheran Church as a true and unadulterated statement and exposition of the Word of God."[1] Therefore, readers will find a distinctively Luthearn approach to understanding the Old Testament in these pages: the proper distinction of Law and Gospel, the centrality of Christ in the interpretation of Scripture and the acknowledgement that God works through the Means of Grace to apply the salvation won by Jesus to fallen, sinful humans—among many other Lutheran distinctives.

Designed primarily for use with a one-semester undergraduate introductory course on the Old Testament, it is also hoped that for many who use this book in that setting or others, it will also serve as a basic reference work once the course has been completed. To that end, instructors will note that the contents are not arranged in order to make planning of one's syllabus straightforward, but in order to organize the material for the benefit of students and other users. The chapters are divided into six sections. The four sections that treat the literature of the Old Testament itself each have an introductory chapter that serves as an overview of important topics that span an entire section of the Old Testament.

Sections 2–5 introduce the individual books of the Old Testament divided in the traditional Christian manner into Pentateuch, Historical Books, Poetry and Wisdom and the Prophets. The sections on Pentateuch and Historical Books are arranged as in Christian Bibles, following the narrative of God's dealing with Israel in chronological order. The section on Poetry and Wisdom also follows the order of these books in the Bible, which one could reasonably argue is also roughly chronological according to their date of composition. However, the section on the prophets follows a chronological, not canonical order. This is intended to help the student place each prophet into his historical context and to better understand the connections among the prophets, especially those who were contemporaries of one another.

---

[1] Constitution of the Lutheran Church—Missouri Synod, Article II.

The final section consists of one chapter that summarizes important issues and historical developments in the intertestamental period. The focus here is on developments and themes that arose out of the Old Testament during this period. At the same time, this chapter begins a transition to the New Testament era and provides an overlap with *Called by the Gospel*, the New Testament introduction in the *Called by the Gospel Series*. This overlap is intentional. That volume contains its own chapter on the intertestamental period, but with a focus on issues and movements that arose during the intertestamental period and had an impact on the New Testament and its times. Thus, the editors have purposely devised these two volumes to dovetail with each other and, hopefully provide a seamless transition from one to the other.

Instructors will also note that several chapters treat more than one book of the Old Testament. Books that belong together by virtue of chronology (i.e., Judges and Ruth or Ezra, Nehemiah and Esther) or because they are from prophets who were roughly contemporary (e.g., Jonah, Amos and Hosea) were grouped this way for the benefit of students. Instructors may wish to distribute the reading assignments for some of these chapters over several class periods (see especially Chapter 27—Jeremiah, Lamentations, Ezekiel and Daniel).

Finally, instructors will note a distinctive feature of this introduction to the Old Testament: not only are isogogical issues discussed for each book of the Old Testament, but also many important pericopes and their meaning as well as their impact on the New Testament are explored. Since this textbook will often serve as the only Old Testament text in the only undergraduate Old Testament course taken by undergraduates who are training either to be workers in the church or are attending a Christian university or college but preparing for other professions, more than a simple isogogical introduction is appropriate. Unlike a seminary introduction that is able to assume that students will take a series of hermeneutically-oriented classes on specific biblical books, courses at the undergraduate level often are the only chance to discuss not only facts *about* the Old Testament, but also specific passages *in* the Old Testament.

This introduction, along with the other three volumes in the *Called by the Gospel Series* is offered to the church in hope that it can help students and other readers to be better equipped to give the world a reason for the hope in Jesus Christ that all Christian possess (1 Pet 3:15).

Soli Deo Gloria.

Andrew E. Steinmann

Abbreviations for Books of the Bible

Gen	Genesis	Matt	Matthew
Exod	Exodus	Mark	Mark
Lev	Leviticus	Luke	Luke
Num	Numbers	John	John
Josh	Joshua	Acts	Acts
Judg	Judges	Rom	Romans
Ruth	Ruth	1–2 Cor	1–2 Corinthians
1–2 Sam	1–2 Samuel	Gal	Galatians
1–2 Kgs	1–2 Kings	Eph	Ephesians
1–2 Chr	1–2 Chronicles	Phil	Philippians
Ezra	Ezra	Col	Colossians
Neh	Nehemiah	1–2 Thess	1–2 Thessalonians
Esth	Esther	1–2 Tim	1–2 Timothy
Job	Job	Titus	Titus
Ps	Psalms	Phlm	Philemon
Prov	Proverbs	Heb	Hebrews
Eccl	Ecclesiastes	Jas	James
Song	Song of Songs	1–2 Pet	1–2 Peter
Isa	Isaiah	1–2–3 John	1–2–3 John
Jer	Jeremiah	Jude	Jude
Ezek	Ezekiel	Rev	Revelation
Dan	Daniel		
Hos	Hosea		
Joel	Joel		
Amos	Amos		
Obad	Obadiah		
Jonah	Jonah		
Mic	Micah		
Nah	Nahum		
Hab	Habakkuk		
Zeph	Zephaniah		
Hag	Haggai		
Zech	Zechariah		
Mal	Malachi		

Section 1
Introduction

1
Reading and Understanding the Bible

The Bible is, probably, the most commonly printed and sold book in the world. It has been read and studied in many languages. It has been and continues to be a book for all people, times and places. Yet each of the books that make up the Bible were originally written for a specific group of people at a particular place at a particular time. Not only do modern readers of the Bible face the challenge of understanding a different time, place and culture every time they open its pages, but most also are reading it in a very different language than the ones in which its authors wrote.

This book is an introduction to the first major portion of the Bible, the Old Testament. As we look at the various books that make up the Old Testament, we will learn to understand the time, place and culture that each book of this collection addressed. In this chapter we will begin by learning some basic principles that have traditionally shaped Christian understanding of what the Bible is and, therefore, how it is to be understood. In addition, we will look at what it means to read the Bible (or any book, for that matter) in languages other than the ones in which it was originally written.

1. Basic Christian Presuppositions About Reading and Understanding the Bible—*What Principles Guide Us in Reading the Bible?*
2. Reading the Bible in English Translation—*What Do Bible Translators Do, and What Does this Mean for the Reader?*
3. Helps for Studying the Bible—*The Types of Resources Available that Aid in Studying the Bible*

1. Basic Christian Presuppositions about Reading and Understanding the Bible

When we pick up something to read—whether it is a book, newspaper, magazine or a letter from a friend—we have a number of presuppositions about what we expect to read and how we will go about the task of understanding the text we will be reading. This is true before we begin to read the first sentence on the first page. As we read we may change our presuppositions because the text we are reading requires us to adjust our expectations, but we always have presuppositions. If we open a newspaper, we expect to find quite different types of texts on the front page, the editorial page, the sports page, the crossword puzzle and the comics. If we have read quite a few newspapers in our lifetime, we know generally what to expect in each of these sections of a newspaper, and we presuppose that the comics will be written primarily to entertain us while the editorials will be primarily written to express an opinion and persuade us. (However, comics may at times seek to express opinions and persuade and editorials may sometimes contain some elements intended to entertain us).

What presuppositions have Christians brought to the reading of the Bible? First, we should note that Christians consider the Bible to be **Scripture**. This term implies that the Bible is holy because it is God's *written* word. (The English word *scripture* comes from Latin *scriptus*, the act of writing). That the Bible is *God's* word and that it was specifically and purposefully *written* for humans to read leads to a number of principles that form the foundation for Christian understanding of what the Bible is and how we should read it. Secondly, we should understand that Christians look to the Scriptures and find that they tell us what they themselves are and how to understand and apply them.

Inspiration

Christians understand the Bible to be inspired by God. (*Inspired* because God placed his *Spirit in* those who wrote.) This **inspiration** means that although the Bible was written by humans in their own language and with their own vocabulary, the Holy Spirit guided them so that the Scripture they wrote is entirely the Word of God in all its parts and in every word. Thus, inspiration affirms both the human and divine contributions to Scripture, but acknowledges that ultimately the Scriptures are not merely a collection of human compositions, but are the actual words used by God to tell us his message to us. Several passages in the Bible affirm this working of God through his chosen messengers:

> These are the last words of David: The oracle of David, son of Jesse, the oracle of the man lifted high, the anointed one of the God of Jacob, the sweet singer of Israel's songs, "The Spirit of Yahweh speaks to me. His words are on my tongue." (2 Sam 23:1–2)

> All this took place to fulfill what was spoken by the Lord through the prophet... (Matt 1:22)

> For prophecy was produced, not by the human will, but men spoke from God as they were carried by the Holy Spirit. (2 Peter 1:21)

This belief in the inspiration of the actual words of Scripture is called **verbal inspiration**. It means that inspiration was more than simply a special guidance that gave the biblical writers their general thoughts. Moreover, it means that although God's people have written many helpful works, only the Scriptures are the inspired Word of God.

The Purpose of Scripture

God inspired the Scriptures—but for what reason? What is the purpose of the Bible? Why should Christians—or anyone else—read it? Christians have always considered the central purpose of the Bible to reveal Jesus and what he has done for all people. From Genesis to Revelation, it is a witness to God's saving activity as it is first promised to God's Old Testament people Israel and then fulfilled in Jesus.

In order to understand this purpose of Scripture and apply it to ourselves, we must understand that through faith in Jesus Christ we receive forgiveness and life. Only when read from this perspective can one truly understand and correctly use the Scriptures. This requires properly distinguishing two important doctrines of Scripture as we read God's Word—**Law** and **Gospel**. The Law tells us what God requires of us. Thus, whenever we read any commands in the Bible, whenever it demands that we behave in a certain way or have proper attitudes, we are reading Law. Whenever a passage in the Bible condemns sin and sinners and threatens God's punishment, it is Law. Thus, when a portion of the Bible tells us about sin and its consequences, especially death, it is Law.

On the other hand, the Gospel (from Old English *Godspell*, good news) tells us what God has done *for* us, especially what he has done in Jesus to deliver us from sin and death. Whenever we read a promise of God to do something for us that we have not earned or deserved, we are reading Gospel. Whenever the Bible reminds us that God is our Savior who has done for us what we cannot do for ourselves, it is Gospel. These two doctrines work together to point us to God's central purpose—to save us from eternal death and make us his people and members of his eternal kingdom. Jesus reminded his contemporaries,

You search the Scriptures because you think that you have eternal life in them, and they testify about me. (John 5:39)

Thus, Christians do not believe that it is enough only to understand the facts presented in Scripture. Those facts must always be related to Jesus and his work of salvation. Moreover, Christians from the beginning have believed that the Old Testament, when rightly understood, also bears witness to Jesus (Luke 24:25–27, 44; John 1:45; 5:39; Acts 26:22–23; 28:23).

In addition, the Scriptures tie the acts of God to save us in Christ to the historical events that take place in its pages. Thus, to question whether the historical events in Scripture took place or to doubt their truthfulness involves questioning the Gospel itself. For this reason, Christians have traditionally accepted the Bible's historical accuracy. We can certainly investigate the Bible's historical claims. When there is sufficient historical records to compare to a historical fact reported in the Bible, those claims will be proved accurate. However, the Bible's authority is not dependent on the judgment of historians but on the authority of God who inspired its writers.

The Gospel

Although the Bible's two outstanding doctrines are Law and Gospel, the Gospel, not the Law is the chief doctrine of Scripture and the center of the Christian faith. The Bible, as God's revealed word, establishes what the Gospel is. Thus, the Gospel is the **material principle** of Christian theology, because it is the substance or *material* of the Christian faith: God's declaration of forgiveness to the sinner who believes in Jesus as the Savior from sin. (Thus, the material principle of any theology is its most important or central principle.) The Scriptures themselves tell us this when they say:

> To this man [Jesus] all the prophets witness that all who believe in him receive
> forgiveness of sins through his name. (Acts 10:43)

The Scriptures provide the **formal principle** of the Christian faith because God's revelation in the Bible provides the *form* for the Gospel as it tells us about all that Christ has done for us through his life, death and resurrection. (Thus, the formal principle of any theology is its source or sources of theological information.) That is why Acts 10:43 speaks of the *prophets* as witnesses to the Gospel.[2]

When reading the Bible it is important not to confuse these two principles. For instance, it is often tempting to make acceptance of the Bible's authority the heart and center of the Christian faith (turning the formal principle of the Christian faith into the material principle). However, it is belief in Christ, not trust in the authority of the Bible, that makes one a Christian. While the Bible's authority is important, Christians do not accept the Scriptures for their own sake. In-

---

[2] Not all Christians recognize the same material and formal principles. For instance in Roman Catholic theology the formal principle is Scripture plus tradition. For some Christian theologies the formal principle is Scripture plus human reason.

stead, the Gospel is the center of Christian belief, and the Bible is the witness to the Gospel.

On the other hand, it is sometimes urged that all doctrines should be judged by the Gospel (turning the material principle into the formal principle). For instance, it is sometimes argued that Christians should believe or act a certain way because of the Gospel, without any clear mandate of Scripture or even contrary to what the Scriptures say. However, the Gospel is not an authority used to distinguish articles of doctrine. Instead, it is the central doctrine taught by God through his Word.

The Authority of Scripture

If the Scriptures are an authority for Christians, what kind of authority do they possess? Most importantly, Christians have understood that as the Scriptures present the Gospel, they have the authority and the power to bring people to faith in Christ. The Bible mentions this **causative authority** of God's Word several times, including John 20:31 and Romans 1:16

> ...these things are written that you might believe that Jesus is the Christ, the Son of God, and that as you believe, you will have life in this name. (John 20:31)

> I am not ashamed of the Gospel, because it is the power of God for salvation to everyone who believes—to the Jew first of all, and then to the Greek. (Romans 1:16)

In addition, Christians, especially Lutherans, have also recognized the Scriptures as the only standard of Christian doctrine and life.[3] It establishes what Christians believe and how they ought to live. This is the **normative authority** of God's Word, because God's Word provides a norm or standard for all Christian doctrine and life. Scripture itself praises those who use it as the only authority for Christian doctrine.

> These Jews [in Berea] were nobler than those in Thessalonica. They received the word with all eagerness, examining the Scriptures daily to see whether these things were so. (Acts 17:11)

---

[3] While all Christians have acknowledged the authority of Scripture, not all of them recognize it as the only authority to establish doctrine. Lutherans, however, recognize no other authority that is able to determine what Christians should believe.

Therefore, as Christians read the Scriptures, they understand them to be the judge of all doctrines, and they use them to distinguish between what is proper for Christians to believe and what is not proper. Christians accept this authority of Scripture by faith. Indeed, non-Christians often read the Bible and reject its claims of authority.

The causative and normative authorities of God's Word are two aspects of same power of the Scriptures. Therefore, one cannot separate them. For instance, we cannot limit the authority of the Scriptures to the power to bring us to faith in Christ, since they not only tell us about Jesus in general terms, but they also specifically tell us the significance of what Jesus did and what it means for us (the Gospel). Therefore the Scriptures have authority not only in what they *do* (bring people to faith), but also in what they *say*.

The authority of Scripture ultimately lies in its nature as God's Word and not because it is the best available source for the history of Israel or the life of Jesus or because it was written by recognized leaders of God's people in the past or because the church has declared it to be authoritative. While these other observations about Scripture may be true, they are not sufficient reasons to establish the Bible as the Christian's ultimate authority. The authority of the Scriptures derives from God himself who inspired them.

Scripture is Without Error

Since Christians accept the Bible as God's Word, they have traditionally also believed its claims to be without error in everything it says. The Bible says of God's Word,

> The sum of your word is true. All of your righteous ordinances are forever. (Psalm 119:160)

> Your word is truth. (John 17:17b)

Thus, the words *inerrant* (without error) and *infallible* (incapable of erring) describe the trustworthiness of the Scriptures.

While some have found what they believe to be contradictions in the Bible, Christians have often viewed these as only items that appear to be contradictions due to our incomplete knowledge of the times, places and cultures that form the setting of the Bible. At other times, the apparent contradictions may be due to someone's misunderstanding of what a passage in the Bible is saying, not because of what the Bible actually says. Thus, many Christians reject the assertions that the Bible contains errors in theology or history or any other area about which they speak. This means that the Scriptures are not only true with respect to the Gospel, but also in all respects—even when they speak of things that affect our view of historical and scientific truth.

Not everyone regards the Scriptures as inerrant and reads them as if they were. However, Christians have often recognized that to read the Bible and allow human reason to determine what is correct and incorrect in its pages is to allow an authority other than God's Word to determine what is true. This endangers the Gospel, since it would mean that humans could determine whether or not any specific teaching of the Gospel was true (for instance, whether Jesus really rose from the dead).

The Unity of Scripture

By collecting the various books of the Bible into one book, Christians have made a statement about the unity of the message throughout these various writings. Although there is a rich variety of language and style in the Bible, and although the books of the Bible were written over a number of centuries at different places, Christians have regarded the Scriptures as united in their message of the one doctrine of the Gospel and all its parts. Traditionally Christians have not looked for conflicting or contradictory theologies in the Bible, but have believed that there is one, united Gospel taught from Genesis to Revelation. Jesus claimed that the Gospel (that we find in the New Testament) was the same as Moses' teaching in the Old Testament when he said,

> If you believed Moses, you would believe me, because he wrote about me. But if you do not believe him, how will you believe my words? (John 5:46–47)

Prophecy and Fulfillment

Because Christians see a unity throughout the Bible, they also see a connection between the Old and New Testaments. The Old Testament points forward to Jesus and his work, while the New Testament tells us how Jesus fulfilled the Old Testament prophecies. Therefore, when the New Testament speaks of an Old Testament passage as fulfilled by Jesus, Christians view this as the full and correct meaning of the Old Testament passage. Moreover, these Old Testament prophecies can only correctly be understood in their fullest sense through their fulfillment in the New Testament. This means that from the beginning Christians have acknowledged that there are Messianic prophecies (from Hebrew *Meshiah* = Greek *Christos* = English *Anointed One*) throughout the Old Testament. It also means that Christians have looked to the New Testament to establish the correct meaning of these Old Testament passages.

Therefore, Old Testament passages are not reinterpreted to be about Jesus by the New Testament, but this was their meaning all along, even if not every ancient Israelite reader of the Old Testament books understood this. Many Israelites and the prophets in particular, however, understood the prophecies to be about the **Messiah**, as the Bible reminds us:

> Your ancestor Abraham rejoiced that he would see my day. He saw it and was glad. (John 8:56)

> Isaiah said these things because he saw his glory and spoke about him [the Christ]. (John 12:41)

> Now a Jew, a certain man named Apollos, a native of Alexandria, an eloquent man, came to Ephesus. He was well-versed in the Scriptures....He vigorously refuted the Jews in public by demonstrating by the Scriptures that Jesus was the Christ. (Acts 18:24, 28)

Historical Methods and Biblical Interpretation

Much of the Bible reports historical events, and we can study the Bible's view of that history. Does this mean that we can use the same methods that historians use to understand past events that the Bible records? We certainly must understand the history of the Bible, and we must place its historical events into their proper setting in time to understand them correctly. However, we cannot simply adopt all of the methods that historians use to study other historical documents. First of all, historians are accustomed to look at each document from history and question the reliability every fact it presents. At times they will discount some passages in documents that have been handed down because they believe they are inaccurate or reflect a bias on the part of the author.

Christians who believe that God is the ultimate author of Scripture (since it is his word) reject the notion that the Bible can be correctly read and examined in the same way that other historical documents are read. While it presents historical information, because Scripture is the Word of God, faith in God and his trustworthiness guides Christians in reading the Bible. Historical information about biblical times is helpful in understanding the Bible, but not all of the presuppositions that secular historians use to examine historical documents apply to the reading and study of the Bible.

For instance, a Christian reading of the Bible rejects the idea that one can assume that God does not intervene in history and, therefore, rejects the assertion that the miracles mentioned in the Bible did not actually take place. This type of thinking, however, has led some to deny miracles, including Jesus' resurrection. Another example would be the denial of any supernatural presence in the Bible, such as denying the existence of angels or of the devil.

These are the principles that Christians have often brought with them in reading the Bible. Not everyone fully accepts these principles, even among those who are members of Christian churches. However, these principles derive from the Scriptures themselves, and guide how Christians by faith in God read the Bible.

Nevertheless, it is important to understand that everyone who reads the Bible reads it from a perspective of faith. For Christians this perspective is faith in Jesus. For Jews who regard only the Old Testament as God's Word, their faith in other principles guides their reading and understanding of the Bible. Non-Christians, many of whom may believe in other gods or in no god whatsoever, may read the Bible with other presuppositions. Yet those different presuppositions are also a form of faith, either in other gods and non-Christian theologies or faith in human ability alone to explain and understand the events and message contained in the Bible. Although some would want us to believe there is a neutral non-faith-based approach to reading the Bible, in reality such an approach does not exist. Thus, it is not a matter of a faith-based approach versus an objective approach to reading the Bible that separates Christians and non-Christians. Instead, it is a matter of what or whom one believes and trusts. Christians base their interpretation of the Bible upon the Gospel as revealed by God. Others have different guiding principles that often lead them to very different understandings of the meaning of Scripture because their ultimate trust is in some other god or in human ability. Christians have rejected these ways of reading the Bible as incorrect because they deny the gift of eternal life won by Christ through his life, death and resurrection.

Historical-Critical Interpretation

Until the eighteenth century, the overwhelming majority of Christians accepted the Bible's own testimony about itself and the historical facts it presents as accurate and truthful. However, with the rise of the Enlightenment in Europe around 1700 a new way of looking and analyzing the Bible arose. Enlightenment philosophers placed humans at the center of thought and knowledge as the judge and measure of all things, the Bible included. This called for a thorough questioning of the Bible and its origins.

Once started, this method of reading and interpreting the Bible led, by the end of the nineteenth century, to the rise of **Historical-Criticism**, also called **Higher Criticism**. This method has as its foundations critical historical analysis with human reason as the ultimate judge to evaluate the Bible's claims. The history presented in the Bible and the Bible itself are subjected to critical investigation, to doubt and to verification, by methods devised by the critics themselves. This is not criticism in the negative sense, but in the academic sense of investigation of literary documents (including the Bible) about such matters as origin, text, composition, and history. This type of criticism is often used to determine the origin of ancient documents.

At the root of the method is the employment of secular, rational thought and the assumption that no document, not even the Bible, is to be automatically trusted as truthful. Instead, it is to be tested, investigated and judged by human standards. Historical-critical investigation may judge some parts to be accurate while other parts are judged to be inaccurate or biased by the writer's ideology and assumptions. Some more important methods used by historical critics include:

3. Helps for Studying the Bible

A number of useful aids for studying the Bible are available. Many of these are printed in various editions of the Bible, while others are separate volumes. Among the most useful are:

Cross–references: Many Bibles contain a center column that lists Bible passages that share similar words, themes, subjects or events with the verses on the page. These references are often keyed to particular verses in the text. These cross-references can help in comparing similar parts of Scripture to one another.

Concordances: A concordance is a list of words that are used in the Bible with a list of passages where they are used. Many Bibles contain abbreviated concordances in the back. These often list only the most important words. Also available are separate books that are complete or exhaustive concordances. These list all the words that occur in a particular Bible translation (except very common words such as *a, an, the, is, are*, etc.). Concordances are useful tools that can be used to study how a word is used or to find a passage that mentions a particular word.

Bible Atlases: While many Bibles contain basic maps relating to the places mentioned in the Bible, more complete and thorough Bibles atlases are available. Often these atlases not only contain a wide variety of maps for every era of biblical history, but they also may contain other information, including background on the history, culture and places relating to the Bible, useful illustrations and photographs, timelines of biblical events and important events in ancient history or other information.

Bible Dictionaries/Encyclopedias: A wide variety of Bible dictionaries or encyclopedias have been published. Some are one-volume works, while others consist of several hefty volumes. These works contain articles related to important themes, persons, places and events listed by topic headings arranged in alphabetical order. Many also have a short bibliography at the end of each article as a guide for those who wish to do further study. The entries in these works are chosen by editors to cover important aspects of the Scriptures and often include subjects relating to the Bible, but not directly from its pages. The articles are often a good introduction to the study of specific questions that arise about the Bible.

Commentaries: Books that explore the setting, purpose and meaning of the Bible or one of its books are useful for detailed study of the Bible. Commentaries come in various sizes and are written for various types of readers, from beginners to biblical scholars. One-volume Bible commentaries are often written to be guides for non-specialists who wish to know more about the Bible's meaning. Some commentaries are more detailed and cover the entire Bible in two or more volumes. Some commentaries are part of a series. These series often have one or more volumes for each of the longer books of the Bible, but may combine comments on several shorter books into one volume. These series can cover either the Old or New Testament or the entire Bible and may be thirty or more volumes. Some commentaries cover only one book of Scripture or several smaller books of Scripture and are not part of a larger series. Commentaries may provide insight into the meaning of the Bible, explain customs and historical events that shaped the biblical test, explore the history of interpretation of the Bible, as well as set forth the view of the writer or of those who share his religious convictions.

Bible Software: A number of software packages are available to enhance study of the Bible. These often include various Bible translations in English or other languages that enable users to perform customized concordance work for words or phrases used in the Bible. Some more sophisticated programs contain the Hebrew and Greek texts of the Bible and related ancient documents. Many also have electronic versions of other Bible helps, including atlases, dictionaries, timelines and cross-references, as well as numbering systems that match words in English translations to the Hebrew or Greek words that they translate. A few also contain lexicons that provide detailed information on the meanings of Greek and Hebrew words that occur in the Bible.

2
Introducing the Old Testament

Before departing on that long vacation in your car you have probably done a good bit of acquainting yourself with the sights along the way. You have looked at the roadmap, checked brochures on the sights you may want to see, and learned a little about the people and places you will be visiting. This type of glance ahead is not only helpful for vacations, but also is useful before plunging into reading the Old Testament. In this chapter we will first check the road map by looking at the Old Testament books as a collection. Then we will become acquainted with the people, places and times that form the matrix against which the stories of the Old Testament are set.

1. The Canon of the Old Testament—*The Collection of Books that Comprise the Old Testament*
2. Geography of the Old Testament—*An Overview of the Places Important for the Old Testament's Story*
3. The Social and Cultural World of the Old Testament—*An Overview of the Human Dimension of the Old Testament*
4. Old Testament History—*An Overview of Old Testament Times*

1. The Canon of the Old Testament

The Old Testament is a collection of books. The word used to describe the set of books that comprise this collection is **canon**. Derived from the Greek word for *measuring rod*, a canon is a collection of authoritative and divinely inspired books accepted as such by an overwhelming majority in a religious community. Several religious traditions recognize the Old Testament canon, though they may differ on the order in which the books are to be listed or whether some additional books are to be placed alongside the books that others accept.

The History of the Canon as a Collection

While the history of how the books of the Old Testament came to be collected is shrouded in the history of ancient Israel, it is clear that at least two centuries before Christ (and perhaps earlier) the collection we now know as the Old Testament had formed. The book of the Wisdom of Jesus Ben Sira, written around 180 BC, made use of nearly every book of the Old Testament, even mentioning the twelve minor prophets (Hosea—Malachi) as a unit. The New Testament recognizes an Old Testament canon (although it does not use that term to describe it). It often mentions "the Scriptures" and quotes from them with the formula "it is written." It divides the Old Testament into smaller units, most commonly the Law (the five books of Moses) and the Prophets (the rest of the Old Testament). In one passage the New Testament, like Ben Sira, mentions the collection of the twelve minor prophets (Acts 7:42). The New Testament treats every book of the Hebrew Old Testament except Esther as Scripture, and no book outside this collection is ever treated as Scripture by the New Testament writers. By the late first century Josephus, a Jewish historian and younger contemporary of Jesus (see Chapter 29), wrote about the Old Testament canon and outlined its contents, giving a description that corresponds to the Hebrew Old Testament we know today.

However, in Josephus' day and in Jesus' day, the Old Testament did not exist as a book, but as a collection of scrolls. During the early centuries of the Christian church's history, bound books became popular, and people began to put the books of Scripture together within the covers of a single volume. At this time Christians, who seldom knew or read Hebrew, relied on Greek translations of the Old Testament books. Along with these translations of various books of the Old Testament, they also read other Jewish books in Greek. By the third century many Christians, especially in the West, began to accept these additional books as part of the Old Testament canon. However, Jews and other Christians continued to treat only the books of the Hebrew Old Testament as Scripture.

During the Middle Ages, most Christians in Western Europe accepted the wider canon that included the additional books, while Christians in the East were divided over the status of these books. At the time of the Reformation Martin Luther and other reformers began to question the canonical status of the additional books. When Luther translated the Bible into German, he removed these books from their accepted place in the Old Testament and placed them between the Old and New Testaments as worthy reading, but not Scripture. The same procedure was followed in English Bibles, such as the King James Version when it was first printed in 1611.

Luther and Reformers argued that no Jew in Jesus' day recognized the additional books as Scripture, and the New Testament evidence demonstrates that Jesus and his apostles accepted only the books of the Hebrew Old Testament. The additional books were labeled **apocrypha** (from a Greek word that means *hidden*). In reaction to the Protestant view, the Roman Catholic Church reaffirmed the canonical status of these additional books, labeling them **deuterocanonical** ("second canon"). Eventually, most Protestant Bibles omitted the Apocrypha altogether (since this made Bible cheaper and less bulky) while Roman

Catholic Bibles continue to include the deuterocanonical books within the Old Testament.

The Canon in Various Religious Traditions

Jewish (24 books)	Protestant (39 books)	Roman Catholic (46 books)
Torah	Pentateuch	Pentateuch
Genesis	Genesis	Genesis
Exodus	Exodus	Exodus
Leviticus	Leviticus	Leviticus
Numbers	Numbers	Numbers
Deuteronomy	Deuteronomy	Deuteronomy
Prophets	History	History
(Former Prophets)		
Joshua	Joshua	Joshua
Judges	Judges	Judges
	Ruth	Ruth
Samuel	1 Samuel	1 Samuel
	2 Samuel	2 Samuel
Kings	1 Kings	1 Kings
	2 Kings	2 Kings
(Latter Prophets)	1 Chronicles	1 Chronicles
Isaiah	2 Chronicles	2 Chronicles
Jeremiah	Ezra	Ezra
Ezekiel	Nehemiah	Nehemiah
The Twelve		Tobit
(as one book)		
Hosea		Judith
Joel	Esther	Esther (with additions)
Amos		1 Maccabees
Obadiah		2 Maccabees
Jonah	Poetry & Wisdom	Poetry & Wisdom
Micah	Job	Job
Nahum	Psalms	Psalms
Habakkuk	Proverbs	Proverbs
Zephaniah	Ecclesiastes	Ecclesiastes
Haggai	Song of Songs	Song of Songs
Zechariah		Wisdom of Solomon
Malachi		Ecclesiasticus (Ben Sira, Sirach)

Jewish	*Protestant*	*Roman Catholic*
Writings	*Prophets*	*Prophets*
	(*Major Prophets*)	(*Major Prophets*)
Psalms	Isaiah	Isaiah
Job	Jeremiah	Jeremiah
Proverbs	Lamentations	Lamentations
Ruth		Baruch (incl. the Letter of Jeremiah)
Song of Songs	Ezekiel	Ezekiel
Ecclesiastes	Daniel	Daniel (with additions)
Lamentations	(*Minor Prophets*)	(*Minor Prophets*)
Esther	Hosea	Hosea
Daniel	Joel	Joel
Ezra-Nehemiah	Amos	Amos
Chronicles	Obadiah	Obadiah
	Jonah	Jonah
	Micah	Micah
	Nahum	Nahum
	Habakkuk	Habakkuk
	Zephaniah	Zephaniah
	Haggai	Haggai
	Zechariah	Zechariah
	Malachi	Malachi

Jewish Canon

The Jewish canon, often called the **Tanak**, an acronym for the three major divisions of its books (Torah, Nevi'im [Prophets], Kethuvim [Writings]), consists of twenty-four books. The first major division, the **Torah** encompasses the five books attributed to Moses. The second division, Prophets, is divided into two sections. The former prophets consist of books primarily concerned with the history of Israel. The latter prophets contain the messages of individual prophets. The book of the twelve prophets is counted as one book, since in ancient times this entire collection of twelve books could be written on one scroll. The Writings contain other books, including poetry, wisdom and historical narratives.

This arrangement of the canon probably arose after the first century in response to Jewish liturgical practices. Before this time all of the books outside of the Torah were generally grouped together as "the Prophets." Later Jewish liturgical practice used a cycle of readings for each Sabbath from the Torah and the Prophets. Books that were not part of this cycle and that were never read in worship or read only on certain festival days became part of the Writings.

The Protestant Old Testament

The Protestant Old Testament of thirty-nine books is identical in content to the Jewish canon, although the books are arranged and counted differently. Samuel, Kings and Chronicles are divided into two books each. The twelve Minor Prophets are counted as twelve books instead of one. Ezra and Nehemiah are counted as two books instead of one.

The **Pentateuch** (from Greek for *five volumes*) is identical to the Jewish Torah. The books that in the first century were called "the Prophets" are divided into three sections. The first presents the history of Israel in roughly chronological order from Joshua, Moses' successor, to Ezra and Nehemiah. The second section contains the major poetic books of the Old Testament (including the wisdom books). The third section contains the messages of the prophets. The larger books plus Lamentations are called the **Major Prophets**, while the small books are called the **Minor Prophets**. (The distinction between major and minor is based on size, not on the importance of the prophet's message.)

The Roman Catholic Old Testament

The arrangement of the Roman Catholic Old Testament is similar to that of the Protestant Old Testament. The Pentateuch begins the collection, making the books of Moses the foundational books in the Jewish canon and in all Christian canons. The remaining books are once again divided into three sections of History, Poetry and Prophets, with the Deuterocanonical books placed in the sections where they most logically fit. The forty-six books of the Roman Catholic canon include not only seven additional books, but also expansions to Daniel and Esther that are found in the Greek versions of those books.

About the Books of the Apocrypha

While Roman Catholics are often familiar with the books they call Deuterocanonical, many other Christians are not acquainted with the Apocrypha. Among Christians from western traditions, Episcopalians are most likely to have heard these books read in worship, although many traditional Lutheran lectionaries once included readings from Sirach and the Wisdom of Solomon.

All of these books date from the period between the end of Old Testament in Ezra's day and the birth of Christ. Although some originally were written in Hebrew or Aramaic, the oldest surviving complete versions are in Greek.

Tobit relates the title character's devotion to the Torah and Jewish customs in Ninevah during Israel's captivity there. His family suffers a number of misfortunes, but God' angel guides his life and blesses his family. Written about 200 BC in Hebrew, the only surviving complete versions are in Greek and Syriac (a dialect of Aramaic).

Judith relates the wiles of a daughter of Israel as she single-handedly rallies her people to victory over the Assyrians after slaying the Assyrian general Holofernes. Judith was probably written around 150 BC.

Additions to Esther are from the Greek version of this book. These additions make Esther a more pointedly religious book and temper its apparent lack of theology by mentioning God, who is never mentioned in the Hebrew version. The Greek additions may date from about 160 BC.

1 Maccabees tells the history of the Jewish revolt against the Seleucid kings of Syria and the struggle against absorption of Jews into the Hellenistic world from 167 to about 127 BC. The rebellion was brought on by the kings of Syria and their attempt to stamp out any distinctly Jewish way of life. The book relates the forty-year struggle led by the priestly **Hasmonean** family of Matthias and his sons, especially Judas and Simon, who were known as the **Maccabees** ("hammerers"). The author clearly shows his admiration for these Jewish heroes and their commitment to Jewish customs and beliefs. Written in Hebrew about 100 BC, the book was preserved for us in Greek.

2 Maccabees covers the period from 167 to 151 BC, overlapping 1 Maccabees 1–7. Instead of writing a strict history, the author relates selected incidents from this period to illustrate the heroism of the Jews and the protection they receive from God. Much more overtly theological than 1 Maccabees, 2 Maccabees was originally written about 124 BC in Greek. Much of it is based on an earlier work by Jason of Cyrene.

Wisdom of Solomon was written by a Hellenized Jew who was familiar with Greek culture. He probably lived in Alexandria, Egypt and wrote about 50 BC. The first part of the book is devoted to encouraging Jews in Egypt to remain faithful in a culture that encouraged pagan worship and mocked the Jews and their trust in the God of Israel. The second part of the book purports to be Solomon speaking in praise of Wisdom. Since Wisdom is personified as God's agent in the world and as sharing his nature, the Wisdom of Solomon is an important link in Jewish thought between Proverbs' portrayal of Wisdom (Prov 8) and Jesus as the incarnate Wisdom of God (1 Cor 1:24).

Ben Sira, known as Sirach in Greek or Ecclesiasticus in Latin, is the wisdom of Jesus Ben Sira, a scribe who trained others in wisdom in Jerusalem. It is mostly pithy sayings about worldly wisdom, common sense and good behavior. Ben Sira was originally written in Hebrew between 190 and 180 BC. It was translated into Greek by Ben Sira's grandson in 132 BC. The Greek version includes the translator's prologue.

Baruch and the Letter of Jeremiah contains four documents, two prose and two poetry. These documents tell us about Jewish devotion to God's Law and their messianic hopes in the Babylonian exile. Although attributed to Baruch, scribe to the prophet Jeremiah, the book of Baruch was probably written in the first century BC. However, the sixth chapter, the Letter of Jeremiah, was written up to one century earlier.

Additions to Daniel, which are extant only in the Greek translation of Daniel and probably date from the second century BC include:

1. *The Prayer of Azariah*: An addition to Daniel 3, the prayer is purported to be by one of the three young Jews condemned to be cast into a furnace by Nebuchanezzzar.

2. *The Song of the Three Young Men*: Also an addition to Daniel 3, this song was supposedly sung in praise to God by the three men in the furnace. The Song of the Three Young Men has had a special place in Christian liturgical use, often having been used as a psalm or song in worship in Roman Catholic, Episcopalian and Lutheran churches.

3. *Susanna*: Often included as Daniel 13 in Greek Daniel, this short story tells how Daniel as a boy in the Babylonian captivity rescued Susanna, who was condemned to death by a plot of certain Jewish elders because she had refused to commit adultery with them.

4. *Bel and the Dragon*: The first part of Daniel 14 in Greek Daniel is a brief account of Daniel's wisdom in action as he proves that the priests of the Babylonian god Bel are frauds and that Bel is a false god. The second part of Daniel 14 in Greek Daniel is a brief story in which Daniel proves that a dragon (a large snake) worshipped by the Babylonians is a false god by destroying it. Because he destroyed their god, some Babylonians forced their king to throw Daniel in a lion's pit. However, Daniel is rescued from the pit where he was protected by an angel who brought the prophet Habakkuk to him.

Eastern Orthodox Old Testament Canons

In eastern Christianity, especially in the churches of the Orthodox tradition, there is a mixed view concerning the Apocrypha. While all of these churches accept the books in the smaller canon recognized by Jews and Protestants, many members of the Eastern Orthodox tradition also accept some or all of the books of the Apocrypha. A few churches among the Eastern traditions accept additional books. For instance, Ethiopic Christians have traditionally accepted a second century Jewish book known as Jubilees as part of the Old Testament canon.

2. Geography of the Old Testament

The history contained in the Old Testament is set in what today we call the Middle East. Historians and others who study this period of time often call this area the Near East. Stretching from Turkey and Egypt in the west to Iran and the Arabian peninsula in the east, this part of the world was home to very ancient civilizations who developed some of the earliest known cities and invented the earliest writing systems known.

The Fertile Crescent

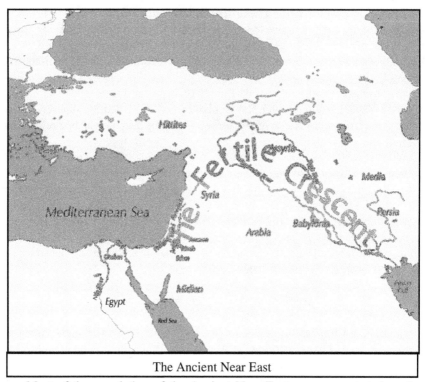

The Ancient Near East

Most of the population of the Ancient Near East was concentrated on the fertile land that stretched in an arc from the Persian Gulf in the east to the Nile River in the west. This was the most inhabitable land in this part of the world since north of this fertile area were mountains, and south of it were deserts.

The eastern leg of the fertile crescent is known as **Mesopotamia**, from Greek for *between the rivers*. Mesopotamia is the land between and around the

Tigris and Euphrates Rivers. Its southeastern end is the Persian Gulf and it extends as far west as Syria. Lower Mesopotamia (the portion lower in elevation and near the Persian Gulf) was the site of some of the earliest known civilizations. The Sumerians built cities here in the earliest recorded history of this region. They invented a writing system known as cuneiform. Later the Babylonians would dominate this region. The Assyrians dominated Upper Mesopotamia near Syria. Terah and his sons Nahor and Abram came from Ur in Lower Mesopotamia and settled in Haran in Upper Mesopotamia (Gen 11).

The western leg of the Fertile Crescent is part of the **Levant**, the eastern rim of the Mediterranean Sea. This part of the Fertile Crescent includes Syria, Lebanon and Palestine (modern Israel and Jordan). This part of the world was home to the ancient Arameans, who lived in Syria, as well as the Phoenicians/Canaanites who lived in Palestine and on the coast of Lebanon and founded the great cities of Biblos, Tyre and Sidon. The very southern end of the Levant is Palestine, where the Edomites, Ammonites, Philistines, Amorites, Moabites and other peoples lived. This was the land promised to Abraham by God and where the Israelites would make their home after leaving captivity in Egypt. Much of the story of Israel as recorded in the books of Genesis, Numbers, Deuteronomy, Joshua, Judges, Samuel, Kings, Chronicles, Erza and Nehemiah took place in Palestine.

Since the Fertile Crescent narrows as one travels south toward Egypt, the Levant saw a large amount of traffic moving back and forth between Asia and Africa in ancient times. Numerous caravans carried goods through Syria, Lebanon and Palestine, and armies frequently marched through this narrow neck of land as they fought for control of kingdoms and empires.

Egypt is on the southern edge of the Fertile Crescent. In ancient times Egypt was simply a narrow strip of land on either side of the Nile River. Like the Sumerians, the Egyptians founded one of the earliest civilizations known and invented their own writing system. Egypt was important throughout the history of the people of Israel from Abraham's day (c. 1900 BC) down to the Babylonian Captivity (586 BC).

Focus on Palestine

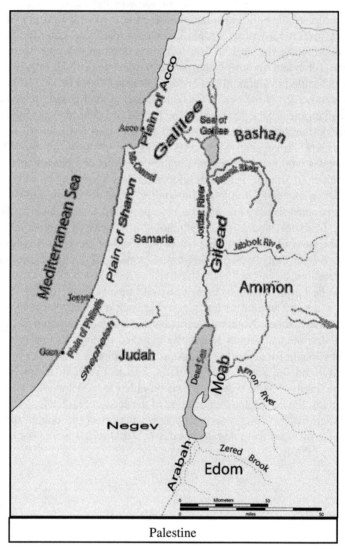

Palestine

    While portions of the Old Testament take place in Egypt, Assyria, Babylonia, Aram and Lebanon, the majority of the Old Testament is focused on **Palestine** or **Canaan**, as it is often called in the Bible. In this small strip of land, about 150 miles from north to south and about 100 miles from the Mediterranean Sea eastward at its widest, the Israelites lived with several other ethnic groups.

Palestine is marked by four major geographical areas that run along a north-south axis along the Mediterranean coast. Along the coast are the *Coastal Plains*. Further eastward are the *Central Hills*. East of the central hills is the *Rift Valley*. The easternmost area is the elevated *Transjordan Plateau*.

Coastal Plains

Along the Mediterranean coast of Palestine are a series of plains. North-ernmost of these is the **Plain of Acco**, named after the port city that dominates this region. This plain, which is directly west of Galilee and extends southward to Mount Carmel, was dominated by the Phoenicians in ancient times.

South of Mount Carmel is the **Plain of Sharon**. Its southernmost point is the port city of Joppa. Mentioned only six times in the Old Testament, in ancient times this plain was mostly marsh and dense forest. A limited area of this plain was useful for pasturing herds of cattle (1 Chron 5:16; 27:29).

Mediterranean Coast Near Ashkelon

The **Plain of Philistia** runs from Joppa in the north to Gaza in the south. This region was named after the Philis-tines, who inhabited this plain throughout most of the Old Testament era. The five Philistine cities of Ashdod, Ashkelon, Ekron, Gath and Gaza were located here.

Central Hills

The hill country east of the coastal plains was home to some of the most densely populated areas in ancient Palestine. The northern section of the central hills is known as **Galilee** and lies directly west and northwest of the Sea of Gali-lee. The region receives its name from the Hebrew word for *circle* or *circuit*. The northern half of Galilee, northwest of the Sea of Galilee and west of Lake Hula is called Upper Galilee because of its higher elevation. It was home to the Israelite tribes of Asher, Dan and Naphtali. In ancient times Upper Galilee was covered by thick forests.

Lower Galilee, directly west of the Sea of Galilee was a prosperous region that was home to the tribes of Issachar, Naphtali and Zebulun. More heavily populated than Upper Galilee, this region was strategically important to the kings of Israel. In New Testament times Galilee was home to Jesus and he spent most of his ministry in this region.

South of Galilee lay the portion of the central hills that came to be known as **Samaria**, after one of its most important cities. The two most populous tribes of Israel—Manasseh and Ephraim—lived in this area.

The Desert of Judah

From Jerusalem southward lay the prominent tribe of Judah. It's territory along with that of the smaller tribes of Benjamin and Simeon became known as **Judah**, or later **Judea**. The western region of Judah toward the Plain of Philistia was known as the **Shephelah**, "lowland," because its hills were lower. The Shephelah is split by several valleys, such as the Valley of Aijalon (Josh 10:12).

The extreme southern portion of the central hills is known as the **Negev** (also spelled *Negeb*), from the Hebrew word for *dry*. This extremely dry wilderness region hosted a very small population, but plays a fairly prominent role in the Bible, being mentioned eighty-three times in the Old Testament.

The Rift Valley

The earth's crust consists of a number of plates. The border between two of these plates is marked by the Rift Valley, a low depression that runs south to the Red Sea and continues into Africa. Because of its steep slopes, rivers and seas, and dense vegetation, the Rift Valley was a natural barrier between the east and west. Therefore, most traffic between Asia and Africa traveled north and south through Palestine to the west of the **Jordan River**.

The Jordan River's headwaters are in the northern part of the Rift Valley. As it flows south, it enters Lake Hula from the north and exits from the south. Later it enters into the **Sea of Galilee**. This large lake (the Sea of Galilee is smaller than any of the Great Lakes) was called Chinnereth, Hebrew for *harp,* by the Israelites, because it is harp-shaped. In ancient times the Sea of Galilee was an important fishing area and several towns grew up on its shore.

The Jordan River continues its southward descent as it flows out of the Sea of Galilee toward the **Dead Sea**. For about seventy miles the Jordan twists and turns until it finally empties into the Dead Sea. The shore of the Dead Sea is the lowest spot on earth, about 1300 feet below sea level. The Jordan and all other streams in this area empty into the Dead Sea, but none leave. Therefore, the

Dead Sea has accumulated all of the salts dissolved in the waters that flow into it, making it more dense than the ocean's waters and uninhabitable for fish and other creatures. The ancient Israelites called it the Salt Sea.

Dead Sea and Mount Nebo

The area around the Dead Sea receives little rainfall each year, making this part of the Rift Valley dry and hot. Consequently, few people lived in the vicinity of the Dead Sea. South of the Dead Sea lies the **Arabah**, the southern reaches of the Rift Valley. The Arabah extends to the Gulf of Aqabah, with the ancient port city of Ezion Geber at its northern tip.

Transjordan Plateau

The high Transjordan Pleateau rises quickly to the east of the Rift Valley. It is cut by four rivers that flow into the Rift Valley: The Yarmuk, Jabbok, Arnon and Zered. This easternmost section of Palestine is divided into four sections.

North of the Yarmuk River is **Bashan**, an extremely fertile area known in ancient times for its rich pastureland and for its wheat fields. South of the Yarmuk to the north shore of the Dead Sea is **Gilead**. The Jabbok River bisects this fruitful area known for its abundant harvests of wheat, grapes and olives. Its eastern side is often called **Ammon** after the Ammonites who lived there.

The plateau east of shore of the Dead Sea was **Moab**, home of descendants of one of the sons of Lot (Gen 19:37). Moab, which is considerably drier than Gilead or Bashan, was known in antiquity for sheep. The Arnon River runs westward through Moab on its journey into the Dead Sea. The southern border of Moab was the Brook Zered.

South of the Zered was **Edom**. The Edomites, descendants of Jacob's brother Esau who was also called Edom, lived in this land south and east of the Dead Sea.

Weather and Seasons

Palestine lies at roughly the same latitude as southern Spain or the state of Georgia. The weather of Palestine is dependant upon the breezes from the Mediterranean that bring rain. Unlike many parts of Europe and the United States, Palestine does not enjoy four distinct seasons. Instead, two main seasons dominate the region: a wet season, roughly corresponding to winter, and a dry season, roughly corresponding to summer.

Since the prevailing winds come from the Mediterranean Sea in the west, rainfall is most plentiful in the west and is captured by the higher elevations in the north with accumulations of about forty inches each year in much of Upper Galilee. Acco receives about twenty-five inches of rain each year. This is roughly the same amount of rain as Victoria, British Columbia or London, England. As one travels south and east rainfall diminishes. Parts of Edom and the Negev as well as the lower Jordan River Valley receive less than ten inches of rain in an average year. Much of Palestine, therefore, is critically dependent on rainfall. Years of drought are far from rare, with several severe droughts mentioned in the Old Testament.

Jerusalem

The wet season lasts from about November through April. During this time precipitation is fairly regular. Rain is the most common type of precipitation. Occasional hailstorms are known (Hag 2:17). Except on the highest mountain elevations in the extreme north toward Lebanon, snow and frost are infrequent, since temperatures below freezing are not common. (The average temperature in Jerusalem in January is about 47° Fahrenheit.) Days on which snow fell were often remembered because they were so rare (2 Sam 23:20; 1 Chron 11:22).

The transition from the wet season to the dry season lasts about six weeks as the rains become less and less frequent. The dry season lasts from mid-June to mid-September. During the months of June, July and August many parts of Palestine will receive no measurable precipitation. In mid-September the rains will begin to return and for six weeks will happen with increasing frequency until November and the return of regular rains.

Because of the small amount of rain received in southern Palestine, issues concerning water were of extreme importance in the Old Testament. In order for a family and their cattle to survive the dry season, a source of water was crucial. A few places in Palestine were blessed with year-round sources of water, such as Jerusalem, which relied on the Gihon Spring (2 Chron 32:30). A common source of water was wells that penetrated the earth down to the water table below. Abraham's dispute with Abimelech over the ownership of wells in

Seasonal Stream in Judah

Beersheba on the edge of the Negev illustrates the importance of controlling a constant supply of water (Gen 21:25–32). Many in Palestine depended on cisterns for water. Dug deep into bedrock and lined with plaster to retain runoff from rain, these holding pits preserved water from the wet season rains.

Much of Palestine is crossed by seasonal streams, called *wadis* in Arabic. Wadis are dry valleys much of the year, but can turn into raging torrents when rain falls. Within a twenty-four hour period a wadi can fill with water from run-off from higher elevations and then return to being a dry river bed.

Way of Life

The geography of Palestine dictated the way of life of most of its residents. While a few could make their living by being merchants who sold manufactured and imported wares and others could be artisans, such as weavers or potters, the large majority were involved in agriculture and animal husbandry. The main grain crops were wheat and barley. Since the nutritional value of wheat is roughly three times that of barley, wheat was the preferable grain to grow. However, wheat needs more water than barley. Therefore, in the north in Galilee, Bashan and Gilead wheat was often the crop of choice. The further south one lived, the more one planted some fields with barley as a hedge against a year with light rainfall. Thus, in Bethlehem in central Palestine, both wheat and barley were commonly planted (Ruth 2:23).

Larger cattle, such as cows and oxen, also require more water per animal than do smaller animals such as sheep and goats. Thus, Bashan in the north was famous for its cows (Amos 4:1). Further south and east many raised only a few cows and oxen and concentrated more on sheep and goats. During the dry season when the grass on one's own fields was used up, it was often necessary to take one's flock some to less inhabited areas in search of a pasture.

Many also made a living harvesting other foods. Vineyards were common, with the grapes used to make wine, vinegar and raisins. Almonds and dates were gathered from cultivated trees. Pomegranates and figs were common fruits. Bee-keepers harvested honey, both to be eaten and to serve as a sweetener in many baked products.

Olive oil was an important source of dietary fat, since meat was not easily preserved and a slaughtered head of cattle could no longer provide milk or wool. Olive trees were cultivated throughout Palestine. Gilead was known for its high-quality olive oil, and the Mount of Olives outside Jerusalem was named after its ancient grove of cultivated olive trees (2 Sam 15:30).

Mount of Olives with
Jerusalem in the Background

Farming in ancient Palestine was hard work, and was done with simple hand-held tools such as sickles to harvest grain and razors to shear sheep. Some work could be done with the aid of draught animals such as oxen to pull plows and carts, but most labor was intensively manual. For this reason, a family often prospered by producing a large number of children to help with the labor. Large families often were viewed as a blessing from God (Ps 128:3). A wife who was barren and produced no children for the family often was seen as a detriment to her husband. The Old Testament stories of Sarah, Rachel and Hannah highlight the pain felt by these women because they could not provide children for their husbands.

3. The Social and Cultural World of the Old Testament

The Israelites lived among the peoples of the ancient Near East and shared many features of their culture with them. Several of these are important for understanding the social and cultural pressures felt by Israel throughout its history.

Pervasive Polytheism

In the ancient world nearly everyone worshipped more than one god. In fact, it was assumed that many gods existed, each with their own sphere of activity that affected the world. This **polytheism** pervaded every endeavor of the peoples among whom Israel lived. While faithful Israelites were the world's first monotheists, believing there was only one God, the One who had called them to be his people, all other nations worshipped many gods and goddesses. Each nation may have had its own pantheon of gods, but they often equated the gods of other nations with similar ones in their pantheon or adopted them as one of their own.

The gods of the nations, though worshipped as powerful, were often depicted with the same ambitions, foibles and follies that beset humans. These gods nurtured rivalries with other gods, ate, drank and slept, and they often chose to favor some humans over others. Most nations had a national god to whom kings declared allegiance and who were thought to protect the king and his kingdom.

There was a rich tapestry of myths about the gods. These myths not only told stories of the creation of the world, but they also helped explain natural phenomena. For instance, Baal was the Canaanite storm god. He rode upon the clouds, which served as his chariot. Baal was thought to bring the rain. (In the Old Testament Israel's God, **Yahweh**, is responsible for all good things, including the rain. Therefore, it is not surprising that Yahweh is depicted at times with imagery similar to that of Baal. See Ps 18:8, 10.) Asherah or Astarte was a fertility goddess, who not only ensured fertility of the land, but also was worshipped as the provider of fertility to women. The Philistines worshipped Dagon as the god of grain, who ensured harvest. These myths often tempted the Israelites to worship of the gods of the nations, since the myths seemed to explain the world, and worship of these gods was thought to ensure prosperity. While many Israelites may have abandoned the worship of the God of Israel altogether, it was often common for many of them to simply make the God one of the many gods they worshipped. Both abandoning God altogether and worshipping him as only one of any number of gods was condemned by Moses and the prophets.

Semitic Culture

The Israelites were one of the many **Semitic** peoples (named after Shem, their presumed ancestor, Gen 6:10) that lived in the Fertile Crescent. The Assyrians, Babylonians, Phoenicians and Canaanites, Moabites, Edomites and Arameans were other Semites who shared many common cultural ties with Israel. Their languages were related to one another. They often had similar customs and mores. Their civil laws often mirrored similar laws given by Moses to Israel. The solar-lunar calendar used by Israel was virtually identical with the calendar used by other Semitic peoples of the Near East. The alphabet was invented by Canaanites in Palestine or Lebanon and became the common inheritance of all western Semitic peoples and was spread abroad to the Greeks and others in Europe. Throughout the pages of the Old Testament we can find many practices of Israel which were shared with her neighbors.

Despite these cultural ties, Israel made a unique contribution to the world—the steadfast faith that there was only one God who made the world and ruled it and who promised a Messiah who would save humans from sin and rule the world in truth and justice. The cultural ties to other Semitic peoples provided a powerful temptation for Israel to abandon this belief. Many in Israel gave into this temptation. However, throughout the Old Testament God preserved in each generation faithful Israelites who, despite the temptation of many features of the general Semitic culture they shared with the nations around them, remained faithful to Him.

Egyptian Culture

From before the time Jacob and his family entered Egypt (Gen 46) to the end of the Old Testament, Egypt was a powerful and influential force in Israelite life. Egypt's prosperity depended on the annual flooding of the Nile that brought renewed deposits of rich soil from the highlands to the south. Because of the need for authority to control and organize irrigation along the Nile, as well as the need to see to the draining of swamps, construction of dams and dikes and maintenance of canals, kingdoms grew up along the Nile very early in recorded human history. The two kingdoms of Upper (southern) and Lower (Northern) Egypt were united around 3000 BC, creating a powerful empire that often dominated its neighbors. By the time Joseph became a slave in Egypt (Gen 37), its culture and society had a rich history, and the pyramids and the Sphinx had been standing for hundreds of years.

Egypt was isolated by the deserts that lay to the east and the west. Nevertheless, the kings of Egypt, the Pharaohs, sought to dominate Palestine so that it would act as a buffer between them and the kingdoms in Mesopotamia. Egypt's isolation had several profound effects upon its culture. The Egyptians developed their own writing system, called hieroglyphics, and developed writing material from the reedy papyrus plant that grew in abundance in the Nile Delta. (Papyrus is the source of our word *paper*.) Egypt's isolation also led to the development of a unique pantheon of gods and goddesses. Whereas Semitic peoples often shared similar gods and myths, the Egyptian gods and myths were distinct and revolved around life as it was lived along the Nile. The Pharaohs, unlike the kings of Mesopotamia and the Levant, were thought to share divine attributes with the gods.

Throughout the Old Testament, Egypt's influence was brought to bear on Palestine. Egyptian art was imitated by artisans in Israel, Moab, Edom, Philistia and Phoenicia. Egypt's armies crossed through Palestine several times during the Old Testament period (1 Kgs 9:16; 2 Kgs 23:29; Jer 37). Solomon entered into a treaty with Egypt by marrying a daughter of one of the Pharaohs (1 Kgs 3:1). Later kings of Israel sought help from Egypt to check the power of empires and kingdoms from the east (1 Kgs 18:2; Isa 30; 36:6). Thus, Israel was often tempted to trust in Egypt's power instead of God's, and Israelites were tempted to adopt Egypt's gods as their own (Josh 24:14; Jer 44:8).

Empire Building

With the development of civilization in the ancient Near East a number of city-states began to dominate the regions around them. At first many of these cities were ruled by their own kings. However, geo-political and economic forces combined with human ambition to move kings to seek domination over larger areas. Eventually, some kings became powerful and influential enough to build empires that would dominate all or large parts of the Near East or Mediterranean basin. The same economic and geo-political forces that enabled empires to rise also brought them to ruin, only to be replaced by other empires. Israel often had to react to the pressure brought to bear from these world powers, whether it be Egypt in the south or various Mesopotamian empires in the north and east. Only during the time of David and his son Solomon was Israel able to expand and build its own sphere of influence by dominating its neighbors. Later Israel would fear the empires from Assyria in Upper Mesopotamia or Babylon in Lower Mesopotamia. The Persian Empire from what is now modern Iran would also rule over Israel during the late period of Old Testament history.

Empire building involved the fearful conquest of armies who often inflicted much damage on the lands in which they fought and brought death and destruction to conquered peoples. Those who were captured in war, including noncombatants, were often enslaved and exiled to other lands. In the ideology of ancient warfare it was often assumed that the national god of the conqueror was stronger than the god of the conquered.

When a land was subdued either by conquest or by capitulation in the face of a powerful army, it was subject to taxes, called tribute, which was paid to the foreign king who claimed the subdued territory as his own. While the conquered kingdoms often were allowed to maintain a native king, that king was required to swear allegiance to his conquerors. Since the required tribute was often so heavy that it reduced the conquered land to near poverty, many conquered nations would rebel when they perceived weakness in the empire that dominated them. This lead to shifting alliances of kings seeking to overthrow whichever empire was ruling them. When two powerful empires were dueling with each other for dominance of the Near East, kings of less powerful nations often sided with one of them to ward off the other.

Israel was told by God that she should not trust the power of any foreign king, but rely on God as her defense. However, the kings of Israel often ignored this invitation by God to trust only him and made alliances with the nations around them. The prophets God raised up for Israel often condemned these worldly alliances and the pagan influences that crept into Israel because of them.

Covenant and Obligation

The fabric of ancient Near Eastern societies was often held together by a strong sense of obligation to one's family and community. While there were those who neglected the responsibilities of community membership, most understood that their honor and the respect of others often rested upon fulfillment of obligations that were placed upon everyone. Family members were expected to look after their weaker and poorer members. One was obliged to respect and defer to the judgment of elders. Since there was often an absence of formal law enforcement, community values, customs and mores dictated everyone's obligations to the community's greater good. This emphasis on the community determined social conventions that were strictly followed in most instances, making honor and shame as important as wealth or poverty.

Covenants were important parts of this social fabric. These mutually binding promises were considered sacred. To break one's covenant was to offend the other parties to the covenant, the community as a whole and the gods one worshipped. Many covenants were sealed with oaths. Swearing an oath meant calling on God or several gods as witnesses who guaranteed the truthfulness and reliability of the oath. If the oath involved a pledge to do something, the person who swore the oath and even his heirs who may have been bound by his oath were expected to carry out his pledge no matter what later circumstances developed. Breaking an oath was a high crime against others and an insult to God or the gods.

Kings often entered into covenants with one another. When the kings were roughly equal in power, a **parity covenant** was agreed upon. In this type of covenant both parties negotiated the terms of the promises and obligations to which they pledged themselves. When one king dominated another, he often imposed a **suzerainty covenant** upon the lesser king (a suzerain is superior king). In this case the terms of the covenant were determined by the more powerful king.

God also entered into a covenant with Israel. His covenant had the form of a suzerainty covenant, since he laid out the terms. However, Israel agreed to the terms of God's covenant (Exod 24:3), which pledged his love and protection to Israel and expected their loyalty to his laws in return. God made several covenants with his people including his covenants with Noah (Gen 9), Abraham (Gen 15 and 17) and David (2 Sam 7). God's covenants were always trustworthy, since God does not lie and will not break his promises. However, the people of Israel often violated God's covenants with them. The prophets frequently warned Israel of the consequences of abandoning the covenant and reminded them that God often kept his pledges to them although they had not kept their pledges to him.

4. Old Testament History

The Old Testament covers details of the history of God's people from several centuries. The book of Genesis alone covers the history of God's people from creation to about 1800 BC. This short introduction will provide us with an overview of Israel's history from Abraham to just before the birth of Christ. The details of this history will be explored in more depth in later chapters as individual books of the Bible are discussed.

From Moses to Malachi

Genesis begins with the creation of the world and traces the early history of God's faithful people down to Abraham. This first part of Genesis quickly covers much history, but only sketches a few details. The narrative slows, however, when we reach the **patriarchs** of Israel: Abraham, Isaac and Jacob.

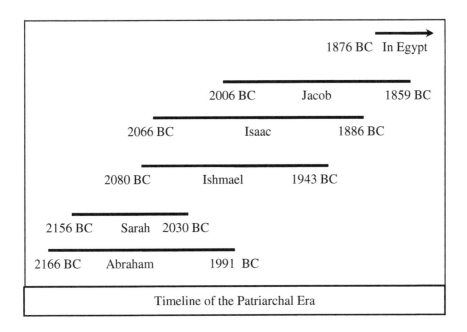

Timeline of the Patriarchal Era

The Patriarchs and Their Times

By the time Abraham was born in Ur in Lower Mesopotamia the Sumerians, a non-Semitic people who had dominated this area during its early history, had lost their power to Semites who now ruled most of the land. In Egypt the Old Kingdom period, which saw the building of the pyramids, had drawn to a close and the First Intermediate Period was underway. It was a time of competing Egyptian dynasties accompanied by decline in Egypt's international status. Abraham would leave Ur with his father's family, settling first in the city of Haran in Aram. After the death of his father, Abraham would move at God's direction to Canaan where his sons Ishmael and Isaac would be born. God's promise to Abraham to make him a great nation and bless all peoples through him was repeated to his younger son Isaac and to Isaac's younger son Jacob. During the years that the patriarchs lived in Canaan, Egypt would again rise in international affairs during what is known as the Middle Kingdom. Eventually, Jacob, whom God renamed Israel, would settle in Egypt with his children, grandchildren and great-grandchildren.

Israel Becomes a Nation: The Exodus and Wandering in the Wilderness

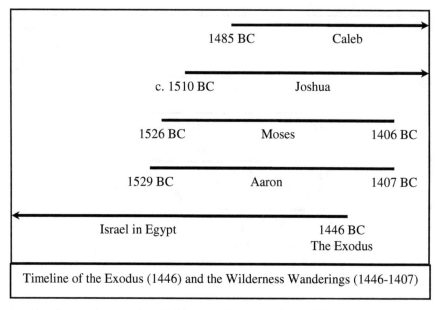

1485 BC	Caleb	
c. 1510 BC	Joshua	
1526 BC	Moses	1406 BC
1529 BC	Aaron	1407 BC
Israel in Egypt	1446 BC The Exodus	

Timeline of the Exodus (1446) and the Wilderness Wanderings (1446-1407)

The descendants of Israel would live in Egypt for over four hundred years, a period about which the Bible tells us little. The Middle Kingdom faded during this time and Egypt experienced the Second Intermediate Period, a time of foreign domination of the Nile delta by a Semitic people known as the Hyksos. Eventually a native Egyptian dynasty would establish itself as the new power in Egypt and the New Kingdom period would begin. During this time, as the book of Exodus tells us, the people of Israel were enslaved and forced into hard labor. The Egyptians, who had expelled the Hyksos, did not look kindly upon the Israelties (who like the Hyksos were Semites).

Moses' birth and early life at the Egyptian Pharaoh's court took place during the prosperity of the New Kingdom. His life is divided into three roughly equal periods of forty years. The final forty years of his life he led Israel out of Egypt through the Red Sea and into the wilderness where, at Mount Sinai, Israel received God's covenant. After failing to enter the land of Canaan, Israel wandered in the desert forty years until the death of Moses and the generation of Israelites who left Egypt with him.

The books of Exodus, Leviticus, Numbers and Deuteronomy cover Moses' life and leadership of Israel. Moses was the foundational prophet for God's people. He gave them God's Law, established their worship practices as God directed, and supervised the building of a portable place of worship, the Tabernacle, including all of its furnishings. The most important of these was the Ark of the Covenant which was God's throne and above which God's glory appeared to the people. Before his death Moses reminded the younger generation of God's promises and laws. This generation had been prepared to enter Canaan to conquer it and take possession of the land as God had promised Abraham, Isaac and Jacob.

Settlement and Strife: Joshua and the Judges of Israel

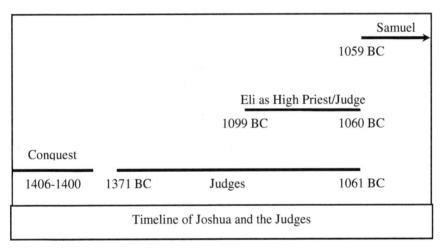

Timeline of Joshua and the Judges

Following the death of Moses, leadership passed to his assistant Joshua. The book that bears Joshua's name relates the initial conquest of the land of Canaan. It also records the dividing of the land among the twelve tribes of Israel. After Joshua's campaigns broke the resistance to Israel's entry into the land, each tribe was responsible for finishing the conquest of the territory given it by God.

After the death of Joshua, the Israelites often abandoned God and began to worship the gods of the Canaanites and other peoples in Palestine. The book of Judges tells us that God allowed other nations to oppress his people, but when they cried out to him for relief, he would raise up a leader, called a judge, to lead them into battle and drive out their oppressors. The book of Judges relates the stories of a number of judges over a period of about 350 years. This was the transition in Palestine from what archaeologists call the **Bronze Age** to the **Iron Age**. During the Bronze Age the most durable metal known for making implements and weapons was bronze, an alloy of copper and tin. Later, people learned how to work with iron, which allowed them to make stronger and more durable implements. However, iron technology did not come to all of the inhabitants of Palestine at the same time. The books of Judges and Samuel tell us that the Philistines possessed iron technology before Israel did. Therefore, the Philistines posed an important threat to Israel during the times of the last judges, Samson and Samuel.

The book of Samuel begins during the end of the rule of the judges. Events from the life of Samuel occupy the first part of the book that bears his name. When Samuel grew old, Israel asked him to request that God give them a king so that they could wage war like the nations around them (1 Sam 8). Though this was a rebellion against God's kingship over Israel, God allowed them to have a king, who was installed into office by Samuel.

The Kingdom of Israel: Saul, David and Solomon

When the kingdom of Israel was established, God chose Saul, a man from the tribe of Benjamin, as Israel's first king. Saul, who reigned from about 1050 to 1010 BC, proved to be an ineffective leader and unfaithful to God according to the book of Samuel. Because of Saul's refusal to listen to God's directions, God instructed the now aged Samuel to anoint another person as king over Israel. Led by God to the family of Jesse in Bethlehem, Samuel was told to choose Jesse's youngest son David as the new king. The book of Samuel traces God's hand in replacing Saul with David as David prospers first as a leader in Saul's army and later as a leader of a band of mercenaries. Though Saul sought to kill David, Saul himself was eventually killed in battle with the Philistines (1 Sam 31).

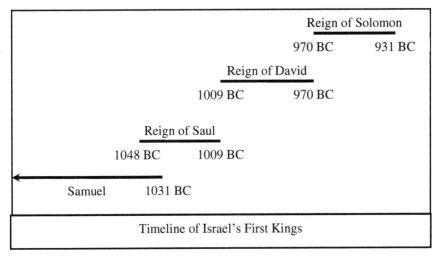

Timeline of Israel's First Kings

At the beginning of 2 Samuel and 1 Chronicles we are told how David became king over his people. His reign lasted forty years, from 1009 to 970 BC. At first David ruled only his own tribe of Judah, because Saul's grandson, Ishbaal remained king over the rest of Israel. Seven years later, after Ishbaal was assassinated, the remaining tribes of Israel acknowledged David as king. The rest of the book of Samuel relates important events from David's reign, including his sins and failures. David not only defeated the Philistines, but also extended his kingdom's dominance over Israel's neighbors, including the Edomites, Moabites and Ammonites.

In the forty years that David ruled over Israel he accomplished many things. He brought the Ark of the Covenant to his new capital city Jerusalem and made plans to build a permanent temple of God there. Despite David's sins, God chose him to be the ancestor of the Messiah. David, though not perfect, was the king whom God favored, because he never failed to repent of his sins and rely solely on God's mercy and forgiveness. The events of David's reign are recorded in 2 Samuel and 1 Chronicles.

When David grew old and was near death, there was a struggle between his two oldest surviving sons to succeed him (1 Kgs 1). God and David had promised the kingdom to Solomon, but Solomon's older half-brother Adonijah attempted to sieze the throne. Through the intervention of the prophet Nathan, God ensured that Solomon was placed on the throne even before David died. Although David had wanted to build a temple for God in Jerusalem, it was Solomon who oversaw its construction. Solomon, whom God blessed with great wisdom, reigned from 970 to 931 BC. Although he built and dedicated the temple in Jerusalem, Solomon also married many foreign women. Because they worshipped the gods of the nations around Israel, in his later years Solomon strayed from God and worshipped the gods of the nations that his wives worshipped. Because of this, God threatened to take ten of the twelve tribes away from Solomon's son after Solomon's death. However, because of God's great love for David and his promise to him, two tribes, Judah and Benjamin, would continue to be ruled by David's descendants.

Israel as Two Nations

		Babylonian Captivity	
		605 BC	538 BC
931 BC	Kingdom of Judah		587 BC
931 BC	Kingdom of Israel	723 BC	

Timeline of the Divided Kingdom and the Babylonian Captivity

Following Solomon's death in 931 BC (1 Kgs 11:43; 2 Chr 9:41), his son Rehoboam sought to establish his authority over all Israel. However, the northern ten tribes of Israel rebelled and placed Jeroboam, son of Nebat on the throne. This split left two kingdoms in Israel. The kingdom consisting of the northernmost ten tribes was known as Israel, whereas the tribes of Judah and Benjamin remained loyal to David's dynasty in what became known as the kingdom of Judah.

Under Jeroboam's leadership Israel quickly fell into idolatry. God expressed his displeasure with the idolatry in Israel through his prophets, especially Elijah and Elisha. However, most Israelites followed their kings into idolatry. During its 208-year history Israel would be ruled by ten different dynasties. However, the writer of Kings tells us that all of them were corrupt and followed the sin of Jeroboam, son of Nebat. In 723 BC Israel was conquered by the Assyrian Empire and its people were taken into captivity.

Judah remained loyal to David's line. Throughout its 344-year history, with the exception of the reign of Queen Athaliah, it would be ruled by a descendant of David. Many of Judah's kings also fell into idolatry. However, a number of notable kings remained loyal to Israel's God. The most prominent of these faithful kings were Hezekiah and Josiah. Hezekiah ruled Judah during the days when Israel fell to Assyria. However, Judah was spared, and the writers of Kings and Chronicles note that this was because of Hezekiah's steadfast faithfulness. Despite Hezekiah's example, Judah immediately fell into idolatry again under Hezekiah's son Manasseh. Of the kings that followed Hezekiah, only Josiah would be faithful to God. Following Josiah's death in battle with Pharaoh Neco in 609 BC Judah quickly declined as the Babylonian Empire replaced the Assyrian Empire as the dominant power in the Near East. Eventually, Jerusalem fell to the Babylonians in 587 BC and her people were carried into captivity in Babylon.

Many important events in the history of the kingdoms of Israel and Judah are recorded in the book of 2 Kings. 2 Chronicles documents this same history, but concentrates only on the kingdom of Judah. Both books set forth the political events that led to the fall of these kingdoms. However, the writers also concentrate on the religious dimension of life in Israel and Judah and constantly remind us that it was not political or economic forces that ultimately led to the fall of these kingdoms. Instead, God's judgment was the decisive factor in the fall of both Israel and Judah. Although God was patient with his people and sent them prophets to turn them back to him, most of the Israelites refused to repent, so God gave other nations power over them, and they destroyed these kingdoms.

The Babylonian Captivity

As prophesied by Jeremiah, the last great prophet to Judah, the people were captives in Babylon for seventy years (Jer 25:11–12; 29:10). The entire ministry of the prophets Ezekiel and Daniel took place during this Babylonian Captivity. However, in 539 BC Babylon fell to the Persians led by Cyrus, who would establish an empire that would stretch from modern Iran in the east to Turkey and Egypt in the west.

Return from the Exile

Cyrus reversed the policy of the Assyrians and Babylonians by allowing exiled peoples to return to their homelands. This included a decree that the people of Judah, now becoming known as Jews, could return to their ancestors' land (2 Chronicles 36:22–23; Ezra 1:1–4). The books of Ezra and Nehemiah report the struggle of those who returned to the land of Judah to rebuild Jerusalem and its temple and to remain faithful to God who had allowed them once again to live in the land promised to the patriarchs centuries earlier. During this period of the Persian Empire the prophets Haggai, Zechariah and Malachi prophesied to the people in Judah and the events of the book of Esther took place. Sometime before 400 BC the last books of the Old Testament were written, and Jews had not only settled again in Judah, but had spread throughout the Near East from Persia and Babylon in the east to Egypt in the west.

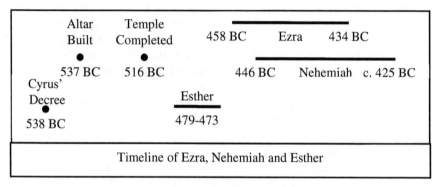

Timeline of Ezra, Nehemiah and Esther

From Persian Province to Roman Territory

The Old Testament ends in the middle of the fifth century BC, but the New Testament does not begin its story until the birth of Jesus in the late first century BC. It is helpful to know the history of this period in order to understand the forces that shaped Jewish life and faith between the end of the Old Testament and the birth of Christ.

The Late Persian Period

Under Persian rule Jews continued to thrive, not only in and around Jerusalem, but also in Galilee and in thriving communities in Babylon and Egypt. The Persian Empire would last until 332 BC, and the peace it provided allowed economic and social prosperity. Not much is known about Jewish history during this period.

Alexander and Greek Empires in the East

In 334 BC a young Macedonian king crossed the Hellespont between Greece and Asia Minor to invade the western reaches of the Persian Empire. This proved to be the beginning of a conquest that would reshape the Near East. Alexander, the Macedonian king, would conquer the entire Persian Empire and beyond into what currently are parts of Afghanistan, Pakistan and India. In Egypt he was hailed as a new pharaoh, and he founded a new Greek city named Alexandria. According to legend, when he approached Jerusalem the Jewish high priest came out to him and greeted him as the conqueror mentioned in the prophecy of Daniel. Alexander, however, would not live to enjoy a long reign over his vast empire. He died in Babylon in 323 BC.

Although Alexander died at a young age, his influence was enormous. Alexander and his successors brought Greek language and culture to the Near East. This began a process of acculturating nations in the eastern Mediterranean to basic Greek ways. This gradual adoption of Greek culture is known as **Hellenization** (from the Greek word for Greece, *Hellas*). In the coming centuries new cities would be built in Egypt and the Near East using the classical Greek city-state as their model. Greek language would become the language of politics, the marketplace and academic discourse. Greek architecture, philosophy and science would be studied and used throughout Asia Minor, Syria, Palestine and Egypt. Eventually, the greatest library of the ancient world would be established in Alexandria for the study of all useful knowledge. Of course, all the books in its collection were either Greek or translated into Greek. Hellenization would also effect the Jews, especially those living in Palestine and Egypt.

Alexander died without an heir. His generals and officials fought over his territory. Eventually, most of Alexander's empire was split into three kingdoms. Antigonus became ruler of Alexander's European territories, Greece and Macedonia. Seleucus gained control over Asia Minor, Mesopotamia and most of Syria, founding the Seleucid Empire. Ptolemy was crowned Pharaoh in Egypt and also ruled Palestine and southern Syria.

The Jews did not always fare well under Ptolemaic rule. At times Jews in Egypt and Palestine were persecuted. Nevertheless, a thriving Jewish community became established in Alexandria. It was probably in Ptolemaic Alexandria that the Old Testament, especially the Pentateuch, was first translated into Greek.

Because they shared a common border, the **Seleucid** and **Ptolemaic** kings often battled one another for dominance of the eastern Mediterranean basin. In 198 BC control of Palestine was wrested away from Ptolemy VI by the Seleucid king Antiochus III. In 175 BC Antiochus IV became king of the Seleucid Empire. He actively sought to Hellenize the populations under his control, including the Jews in Palestine. Although he met resistance from many, he insisted that they adopt Greek ways and worship Greek gods. He forbade Jews from practicing circumcision and turned the Temple in Jerusalem into a place for sacrifice to the Greek gods.

The Maccabean Revolt and the Hasmonean Dynasty

Active resistance to Antiochus' policy became open revolt in 165 BC. At first the revolt was led by Matthais, a Jewish priest at Modien in Palestine. His family was known as the Hasmoneans. However, Matthais died shortly after the rebellion began and the leadership passed to one of his sons, Judas. Judas was also known as Maccabeus ("the hammerer"). Judas led his undermanned Jewish forces in several stunning defeats of the Seleucid armies sent to dispel the rebellion. Eventually, Judas recaptured most of Jerusalem from the Seleucid rulers. On December 14, 164 BC, exactly three years after Antiochus had desecrated the temple in Jerusalem, Judas and his followers rededicated the temple. This rededication is the source of the Jewish festival Hanukah, which is mentioned in the New Testament (John 10:22). Judas was killed in battle in 160 BC, and the leadership of the rebellion passed to his brother Jonathan, also called Maccabeus. Jonathan was able to establish a semi-autonomous Jewish state in Judah and eventually expanded his realm to include Samaria. He would claim the titles of governor and general, and as a member of a priestly family, high priest. When he died in 143 BC, a third brother, Simon was made ruler. Simon was declared high priest by the Jewish people.

Simon and his sons continued to expand this Jewish state. Under their leadership the Jews were able to make a defense treaty with Rome to guarantee Jewish independence. **Hasmonean** kings also served as high priests in Jerusalem. The Hasmonean kingdom reached the height of its power during the reign of Alexander Janneus (103–76 BC).

Eventually Hasmonean power waned due both to internal struggles among the Jews as well as Roman expansion into the eastern Mediterranean. The Hasmonean Jewish state in Palestine came to an end in 63 BC when the Roman general Pompey annexed Palestine to the Roman Empire. The Hasmoneans attempted to regain their former glory, but were unable to defy the Romans. In 37 BC Herod the Great, an Idumean (Edomite) married into the Hasmonean family. Herod was appointed king of Judea by the Romans, bringing a final end to the Hasmonean dynasty, though his descendants could claim to have Hasmonean blood through his wife.

The Origin of Jewish Sects

The first historical accounts to mention Jewish sects place them during the early years of the Hasmonean dynasty. These sects probably arose as a result of several historical pressures, including the need for a Jewish response to Hellenism. Ancient sources tell us of three prominent Jewish sects that survived into the New Testament era.

The Sadducees were mainly an upper class movement. Many prominent priests became **Sadducees**. Sadducean beliefs were heavily influenced by Hellenistic philosophy. Therefore, the Sadducees denied the resurrection of the dead and the existence of angels (Acts 23:8).

Pharisees enjoyed popular support among the Jews in Palestine. They resisted Hellenistic influence in Jewish religious belief and practice. The Pharisees' religious practice was guided by their detailed tradition about the meaning of the laws given by Moses in the Pentateuch.

The **Essenes** were a very small sect. They refused to sacrifice at the Temple in Jerusalem, since the considered the Jewish priesthood in their day and its rites to be corrupt. They were very careful to keep the ceremonial laws of Moses in order to avoid the corruption they saw among the priests. Essenes were mainly adult males, and their beliefs encouraged celibacy. While the Pharisees and Sadducees are mentioned in the New Testament, the Essenes are not. However, there may have been some Essenes among the Herodians (Matt 22:16; Mark 3:6; Luke 12:13), since the Essenes supported Herod and his descendants.

Each of these sects sought to follow the ancient laws of Moses and to live by what they viewed as good Jewish customs. It was into their religious world that Jesus and his disciple came, proclaiming the nearness of God's kingdom.

The Rise of Rome

While the Ptolomaic and Seleucid empires were dying and the Hasmonean kingdom was dissolving, a new power was beginning to dominate the Mediterranean world. Rome, which began as a republic, was establishing an empire that would rule most of western Europe and all of the lands that touched the Mediterranean shore. In 27 BC the Roman Senate declared Octavian the first Roman emperor. Octavian, who changed his name to Augustus, ruled until AD 14. Many Jews found themselves under what they considered to be the harsh yoke of Roman rule. Into this world Jesus was born (Luke 2:1).

Section 2
The Pentateuch

3
Introduction to the Pentateuch

Anyone who erects buildings for a living will testify that the first and often most important task in the actual construction is the laying of a solid foundation that can support the structure throughout its expected life. The most massive building requires the most solid and stable foundation. Like the foundation of a large building, the Pentateuch serves as a solid foundation that supports the entire Old Testament. It is not surprising, therefore, that these five books introduce readers of the Old Testament to most of its major concepts and to its most important prophet, Moses.

1. The Contents of the Pentateuch—*A Overview of the History of Israel from Abraham to Moses*
2. The Foundation of the Old Testament—*The Pentateuch Is Where Old Testament Theology Begins*
3. Authorship of the Pentateuch—*When and Where Did These Five Book Originate?*

1. The Contents of the Pentateuch

The first five books of the Old Testament are sometimes called by their Hebrew name, the **Torah**. This word is often translated *Law*, although it more properly means *instruction*. Throughout the Bible these books are called the "Law of Moses" or simply "the Law." Another name for these books often used among Christians is the **Pentateuch**, from the Greek for "five books."

The Pentateuch taken as a whole tells the story of God's people from Creation to the death of Moses. Genesis begins the story by progressively narrowing the focus from the created world to humans to the family of Abraham, Isaac and Jacob that became the people of Israel. The first chapters of Genesis tell of God's creating the world and the first humans and their fall into sin. This is followed by the so-called **Primeval History**, the struggles of Adam and Eve's descendants to cope with the curse of sin in a fallen world. Eventually God gives humanity a new start with the flood that saves the faithful Noah and his family. However much the flood reduced sinfulness in the world, it did not wipe out the sinfulness that had infected the world, so the problem persisted for humanity.

Genesis quickly moves through only a few incidents after Noah to arrive at Abraham. Here the story slows as Genesis tells us of God's choice of Abraham and his son Isaac and his grandson Jacob as his people. Many details of the lives of these fathers or **patriarchs** are given in the **Patriarchal Narratives** in Genesis. Most importantly we follow the promise of God to his people as we read the lives of these men and their families. God promises the Patriarchs that through them will come a blessing for the entire world. He also promises them that their descendants will possess the land of Canaan. The Patriarchal Narratives conclude with Jacob (whom God renamed Israel) and his twelve sons and their families in Egypt with Jacob's second-youngest son, Joseph, as second only to the Egyptian pharaoh himself in authority in Egypt.

The second book of the Pentateuch, Exodus, begins almost four hundred years after the end of Genesis. The people of Israel have been reduced to the status of slaves in Egypt. The opening chapters of Exodus tell us of the birth and early years of Moses until God called him to lead Israel out of Egypt. The account of God's mighty hand sending plagues on the Egyptians to convince them to allow the Israelites to leave Egypt is the most well-known part of this book. It culminates with the tenth plague, the death of every firstborn male among the Egyptians followed by the exodus from the land of the Nile and God's deliverance of his people as he leads them across the Red Sea.

However, Exodus does not end here. It continues with the account of Israel's journey to Mount Sinai. At this mountain, also called Horeb, God takes Israel to be his own people, a special nation. He gives them his holy law, including the well-known Ten Commandments (Exod 20). He also calls Moses up the mountain and gives him detailed laws to govern God's Old Testament people Israel as well as instructions for building a portable sanctuary for worship, the Tabernacle.

Despite God's great work for them and his grace in making Israel his people, they continue to rebel and sin, first in the desert of the way to Sinai and then at the foot of the holy mountain itself as they make and begin to worship a golden calf. Yet God did not reject his people. Moses pleaded with the Lord to remember his promise to the Patriarchs, and in his grace, God does forgive his people and once again take them to be his own.

Exodus concludes with God's detailed instruction for constructing the Tabernacle and its furniture and the construction and dedication of the Tabernacle. As Exodus closes God presence is seen in the Tabernacle as he now dwells among his people.

Leviticus, the third book of the Pentateuch, is set entirely at Mount Sinai. It contains God's laws for his people with a heavy emphasis on the laws of worship and sacrifice that will convey God's grace to his people throughout the Old Testament.

The book of Numbers begins at Sinai and tracks the movements of God's people for forty years in the wilderness before they enter Canaan. God's original plan was to have his people leave Sinai and enter the land of Canaan from the south, where he would lead them in conquest of the land promised to Abraham, Isaac and Jacob. However, due to the people's rebellions and refusal to enter the land under his guidance, God condemned the people to wander in the wilderness south of Canaan for forty years until every adult of that generation died. At the end of the forty years God has Moses lead Israel to the brink of entering the Promised Land. Numbers reveals to us many incidents concerning Israel's continual rebellion against God, thereby also emphasizing God's mercy and love as he forgives and receives his people back into fellowship with him. Unfortunately, because of the sins of Moses and his brother Aaron, Israel's high priest, these two men will not live to enter Canaan. Numbers records Aaron's death.

The last book of the Pentateuch, Deuteronomy, consists of Moses' final addresses to the people of Israel. He reminds them of God's Law, points them to God's promise and mercy, and prepares the new generation of Israelites to enter the land promised to the Patriarchs. The final chapter of Deuteronomy records the death of Moses, the prophet unlike any other in the Old Testament, with whom God spoke face-to-face.

Creation Primeval History Patriarchal Narratives	**GENESIS**
Moses' early life The Exodus from Egypt The Covenant at Sinai The Tabernacle	**EXODUS**
Laws for God's People (especially concerning worship)	**LEVITICUS**
Forty Years in the Wilderness	**NUMBERS**
Moses' last instructions for Israel The Death of Moses	**DEUTERONOMY**

2. The Foundation of the Old Testament

The Origin of Israel and Its Institutions

The Old Testament is a collection of books that from beginning to end document the history, institutions, culture and faith of ancient Israel. The Pentateuch lays the foundation for the remaining books of the Old Testament by chronicling the origin of this people and its institutions. This origin is rooted in God's work of calling Israel to be his people, making them his special nation, granting them access to him and his mercy through worship and governing them through rulers that he appointed.

The book of Genesis begins this focus on Israel by its recording of how God chose his people from all the nations by calling Abraham to be his servant and promising to make him a great nation. This promise is passed down to Abraham's son Isaac, whom God chose although Abraham had an older son, Ishmael. The promise is passed on to Jacob, one of two twin sons of Isaac, even though his brother Esau was born first. The book of Genesis serves to define who the people of Israel are: the recipients of God's choice and promise to Abraham through his descendants Isaac and Jacob, whom God named Israel.

Although Genesis defines the people of Israel, it is left to Exodus to tell of their origin as a nation whom God claims as his own among all the nations of the world. God's claim on them as his people is a result of his rescuing them from the power of the Egyptians. He solidifies this claim through the covenant given on Mount Sinai where he grants them the special status of his treasured possession, his royal priesthood, his holy nation (Exod 19:5–6). The laws he gave them were designed to guide them in holy living that demonstrated their special status as God's people. The Tabernacle was designed to be a place where God dwells with his people and his people can come to him for forgiveness when they have sinned. All this points to Israel as recipients of God's mercy and favor. They are his creation, and he not only makes them his own, but also in his great love he provides a way for them to be restored to holiness before him when they fail to live as the holy people of God.

This theme continues into Leviticus where God now grants his people laws for various sacrifices that would be offered to him in the Tabernacle. Far from placing a burden on Israel, these laws of sacrifice are a consequence of his love and mercy, since they provide a way for sinners to come into the presence of the holy God. Though the sacrifices commanded by God through Moses are similar to the sacrifices offered by the surrounding nations to their gods, Israel's sacrifices are unique in both the details of their performance and in their significance as means provided by God to communicate his forgiveness to his people.

Moreover, God provided a priesthood that was authorized to represent God to the people and bring the people's offerings to God. Moses' brother Aaron was installed as the first high priest and God provided for a continual line of priests by bestowing the priesthood only upon the male descendants of Aaron. This was not God's way of restricting access to him. Rather it was a way of reassuring the people of Israel that their offerings would be accepted by him. Unless God chose priests, the people would never be certain that God was pleased with their sacrifices. Whenever the Aaronic priest offered a sacrifice in accordance with the laws given by Moses, the worshipper who brought the sacrifice could be certain that God had approved of it and would receive it as he promised. The worshipper could be confident that God had forgiven him and made him his child and heir of his eternal kingdom.

Leviticus also speaks of other religious institutions in Israel such as the yearly festivals of Passover, the Day of Atonement and the Festival of Booths as well as the weekly Sabbath. It also goes beyond laws of worship to command laws for daily living among God's people, demonstrating to Israel and to us that worship is not simply an activity performed at a special place of worship, but that forgiveness received in worship transforms the lives of God's people so that all of their activities become holy acts dedicated to the God who loved them, rescued them and made them his holy people.

Numbers reminds us that although Israel was now a nation, it was a nation without a homeland. It allows us to see that Israel rejected God's provision from a homeland, but God did not reject his people. They would wander the wilderness for forty years, often rebelling against God and failing to trust him, but God continued to remember his promise to Abraham, Isaac and Jacob. He patiently loved Israel through these forty years. Even when the new generation fell into idolatry and began to worship the pagan God Baal at Peor as God was leading them to the promised land of Canaan, the Lord did not reject his people (Numbers 25). He granted them victory in battle over the Amorite kings Sihon and Og who sought to keep them out of Canaan (Numbers 21), and he brought them to the edge of the land he had promised to give them.

Finally, in reminding Israel of God's work for them from the time they left Egypt, Moses emphasizes once more that God is "merciful and gracious, slow to anger and abounding in steadfast love and faithfulness" (Exod 34:6). He had shown this to Israel from the time they left Egypt until the day that Moses died, and God would continue to show his mercy and favor to Israel even after Moses' death (Deut 34). Therefore, as they stood on the threshold of the land promised centuries earlier to Abraham, Moses laid before them two ways: the way of life and the way of death, the ways of blessing and curse (Deut 30). Trusting in God and living by his instruction ("torah") would lead to life. Abandoning God and his ways would lead to death. So Moses urged the people:

"...choose life, that you and your descendants may live, loving Yahweh your God, obeying his voice and holding fast to him, for he is your life and length of days, that you may dwell in the land that Yahweh swore to give to your fathers, to Abraham, to Isaac, and to Jacob,." (Deut 30:19–20)

Therefore, the Pentateuch tells us of Israel's origins. It explains from where they came and how and why they lived and worshipped using their own special institutions and customs. In doing this the Pentateuch never focuses us on Israel alone, but on God who created and sustained his people and brought them to the place he promised them. For the reader of these five books the message is clear: God's people are his creation, and as we share in the blessing of forgiveness and life with Yahweh's ancient people, we, too, know that it was God who rescued us from bondage to sin and death and made us his own, just as he rescued Israel from bondage in Egypt and claimed them as his special possession.

The Messianic Promise

As much as the Pentateuch tells us about Israel's beginnings, there is another theme that runs through it and gives us the reason that God chose Israel as his people: the promise of a Savior from sin. This promise is traced through the book of Genesis as God was choosing a people for himself. The promise of a Savior is first given to Adam and Eve immediately after they sinned. God promised that one of Eve's descendants would crush the serpent's head (Gen 3:15). Later, Noah as he praised God in a prophecy to his sons, promised blessing to Shem (Gen 9:26–27). Genesis quickly moves to Abraham, one of the descendants of Shem. Several times God promised him that all nations would be blessed through him, a promise that he would be the ancestor of the Savior (Gen 12:3; 22:18; see Gal 3:16). This promise is given to Abraham's son Isaac (Gen 17:18–21; 26:2–4) and then to Isaac's son Jacob (Gen 28:13–15). Finally, among the sons of Jacob, Judah receives the promise in Jacob's prophecy to his sons shortly before his death (Gen 49:8–12). Therefore, while Genesis is telling the story of how the nation of came to be, it is also tracing the reason for that nation's existence—to bring the Messiah, the promised Savior of all sinful humans, into the world.

The Messianic promise is then expanded as the remaining books continue to point Israel to the coming Messiah. The exodus from Egypt itself is merely a foretaste of the deliverance from sin that the Messiah will accomplish when he comes. In the book of Exodus as God gives laws pertaining to Israel's worship, he points them to the Messiah. This can be seen most clearly in the Passover lamb (Exod 12; see John 1:29, 36; 1 Cor 5:7), but is also evident in the annual festivals God commands for Israel—the Festivals of Unleavened Bread,

Firstfruits and Harvest (Gen 23:14–19), each of which points to some aspect of the Messiah's work (Luke 10:2; Rom 1:13; 1 Cor 5:6–7; 15:20, 23). The Sabbath, first commanded by God in Exodus (Exod 20:8–11), is also a picture of the Messiah, Sabbath rest of God's people (Matt 11:28). The Tabernacle that provides access for Israel to God is a foreshadowing of the work of the Messiah who will provide access to God for all people through his ministry.

In Leviticus both the sacrifices and the priesthood as they were carried out in the Tabernacle are reminders of the work of the Messiah, who will be both great high priest as well as sacrifice (Heb 4:14; 9:1—10:18). Numbers, likewise, points to the Messiah, both in the prominence of Judah as leader of the tribes as they march (Num 10:14) as well as its continued emphasis on the Passover (Num 9:1–14; 28:16–25).

Finally, Deuteronomy contains Moses' promise of a great prophet like him who will come (Deut 18:14–22). This is a promise that the Messiah will not only be a priest, but also a prophet, and was fulfilled in Jesus (John 6:14; Acts 3:22–26; 7:36).

The Messianic promise, therefore, runs throughout the Pentateuch as a golden thread that unites its fabric. The Messiah is the reason for God's love and patience with Israel, as he promises them and the world a Savior from the sin that has infected humans from the earliest pages in the Pentateuch (Gen 3). God calls Israel to be his own so that they will bring forth the Messiah through whom people of all nations can become God's new Israel (Gal 6:16).

3. Authorship of the Pentateuch

Traditionally both Christians and Jews have attributed the Pentateuch to the pen of Moses. This tradition was not simply an invention based on Moses' prominence in the Pentateuch, but was derived from the witness of the Scriptures themselves to Moses' work as an author.

First of all, all of the books of the Pentateuch except Genesis claim to have derived wholly or in part from Moses (Exod 17:14; 24:4; 34:27; Lev 1:1; 27:34; Num 33:1–2; Deut 1:5; 31:9, 22, 24). Leviticus itself states over fifty times that "the Lord spoke to Moses." It is difficult to understand how all of these conversations of God with Moses came to be written down unless Moses himself recorded them or dictated them to someone.

Secondly, the other books of the Old Testament frequently refer to parts of the Pentateuch as commanded by Moses. At Joshua 8:35 we are told that what Moses commanded, Joshua *read* to the people. Moreover, the Pentateuch as a collection is repeatedly called the Law (Hebrew *Torah*) and quite often this Law as a written document is ascribed to Moses:

Reference to the Pentateuch	*Scripture References*
"The Law of Moses"	Josh 1:7; 8:32; 1 Kgs 2:3; 23:25; 2 Chr 23:18; 30:16; Ezra 3:2; 7:6; Dan 9:11, 13
"The Book of the Law of Moses"	Josh 8:31; 23:6; 2Kgs 14:6; Neh 8:1
"The Law, the Book of Moses"	2 Chr 25:4
"The Book of the Law given through Moses"	2 Chr 34:14
"The Book of Moses"	2 Chr 35:12; Ezra 6:18; Neh 13:1
"The Law that the Lord commanded Moses"	Neh 8:4
"God's Law given by Moses"	Neh 10:29
"The Law of my servant Moses"	Mal 4:4

The New Testament continues this ascription of the Law to Moses, often grouping it with the rest of the Old Testament, which is called "the Prophets."

Reference to the Pentateuch	*Scripture References*
"Moses and (all) the Prophets" "The Prophets and Moses"	Luke 16:29, 31; 24:27, 44; John 1:45; Acts 26:22
"The Law of Moses"	Acts 13:39; 15:1, 5; 1 Cor 9:9; Heb 10:28
"he (Moses) is read"	Acts 15:21; 2 Cor 3:15
"The Law of Moses and the Prophets"	Acts 28:23

Jesus himself refers to these books as authored by Moses, saying to his contemporaries, "Moses accuses you," (John 5:45–46) and, "Moses has given you the Law" (John 7:19). The conviction that Moses wrote these books was shared by Jews in the first century, as indicated at Acts 6:14 when Jewish authorities refer to "customs Moses delivered to us." The writer to the Hebrews assumes that he and his readers accept the Pentateuch as a collection that can be read and studied when he says that "Moses said nothing about" a priest from the tribe of Judah (Heb 7:14; see Heb 9:19).

In addition, in many places in the New Testament Jesus, the Apostles and their contemporaries refer to specific passages of the Pentateuch as being authored by Moses:

Reference to a Passage from the Pentateuch	*Passage in the Pentateuch*
Matt 8:4; Mark 1:44; Luke 5:14	Lev 14:1–32
Matt 19:7–8	Deut 24:1–4
Matt 22:24	Deut 24:5–10
Mark 7:10	Exod 20:12; 21:17; Lev 20:9; Deut 5:16
Mark 10:4	Deut 24:1, 3
Mark 12:19; Luke 20:28	Deut 25:5
Mark 12:26; Luke 20:37; Acts 7:32	Exod 3:6
Luke 2:22	Lev 12:6–8
John 8:5	Lev 20:10; Deut 22:22–23
Acts 3:22	Deut 18:15, 18
Acts 7:37	Deut 18:15
Rom 9:15	Exod 33:19
Rom 10:5	Lev 18:5
Rom 10:19	Deut 32:21
1 Cor 9:9	Deut 25:4
Heb 10:28	Deut 17:6
Heb 12:21	Deut 9:19

While there is no direct reference to any passage in Genesis as coming from Moses, this is a reasonable assumption since it is clearly included in references to "the Law," and the rest of the Pentateuch, especially the opening verses of Exodus, assumes that readers have access to Genesis and have read it.

While this strong evidence from the Bible itself ascribes authorship of the Pentateuch to Moses, many scholars who hold to this belief today recognize that some parts of the Pentateuch may have received updating at the hands of later prophets. This can be seen already in the book of Joshua where we are told, "Joshua wrote these words in the Book of the Law of God" (Josh 24:26). The most obvious of these updatings is Deuteronomy 34:1–12, the account of the death of Moses, which could hardly have been written by Moses himself. The end of Deuteronomy 34 notes, "no one knows the place of his burial to this day" and "since that time, no prophet has risen in Israel like Moses." These statements from the author certainly indicate that a considerable number of years have passed between Moses' death and the composition of the account of his death. Other passages that indicate later updating include Genesis 14:14 where the city of Lachish is call "Dan" (see Judg 18:29), Genesis 36:31 which mentions kings of Israel, and Genesis 47:11, Exodus 12:37 and Numbers 33:3, 5 which call the region of Goshen, "the land of Rameses," after a later Egyptian pharaoh.

4

Genesis

Viewing the beginning of a movie is obviously important for understanding the remainder. Just think how confused and uninformed a person who misses the first fifteen minutes would be. This initial movie segment portrays the setting, introduces the characters, and explains vital events for all subsequent scenes. Becoming familiar with the book of Genesis is all the more important for understanding the rest of the Bible. Genesis introduces Yahweh in His role as creator. It identifies who people are in relation to Yahweh. Genesis also depicts the created world and humanity's role before Yahweh. Genesis then communicates the disastrous entrance of sin into the world. Yet, God promises favor to his people, especially through a Savior. Genesis then proceeds to describe Yahweh's faithfulness to this promise throughout the generations, beginning with Abraham and continuing with his descendants. Genesis receives much attention in the Old Testament as well as the New Testament. The God who creates is also the God who saves. Understanding Genesis provides the foundation to comprehend the work of Christ.

1. Date of Writing—*When Was Genesis Written?*
2. Date of Events in the Book—*What Time Period Does Genesis Cover?*
3. Themes—*Foundational Concepts in the Old Testament*
4. Overview of the Events in the Book—*From Creation to the Sons of Jacob*
5. Important Passages—*Tracing the Beginnings of God's People*

1. Date of Writing

Traditionally, Christianity and Judaism have affirmed Moses as the author of the first five books of the Bible. This collection of the first five biblical books is known as the Pentateuch. The date of Moses' authorship of Genesis, as well as the rest of the Pentateuch, relies heavily upon 1 Kings 6:1. According to that passage, the fourth year of Solomon's reign over Israel comes 480 years after the Israelite exodus from Egypt. This year in Solomon's reign is known to be

966 B.C., which places the exodus at 1446 B.C. Thus, the forty years of wandering and the likely parameters for the composition of the Pentateuch occur between 1446–1406 BC, since Moses died just before the Israelites entered the Promised Land (Deut 34).

2. Date of Events in the Book

When did creation take place? The biblical text clearly indicates a young earth which arose through Yahweh's creative word. The Bible does not support macroevolution, which asserts huge developmental leaps from the simple life forms to more complex ones over billions of years. Nor does the biblical creation account agree with **theistic evolution**, according to which God directed macroevolution. The assumption of a young earth receives support, for example, from the word *day* in Genesis 1 as Yahweh created the world in six days and rested on the seventh (1:5, 8, 13, 19, 23, 31; 2:2). In this context, *day* simply refers to the transition of light and darkness, at first without sun and moon (Gen 1:14–19). But how long was this rhythmical day? Although *day* in the remainder of Scripture can at times have figurative meanings (e.g., Ps 90:4; 2 Pet 3:8), the literal interpretation and most natural reading of *day* in Genesis 1 is the typical twenty-four hour day. Additionally, some English translations appropriately render the end of Gen 1:5 as "one day" instead of "the first day." This "one day" translation specifies the creation day as the transition of light and darkness, not multiple days or years. Although the literal twenty-four hour day precludes the origin of the earth millions or billions of years ago, dating creation includes challenges. A major source of dating this early period is the genealogies in Genesis (e.g., Gen 5; 10—11). However, biblical numbers can at times be symbolic, and the term *son* can have the generic meaning of *descendant*. While a very literal reading of the numbers would date the earth around six thousand years old, an older age of additional thousands of years is certainly plausible. While specifying an exact date of creation is impossible, it is clear from the biblical text that God created a mature earth in a six-day period.

Dating the remainder of the book of Genesis does not lack some challenges. Even conservative Christian scholars differ significantly regarding dating. What follows is a reasonable construction of the data. The remainder of the events in Genesis 1—11 take place before 2200 B.C. Abraham lives from 2166–1991 B.C. During this time he moves to Canaan in 2091 B.C, and Sarah bears Isaac in 2066 B.C. After the attempted sacrifice of Isaac in 2050, Isaac lives until 1886 B.C. During the life of Isaac, Jacob and Esau are born in 2006 B.C. Jacob flees to Haran in 1929 B.C, settles in Egypt in 1876 B.C. and dies in 1859 B.C. Joseph's birth takes place in 1915 B.C. His brothers sell him into slavery in 1898 B.C, and he dies in 1805 B.C.

3. Themes

Creation

A vital theme of Genesis is Yahweh's act of creation. As the first chapters of Genesis unfold, several truths become obvious. First, creation answers who God is. Second, creation is a miracle of God's benevolence, artistry, and power. Third, creation answers who we are before God.

Indeed, the creation account answers who God is. He is the only one uncreated. Before the created world or anything else came into existence, He existed. Genesis assumes this truth without feeling the need to explain it. He is the single creator without competition. Yet, within this singularity, the Genesis account reveals a plurality. The first words of Genesis declare, "In the beginning God created..." (Gen 1:1). Although the verb "created" is singular in the Hebrew language, the word for "God" (*Elohim*) is plural. This plurality also becomes apparent when He begins to create humans. "Then God said, 'Let *us* make man in *our* image, in *our* likeness...'" (Gen 1:26). Specifically, Scripture reveals in the creation account that the one God consists in three persons: Father, Son, and Holy Spirit. The Father creates through His Word. The Son is the Word which issues forth from God to create. Throughout Scripture, we best come to know the heart of God through the Son, who becomes the Word in human flesh for our salvation (John 1:14). The Spirit hovers over the surface of the deep to support creation (Gen 1:2). Indeed, the biblical testimony of creation makes Yahweh's identity clear and emphasizes His action.

Second, creation is a miracle of God's benevolence, artistry, and power. The world, the universe, all creatures, humanity, and heavenly beings are objects of his creative work. Yahweh does not create from existing material. He creates from nothing and then puts in order what He made. He does not use a process of billions of years. Rather, His divine power becomes obvious, since in six days He created a mature earth. Creation happens by His mighty, creative Word. He speaks, and it comes into being. The Genesis account reveals His masterful, determined plan of creation and how it goes from broad design to the more ordered and complex. He creates and moves all toward order. In the first three days He creates empty structures by His acts of separation. In the latter three days he fills those empty structures with created things. Created last, humanity stands as the climax and the crown of creation, made in the image of God. All was made perfectly; all was good in the sight of God.

Third, the creation account reveals who we are before God. We are creatures of God and exist by His power. Humanity would not have its exalted existence without Yahweh's detailed attention in forming humanity and giving it the breath of life (Gen 1:26–29; 2:7–24). Humanity does not define its own identity and existence. Rather, we receive such gifts as God has given them. He has given us our bodies, lives, and all faculties. He made us and preserves us. He directs creation to provide all the necessities of life for us. God has given us a high purpose in life under Him. We have the vocation of representing God in caring for the earth. We act as His stewards or managers to maintain order in this world (Gen 1:26–29). This high status becomes apparent by the gift of naming things in creation (Gen 2:19–20). In creation, God's reveals His intended order for the family. Male and female are meant for each other in God's plan. He makes known the relationship between husband and wife. Adam, as head of the household, was created first (Gen 2:7; 1 Cor 11:8). Eve is a helper suitable for him (Gen 2:18). God encourages the procreation of children in a marriage and blesses a couple with them (Gen 1:28). In this way, Yahweh established humanity's existence, identity, and purpose in life before Him. When we define who we are apart from God, as Eve does, all goes awry. All moorings of identity, truth, purpose, and morality fall asunder without assuming God as creator.

A final note is appropriate regarding Christ and creation. Emphasizing Christ's role in creation is a vital part of Christian theology. Maintaining the link between Christ and creation upholds the incarnation, where Christ took on creation and suffered for us in the flesh on the cross. This link also affirms His presence in the physical elements of the sacraments as well as His kingly office of having all creation under His feet. Thus, creation theology and **Christology** have a vital connection.

Sin

Sin is very apparent in the book of Genesis. Although Yahweh perfectly created the world and all people, the rebellion of Adam and Eve wrought by the devil brought sin into the world. This caused corruption, death, conflict, and every other sort of evil. Sin in its two forms appears clearly in Genesis. First, **original sin** is a corrupted condition affecting our very human nature. Second, **actual sin** involves every evil thought, word, and deed, which flows from the condition of original sin. Humanity's original sin and actual sin are damnable and deserve nothing but God's divine wrath.

Indeed, original sin is the corruption of human nature since the fall of Adam, so that people are full of evil and have evil inclinations from the moment of conception.[4] Sin is not the creative work of God. Rather, the corruption of human nature is the devil's work, as seen by the fall (Gen 3:1–19). With this fall, humanity loses its original righteousness before God, including the loss of perfect fear, love, and trust of God. Now Adam and Eve feel shame before their

---

[4] Augsburg Confession, Article 2.

maker (Gen 3:7, 10). They no longer possess the image of God given at creation (Gen 1:26). In Adam, this corrupted condition passes from one generation to another (Gen 5:3). Even after the fall, although God does not cause evil, He still creates and sustains human nature.

Actual sin involves thoughts, words, and deeds which people commit as a result of original sin. Actual sin also involves omission of the good that we should have done. God has created the world and still preserves it. Yet, He is not the source of actual sin just as He is not the source of original sin. Actual sin arises from the corrupted human will and the will of the devil.[5] The initial actual sin of mistrusting Yahweh and eating the forbidden fruit results in brokenness between God and people. That brokenness then shatters the relationship between Adam and Eve. Instead of admitting blame for the fall into sin, Adam shifts the blame to his wife in a self-centered manner. He even blames Yahweh for giving him this woman (Gen 3:12). Sins continue with the tragic first murder when Cain acts in jealousy against his brother Abel (Gen 4:8). The wickedness of people becomes so great that Yahweh destroys the entire world in the great flood at the time of Noah (Gen 6—9). This event demonstrates what humanity deserves as a result of sin; it also demonstrates God's just wrath. Unfortunately, the sinful trend only continues as the people at the Tower of Babel seek to give themselves ultimate glory rather than giving it to God. Yahweh brings righteous judgment by confusing their language (Gen 11:1–9). Sinful acts continue throughout Genesis, whether in people who reject Yahweh or even among the patriarchs themselves. With fear and mistrust in Yahweh's protection, Abram withholds the truth about his marriage to Sarai (Gen 12:10–20; 20:1–18). With mistrust in Yahweh's ability and faithfulness, Abram tries to gain an heir through Hagar instead of Sarai (Gen 16:1–19). Isaac deceives Abimelech of the Philistines in a manner similar to Abram (Gen 26:1–11). Jacob acts with trickery toward his brother and father (Gen 25:27–34; 27:1–40). Jacob's two sons Simeon and Levi deceitfully kill the men of Shechem (Gen 34:25–29). A group of Jacob's sons then sell Joseph into slavery and lie to Jacob about the matter (Gen 37:12–36). Thus, Genesis and the entire Bible do not emphasize human virtue, but instead they emphasize a merciful God.

Sin not only corrupts human nature and human action, it also affects the rest of the created world. Although Yahweh created all things perfectly, matters change with the entrance of sin. Just as sin in people brings hardship, so also the created world under sin causes hardship. The ground produces thorns and thistles for Adam so that he must acquire food with much toil (Gen 3:17–19). This condition of the ground appears to be worsened in the punishment against Cain after the murder of Abel (Gen 4:10–12). Water brings death instead of life dur-

---

[5] Augsburg Confession, Article 19.

ing the world-wide flood at the time of Noah (Gen 6—8). The animals will have fear and dread of people rather than the original harmony (Gen 9:2). A famine causes hardship among many nations at the time of Joseph (Gen 41—44). Creation groans under sin and hopes for the promised redemption of God's people so that it also might be free from sin (Rom 8:20–25).

Redemption through the Promised Savior

Redemption involves the payment of a price to gain the freedom for a captive or for one's property. As Scripture articulates redemption, the nearest relative (called a **kinsman redeemer**) is to pay the redemption price to win this release (Deut 25:5–10; Ruth). The need for redemption from sin directly affects the human condition, since we all are corrupted by sin and enslaved to it. We are additionally under the curse of the Law for breaking it, under the power of the devil, and deserving God's wrath of eternal punishment. Humanity does not have the ability to pay this redemption price. Therefore, Christ pays the redemption price with His own life. By His humanity He suffers in our place; by His divinity His sacrificial life and death count for all people. Jesus suffers to pay for the debt of our condition of original sin as well as our actual sin.

The first indication of redemption through a Savior occurs in Genesis 3:15 where God promises an offspring of Adam and Eve, who will crush the serpent's head. That is, he will destroy the devil and nullify his power over humanity. However, in the process of this victory, a price is paid. The offspring will suffer harm as he subdues the devil. Admittedly, this description lacks the detail which a reader may want. Yet, in these words of Yahweh, the plan of redemption begins to unfold in Genesis. Next, just after Genesis 3:15 Yahweh covers the shame of Adam and Eve by making garments of animal skin for them. Covering their sin thus required a very high cost, namely, a death. This could be a typology of future animal sacrifices, which formed the sacramental life of the Old Testament people. These sacrifices prepared the Old Testament church for the coming of the ultimate sacrifice of Christ. The redemption price becomes especially poignant in Genesis in the attempted sacrifice of Isaac (Gen 22:1–19). In this event, the text does not emphasize the faith of Abraham. Rather, it focuses on God's plan to sacrifice His own son, a price He would never require of Abraham or anybody else. At this event the Angel of the Lord—assumedly the pre-incarnate Christ—stops the attempted sacrifice of Isaac (See also Gen 16:6–16). He says that the Lord will provide the sacrifice instead. The sacrificial price would be His own life.

Although not directly specifying a redemption price, other texts also unfold the plan of salvation and show the messianic trajectory of Genesis. First, this appears in the contrast of the first Adam to the second Adam. Scripture refers to

Christ as the second Adam, since He has such a formative effect on humanity like Adam (Rom 5:12–21; 1 Cor 15:21–28). Just as the first Adam brought sin into the world and death through that sin, so also Christ's price of obedience on the cross brings forgiveness and life. Second, Yahweh particularly blesses the line of Shem, the Semites, from which the heritage of Christ comes (Gen 9:27). Third, in Abraham and his *seed* (i.e., descendent), all the nations of the earth will be blessed (Gen 12:2–3; 17:19; Gal 3:16). This promise of a seed to bring great blessing revisits Yahweh's words about a Savior after the fall (Gen 3:15). Fourth, the book of Hebrews interprets the high priesthood of Melchizedek as a **type** of Christ's priesthood, one to overshadow the imperfect and incomplete Aaronic priesthood (Gen 14:18–24; Heb 5:1–9; 7:1–28). Finally, when Jacob delivers his last blessing to his sons, he speaks on behalf of Yahweh to favor the line of Judah from which the Christ would come (Gen 49:8–12).

Justification through Faith

Justification involves the declaration of pardon from guilt in an implied courtroom setting. In the Bible, such a declaration comes from an outside source, Yahweh, who undeservedly confers this gift upon someone. Justification is received through the gift of faith. Faith contributes nothing to the act of justification but only receives. This pardon is free but comes at a high cost to God who declares it. Namely, this pardon from the guilt of sin is possible, since the punishment is transferred to the Savior. In this act of justification, the sinner receives a status of righteous before God. This is not the inherent or natural righteousness, which Adam and Eve possessed at creation. Rather, it is an imputed righteousness, which God graciously credits to a person by the merits of Christ Jesus.

Justification through faith in the book of Genesis becomes particularly clear through Abraham. He believes the gracious promise of Yahweh, particularly that in him and his seed all the nations of the earth would be blessed (Gen 12:2–3; 17:19; Gal 3:16). Although Abraham does not have all the details regarding this coming Savior, he trusts in the gracious plans of Yahweh. Through faith in the promise Abraham receives the gift of justification. "Abram believed the Lord, and he credited it to him as righteousness" (Gen 15:6). Especially in this example of Abraham, St. Paul wishes to make clear that this faith does not count as merit before Yahweh. Faith is not a meritorious work. This righteousness through faith should not be confused with the immature righteousness of life, which is always imperfect in a human. Paul excludes works in the context of justification. Good works do not precede faith (Rom 4:3–25; see Heb 11:8–12). In this way, Paul emphasizes the patriarch Abraham as an archetype of how one is saved.

While Genesis accentuates justification through faith particularly in the person of Abraham, the book of Hebrews highlights additional persons in Genesis who have this righteousness through faith. Although Genesis says little about Abel, Hebrews indicates that he was righteous through faith. "By faith he was commended as a righteous man, when God spoke well of his offerings. And by faith he still speaks even though he is dead" (Heb 11:5b). Regarding Noah, after recounting the building of the ark, Hebrews declares: "By faith, he condemned the world and became heir of the righteousness that comes by faith" (Heb 11:7). Thus, additional Old Testament heroes in Genesis exemplify justification through faith.

Origin of the People Israel

The name *Israel* is a mark of Yahweh's covenant grace. Yahweh gives this name to Jacob as the promise passes from Abraham, to Isaac, and now to him. This name designates Jacob, his children, and all their descendants as objects of Yahweh's mercy. In this way, the name resembles a baptismal name.

Jacob first receives this name in the momentous wrestling with God. Jacob asks for a blessing before God departs. In that context of blessing, God renames him Israel. "Then the man said, 'Your name will no longer be Jacob but Israel because you have struggled with God and have overcome'" (Gen 32:28). Here the meaning of the Hebrew name Israel becomes vital. Indeed, the immediate rendering of Israel would be *he struggles with God*. This translation fits the context, since a noteworthy wrestling match has just taken place. Yet, being a context of blessing, one might expect a pure Gospel meaning associated with Israel as it later receives (Gen 35:10–13; 2 Chr 9:8; Isa 11:12; 27:6; 44:21; Jer 31:31). It is possible that the text includes double meaning in Genesis 32:28 in light of the wider Gospel baggage of Israel as well as the Hebrew wording here. A slight variation of the Hebrew word for Israel can mean *El (God) has made righteous*, and the subsequent explanation of the name would be "Because you are right with God, with men you will prevail." Assuming such a double meaning nicely fits the immediate context as well as the wider Gospel context. This name change indicates an act of mercy and redemption by Yahweh. Formerly, he had the name Jacob which means *he deceives*. Now his name is *God has made righteous*. The deceiver stands forgiven and blessed to be an instrument of the promise. It seems noteworthy that this act of reconciliation between Yahweh and Jacob correlates with the reconciliation between Jacob and Esau (Gen 33:1–19).

Jacob receives the name Israel a second time in Genesis 35:10. "God said to him, 'Your name is Jacob, but you will no longer be called *Jacob*; you will be *Israel*'" (Gen 35:10). The text then includes only promises of divine favor as He made to the previous patriarchs. God promises to make his descendants abundant. A great nation and kings will issue forth from him. Yahweh will grant them the promised land (Gen 35:11–13). In such a context the definition of Israel as *God has made righteous* would fit well, whereas *he struggles with God* would not.

After Jacob, Yahweh then carries on the promise not in one person but in the sons of Israel and their descendants, who also have the designation *tribes* or *children* of Israel. Yahweh carries out the great redemption of Israel in the Exodus. Although initially a correlation between the name Israel and the bloodline of Jacob, the term Israel is not inherently nationalistic, even though Church and state are together in the Israel of the Old Testament. Belonging to Israel does not require a certain heritage. Rather, the name is a gift to anyone. This fact becomes evident not only by the covenant baggage just mentioned in the name Israel but also by the fact that foreigners can become a part of Israel (Ex 12:48–49; 20:10; 23:12; Lev 16:29–30; 19:33–34; Deut 29:11; 31:10–13; Josh 8:33; Ps 146:9; Ezek 47:22–23). Essentially, Israel is the name for the Old Testament Church. This name also pertains to the New Testament Church (Rom 9—11; Gal 3—4).

Since Israel was represented by one person, Jacob, this easily illustrates how another single person can represent Israel as well. Christ is the substitute and representative of the true Israel, that is, the Church. He is Israel boiled down to one. Whereas Israel failed in its arrogance and rebellion, Christ the substitute made up for this by His perfect life and death for us. Our sins were placed on Him, and we receive His baptismal grace. Christians are the new Israel in the long line of those who belonged to Israel by the mercy of God (Gal 6:16).

4. Overview of the Events in the Book

The book of Genesis reflects a distinctly genealogical structure. The various parts of this structure are marked by the Hebrew word *toledoth*, which means *generations* or *historical accounts*. The progression of these generational lines marks the passing of the promise from one generation to the next. Each major generational line ends with a concluding genealogy as the promise passes to the next line. This generational succession emphasizes patriarchal individuals until the promise passes to all Israel, particularly as Genesis flows into Exodus. One can categorize these *toledoth* or historical accounts into three eras: the Pre-Patriarchal History (Gen 1—11), Patriarchal History (Gen 11:27—37:1), and the History of Joseph (Gen 37:2—50:26). Some minor *toledoth* also exist in Genesis which concern secondary individuals not in the line of the promise (Ishmael in 25:12–18; Esau in 36:1—37:1). Although having a genealogical structure, Genesis does not emphasize people, since all fall short of God's perfect standard.

Yahweh is the focus of Genesis. His actions are primary as He graciously enters into human history.

Genesis 1—11 records the period before the major patriarchs. This Pre-Patriarchal period also has the title "primeval history," not because it is myth or unhistorical. Rather, it does not readily lend itself to historical investigation as later periods. Yet, the revelation is absolutely true and historical. This era before the patriarchs commences with Yahweh creating the heavens and the earth (Gen 1:1—2:3). The first occurrence of the word *toledoth* actually occurs in Genesis 2:4, when it introduces the "account of the heavens and the earth" (2:4—4:26). Complementing the universal creation account in Genesis 1, Genesis 2 includes a creation account which emphasizes humanity. After Yahweh's perfect creation, the tragedy of sin breaks in and causes death, including the death of Abel at the hand of his own brother Cain. The next genealogical line (*toledoth*) is that of Adam (5:1—6:8). With little historical narrative, this section primarily recounts Adam's genealogical line as it passes through Seth (not Cain, Gen 4:17–26) and finally to Noah. The promise then proceeds through the *toledoth* of Noah (6:9—9:29) as Yahweh instructs him to build an ark to preserve his family and representatives of all living things to preserve them from a universal flood. In His mercy, Yahweh articulates a portion of the promise in an unconditional covenant never to destroy the earth by flood again (Gen 9:8–17). The next *toledoth* refers to Noah's three sons (Shem, Ham, and Japheth), of which Shem continues the promise (10:1—11:9), not his brothers (Gen 10:2–4, 5–20). The descendant list of Genesis 10 is often called the Table of Nations. The subsequent *toledoth* is "the account of Shem" which traces his line all the way to Abraham's father Terah (Gen 11:10–26).

> MAJOR *TOLEDOTH* IN GENESIS
> Heavens and Earth, 2:4—4:26
> Adam, 5:1—6:8
> Noah, 6:9—9:29
> Noah's Sons, 10:1—11:9
> Shem, 11:10—11:26
> Terah (Abraham), 11:27—25:12
> Isaac, 25:19—35:29
> Jacob (Joseph), 37:2—50:26

The second major section of Genesis is the Patriarchal History (Gen 11:27—37:1). The genealogical account (*toledoth*) which begins the patriarchs concerns Terah. Although Abraham is the initial major patriarch, his family line occurs under his father. At an initial encounter with Abram, Yahweh promises his covenantal grace and calls him to leave his father in Haran and settle in Canaan (Gen 12:1–9). Since Abraham and his nephew have difficulties sharing the same land, they and their servants part ways (Gen 13:1–18). When opposing kings capture Lot, Abraham uses military might to retrieve him. In the process, Abraham meets the priest Melchizedek who blesses him (Gen 14:1–24). After God makes a covenant with Abraham (Gen 15:1–17:27), Abraham intercedes for the cities of Sodom and Gomorrah, since Yahweh intends to destroy these wicked cities. With no righteous people in those cities, the citizens obtain their due punishment (Gen 19:1–38). Although Abraham receives an heir in the person of Isaac, God tests Abraham by asking him to sacrifice Isaac. Yet, Yahweh does not go through with the sacrifice. He actually intends to foreshadow the sacrifice of Christ in this event (Gen 21—22). When Abraham dies, the promise passes to Isaac, whose *toledoth* begins the next patriarchal section (25:19—35:29). Isaac's wife Rebekah bears twin sons, Esau and Jacob. Although Esau is the elder, Yahweh favors Jacob in spite of his conniving nature. When Jacob tricks Esau for the birthright, Jacob flees to his uncle Laban, whose daughters Rachel and Leah he marries (25:19—33:20). Jacob, also called Israel, has twelve sons, who become the leaders of the tribes of Israel. In such a way, the promise passes from one individual to another until Yahweh brings forth the people Israel.

The third and final section of Genesis is the History of Joseph (Gen 37:2—50:26). Although this *toledoth* is ascribed to Jacob (Gen 37:2), the text focuses upon Joseph, since he carries on the promise for his family. When Joseph receives the favor of Jacob, his brothers become jealous and spitefully sell him into slavery in Egypt (Gen 37:2–36). There Yahweh brings Joseph through some significant setbacks to a position of high authority in Egypt (Gen 39—41). In this position Joseph prepares Egypt for a major famine by storing grain during bountiful years. Thereby Yahweh provides a haven for the children of Israel in this crisis. When Joseph's brothers come down to buy grain in Egypt, Joseph eventually reveals his identity to them and brings them all to settle in Egypt. Thus, Genesis anticipates the book of Exodus by answering how Israel arose and how they come to live in Egypt. Genesis also prepares for Yahweh's great Old Testament act of salvation from Egypt.

Creation and Evolution

Creation and the theory of evolution are polar opposites of each other. Creationism accepts the word of Scripture regarding the existence of God, the six-day creation of a mature earth, and the place of humanity as the crowning touch of Yahweh's hand. The more generic "Intelligent Design" has overlap with Crea tionism, since it asserts that some intelligent being must be behind the origin of such a complex universe. Evolution in its classic form accepts no god but relegates all existence to naturalistic causes and views humanity as the most evolved animal. Those who assert evolution against creation vehemently claim this as a debate of science versus religion. However, such is far from the truth. The theory of evolution goes beyond the parameters of science and actually becomes a religion. As a religion, evolution falls far short of Scripture's elevated message. In this comparison of creation versus evolution, it will become apparent how evolution falls short as a science as well as a religion.

Evolution indeed is lacking as a science. This becomes apparent on several grounds. First, the scientific method seeks to test and answer questions in an empirical manner. This involves stating a question, forming a hypothesis, doing experiments to test the hypothesis, and interpreting the data. In the question of "how did life originate?" scientists cannot recreate the scene of the universe's origin nor empirically demonstrate that it occurred in an evolutionary manner. Certain large leaps of faith are required in evolution such as how the Big Bang (or now Inflationary Universe Theories) resulted in greater order whereas every other explosion resulted in greater disorder or how matter arose for this explosion when previously nothing existed.

Second, while science can demonstrate microevolution (natural variation among like creatures), it cannot prove macroevolution (drastic leaps from the simple to the complex). Creationists concur that microevolution exists among creatures. For example, humans have varied eye color, skin color, differences in height and width, and so forth. However, genetic boundaries exist to this variation. People do not sprout wings nor do cats grow gills. Evolutionists assume the existence of transitional species, which demonstrate the upward evolution across types of living beings. However, no such transitional species or "missing links" have ever been found among fossil records.

Third, whereas evolutionists assert natural selection as the means by which simplicity becomes complexity, such cannot be demonstrated. On the contrary, mutations result in a harmful, downward trend within a species.Fourth, radiometric dating processes such as Potassium-Argon, Argon-Argon, and Uranium-Helium dating proceed with certain assumptions regarding the existence of a given substance within an artifact. However, the assumptions of these dating methods are being shown to be tenuous. Many more points could receive mention about how evolution is still a theory and not fact. Evolution rests upon many assumptions or leaps of faith. When faith is required in matters such as the origin of life, evolution is not a true science but indeed becomes a religion.

Evolution falls short as a religion in contrast to the true message of Scripture. First, evolution naturally results in atheism. Thus, humanity becomes a god, namely, the source of identity, security, and meaning in life. This is the sin of Adam and Eve. Second, without acknowledging the existence of God, humanity becomes the measure of all truth, including the value ascribed to life. With a myriad of different people and points of view, relativism becomes inevitable. Third, without God as creator, humanity does not possess its dignified, valued position by divine design, but has rather usurped this position through rising from a so-called primordial soup. Fourth, evolution wishes to create the façade of constant improvement. In contrast, Scripture indicates the truth that sin has corrupted the world and is making the matters continually worse. The world greatly needs rescue. This leads to the fifth and final point that rejecting God as creator ultimately means rejecting Christ as Savior. Evolution sees no need for salvation as promised in Christ. Thus, evolution provides no hope for humanity other than in itself. In contrast, the salvation promised in Christ through the forgiveness of sins provides hope in a fallen world. Indeed, the religion of Scripture far outshines the religion proposed in evolution.

Ancient Creation Accounts

Besides Genesis 1—2, other ancient creation accounts exist, some having significant parallels with the Genesis creation accounts. These additional texts primarily come from ancient Egypt and Mesopotamia. The Egyptian the texts originate from the cultic centers of Memphis, Helipolois and Hermonpolis, each of which worshiped its respective god and ascribes a role in creation to it. The most famous text from Egypt is the *Memphite Theology*, whose original possibly dates from the thirteenth century before Christ. The primary texts from Mesopotamia are the *Epic of Atrahasis* and the *Enuma Elish*. While these texts may demonstrate some familiarity with a common biblical tradition, they lack the lofty nature of the Genesis account. For example, only the Genesis text assumes that the creator is eternal and made the universe out of nothing. The *Papyrus Leiden* I 350 from Hermopolis asserts that the first god Amun came forth from the waters. Waters and darkness already existed, and the gods merely come onto the scene to bring order. In the *Enuma Elish*, the god Marduk kills Tiamat, the goddess of the primeval oceans. Marduk then divides her carcass to make the heavens and the earth. Second, in the Genesis account Yahweh solely is at the scene without competition or enemy, whereas the other accounts have a deified or personified opposition at the scene of creation. Tiamat brings chaotic opposition against Marduk. The Egyptian chaotic source is the ocean god Nun. Third, the identity and role of humanity significantly differs as well. According to the

Epic of Atrahasis, clay and the blood of slain rebel gods are mixed together to form people. In the Enuma Elish, Marduk takes the blood of Tiamat to create people. Rather than the lofty role of humanity in Genesis, Marduk makes humanity for the purpose of hard labor so that the gods need not toil. In summary, while similarities may exist between Genesis and other texts from the Ancient Near East, these extra-biblical accounts are imperfect and often corrupted reflections of the Bible.

5
Exodus

Normally every year the newspapers report a miraculous rescue of somebody trapped, perhaps in a cave, a mine, or an abandoned well. While trapped, the person suffered the pangs of confinement and feared for his or her life. Suddenly after all hope seemed hopeless, the rescue team came and lifted the person to safety. What joy that person certainly experienced in the gift of freedom! What thanks the rescued person showed to the members of the rescue team because of this life-changing event! The book of Exodus proclaims a similar story of an entire nation. The Israelites are trapped in slavery under the oppressive nation of Egypt. Yahweh comes to rescue the people by the mediation of Moses. Through great miracles, including the parting of the Red Sea, the Lord brings the people to safety. He then describes the new identity they have in Him and how God's people live. Yahweh also provides the Tabernacle where He locates His name to grant forgiveness. These events provide a preview of the great rescue in Christ. Through His life, death, and resurrection He saved us from the sin, death, and the devil. He grants these gifts today where He has located His name, that is, in His Word and Sacraments.

1. Date of Writing—*When Was Exodus Recorded?*
2. Date of the Events of the Book—*When Did the Exodus Take Place?*
3. Themes—*Important Motifs that Characterize Exodus*
4. Overview of the Events in Exodus—*What is Contained in Exodus?*
5. Important Passages—*Pivotal Portions of Exodus*

1. Date of Writing

The date of writing of Exodus depends upon the assumed author of the book. According to the text of Exodus (Exod 17:14; 24:4; 34:27), Yahweh gives His revelation to Moses, who then puts this revelation into written form. Additionally, Joshua 8:31 confirms that Moses wrote the words of Exodus 20:25. The New Testament also ascribes portions of Exodus to Mosaic authorship (Mark 7:10; 12:26; see Luke 2:22–23). Historically, Christianity and Judaism have accepted Moses as the author of Exodus as well as the rest of the Pentateuch. Since the traditional date of the Exodus is 1446 BC (see below for evidence) and the

Israelites wandered with Moses forty years until his death (Deut 34), the book of Exodus was written between 1446 and 1406 BC.

2. Date of the Events in the Book

The Biblical data provides primary input regarding the date of the Exodus. I Kings 6:1 states, "In the four hundred and eightieth year after the Israelites had come out of Egypt, in the fourth year of Solomon's reign over Israel, in the month of Ziv, the second month, he began to build the temple of the Lord." This year in Solomon's reign is known to be 966 BC. Taking the 480 years literally places the Exodus at 1446 BC, and 1406 BC would mark the end of their wilderness wanderings, the death of Moses, and entry into the promised land. In Judges 11:26 the Judge Jephthah indicates that Israel had occupied particular cities in Canaan for 300 years since the conquest of that land. (Jephthah was probably using 300 as a round number.) Knowing that the date of Jephthah began his judgeship around 1088 BC and adding 300 years to that would fit nicely with end of the conquest in 1400 BC. Exodus 1:11 states that the Israelite slaves built the city of Rameses. This apparently poses a problem with the 1446 dating, since Rameses II reigned from 1304–1237 BC. However, one could reasonably say that the name *Rameses* existed before Rameses II or perhaps there was an editorial updating that occurred in the Exodus text after Moses' time. Taking this Biblical evidence and a high chronology of Egyptian dating, the Pharaoh of the Israelite oppression was Thutmose III (1504–1450 BC), while the Pharaoh at the time of the actual Exodus was Amenhotep II (1450–1425 BC).

Additional chronology of this time period can be gleaned from the Biblical text. According to Deuteronomy 34:6, Moses died at the age of 120. Acts 7:23 tells that Moses was 40 years old when he killed the Egyptian and moved to Midian. According to Acts 7:30, Moses had been in Midian forty years when Yahweh appeared to commission him for the Exodus (see also Exod 7:7). The three periods of forty years, for a total of 120 years, may be rounded numbers. However, taken literally, his birth would have been in 1526 BC and flight to Midian in 1486 BC, knowing that the Exodus was in 1446 BC and death in 1406 BC.

Examples of some extra-biblical evidence also support the 1446 date of the Exodus. First, an Egyptian inscription from Pharaoh Merneptah records a military victory poem during the fifth year of his reign, around 1207 BC. This inscription called either the "Merneptah Stela" or "Israel Stela" contains the earliest extra-biblical reference to "the people of Israel," whom Merneptah purportedly defeated. Many would argue that the Israelites were certainly in the land for centuries to be recognized by Pharaoh as an established ethnic group. Second, the 382 letters of the .Amarna Tablets describe the political situation in Canaan during the fourteenth century BC. These texts speak of political chaos caused by the *Habiru*, which is likely the Hebrew Israelites. This would characterize well the situation at the conquest of Canaan. Third, excavations at cities such as Jericho and Hazor indicate destruction shortly after the 1406 BC arrival of the Israelites according to some archaeologists. Fourth, the Dream Stela of Thutmose IV (1425–1417) tells that he was not the original legal heir to the throne. Thutmose IV is the one who followed Amenhotep II (1450–1425 BC), the Pharaoh of the Exodus. Amenhotep II would logically not have a first-born son, since he died in the tenth plague.

Selected Evidence for the Exodus in 1446 BC

Source	Contents
1 Kings 6:1	The Exodus occurred 480 years before Solomon built his temple in 966 BC
Judges 11:26	Jephthah (1088 BC) says that the conquest occurred 300 years previously.
Merneptah Stela (1207 BC)	The term *people of Israel* likely indicates that the Israelites had already been in the land for centuries.
Amarna Tablets (14th Century BC)	The "Habiru" are causing havoc in Canaan.
Jericho and Hazor excavations	Evidence shows destruction at the assumed time of the conquest.
Dream Stela of Thutmose IV (1425–1417)	Thutmose IV was not the originally intended legal heir.

3. Themes

Redemption

Redemption involves rescuing or ransoming someone or something in jeopardy. The classical Biblical definition of redemption in civil legislation is found in Leviticus (Lev 25:25–28, 47–49; see also Num 3:51, Neh 5:8). According to Leviticus, in cases of property foreclosure or slavery caused by severe indebtedness, the closest relative or **kinsman-redeemer** is obligated to pay the redemption price to acquire release. In Exodus the great Old Testament redemption takes place when Yahweh rescues Israel, which is being held in slavery under an evil ruler. In Exodus 6:6 Yahweh defines this redemption through parallel statements: "Therefore say to the Israelites: 'I am the Lord, and I will bring you out from under the yoke of the Egyptians. I will free you from being slaves to them, and I will redeem you with an outstretched arm and mighty acts of judgment.'" (See Deut 9:26; 2 Sam 7:23; 1 Chr 17:21) That is, Yahweh graciously assumes the role of kinsman-redeemer. He makes Israel His own people to bring them out of this oppressive slavery and grant them the land promised. The Israelites were "baptized" as His people through the Red Sea (1 Cor 10:2). They become His Old Testament Church. Yahweh is known throughout the Old Testament as Israel's redeemer in various situations (e.g. Job 19:25; Ps 19:14; 34:22; 78:35, 52; Isa 44:6; 48:17; 52:3, 9; 63:9). While the Exodus redemption may not appear to have a redemption price paid to gain the Israelite freedom, one can indirectly point to the lives of the first-born males in Egypt as the ultimate price which led to the Israelite release from slavery.

The life of Jesus, the only-begotten Son of God, was our redemption or ransom price (Acts 20:28; 1 Cor 6:19–20; Gal 3:13; 4:4–5; Eph 1:7; Col 1:14; 1 Tim 2:5–6; Tit 2:14; Heb 9:12; 1 Pet 1:18–19; Rev 5:9). He purchased and won our freedom from slavery to sin (Rom 7:23), death (Isa 25:8; John 5:24; Rom 7:24–25), the curse of the law (Gal 3:13), and the evil ruler Satan (Heb 2:14; 1 John 3:8). Jesus assumed the role of our kinsman-redeemer when He took on human nature. He makes people His own in Holy Baptism, a sacrament where people are rescued through water connected with God's Word. There He creates a people for Himself, the New Testament Church, the new Israel. He will lead them to their promised land in the resurrection of the body and the everlasting life. The Exodus, the great redemption act of the Old Testament, points forward to the greater redemptive act of the New Testament.

Covenant and Testament

Yahweh made two types of covenants with His Old Testament people. One type is a conditional agreement between Yahweh and people, while the other is an unconditional promise of divine favor. The former is a Law covenant, since it depends to some extent on human effort. The latter covenant of pure promise is Gospel. The general nature of these two types of covenants has significant overlap with alliances made by kings of the Ancient Near East. A "Suzerain-vassal Covenant" was a conditional alliance made by a great king (**suzerain**; see Deuteronomy "Overview of book") with a lesser king (**vassal**). A "Royal Grant Covenant" was a king's unconditional promise of favor to a loyal servant for particular faithfulness. Yet, the content of Biblical and secular covenants is not identical. Yahweh's relationship with Israel is much deeper than the relationship of a political alliance or benevolent act of a king. Yahweh is their loving God, and they are His chosen, beloved people. The content of the Old Testament emphasizes sin, grace, and a life of sanctification rather than political fidelity. In the table below the major covenants between Yahweh and His Old Testament people are listed and identified.

Covenant Type	Reference	Recipient	Description
Unconditional	Gen 9:8–17	Noah	Yahweh promises never to destroy the earth with a flood again.
Unconditional	Gen 12:2–3	Abram	Yahweh promises that He will make Abram into a great nation, bless, and protect him.
Unconditional	Gen 15	Abram	Yahweh promises many offspring and the land of Canaan.
Conditional	Gen 17	Abraham	Yahweh promises offspring, faithfulness, and land on the condition of fidelity illustrated by circumcision.

Conditional	Exod 19—24	Israel	Yahweh promises to be their God with the condition of Israel's fidelity to Him.
Unconditional	Num 25:10–31	Phinehas	Yahweh promises an enduring priesthood for this family.
Unconditional	2 Sam 7:5–16	David	Yahweh promises to bless David and his kingdom and continually provide a king like David.
Unconditional	Jer 31:31–34	Israel	Yahweh promises a new covenant to forgive sins and write His law on His people's heart.

A testament has much overlap with a covenant, particularly the unconditional, Gospel type of covenant. In a testament the stipulations of a will are carried out at one's death. Thus, the death of the testament's author is required for beneficiaries to receive the gifts. While the Old Testament covenants above at times use blood for ratification (Gen 15; Exod 19—24), the covenant author does literally not give up his life. It became apparent that the conditional covenants would not suffice (Jer 31:32). Because of their sinful condition, the Israelites could not be faithful to uphold their end of the covenant. Therefore, a new covenant would be necessary, based partially on the previous unconditional covenants (Gal 3—5). Yahweh speaks about this new covenant in Jeremiah 31:31–34. This is a covenant founded solely on the Lord's divine favor, emphasizing the forgiveness of sins. As this covenant was fulfilled in Christ, it became obvious that this was also a testament. Jesus said at the institution of the Lord's Supper, "This cup is the new covenant in my blood which is poured out for you" (Luke 22:20b; see 1 Cor 11:25). The death of Jesus brought into effect the benefits of the new covenant/testament: forgiveness of sins, life, and salvation. The Old Testament unconditional covenants give a preview of the promise fulfilled in Christ.

Sanctification

Sanctification in its narrow sense is the inward spiritual transformation of a believer by the miraculous working of the Holy Spirit through the means of grace. After God graciously pardons our sins through the work of Jesus Christ (justification), Christians are not yet perfect inside. Although viewed as righteous in God's eyes through Christ's atoning work, the sinful side of us, known as the Old Adam, yet remains. Sanctification is that process through which the Old Adam is daily put to death in baptism and the new man daily arises in Christ (Rom 6:4). That is, a Christian is simultaneously saint and sinner (a thought often summarized in the Latin phrase *simul iustus et peccator*). In sanctification, God kills the sinner but raises the saint. The Law of God kills the Old Adam as it exposes sin, whereas the Gospel enlivens the new self. This is the rhythm of confession and forgiveness. Motivated by the Gospel, the new self then gladly follows the Law of God.

Yahweh's pattern of killing the sinner to give life to the saint becomes commonplace in Exodus. The Israelites become accustomed to observing this pattern outside themselves when Yahweh causes death among the Egyptians to give life to the saints of Israel. This previews what will happen within their hearts as Yahweh brings sanctification by killing the sinner and raising the saint within them. In the first nine plagues, the Israelites observe the context of death among the Egyptians by the appearance of blood instead of water (Exod 7:14–24), the dead frogs (Exod 8:12–14), the livestock (Exod 9:6), the destruction of crops from a hailstorm (Exod 9:24–26), and the destruction of crops from the locusts (Exod 10:15). These occur in the process of Yahweh giving freedom and new life to His saints of Israel. The tenth plague demonstrates this pattern even more poignantly, since the Egyptian first-born males die as archetypes of those who reject Yahweh. Yet, the saintly Israelite children come forth alive in this death context because of the blood of the lamb (Exod 11:1—12:30). The most illustrative example of this pattern occurs at the Red Sea. Both the heathen Egyptian armies and the Israelites enter the water. Yahweh kills the sinners, yet raises the saints through the water. This water of the Exodus resembles baptism (1 Cor 10:2) as Christians are baptized into Christ's death and the old self dies. In Christ's resurrection the baptized saints in Christ come forth alive (Rom 6:2–11).

Having been "baptized" as God's people in the Red Sea, the Israelites come to realize how sanctification also happens among themselves as well. The book of Exodus illustrates how the Israelites are still sinners as well as saints. Thus, death is threatened for various sins such as murder, attacking one's parents, kidnapping, or cursing one's parents (Exod 21:12–17; see also Exod 22:18–24). When the Israelites rebel by worshipping a golden calf instead of Yahweh, the

Lord brings death to a token amount of these Israelite sinners (Exod 32:27–29) who were also declared to be saints. The sin-exposing Law has done its task by leading to confession. Moses confesses the sin of the people before Yahweh on their behalf (Exod 32:31–32). Although the people suffer some natural consequences of their offences (Exod 32:35), Yahweh does forgive them. He renews the covenant and continues to be their God to lead them to the land of Canaan (Exod 34:1–28). Yahweh initiates this renewal with the words, "The Lord, the Lord, the compassionate and gracious God, slow to anger, abounding in love and faithfulness, maintaining love to thousands, and forgiving wickedness, rebellion and sin..." (Exod 34:6b–7a). With these events the Israelites come to know the rhythm of confession and forgiveness, death and life, as the pattern for the entire Christian life.

The Israelites also learn the motivation for following Yahweh's Law in their life of sanctification. It is the saving Gospel, which granted them a new identity as His people and now moves them to live in that identity. The context of the Ten Commandments illustrates this particularly. Yahweh begins that context with the Gospel words, "I am the Lord your God, who brought you out of Egypt, out of the land of slavery" (Exod 20:2). After this Gospel statement of their identity, the Ten Commandments appear. Originally called the "Ten Words," they are actually statements of how a saint lives, not commands to coerce. The saint gladly and naturally follows this life into which he was baptized. Here the Law has a teaching function to show the content of what is God-pleasing. This is known as the **third use of the Law**. The new identity based on the Ten Words is further explained for the Israelite context in the "Book of the Covenant" (Exod 20:22—23:19). However, since the saint is also sinner, these Ten Words also continually convict the old self as well. The convicting function is the **second use of the Law**. The Gospel motivation becomes apparent in one final example, the initial ratification of the covenant. After the great salvation by Yahweh and the shedding of the blood to ratify the covenant, the Israelites are moved to say, "We will do everything the Lord has said; we will obey" (Exod 24:7b).

Worship

The worship life of Israel was located at the Tabernacle, a large and portable tent structure with many fixtures inside. Yahweh's directions for Tabernacle and fixture construction appear in Exodus 25—31. Subsequently, Exodus 35—39 details how the Israelites carried out these exact instructions. The descriptions of the Tabernacle illustrate three points. First, the Tabernacle and worship life of Israel is centered around the presence of Yahweh and His divine action for the people. Second, all parts of the tabernacle are very ornate in accordance with their holy purposes. Third, everything regarding Tabernacle construction and usage is very orderly.

First, the Tabernacle and worship life of Israel are indeed centered around the presence of Yahweh and His divine action for the people. That is, the action of the people is not the primary focus point in the worship life of Israel. Everything about the Tabernacle flows from the specified wishes of Yahweh, not the people's input. The introductory words for Tabernacle construction specify its purpose as a dwelling place for Yahweh among His people (Exod 25:8). Yahweh has similar words concerning its consecration: "So I will consecrate the Tent of Meeting and the altar, and I will consecrate Aaron and his sons to serve me as priest. Then I will dwell among the Israelites and be their God" (Exod 29:44–45). The climax of the Tabernacle and the closing touch of Exodus is when the glorious presence of Yahweh descends upon the Tabernacle. Although He is certainly everywhere, Yahweh chooses specifically to be located here for Israel, His Old Testament Church. This "real presence" of Yahweh located at the Temple is primarily merciful. He associates His gracious presence at the Tabernacle with His rescue in the Exodus (Exod 29:46). Importantly, Yahweh's first directions for the Tabernacle were to construct the Ark of Testimony (also called the Ark of the Covenant), particularly the atonement cover, where forgiveness would be granted through blood (Exod 25:10–22; Lev 16:14– 17). Additionally, bread of the Presence on the special table is in the presence of God to bring blessing (Exod 25:23–30; 33:14–15; Isa 63:9). The horns of the altar are connected with help, refuge, and atonement in the sacrifices (Exod 29:12; Lev 4:7, 18, 25, 30, 34; 8:15; 9:9; 16:18; 1 Kgs 1:50; 2:28; Ps 18:2). The emphasis on Yahweh's action in the Tabernacle becomes very vivid in the consecration of the priests as they have a very passive role. The priests just stand and receive the gifts of the holy office and the articles for priestly service (Exod 28—29). Finally, Yahweh specifies that *He* decides when and how He meets people at the Tabernacle (Exod 29:42–43).

Second, all parts of the Tabernacle are very ornate in accordance with their holy purposes. The materials used in construction are the most precious available: gold, silver, bronze, fine linen, acacia wood, various gems, and so forth. (Exod 25:3–7). The amounts of these fine materials used are vast (Exod 38:21–31). The Tabernacle and its furnishings are also finely crafted from these precious materials. For example, the Ark of Testimony consists of acacia wood, overlaid with gold inside and outside. The poles used to carry the ark have gold overlay, and the rings for the poles are pure gold. The atonement cover is pure gold, having two ornate gold cherubim on top (Exod 25:10–22). The Lampstand is made of one talent of pure gold (about 75 pounds), ornately constructed with branches, buds, and blossoms (Exod 25:31–40). Finally, Yahweh selects the most skilled craftsmen for construction (Exod 31:1–11).

Third, everything regarding Tabernacle construction and usage is very orderly. Yahweh gives very specific details and insists on this pattern (Exod 25:8). Nothing is haphazard or spontaneously done. For example, Yahweh specifies exactly four gold rings for the Table and how to fasten then to the four corners (Exod 25:26–27). All eleven curtains of the Tabernacle must be the same size (Exod 26:8). The priestly garments are described in great detail in an organized way. Yahweh introduces the breastpiece, ephod, robe, woven tunic, turban and sash. Then He proceeds to describe exactly how each should look (Exod 28). Moses inspects the constructed Tabernacle and furnishings to ensure that every detail is exact (Exod 39:32–43). Not only is the construction orderly and consistent, but also the rituals to take place in the Tabernacle display the same orderliness. Every single day, the high priest offers two lambs, each a year old—one in the morning and one in the evening—in a particular way with fine flour, oil and wine. This is a daily practice for generations to come in Israel (Exod 29:38–43). Additionally, the high priest must burn fragrant incense on the altar every single morning (Exod 30:7–8). Aaron's same sacred garments are consistent for succeeding generations (Exod 29:29–30).

Such a description of worship in Israel provided a preview of Christ and a pattern for the Christian Church. The divine presence of Yahweh with the physical structure of the Tabernacle foreshadows the incarnation of Christ, where God dwelt among His people, having taken a human nature upon Himself. Forgiveness is located with Christ just as with the atonement cover (also called "mercy seat") in the Tabernacle (Rom 3:25). Christ would offer Himself as the ultimate sacrifice in the heavenly Tabernacle, of which the Israelite Tabernacle was a copy (Heb 8:2; 9:24–25). Thus there exists an intentional parallel between the earthly Tabernacle/Temple and the heavenly one. Christian worship emphasizes the presence and action of God as He comes in Word and Sacrament today. His real presence of His body and blood is truly in, with, and under the bread and wine. Today also, worship is appropriately ornate and orderly. Frequent repetition of receiving God's gifts in Word and Sacrament is vital for the Christian life.

Moses as the Foundational Prophet of God in the Old Testament

Moses indeed was the Old Testament's foundational prophet. Whereas other prophets received revelation through visions and dreams, only Moses received revelation directly from the mouth of Yahweh (Num 12:6–8; Deut 34:10). Additionally, Moses wrote the large and foundational portion of Scripture called the Pentateuch, the first five books of the Bible. The characteristic roles of the prophetic office in the Bible are "foretelling" and "forthtelling," namely, revealing future events and proclaiming Yahweh's immediate revelation. While Moses' prophetic work is not devoid of foretelling (e.g., Deut 18:14–20; 31:14–29), Moses' primary contribution is proclaiming the message of Yahweh. Through Moses, Yahweh reveals instructions for specific situations at that time in Israel (e.g., Exod14:1–4; Num 9:1–5; 16:23–24) as well as legislation with ongoing scope (e.g., Exod 20:22—23:33; Lev 1:1—7:37). He conveys God's revelation both verbally and in written form (e.g., Exod 24:4; 31:18; 32:15–16; 34:28; Deut 31:24). He conveys Yahweh's message of Law (e.g., Exod 23:1–13; 32:19–29; Lev 20; Deut 4—5) and Gospel (e.g., Exod 6:6–8; 15:1–21; 20:1; 24:1–11; Lev 16) in pivotal moments early in Israel's history. Like many prophets, Moses also performs miracles (e.g., Exod 5—11; 14; 15:22–27; Deut 34:11–12). The ongoing vital role of Moses becomes obvious when only He and Elijah appear with Jesus on the mountain of His transfiguration (Matt 17:1–13; Mark 9:2–13; Luke 9:28–36). Finally, Christ is the fulfillment of a future prophet, who is greater than Moses (Deut 18:14–20; Acts 3:22–23, 7:37).

4. Overview of the Events in Exodus

The name *Exodus* means *road out*, referring to Israelite departure from Egypt by Yahweh's great acts of power and mercy. This departure is the central topic of Exodus and the foremost act of Old Testament salvation, which anticipates a greater act of salvation in Christ. Jesus gives a glimpse of this salvation at the time of His transfiguration when He reveals His divine glory (Luke 9:28–36). There He speaks with Moses and Elijah about His departure, namely, His death (Luke 9:31). The Greek word for departure is the word *exodus*. Therefore, just as Moses would rescue the Israelites through His role as mediator, so also Christ would mediate an even greater rescue from sin and death by His own death on the cross. When Christ came forth victoriously on Easter, this exodus from the tomb sealed life and freedom in Christ as the final verdict for God's people.

Exodus begins by recounting the names of the Israelite tribes that settled in Egypt. From these original seventy people Yahweh greatly multiplies the number of Israelites, a partial fulfillment of Yahweh's original promises to Abraham (Gen 12:2). After a change in Egyptian dynasties, the new Pharaoh becomes nervous about Israel's prosperity in numbers. The Egyptians, therefore, enslave the Israelites and oppress them in hard labor. Pharaoh even attempts to exterminate the Israelite male babies in order the curb their population growth (Exod 1:1–22). In Yahweh's great mercy and in remembrance of His covenant promises, He sends a child who would grow up to be their deliverer, Moses. Because of Pharaoh's attempts to kill Israelite male babies, Yahweh works through various individuals to ensure his safety, including Pharaoh's daughter who raised Moses in Pharaoh's household. When Moses reaches adulthood and sees the oppression of his people, he unleashes his anger by killing an Egyptian who was abusing an Israelite. After Pharaoh hears of this treasonous act and threatens punishment, Moses flees to the land of Midian for refuge and establishes a family there (Exod 2:1–25).

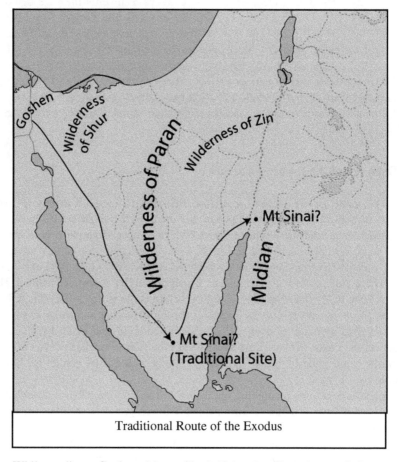

Traditional Route of the Exodus

While tending a flock on Mount Sinai, Yahweh calls and commissions a reluctant Moses to confront Pharaoh and deliver His people from slavery (Exod 3:1—4:17). When Pharaoh refuses a request for the people to depart, Yahweh sends a series of plagues through the hand of Moses, the last plague culminating in the death of first-born males of the Egyptians (Exod 4:18—11:10). This last plague and Israel's imminent departure provide the context for the institution of the Passover (Exod 12:1–30). With such a devastating plague, Pharaoh finally relents and lets the Israelites leave. Pharaoh, however, changes his mind and pursues the Israelites as far as the Red Sea. There Yahweh parts the waters and allows the Israelites to cross on dry ground while the Egyptian military is held at bay. When the Egyptians are finally allowed to pursue them into the dry seabed, Yahweh again brings the waters to their original state, thus drowning Pharaoh's military. Moses and Miriam then lead the Israelites in praise to the Lord for this great deliverance (Exod 12:31—15:21).

The remainder of the book concerns the difficult travels to Mount Sinai, the covenant and rebellion at Sinai, and consecration of the Tabernacle. Along the path to Sinai, troubles already begin. As the Israelites become hungry and thirsty, they complain to Moses and wish they were back in Egypt. Yet, Yahweh graciously provides daily, miraculous sustenance for them (Exod 15:21—17:16). They arrive in Sinai three months after their departure from Egypt. At Mount Sinai Yahweh instructs Moses to have the people consecrate themselves. They must wash their clothes to be in the presence of Yahweh as He reveals His covenant word to them. This is reminiscent of the liturgy when Christians are cleansed by confession and absolution to be in the presence of God as He reveals His word (Exod 19). Then Yahweh begins His words with a reminder of His gracious rescue from Egypt. After this Gospel word, He proceeds to describe the identity of a covenant people in the Ten Commandments (Exod 20:1–21). Yahweh then reveals the "Book of the Covenant" (Exod 20:22—23:19), which elaborates the application of the Ten Commandments as they would be lived by the Israelites in their setting in the ancient world. All this revelation takes place in the context of the covenant ratification. Accordingly, the people affirm their adherence to Yahweh's covenant words. Moses sprinkles blood on an altar and on the Israelites to mark them as a forgiven people and to seal the covenant (Exod 24:1–11). He once again ascends Mount Sinai to receive revelation concerning the Tabernacle, its furnishings, rituals at the Tabernacle, and the priesthood (Exod 24:12—31:18). Unfortunately, the Israelites quickly forget their promise to live as a people faithful to Yahweh. When Moses is delayed on the mountain, they ask Aaron to make an image of a calf as a substitute god for Yahweh. Aaron and the elders surprisingly comply. Yahweh's anger justly burns against the people, but Moses intercedes to beg forgiveness for them. Yahweh relents and renews the covenant promise made to their ancestors to lead them to the promised land (Exod 32—34). The Tabernacle and everything associated with it is then constructed according to the words of Moses. After its completion the glory of the Lord settles upon the Tabernacle (Exod 35—40). This is His real presence among them associated with a physical object. This gracious presence foreshadows Christ living among His people, having taken physical humanity to Himself.

I. The Exodus (1:1—15:21)
    A. Israel oppressed in Egypt and Moses' early life (1:1—2:25)
    B. Moses called by God (3;1—4:17)
    C. God delivers His people from Egypt (4:18—13:16)
       1. Moses returns to Egypt (4:18–31)
       2. Moses and Aaron confront Pharaoh (5:1–21)
       3. God reassures Moses (5:22—6:12)
       4. The genealogy of Moses and Aaron (6:13—27)
       5. God reassures Moses again (6:28—7:7)
       6. Moses and Aaron confront Pharaoh again (7:8–13)
       7. Ten Plagues
          a. Water turned to blood (7:14–24)
          b. Frogs (7:25—8:15)
          c. Gnats (8:16–19)
          d. Flies (8:20–32)
          e. Livestock (9:1–7)
          f. Boils (9:8–12)
          g. Hail (9:13–35)
          h. Locusts (10:1–20)
          i. Darkness (10:21–29)
          j. Firstborn die (11:1–10)
       8. The Passover (12:1–30)
       9. The Exodus (12:31–42)
       10. Passover regulations (12:43–51)
       11. Consecration of the firstborn (13:1–16)
       12. Crossing the Red Sea (13:7—14:31)
       13. The Song of Moses (15:1–21)
II. In the Desert (15:22—40:38)
    A. God provides for his rebellious people (15:22—18:27)
       1. Water at Marah and Elim (15:22–27)
       2. Manna and quail (16:1–36)
       3. Water from the rock (17:1–7)
       4. Defeat of the Amalekites (17:8–16)
       5. Jethro visits Moses (18:1–27)
    B. Preparation for God's presence on Mount Sinai (19:1–25)
    C. Ten Commandments (20:1–21)
    D. The Book of the Covenant (20:22—23:33)
    E. The Covenant Affirmed (24:1–11)

F. Instructions for constructing the Tabernacle (24:12–32:18)
G. The Covenant broken, but reaffirmed (32:1–34:35)
    1. Israel worships a golden calf (32:1–33:6)
    2. Moses and the Tent of Meeting (33:7–11)
    3. Moses sees the Lord's glory (33:12–23)
    4. New stone tablets (34:1–28)
    5. Moses' shining face (34:2–35)
H. Worship and the constructing of the Tabernacle (35:1—40:38)

The contents of Exodus demonstrate a strong link particularly with Genesis as well as the subsequent books of the Pentateuch. The links with Genesis are obvious, for example, by the opening words of Exodus which link with the genealogy of Genesis 46:8–27. Just as Israel lived in Egypt, including a confrontation with Pharaoh as well as plagues, so also Abraham and Sarah experienced a similar situation (Gen 12:10–20). The events in Exodus are already prophesied in Genesis (Gen 15:13–14). Also, the fulfillment of God's promise of many descendents in Exodus (Exod 1:7) is promised in Genesis (Gen 17:6; 22:17). Exodus fits well with Leviticus which immediately follows. Exodus ends by telling where the liturgical life of Israel takes place. Leviticus tells how it takes place. Numbers commences with additional revelation at Mount Sinai. It then continues the travels of Exodus by recounting their journey from Mount Sinai to the plains of Moab at the border of the promised land of Canaan. Deuteronomy emphasizes Yahweh's acts of salvation from Exodus to a new generation and revisits the Ten Commandments.

6
Leviticus

Does a traditional, liturgical church service seem boring? Does it sometimes appear that the rituals of such a service have little meaning, just going through the motions? This can often be a first impression of a liturgical service. One might have a similar reaction when reading the book of Leviticus. With little explanation Leviticus gives rubrics or directions concerning the church services and daily life of the Old Testament Christians. What may appear to be empty ritualism is actually full of richness from God's Word. What may appear to be cold, stagnant directions on a holy life actually characterize the joyful identity into which the Israelites were "baptized" when Yahweh chose them and led them through the waters of the Red Sea. In Leviticus, the reader is invited to enter a different culture and a different way of thinking as the Old Testament gifts of Yahweh are given to an undeserving people. These Old Testament gifts of forgiveness, life, salvation, and a corresponding holy life find their fulfillment in the holiness, which Christ won for us on the cross. When one learns the rituals of the Old Testament, one receives a glimpse at how they point forward to Christ. When one learns and appreciates the rituals of the Christian Church, one receives a profound depth of God's revelation in Christ. Leviticus is characterized by the gracious word and action of Yahweh connected with a physical means such as an animal sacrifice. Similarly, the sacraments of the Church involve God's action with His Word, connected to a physical means, to grant forgiveness.

1. Date of Writing—*When Were These Laws Given to Israel?*
2. Themes—*Important Motifs in Leviticus*
3. Overview of the Book—*What Is Contained in Leviticus?*
4. Important Passages—*Pivotal Portions of Leviticus*

1. Date of Writing

The date of composition of Leviticus depends upon the assumed authorship of the book. As the other books of the Pentateuch, Mosaic authorship is traditionally accepted. Leviticus contains several verses which clearly affirm this claim. Immediately, the first verse of the book indicates that God speaks directly to Moses in the context of Mt. Sinai. In response, Moses communicates the word of Yahweh to the people. This verse (Lev 1:1) sets the character of the entire book in general and begins the section on the five main offerings in particular (Lev 1—7). The concluding section on the offerings also asserts that God gave these regulations to Moses to relay to the Israelites (Lev 7:37–38). Finally, the book of Leviticus also concludes with a similar claim of authorship. "These are the commands the Lord gave Moses on Mt. Sinai for the Israelites" (Lev 27:34). These beginning and ending statements of divine authorship through the mediation of Moses make the authority of this book unmistakably clear. These verses serve as pillars to characterize the nature of Leviticus.

Having determined the author of Leviticus, the date of the book depends upon the dating of Moses' life, particularly through the dating of the Exodus. As noted regarding other books of the Pentateuch, 1 Kings 6:1 helps determine the traditional date of the Exodus at 1446 BC. According to the text (Exod 19, Lev 7:38–39, 27:34, Num 10:11), Yahweh revealed the divine regulations in Leviticus, given at Sinai, within twenty-six months after the Exodus. Since Moses subsequently died in 1406 BC, the book of Leviticus was written during those remaining years of Moses' life.

2. Themes

Sin and Grace

The existence of sin and its ramifications become blatantly obvious in the book of Leviticus. Several observations are noteworthy. First, sin is not a superficial rash, which can be ignored or easily cured. As seen by the frequent death of animals to bring forgiveness, sin is drastically serious. Second, having diagnosed its seriousness, Leviticus clearly indicates that sin must be dealt with. The rubrics for the sacrifices of Leviticus 1—7 show the immediacy of dealing with sin when it occurs. Confession and forgiveness, death and yet the gift of life, are the integral rhythm of Israelite life before God and fellow Israelites. Third, Leviticus illustrates that sin affects the whole person, both body and soul, both physical and ethical. The very physical nature of sin becomes obvious as its remedy is also very physical. The ethical nature of sin is apparent as it touches upon matters of civil relations between people. Fourth, Leviticus exemplifies the stark correlation between sin and death. In the context of sin, there is death. However, Leviticus also indicates that death can be passed to another through confession and forgiveness granted in the sacrifices.

The distinction between **original sin** and **actual sin** is articulated in Leviticus. Original sin is the corruption of our very human nature, a condition inherited by every generation after the fall of Adam. This corrupted nature possesses an inclination toward evil. Although this fallen nature has free will in civil matters among people, it has no free will to come to God. One with original sin is dead in sin. Actual sin concerns the rebellious acts which flow from original sin. These acts defy God's perfect Law set forth in Scripture.

Leviticus is replete with many examples of actual sin. Leviticus 6 speaks of unethical behavior with one's neighbor by deception, swearing falsely, extortion, and neglect (Lev 6:1–4). The breadth of sinful acts is indicated when Yahweh includes sins of which one is not even aware (Lev 5:1–4). The correlation between sin and a death penalty occurs also with actual sins in a myriad of sexual offenses (Lev 20:10–16), offering children to idols (Lev 20:2), cursing one's parents (Lev 20:9), blasphemy (Lev 24:16–23), and priests showing disrespect for Yahweh (Lev 10:1–5). Leviticus 26 is a culminating chapter at the end of Leviticus. It speaks about rewards for obedience and punishments for disobedience. In the section on God's wrath for disobedience a very noteworthy verse states "If you remain hostile toward me and refuse to listen to me, I will multiply your afflictions seven times over, as your sins deserve" (Lev 26:21). Thus, in punishing sins, Yahweh is merely acting as a just judge. Leviticus 26 consists of units where Yahweh first states that if the Israelites continue to disobey him, His wrath will increase exponentially (Lev 26:14–17, 18–20, 21–22, 23–26, 27–39). Toward the end of Leviticus 6, Yahweh speaks of the desired outcome of the Law's application, that is, confession (Lev 6:40–43). He describes how ready He is to forgive sins when the Law has removed their pride. Finally, Leviticus makes a distinction among sins for the sacrificial system. Only once a year, the Day of Atonement takes place to make atonement for intentional sins, that is, premeditated sins, which purposely plan to bring harm. In contrast, sacrifices and the resulting forgiveness for unintentional sins can occur as needed.

Leviticus also contains passages which describe the fallen condition of original sin. This is the root of all actual sin. For example, the Israelites suffer from stubborn pride (Lev 26:19) and uncircumcised hearts (Lev 26:41). At times, Yahweh changes from singular to plural when describing the sin and sinful acts of the Israelites. The singular can indicate the condition, whereas the plural can refer to the acts which flow from the condition (Lev 16: 16, 21–22). Moreover, the concept of a condition becomes apparent through Leviticus' emphasis on cleanness and uncleanness, purification, holiness and lack of holiness (Lev 5, 11—15, 20—21). In these chapters of Leviticus, one noteworthy manifestation of uncleanness before Yahweh is skin disease (Lev 13:1–46, 14:1–32). In this way, a correlation exists between the condition of original sin and a condition of uncleanness through such a disease. The whole person is unclean through both conditions. This form of uncleanness through a disease is just another indication that the sinful condition manifests itself not merely in thought, word, and deed. Such disease and other sources of uncleanness point to the underlying imperfection in people. In preparation for the great Day of Atonement, Aaron must be clean (a condition) in order to make atonement for the people. That is, his uncleanness must be ceremonially washed away (Lev 16:4, 26, 30). When one sins, Leviticus often includes the comment that the person is "guilty" (Lev 4:22, 27, 5:2–4). Again, unclean actions do not leave a person unscathed. They affect the whole person. Finally, the uncleanness of sin so much affects the whole person that one must stay outside the camp of the righteous, the Old Testament Church. One is banished from the presence of Yahweh because of sin. Either the unclean person must permanently stay outside the camp or wait until the uncleanness has passed (Lev 10:4; 13:1–46; 14:1–32; 16:21–22).

This discussion about sin being cast outside the camp is important to understand what Christ did for us regarding sin. It also provides a bridge to move from the discussion about sin to the grace of God in Leviticus. 2 Corinthians 5:21 says concerning Christ, "God made him who knew no sin to be sin for us, so that in him we might become the righteousness of God." Christ took upon himself all our deserved punishment for sin, including banishment from God and people. The book of Hebrews emphasizes this when it declares, "And so Jesus also suffered outside the city gate to make people holy through his own blood" (Heb 13:12). In Leviticus, being banished outside the camp meant to be shunned and distanced from God's favor. That is what Christ suffered for us. This banishment reaches it apex on the cross when Jesus cries out, "My God, my God, why have you forsaken me?" (Matt 27:46) There Christ suffered the pangs of hell itself—utter desertion and separation from God—so that we would not need to suffer such punishment for our sin.

Leviticus overflows with the grace of Yahweh toward His people. First, an emphasis of grace is Yahweh's divine initiative. Grace is truly a gift, not something earned. God's gracious initiative appears even in the first verse of Leviticus where Yahweh approaches Moses. There he tells Moses to speak to the people about the divine means of forgiveness of sins through the sacrificial system. This divine initiative flows throughout the book, even to its conclusion. Leviticus 26 culminates with Yahweh's relentless favor for His people in spite of their continued failure to recognize their sin, even when God's wrath rightfully touches them: "Yet in spite of this, when they are in the land of their enemies, I will not reject them or abhor them so as to destroy them completely, breaking my covenant with them" (Lev 26:44). Similarly, the divine initiative culminates in Christ. His relentless pursuit of sinners in order to have mercy on them, as foreshadowed in Leviticus, is visible in Romans, where we read, "For if, when we were God's enemies, we were reconciled to him through the death of his Son, how much more having been reconciled, shall we be saved through his life?" (Rom 5:10).

Second, Leviticus emphasizes the very objective, external nature of grace. Forgiveness is not assured through a subjective look into one's heart. Rather, an objective sacrifice guarantees forgiveness. Such means give Yahweh's gracious declaration of righteous—clean, pure, and forgiven—upon the sinner. The Projection of sins onto a sacrificial animal and then the slaughter of the animal very concretely demonstrate the nature of sin and salvation. Sin has corrupted the whole person, both body and soul. Therefore, the remedy cannot ignore the external and physical. The means of forgiveness are to involve both physical and spiritual. Likewise, the objective sacrifice of Christ on the cross is the source of our salvation. The benefits of the cross are objectively given as a gift in the means of grace, Word and Sacrament. Yahweh's forgiving presence is located where He deems it to be located, not where people seek its location outside of Yahweh.

Third, there is an inseparable connection between grace and blood, between forgiveness and life. "For the life of a creature is in the blood, and I have given it to you to make atonement for yourselves on the altar; it is the blood that makes atonement for one's life" (Lev 17:11). The sacrifices in Leviticus epitomize this connection between blood and forgiveness, since the shedding of blood results in life and forgiveness. Of course, all the forgiveness granted through the blood of animals in Leviticus only is valid through the blood of Christ (1 John 1:17).

Fourth, grace involves the punishment for sin being transferred to an innocent victim. Justice must be done; the sin must be punished. In God's gracious plan the sacrificial animal receives the death sentence; yet the person receives the gift of life once again. Scripture's fulfillment of this plan is found in Jesus as the "Lamb of God, who takes away the sin of the world" (John 1:29).

Fifth, confession brings sin to a death situation, since sin is death. Confession involves saying back to God what He has said to us. God has clearly revealed that we are sinners, deserving nothing but death. Confession admits this to God. Confession invites death. In the Leviticus sacrifices, the application of death occurs as the confessor brings the sacrifice as the remedy for his sin and the death actually occurs. Confession is part of the rhythm of confession and forgiveness in the sacrificial context (Lev 5:5, 16:21, 26:40). In the Church today, confession once again joins us to baptismal forgiveness. Christians are, thereby, connected to the death and resurrection of Christ that the old self might die and the new self might rise.

Finally, as seen in Leviticus, every part of life is centered around the rituals of sin and forgiveness. Whether childbirth (Lev 12:1–8), skin disease (Lev 13:1–46, 14:1–32), harvest (Lev 23:9–22), wealth and poverty (Lev 25:8–55) and more, the Israelite receives his salvation and identity in the means of grace. Similarly, although a Christian carries out his vocation(s) in the civil arena, this Christian life is founded upon salvation in Christ. This salvation and every aspect of Christian life receive its sustenance in the Church as one receives Word and Sacrament there.

Office of the Ministry

The office of the holy ministry in the New Testament Church is, in part, foreshadowed by the office of priest in the Old Testament. The office of the ministry, however, encompasses more than just the role of the Old Testament priest. The holy ministry in the New Testament also includes aspects of the Old Testament offices of patriarch, prophet, and king. Actually, the most appropriate starting point for the office of the ministry in the New Testament is found in the person and work of Christ himself. He called the apostles and established them as His representatives. They were shepherds under the great shepherd, Jesus Christ. While not holding the apostolic office, those holding the office of the holy ministry in the Christian Church have the subsequent, divinely appointed office of preaching the apostolic word and administering the sacraments.

The Old Testament priests indeed held a divine office to serve at a divinely appointed place in matters determined by Yahweh. By the blessing of Yahweh, they held an office to represent Him in the presence of the people (Lev 4:35, 5:13, 6:6–7) and the people in the presence of Yahweh (Lev 2:2, 3:5). They served at the Tabernacle, and later at the Temple, to administer His grace given in the sacrificial system. Yahweh determined this location as the place of mercy and the place of the priestly office (Lev 17:1–9). The office of priest was established to deal with matters of sin, uncleanness, and impurity on the one hand and holiness, cleanness, and purity on the other. On Yahweh's behalf they would declare someone unclean or clean (Lev 12:1–8, 13:1–46, 14:1–32, 15:1–32). It is illustrative when Yahweh addresses the priests in this manner: "You must keep the Israelites separate from things that make them unclean, so that will not die in their uncleanness for defiling my dwelling place, which is among them" (Lev 15:31). In the process, the priests would explain the laws concerning cleanness and uncleanness (Lev 10:10–11, 11:47) and how the uncleanness is purged through the sacrifices. That is, the priest communicated and applied Law and Gospel (Lev 4:1—6:7, 9:22 16:1–19).

The institution and consecration of the priesthood is a vital part of Leviticus (see also Exod 28—29). In the ordination and installation of Aaron and his sons (Lev 8—9), they are truly receiving this office as a gift, not grasping for a right. In most parts of this ceremony, Aaron and his sons appear as passive recipients. Throughout the ritual, Moses acts on Yahweh's behalf by bringing Aaron and his sons (Lev 8:1), washing them with water (Lev 8:6), putting the tunic and other article of priestly clothing on Aaron and his sons (Lev 8:7–9, 13), and anointing them with oil and blood as additional signs of consecration and for-

giveness (Lev 8:12, 30). Then Moses himself offers Sin Offerings on their behalf to cleanse them from their own sin (Lev 8:14–17). In the ceremony, Moses
also sacrifices a Whole Burnt Offering for worship and places some of the blood
on Aaron's ear (Lev 8:18–30). Their official service begins in Leviticus 9. Yet,
it once again begins with a sin offering for the priests' sins, as well as a Whole
Burnt Offering and Fellowship Offering (Lev 9:1–14). Only then does Aaron
present a sin offering to atone for the people. The initiation into service concludes with Aaron, as well as Moses, blessing the people on behalf of Yahweh
in His glorious presence (Lev 9:15–24). Noteworthy in this ordination of the
priests is the connection between the office and the person holding the office. At
times, the requirements for the priest are more stringent than for the average Israelites (Exod 30:17–21; Lev 10:8–9; 21:1—22:16). The person is obviously
still a sinner with sinful actions often threatening (Lev 4:3; 21:1—22:33). He
must be washed clean through various ceremonies. Yet, these are done to consecrate him for a holy office of service, which represents Yahweh in matters of sin
and grace. Thus, the people are to deem them as holy because of their service for
Yahweh (Lev 21:8).

In their service, the priests encountered people in everyday life events for
which sacrifices were appropriate or necessary. In their guilt, people would
come to them as mediators of the divinely-given forgiveness in the Sin Offering
and Guilt Offering. Priests would mediate a gift of thanksgiving in response to
Yahweh's gifts of mercy in the Whole Burnt and Grain offerings. Fellowship
with other worshippers is an emphasis of the Communion Offering. Since the
people meet the priests in the context of these life events, the priestly office does
not emphasize ethereal thought devoid of the physical. Thus, spiritual and physical are integrally connected in the priestly service of the sacrifices. Also, Leviticus notes that just as priests deal with daily issues of sin and forgiveness, so also they receive earthly benefits from their priestly service. Their portion is specific allotments of the sacrifices (Lev 6:16, 26; 7:7–10; 28–37).

Most notable among the priests is the high priest. Aaron, brother of Moses,
first held this office. To note his high office Leviticus frequently mentions him
first in a list of priests or by himself (Lev 8—10). The high point of the Old Testament liturgical year and most prominent duty of the high priest is his service
on the Day of Atonement (Lev 16:1–34). On this day, the high priest enters the
most holy place of the Tabernacle to atone for all the sins of the people, including the intentional sins. The day includes sacrifices for the sins of the priest as
well as the people. The book of Hebrews emphasizes Christ in his office as a
greater high priest than Aaron or any successors (Heb 4:14—5:10, 7:1—10:18).
Christ is fulfillment of the Old Testament office of priest. Unlike previous high
priests, who would need to offer sacrifices for themselves, Christ was sinless
(Heb 4:15; 7:26–28). Whereas the Aaronic line of priests was imperfect, Christ

is of the superior line of Melchizedek (Heb 5:6–10; 7:1–28). Whereas previous priests needed to offer numerous provisional sacrifices, Christ offered himself once and for all (Heb 7:27; 9:26–28; 10:1–18). He is the mediator of a superior covenant (Heb 8:1–13; 9:15). Unlike priests who offered animals, Christ offered himself, the only sufficient sacrifice for the sins of the world (Heb 9:11–14). Therefore, all the Old Testament sacrifices and priests foreshadow Christ and anticipate their ultimate fulfillment in Him. The sacrifices offered by Old Testament priests only have validity because of the coming sacrifice of Christ. Thus, the Israelites—Old Testament Christians—were saved by the sacrifice of Christ to come on the cross, whereas New Testament Christians are saved by the sacrifice already accomplished on the cross.

Holiness

Holiness is an attribute of Yahweh, according to which he is distinct and distanced from that which is secular, common, unclean, or profane. Likewise, He demands that those associated with Him are not characterized by such descriptions. "I am the Lord your God. Consecrate yourselves and be holy, because I am holy. Do not make yourselves unclean...I am the Lord who brought you out of Egypt to be your God. Therefore be holy, because I am holy" (Lev 11:44–45). When Yahweh manifests His holiness to people, the term *glory* is often associated with it. That is, Yahweh's glory is a revelation of His holiness. When this revelation occurs in the Old Testament, it is typically associated with a physical object such as the Tabernacle or Temple. This prefigures the revelation of God's Son, the God-man Jesus, when the Son of God took physical human nature upon Himself. For example, as He manifests His glory in the healing of a possessed man, also the demons recognize Him and call Jesus the "Holy One of God" (Mark 1:24). The incarnation in general involves a revelation of His glory. "The Word became flesh and made his dwelling among us. We have seen his glory, the glory of the One and Only, who came from the Father, full of grace and truth (John 1:14). As seen from Leviticus 11:44–45 as well as the New Testament passages, there is a frequent connotation of Yahweh's mercy attached to holiness (see also Deut 7:6; Isa 43:14). His judgment is also associated with His holiness (Lev 10:3; Ezek 28:22; Mark 1:24 against the demons,). Thus, one can again observe Yahweh's revelation of Law and Gospel in His holiness. Finally, the term "holy" is associated with Yahweh's *name*, a term vitally connected with His divine presence (Lev 20:3; 22:2, 32).

Regarding people, holiness involves both a status of consecration, which Yahweh grants to His people, as well as the consecrated life which follows. "Consecrate yourselves and be holy, because I am the Lord your God. Keep my decrees and follow them. I am the Lord, who makes you holy" (Lev 20:7–8; see also 20:26; 22:16, 32 regarding the Israelites and 21:8, 15; 22:9 regarding priests). That is, holiness touches upon both justification and sanctification, both the objective and subjective. It involves both God's grace given to His people and the Christian life, flowing from that gift. This status of holiness arises not only from the gracious call of Yahweh to be His people but also from the fact that He Himself is holy. "You are to be holy to me because I, the Lord, am holy, and have set you apart from the nations to be my own" (Lev 20:26). The motivation for the Israelites to be holy in their lives arises from the gift of grace in the Exodus from Egypt, an act in which Yahweh showed His holiness (Lev 11:45; 22:31–33). In the New Testament and the Church today, the holiness ascribed to Christians becomes apparent in the word *saint* (from Latin *sanctus* = holy; Rom 8:27; 1 Cor 6:2; Eph 1:15, 18; 6:18; Phlm 7; Rev 5:8; 19:8). All Christians are saints in Christ.

In Leviticus a close connection between holiness and cleanness appears. This holiness regarding people can be further described as a holism of body and soul, both physical and spiritual. Holiness involves both ritual cleansing through the sacrifices as well as ethical matters. In these ethical matters, Israel declares itself distinct from its pagan neighbors. In the section of Leviticus known as the Holiness Code (Lev 17—26), matters of cleansing from uncleanness are a major theme. In 11:43–45, Yahweh seems to use the words *holy* and *clean* interchangeably. Indeed, holiness and cleanness come through the sacrifices after one has become unclean (Lev 5:1–13). This includes purification after childbirth and cleansing from skin diseases, which exemplify that ritual uncleanness and a lack of holiness is not purely spiritual (Lev 12:1–7; 13:1–46; 14:1–32). The ethical nature of holiness/cleanness becomes apparent particularly in the Holiness Code with its regulations on various aspects of life, including sexual relations (Lev 18:1–30), a repetition and elaboration upon the Ten Commandments (Lev 19:1–37), as well as punishments for ethical defilement (Lev 20:1–27). The introduction to Leviticus 19 is noteworthy when it enjoins the Israelites to be holy and then discusses proper relations with other people as well as with Yahweh. Similarly, the priests, who mediate cleanness on Yahweh's behalf are to pay particular attention to holiness for themselves. Priests are to marry pure virgin women, since priests are holy to Yahweh (Lev 21:7, 13–14). The people should consider them holy because of their office and service in the Tabernacle (Lev 21:8).

Sacrifice and Worship in the Old Testament

General Comments: Sacrifice and worship are common themes throughout the Old Testament, even before the Tabernacle. For various reasons and in various places individuals such as Cain and Abel (Gen 4), Noah (Gen 8:20, 21), Abraham (Gen 12:7–8; 22:13) and Jethro (Exod 18:12) all made offerings, usually at a solitary altar. However, the book of Leviticus (Lev 1–7) most clearly elucidates the five major Old Testament sacrifices to take place at the Tabernacle and the subsequent Temple. These five sacrifices incorporate the purposes of a gift of thanksgiving, fellowship, and purging sin. Specific sacrifices emphasize one aspect above the others, although each aspect is likely present to some degree in all. Both the priest and worshipper have roles in these rituals. The actions of the worshipper in these sacrifices would be in the realm of sanctification, whereas the actions of Yahweh, as mediated through the priest, would be in the realm of justification. While these sacrifices might superficially overlap with others in the Ancient Near East, their function is totally different. They are the Old Testament sacraments, which have their fulfillment in Christ.

Whole Burnt Offering (Lev 1; 6:8–13; 8:18–21; 16:24): A voluntary gift of thanksgiving, atonement for sin, and dedication to Yahweh are emphases of this sacrifice. The worshipper brings a perfect bull, ram or lesser animal, according to one's income. He lays his hand upon the head and slaughters it. The priest sprinkles the blood upon the altar and wholly burns the animal.

Grain Offering (Lev 2; 6:14–23): A voluntary gift of thanksgiving for Yahweh's goodness as well as dedication to Yahweh are emphases of this sacrifice. The worshipper brings grain or flour without yeast and puts oil and incense on it. The priest burns a portion and receives the rest as food for his family.

Fellowship Offering (Lev 3; 7:11–34): A voluntary ritual of fellowship between the worshipper(s), priest, and Yahweh as well as a gift of thanksgiving are emphases of this sacrifice. The worshipper brings an animal without any defect (or some bread), lays his hand upon it, and slaughters it. The priest sprinkles its blood against the altar. Those present may eat the remains.

Sin Offering (Lev 4:1—5:13; 6:24–30; 8:14–17; 16:3–22): An obligatory atonement for unintentional sin or cleansing from ritual uncleanness are emphases of this sacrifice. Various animals are brought, depending upon the guilty party, whether it be the priest, the whole community, a community leader, or individual. After the sin is transferred to the animal by laying hands on it, it is slaughtered. After the priest sprinkles blood on the altar, he burns some of the animal and may eat the rest.

Guilt Offering (Lev 5:14—6:7; 7:1–6): An obligatory atonement for unintentional sin involving restitution and cleansing from ritual uncleanness are emphases of this sacrifice. The worshipper brings a ram or lamb and the amount of money for restitution plus 20%. After the animal is slaughtered, the priest sprinkles the blood upon the altar, burns a portion, and receives the rest as food.

3. Overview of Book

Initially, it may seem that the book of Leviticus interrupts the flow which Exodus began and Numbers continues. After all, Exodus brings the Israelites to Sinai and describes the Tabernacle as the center of their life. Numbers continues the historical account at Sinai where Exodus ends. Why is Leviticus necessary at all? Leviticus plays a vital role in the flow of Yahweh's revelation at this time. The latter part of Exodus tells where the sacramental life of Israel takes place. Leviticus articulates how it takes place and how the gift of holiness affects the lives of the Israelites. Leviticus gives identity, restoration, security, and direction for their life at Sinai and beyond.

Leviticus 1—16 describes the provisions of Yahweh to cleanse the people from the contamination of sin. Within this section, Leviticus 1—7 contain rubrics for the specific sacrifices: the Whole Burnt Offering (Lev 1:1–17), the Grain Offering (Lev 2:1–16), the Communion or Fellowship Offering (Lev 3:1– 17), the Sin Offering (Lev 4:1—5:13), and the Guilt Offering (Lev 5:14—6:7). Leviticus 8—10 record the ordination and installation of Aaron and his sons into the priestly office. Unfortunately, the joy of the event is interrupted by the sin of Aaron's sons, Nadab and Abihu, when they arrogantly introduce unapproved, unclean fire into the Tabernacle ritual and suffer the consequence of death (Lev 10:1–7). Leviticus 11—15 articulate the laws about ritual uncleanness, whether the defilement comes through food (Lev 11:1–47), childbirth (Lev 12:1–8), skin diseases (Lev 13:1–46; 14:1–32), or other sources. The defilements in Leviticus 1—15 find their ultimate resolution in Leviticus 16, the great Day of Atonement. On this holy day, the high priest enters the most holy place once a year to bring purification for sins not atoned during the year, particularly the intentional sins. A noteworthy component of the day is the ritual of the scapegoat. After the high priest transfers the sins of the people to His head, the goat is sent outside the camp to die. This ceremony, as also the entire Day of Atonement, prefigure Christ especially poignantly.

Leviticus 17—26 is known as the Holiness Code. Since the Israelites have been blessed to receive the holiness of Yahweh in the Tabernacle rituals, their life is to reflect that holiness. Thus, the Holiness Code describes the identity of the Israelites as holy people of Yahweh. The text emphasizes proper ritual life at the Tabernacle and the ethical life among the community. Important topics include the restriction on blood only as a means of forgiveness (Lev 17:1–16), propriety in sexual relations (Lev 18:1–30; 20:1–27), proper treatment of one's neighbor to reflect love for Yahweh (Lev 19:1–37), rules for priests (Lev 21:1– 33), and observance of various feasts and holidays (Lev 23:1–44), including the Sabbath year and Year of Jubilee (Lev 25). Leviticus 26 sums up the Holiness Code with rewards for obedience and punishments for disobedience. Leviticus

27 appears to be an appendix, which concerns appropriate compensation for re-deeming various things.

7

Numbers

In an average day we see many numbers: telephone numbers, account numbers, social security numbers, serial numbers, and many more. Such a preoccupation with numbers is very indicative of our culture. It might at first seem puzzling that a book of the Bible is called "Numbers," since this Biblical book comes from a very different era and culture. Were the ancient Israelites as obsessed with numbers as people today? Actually, the title "Numbers" arises from the census lists which appear only twice in the book (Numbers 1, 26). Perhaps a more descriptive title for this Biblical book is its Hebrew title *bemidbar*, which means "in the desert." The book of Numbers primarily tells of the Israelite wandering in the wilderness after the Exodus, including much rebellion by the people and the steadfast faithfulness of Yahweh.

1. Date of Writing—*Moses Writes During the Wilderness Wanderings of Israel*
2. Themes—*A Continual Focus on the Mercy of God*
3. Overview of book—*Focus on the First and Last Years of the Wilderness Wanderings*
4. Important Passages—*Events in the Wilderness that Show Us How God Deals with His People*

1. Date of Writing

The issue of the date of writing for Numbers depends upon the era of the author. As mentioned in previous chapters the author is assumed to be Moses. This assumption is based upon Biblical passages which state that God spoke to Moses, and Moses recorded the contents of that divine revelation. In the book of Numbers occurrences of Yahweh's self-disclosure are quite prominent. Over 150 times beginning with the very first verse Numbers indicates that Yahweh spoke to Moses. Not surprisingly, one Hebrew name for Numbers is *wayedabber* ("And He [Yahweh] spoke"). Numbers 33:1–2 specifically notes that Moses subsequently wrote down this divine word by Yahweh's command.

The date of Moses' authorship of Numbers, as well as the rest of the Pentateuch, relies heavily upon 1 Kings 6:1. According to that passage, the fourth year of Solomon's reign over Israel is also 480 years after the Israelite exodus from Egypt. This year in Solomon's reign is known to be 966 BC, which places the exodus at 1446 BC. Thus, the 40 years of wandering and the likely parameters for the composition of the Pentateuch were between 1446–1406 BC, since Moses died just before the Israelites entered the promised land (Deut 34).

While the vast majority of Numbers comes from the hand of Moses during the dates indicated, minor glosses likely originate from subsequent editorial work. For example, Numbers 12:3 tells that Moses was a very humble man, an unlikely statement from the author himself. Such editorial glosses usually involve only peripheral changes to relate to an audience after the time of Moses. Since the Holy Spirit could use subsequent editors to complete the text that He desired, such additions do not diminish the verbal inspiration of Scripture.

Num 9:1	Passover in wilderness of Sinai	April 1445
Num 1:1, 18	Census Taken	April/May 1445
Num 10:11	Israel leaves Mt. Sinai	May 1445
Num 20:1	Israel arrives at Wilderness of Zin	April/May 1407
Num 33:38	Aaron dies	July/August 1407
Some Dates from Numbers		

2. Themes

Israel's Repeated Rebellion (Sin)

The emphasis of Holy Scripture is indeed upon a merciful God, not on virtuous people who serve as moral examples. The book of Numbers poignantly demonstrates this by the repeated rebellion of the Israelites. As the visible church of the Old Testament, Israel obviously contained blatant sinners. Even the most noteworthy Old Testament saints demonstrated their sinfulness. Israel's behavior exemplified a fallen human nature with its inclination toward evil in thought, word, and deed. Thus, the hope for salvation is clearly outside oneself.

Numbers is replete with examples of rebellion. Immediately upon leaving Sinai, the Israelites complain about the hardships of their journey (Num 11:1–3). The complaint against Yahweh's provisions of food and drink for them is a frequent event (e.g., Num 11:4–6, 20:1–5). Mistrusting Yahweh's care even goes to the point of wishing they were dead rather than waiting for the Lord's provisions (Num 20:3). Having been sent by Moses to explore the Promised Land, the twelve spies return glowing reports of its fertility. Yet, only two of the spies confess their trust that Yahweh can deliver it into their hands (Num 13:26–33). Korah and his followers challenge the authority of Moses, the Lord's chosen mediator (Num 16:1–50). Thus, they challenge Yahweh Himself. The Moabites entice the Israelites to worship their gods, and some easily comply (Num 25:1–

9). In this act, the Israelites commit violence against the loving relationship which Yahweh established with them. Frequently in Numbers, Yahweh justly punishes the Israelites. Yet, He never allows His full, deserved wrath to fall upon them. That curse would fall upon Jesus.

Israel's rebellion stands in stark contrast to Yahweh's great Old Testament act of salvation, the Exodus. In this event, He rescued them from bondage and freed them from the evil grasp of Pharaoh. They were "baptized" as God's people when he led them through the water of the Red Sea (1 Cor 10:1–4). Thus, He made a chosen people for Himself. They were set free and set apart as Yahweh's holy nation for sacred purposes. Yet, they choose not to live as holy people.

The rebellion of the Israelite leadership is particularly disappointing. Miriam and Aaron challenge the special role which Yahweh gave to Moses (Num 12:1–16). So also Moses honors himself rather than Yahweh at **Kadesh** when the water came from the rock (Num 20:9–13). Particularly in the sin of Moses, Scripture dissuades its readers from confidence in human virtue. Even the great rescuer Moses is not an object of trust. Rather, Scripture points to a savior greater than Moses who would rescue people from bondage to sin and death—Jesus Christ (John 1:17).

The sin of Israel in the wilderness closely resembles the rebellion of their original parents, Adam and Eve. Although Yahweh created Adam and Eve and richly provided for them in the Garden of Eden, they disregarded Yahweh's gracious gifts, doubted His intentions for their welfare, and looked for the greatest good outside of Him. Similarly, in the book of Numbers, the Israelites discount the gracious gift of rescue in the exodus. For example, they claim that conditions were better in Egyptian slavery (Num 11:18). They doubt Yahweh's intentions for their welfare by worrying about food and suspecting that Yahweh brought them out with the purpose of letting them die (Num 14:3, 21:5). Finally, they look for the greatest good outside of Him by seeking other gods (Num 25:1–3), choosing their own course of action (Num 14:4, 41–45), and by rejecting Moses, His chosen mediator (Num 14:4, 20:2). With the sin of Adam and Israel, Scripture anticipates a greater Adam, Christ, who would reverse the effect of sin (Rom 5:12–21).

God's Faithfulness to His Promise and Patience with His People

In spite of the unfaithfulness of Israel, Yahweh remains faithful to His promises made to the patriarchs. He patiently continues to preserve a chosen people for Himself. He continues to bless them, and steadfastly leads them to the Promised Land. This mercy in Numbers is often administered through His chosen mediator, Moses, and well as the members of the priesthood, particularly Aaron.

His faithfulness and patience, for example, come in the form of earthly blessings of food and water, despite Israel's ingratitude. With the number of military men listed as 603,550 (Num 2:32), nothing short of daily miracles feed these people along their journey. Although the people complain, wish they were dead, and want to return to Egypt, He still provides for them. In one instance when the people are disgruntled with the variety of the cuisine, the Lord begins to send them quail (Num 11:4–35). In another instance of dissatisfaction with the type of food and amount of water, Yahweh instructs Moses to speak to a rock, which would provide all the life-giving water needed (Num 20:1–5).

Yahweh's faithfulness and patience are obvious as He continually leads a stubborn people on their way to the Promised Land. A turning point in Numbers occurs when the people come in close proximity to the Promised Land. The twelve spies give their report concerning Canaan, and the people consider conquest impossible (Num 13:26–33). On the brink of receiving a covenant gift, the people doubt that Yahweh can actually deliver it to them. Yahweh could have justly allowed Israel to perish. Yet in His mercy only the original adult generation from Egypt will die in the wilderness. He would allow the following generation to inherit the land (Num 14:26–35).

Yahweh's faithfulness poignantly becomes apparent by Numbers' overarching emphasis on salvation from Egypt as well as the salvation to come in Christ. In the very first verse, time itself is marked in light of God's saving act. Numbers 1:1 states:

> "The Lord spoke to Moses in the wilderness of Sinai, in the tent of meeting, on the first day of the second month, in the second year after they had come out of the land of Egypt, saying…"

The Israelites live every day in light of Yahweh's rescue, just as Christians enjoy every day in the light of their baptism. The observance of the Passover at strategic points also highlights Yahweh's salvation and makes it immanent in the life of Israel. Just before the Israelites leave Sinai on the way to the Promised Land, Yahweh instructs them to observe the Passover, the commemoration of the lamb's blood which saved them from death (Num 9:1–14). When they are about the enter Canaan, Yahweh once again instructs them regarding observance of the Passover (Num 28:16–25). These occurrences of the Passover stand like bookends to mark the gracious character of Yahweh in Numbers. Just as Israel in this manner looks back at the Exodus, Israel would look forward to the ultimate Lamb of God who brings salvation for His people. The Christological character of the wilderness wanderings is also apparent by remarks concerning the tribe of Judah, the tribe from which Christ comes. When Yahweh issues marching instructions, Judah appears first in the list of tribes and stations itself at the east (Num 2:3–4) to lead the nation forward on their journey to the promised land (Num 10:14). Judah's position at the east (Num 2:3) is reminiscent of the messianic verse regarding the "sun of righteousness" who will rise with healing in His wings (Mal 4:2).

Yahweh's mercy is also obvious by allowing His mediator, Moses, to still His wrath against the people. When the Israelites doubt that Yahweh can deliver the Promised Land to them and He justly becomes angry, it is Moses who pleads with the Lord. Moses reminds Yahweh regarding His transcending grace, even in the face of just wrath (Num 14:13–19). As noted, only the original adult generation dies. In the Korah event Moses, as well as Aaron, plead for the people. In response, Yahweh only allows a small percentage of Israel to perish. Also, when the people complain about wilderness, water, and food, Yahweh justly allows poisonous snakes to come and bite the people. When Moses prays for the people, the Lord instructs Moses to set up a bronze snake on a pole. Anyone who looks at the serpent would live (Num 21:4–9). Jesus relates this account to Himself in His conversation with Nicodemus (John 3:14–15). The Son of God would be lifted up on a cross so that all who believe in Him might live eternally. Thus, these passages about Moses as mediator point forward to the greater mediator who would still the wrath of God by dying on a cross. The Old Testament people received mercy in Christ's sacrifice, since God must take sin seriously (Num 14:17–19). Christ still pleads for us now in His state of exaltation.

Yahweh's faithfulness resembles the unmovable commitment of a spouse. Scripture frequently compares the love of God to a husband for His wife. In particular Christ is called a bridegroom who saved His bride, the Church. Israel as the Old Testament church and Yahweh's bride is the beneficiary of Yahweh's acts of salvation (Eph 5:23). The Old Testament at times refer to the wilderness wanderings as a honeymoon period in which the bridegroom Yahweh woos His bride in a place of her undivided attention (Hosea 2:14–23). Thus, the emphasis of the wilderness period is His undeserved grace to His people.

An important trend appears in the Pentateuch, including Numbers. Yahweh emphasizes physical means for His saving work. To give them water He uses a rock (Num 20:8). As He leads them through the wilderness, His presence is associated with a pillar of cloud by day and a pillar of fire by night (Num 14:14). Numbers speaks often of forgiveness of sin through the sacrificial system, the Old Testament sacraments. For example, when a plague justly strikes the camp, Aaron makes atonement to still Yahweh's wrath (Num 16:46–50). These animal sacrifices only have validity because their fulfillment is in Christ's sacrifice. His gracious presence is to be found at the Tabernacle, which proceeds at the center of the Israelite camp, an indication of the Tabernacle's importance. This association of Yahweh with something physical foreshadows the time when the Son of God took a human nature to Himself to work salvation. As we later read in 1 Corinthians 10:4, a sustaining rock in the wilderness is also a manifestation of Christ's "real presence" with them. Likewise, His gracious presence connected with something physical in the Old Testament points to the sacraments of baptism and the Lord's Supper today.

Office of the Ministry as God's Institution

The actual foundation for the Office of the Ministry is most directly found in the person and work of Christ as He calls the twelve and entrusts them to be His representatives. The same continues as He later appoints bishops and overseers in New Testament congregations, although through human agents. Yet, offices in the Old Testament preview and overlap with the Office of the Ministry in the New Testament. In Numbers, these are the prophetic office of Moses and the priestly office of Aaron and his sons. In particular, two areas of overlap are noteworthy in the Old Testament:

1. Yahweh's divine appointment or call into the respective office.
2. Being entrusted by Yahweh to proclaim His message of Law and Gospel and/or administer forgiveness through the Old Testament sacraments, the sacrificial system.

These Old Testament offices, which include aspects of the Office of Ministry, are indeed God's institution. Those who hold these offices do not receive authority from below, that is, from people. People do not determine nature and content of the office, not even Moses. Moses indicates this in the Korah event, "And Moses said, 'Hereby you shall know that the Lord has sent me to do all these works, and that it has not been of my own accord'" (Num 16:28). Rather, the men are called and entrusted by Yahweh and bear the authority of the one who called them. When they speak the message of Yahweh, the message brings His authority, whether Law or Gospel. When forgiveness is granted through a sacrifice administered by the priest, that forgiveness is valid before Yahweh.

Scripture immediately communicates Yahweh's hand in Moses' office in the first verse of Numbers. "The Lord spoke to Moses in the wilderness of Sinai, in the tent of meeting..." Thus, at the outset one observes that Moses in His office represents Yahweh. Importantly, the conveyed message is received in the place of His divine presence, the Tabernacle. Examples of Moses communicating Yahweh's message of Law and Gospel are replete in Numbers (i.e., Num 14:17–19, 14:41–43, 16:30, 19:1–22, 21:4–9). With such an introduction to the office and work of Moses, it is not surprising that Miriam and Aaron receive punishment when they act against Moses and jealously attempt to place themselves into the office God had given only to Moses (Num 12:1–16). Yahweh becomes angry when the people want a different leader, since that indicates rejection of Yahweh (Num 14:1–25).

Yahweh establishes the priesthood of Aaron and his sons in Exodus 28. The office is a gift of God and its parameters are determined by Him. The priests serve in the Tabernacle and administer forgiveness to those who confess their sin. The forgiveness occurs through the shedding of blood in the sacrifices. Yahweh also confers His divine blessing, name/presence, and peace through the priests with the **Aaronic benediction** (Num 6:22–27). Where Yahweh locates His name, there is also His gracious presence. Note that only the priests are authorized to speak this blessing. In Numbers, Yahweh's determination of the priestly office is seen by the frequent instruction regarding the activities of the priests (i.e. Num 6:22–27, 18:1–32, 19:1–22, 29:1–40). Yahweh also identifies the Aaronic priesthood as a divinely established office by allowing Aaron's rod to blossom and produce almonds (Num 17:8). Finally, Yahweh reacts starkly when Israelites oppose the priesthood or wish to place themselves in the priestly office, since they in essence oppose Him (Num 16:10–11, 40; 18:7).

3. Overview of Book—Focus on the First and Last Years of the Wilderness Wanderings

Numbers can be divided into three major sections: 1:1–12:16, 13:1—20:13, and 22:2—32:42. Each of the three sections emphasizes a geographical location: Sinai, Kadesh, and the Plains of Moab respectively. The first two sections contain a bridge (Num 10:11—12:16 and 20:14—22:1), which leads the reader geographically and thematically to the following section. The final section ends with a bridge (Num 33:1—36:13) to the books of Deuteronomy and Joshua. One will notice that legal sections on various topics appear interspersed with historical narrative in all three sections. Also, there is little mention of the forty-year wilderness wanderings. Rather, the text contains much more material about the first and last years of travels to Canaan.

Chapters	Location	Contents
1:1—10:10	Sinai	Preparation to travel to the promised land: Census, Construction of the Tabernacle, Commands for purity, Journey to Kadesh
10:11—12:16	*From Sinai to Kadesh*	*Bridge: Transition from Preparation to Rebellion*
13:1—20:13	Kadesh	Rebellion and wandering: Twelve spies, Rebellion of Korah, Wandering in the wilderness
20:14—22:1	*From Kadesh to the Plains of Moab*	*Bridge: Transition from Rebellion to Preparing to Enter the Promised Land*
22:2—32:42	The Plains of Moab	Preparations to enter the promised land: Victory over Sihon and Og, The bronze snake, Oracles of Balaam,
33:1—33:13	*The Plains of Moab*	*Bridge to Deuteronomy and Joshua: Review of the past, Land allotment*

In the first section (Num 1:1—12:16), we encounter Israel in the middle of preparations to leave Sinai. Yahweh had mercifully brought Israel from Egypt to Sinai. At that location, as reported in Exodus and Leviticus, Yahweh revealed His messages of Law and Gospel to them. Now as they prepare to leave, Yahweh orders a census of the men available for battle (Num 1). The tally shows 603,550 in the army of Israel. Numbers 2—4 indicate the centrality of the Tabernacle in the life of Israel, particularly by the Tabernacle's location at the center and the dedication of the tribe of Levi for the Tabernacle's care. Such is not surprising, since Yahweh's "real presence" is associated with the Tabernacle. Numbers 5:1—6:27 involve commands of Yahweh concerning purity of the people in matters of disease, marriage and Nazarites. Numbers 7:1—8:26 concern various offerings of community leaders for the Tabernacle and more of the Levitical role in the Tabernacle. The celebration of the Passover occurs next (Num 9:1–14). As previously mentioned, the Passover remembers the great acts of salvation in the Exodus. This remembrance also assures the Israelites of Yahweh's deliverance in the immediate future. From 9:15—10:10 the text describes Yahweh's presence with the cloud and fire to lead Israel as well as instruction regarding the trumpets to direct their travels.

As mentioned, 10:10—12:16 is a bridge to the next section, both geographically and thematically. Geographically, Israel makes the transition from Sinai to

Kadesh. Thematically, the text moves from preparations to rebellion. In Numbers 11 the people complain about their food. While Yahweh shows His just wrath, His mercy prevails by sending them quail. In the midst of the complaining, Moses finds the burden too great. Therefore, Yahweh again shows kindness by distributing to seventy elders the Spirit which He had placed upon Moses. Thus, Moses has many assistants in dealing with the contentious people. Surprisingly, the contentiousness also is found among Miriam and Aaron (Num 12).

The second section of Numbers emphasizes events at Kadesh, particularly rebellion (Num 13:1—22:1). It begins with Moses sending the twelve spies to scout Canaan. The majority, except for Joshua and Caleb return with doubts about the possibility of conquest. Numbers 14 marks a major turning point. The lack of trust in Yahweh's kind intentions is blatant. As a result, the present generation will not enter the Promised Land. Rather, they wander in the wilderness. In the midst of such sin, Numbers 15 speaks of offerings in response to Yahweh's gift of the Promised

Kadesh-barnea

Land as well as mercy granted in the sacrificial system. Unfortunately, more corruption erupts in the rebellion of Korah, Dathan, and Abiram in their opposition to Moses (Num 16:1–50). The earth splits apart and swallows these men, their households, and their followers. To demonstrate the Yahweh has indeed chosen Aaron, Yahweh makes Aaron's staff sprout in contrast to other tribes' staffs (Num 17:1–13). Then, in the midst of that sin, the text retreats to matters of the Tabernacle again, including the red heifer (Num 18:1—19:22), whose ashes are mixed with water for purification of sin. In its erring ways, Israel is directed back to the place of Yahweh's forgiving presence at the Tabernacle. Finally, Yahweh grants water from a rock in spite of Israelite complaining. But Moses in the process directs the credit to himself rather than Yahweh (Num 20:1–13).

To reflect on the second section thus far, it seems that Israel has indeed made little progress. The section begins at Kadesh. Toward the end, they find themselves again at Kadesh (Num 20:1). Forty years of wandering have occurred in these chapters of Numbers as a result of sin. Interestingly, the text mentions relatively little about those years of punishment. Certainly, the Israelites suffer much hardship and confusion as one generation passes away and another one arises. Rather, the emphasis is the first and last years of wilderness wanderings, that is, Yahweh resolutely remaining faithful to bring the people to Canaan.

The second section ends with a bridge once again, 20:14—22:1. Geographically, the venues changes as the Israelites move from Kadesh to the Plains of Moab. Along the way, the Israelites do not receive free passage through Edom and travel a less direct route (Num 20:14–21). They are not allowed to attack their Edomite relatives. In contrast, Yahweh does lead the Israelites to victory over the king of Arad as well as the Amorite king Sihon and Og of Bashan (Num 21:1–3, 21–35). Meanwhile, the people's discontentment results in the arrival of poisonous snakes. When Moses prays for the people, Yahweh grants rescue in the form of the bronze snake (Num 21:4–9).

The third section (Num 22:2—32:42) geographically takes place at the Plains of Moab. Thematically, it concerns final preparation to enter Canaan, including a census of the new generation (Num 26:1–65) and the commissioning of Joshua to succeed Moses (Num 27:12–23). In the midst of such preparations, the important account of Balaam and Balaak occurs with a wonderful Christological prophecy (Num 22:1—24:25). The text then returns to matters of Tabernacle centrality by instructions about the festivals and sacrifices for this new generation in their new land (Num 28:1— 29:40). A bridge portion occurs once again (Num 33:1—36:13), this time looking toward the books of Deuteronomy and Joshua. In Numbers 33 there is a review of the past journey with a view toward the future. Finally, the text includes matters of land allotment 32:1–42, 34:1—36:13. Here Moses lays down the principles by which Israel will divide the Promised Land among the twelve tribes. (See also Num 27:1–11).

8

Deuteronomy

Students preparing for a test often have a review session with other students. They find it helpful to join with others to recount the important aspects of the course. The book of Deuteronomy is somewhat similar. Moses gathers the people together to review the events in the life of Israel, particularly from the Exodus until their present location on the brink of the Promised Land. Thus, Deuteronomy revisits the previous books of the Pentateuch. Yet, Deuteronomy is more than just review of past events. It engages the theological themes of Yahweh's gracious interaction with His people. Yahweh upholds and protects Israel in spite of its erring ways. Moreover, Deuteronomy provides a historical and theological bridge from the Pentateuch to the books of Joshua, Judges, and beyond. It addresses the future as God's people receive the gift of the Promised Land.

1. Date of Writing — *When Did Moses Write This Book?*
2. Themes — *Important Concepts in Deuteronomy*
3. Overview of the book — *What Does the Book Contain?*
4. Important Passages in Deuteronomy — *Things Israel Needed to Know Before Entering the Promised Land*

1. Date of Writing

Determining the author of Deuteronomy is pivotal for dating the book. Deuteronomy itself indicates Moses as the author. Already in 1:5 the text introduces direct quotations by Moses. Thereafter, much of Deuteronomy continues in the first person address by Moses. Several other Deuteronomy texts specifically say that Moses wrote the words of the text (Deut 31:9, 22, 24). Jesus corroborates Mosaic authorship when he alludes to Deuteronomy (Matt 19:7–8, Mark 10:3–5). Additional Old and New Testament passages affirm his authorship as well (1 Kgs 2:3, 8:53; 2 Kgs 14:6, 18:12; Acts 3:22–23, 7:37–38; Rom 10:19).

Since Moses indeed wrote Deuteronomy, dating the life of Moses is vital for discerning when he wrote Deuteronomy. According to 1 Kings 6:1, the Exodus occurred 480 years before the fourth year of Solomon's reign. This year in Solomon's life is known to be 966 BC, which places the Exodus at 1446 BC. Since the wilderness wanderings lasted forty years, and since this book tells of Moses' last days, Moses likely composed Deuteronomy around 1406 BC.

Portions such as the introduction to Deuteronomy (Deut 1:1–5) as well as the account of Moses' death (Deut 34:1–12) may be glosses added by a later author. This does not discount the certainty of Mosaic authorship for the rest of Deuteronomy nor does it endanger its inspiration. The Holy Spirit can use the hand of a later author to put final touches on such a great book. (Note, for instance, that Moses' successor Joshua wrote some words on the scroll of the Law of Moses [Josh 24:26].)

2. Themes

God's Love for His People

The love of Yahweh for His people is indeed an overarching theme in the book of Deuteronomy. The reason for such favor is the character of Yahweh. In His love, He chose Israel as His own people (Deut 10:15). Although He certainly confronts and punishes sin, love is Yahweh's favored disposition toward His people (Deut 4:31). Both the Old and New Testaments proclaim that this loving disposition did not come cheaply. The cost was the precious blood of Jesus Christ. Having positively stated the reason for His favorable disposition toward Israel, Deuteronomy discounts any human quality or achievement as the reason for His favor. He does not love them because they are numerous (Deut 7:7), nor because of their own righteousness (Deut 9:4), nor because of the uprightness of their own heart (Deut 9:5). Yahweh is gracious in spite of His people (Deut 9:6). So also the Lutheran Confessions state both the positive and negative in a given argument in order to avoid any misunderstanding. The Confessions typically do this to preserve the Gospel just as Deuteronomy does here.

Upon telling the reason for Yahweh's love, the book of Deuteronomy richly enumerates His acts, which demonstrate His love. These acts center on the covenant which Yahweh made with their ancestors. The covenant provides the context for His relationship with the people about to enter Canaan. Here the word **covenant** indicates a promise rather than a mutual agreement which is contingent upon the faithfulness of Israel. Although the original generation of the Exodus has passed away, Yahweh wishes to renew this covenant and assure them that they are beneficiaries of this covenant relationship as well (Deut 5:2–4). The main covenant promises of the past (see Gen 12:1–3; 15:1–19; 17:2; Exod 6:1–8) which are realized in divine action in Deuteronomy are the declaration that Israel is His chosen people, the gift of the Promised Land, and prosperity in power and number. As the people in Deuteronomy are about to enter this Promised Land, they are intimately connected with Yahweh's acts of favor in the past. These past acts provide a foundation for their identity and assurance of favor in the present and future.

Indeed, God graciously acts to claim Israel as His own. He has called them His inheritance (Deut 4:20). He chose them as His own (Deut 7:7). Out of all the peoples on the earth Yahweh declared Israel to be His treasured possession (Deut 7:6; 26:18), a holy people set apart for Him (Deut 14:2; 26:19). Here one must remember that Israel is distinct from the political entity of Israel today. Israel in the Old Testament is the name for the Church (See Gal 3—4). Israel of the Old Testament is equivalent to the bride of Christ, the Church, in the New Testament (Eph 5:25–33, Rev 21:2, 9–14). The Holy Christian Church is chosen in Christ as His own, declared righteous in the death of Christ, and holy as a result of His forgiveness.

The land of Canaan in Deuteronomy is a central gift of Yahweh's love, a gift promised for generations (Deut 1:8; 4:38; 9:1, 4). Now in Deuteronomy the people are on the verge of receiving that gift. At this pivotal point in history, Yahweh assures them of His favor. God cares for this land (Deut 11:12). He promises to bring Israel prosperity. Every place where they set foot, they will take possession (Deut 11:24). The native people of the land will fear them and, thus, yield to them (Deut 2:25; 11:25). This is the case, since the Lord is with them and will fight for them (Deut 1:30). Such gifts of Yahweh are certainly part of what Luther describes in his explanation of the First Article of the Apostles' Creed: "He also gives me clothing and shoes, food and drink, house and home, wife and children, *land*, animals and all I have. He richly and daily provides me with all that I need to support this body and life." God grants such earthly blessings to all His creatures.

Yet, there is more involved in Yahweh's favor to Israel, which other nations do not receive. Old Testament Israel is both Church and state. As such, earthly blessings are naturally part of God's gifts to His Old Testament Church. This gift of land clearly indicates Yahweh's favor to His Church. Moreover, the other nations are not favored and are being driven out, since they are wicked (Deut 9:5). That is, they do not have the benefit of being declared righteous before God in the coming Messiah. The Christian Church today does not include the political state by divine plan. Yet, Christians have a fulfillment of such a Promised Land. It is located where His favor is located today, namely, in His Word and Sacrament in the Christian church. There God's favor is given, and the powers of evil are thwarted. Christians look forward to the ultimate fulfillment of this Promised Land when Christ will come again and bodily raise all Christians to life to grant them a new heaven and a new earth (2 Pet 3:13; Rev 21:1–4).

Another sign of Yahweh's love in Deuteronomy, as well as a fulfillment of the covenant, is the blessing of many people in Israel. Yahweh made this promise initially to Abram (Gen 15:4–5). Now on the verge of entering Canaan they are as numerous as the stars of the heaven (Deut 1:10). Israel also has Yahweh's loving promise to multiply them even more (Deut 7:13). In Christ this promise is fulfilled as people are brought into His people through the sacrament of baptism. Those brought to faith are numerous and increasing as the Holy Spirit works His miracle of water and the word. One day countless members of the Church triumphant will stand before the heavenly throne to praise the Lamb who was slain for them (Rev 7:9).

As the people in Deuteronomy are about to enter this Promised Land, they are intimately connected with Yahweh's acts of favor in the past. These past acts provide a foundation for their identity and assurance of favor in the present and future. Yahweh, writing through Moses, richly reminds them of the rescue in the Exodus event (Deut 4:20; 6:20–25; 7:8). In this great act of salvation from the evil forces of Pharaoh, Yahweh brought them out as His people. They were, so to speak, "baptized" in the waters of the Red Sea to be His own (1 Cor 10:1–4). In Deuteronomy 6:20–25 Yahweh encourages the people to remember this defining event just as Christians today remember their baptism and its defining significance for life (Rom 6:1–14). Another past event of God's love which Deuteronomy repeats is the victory over Sihon and Og (Deut 2:24). Although a relatively recent event, it demonstrates Yahweh's faithfulness and favor to them.

Sanctification

Sanctification in its narrow sense is the inward spiritual transformation of a believer by the miraculous working of the Holy Spirit through the means of grace. After God graciously pardons our sins through the work of Jesus Christ (justification), Christians are not yet perfect inside. Although viewed as righteous in God's eyes through Christ's atoning work, the sinful side of us, known as the Old Adam, yet remains. Sanctification is that process through which the Old Adam is daily put to death in baptism and the new man daily arises in Christ (Rom 6:4).

In the book of Deuteronomy, several facets of sanctification become apparent. First, Christians are *simul iustus et peccator*, that is, simultaneously saint and sinner. Both the Old Adam and new man are constantly present until death and fight against each other (Rom 7:7–25). In Deuteronomy God declares His people Israel to be His saints, *iustus*. They are chosen by Him and precious in His sight (Deut 7:6; 14:2). They are a holy people set apart out of all the people on earth (Deut 14:2). Similarly, a saint's good works are righteous works, since they are done in Christ. In this way Moses describes Caleb, son of Jephunneh, as one who has wholly followed the Lord (Deut 1:36). Similar wording appears regarding all Israel potentially seeking Him with their whole heart (Deut 4:29). Of course, the works of Christians do not contribute to their salvation. They demonstrate that one is in Christ, who won that salvation for us.

Having described the Israelites as saints, Deuteronomy indeed portrays their fallen, sinful nature (*peccator*). The heart has a predisposition toward evil as Yahweh describes. "For I know what they are inclined to do even today, before I have brought them into the land that I swore to give (Deut 31:21b). A few verses later the same is communicated: "For I know how rebellious and stubborn you are... (Deut 31:27a)." This predisposition becomes apparent in the past actions of the Israelites. Moses describes such previous sins in the wilderness. For example, when the spies had gone to explore the land and people were to conquer it, they rebelled by doubting God's gracious intentions for them (Deut 1:26, 32). Not only does the past reveal the Israelites as *peccator*, Yahweh readily states the likelihood and even the certainty of future sinful acts. After Moses recounts God's gracious deliverance from Egypt, care in the wilderness, and impending conquest of Canaan, Moses says, "Take care lest you forget the Lord your God by not keeping his commandments...(Deut 8:11a)." In the same context, Yahweh warns the Israelites not to forget their source of blessing: "Beware lest you say in your heart, 'My power and might of my hand have gotten me this wealth'" (Deut 8:17). They will be tempted to serve other gods and will actually follow that temptation (Deut 4:28, 31:16, 20). Many remaining examples concern punishment for transgression of religious/civil law. Instances include punishment for robbery and murder (Deut 19:11–13), dishonesty in property boundaries (Deut 19:14), a son who rebels against parents (Deut 21:18–21), and various forms of adultery (Deut 22:22–30).

Another facet of sanctification is good works as a fruit of faith. That is, works are motivated by the mercy of God in Christ. The Law cannot change a person; only the Gospel has that ability as the Spirit works in Christians. In Deuteronomy 4 Moses pleads with the people to avoid idolatry in the future. In all the wilderness wanderings they cannot ascribe any of their blessings to things in nature, which pagans have made into gods. At the end of this section, Moses' appeal for these fruits of faith is on the basis of Yahweh's mercy: "But the Lord has taken you and brought you out of the iron furnace, out of Egypt, to be a people of his own inheritance" (Deut 4:20). Later in Deuteronomy 4, Moses describes the love which Yahweh demonstrated to Israel's ancestors, including the defeat of mighty nations to grant them the Promised Land (Deut 4:37–39). On that basis Moses continues, "Therefore, you shall keep his statutes and his commandments, which I command you today... (Deut 4:40)."

Deuteronomy includes images of **catechesis**—the teaching of the faith—in the family. In Deuteronomy 6, when a son asks about the meaning of the Lord's statutes, the father is to tell of the miracles that Yahweh did to free the Israelites from the Egyptians. Then He fulfilled His promise to grant the land. Immediately thereafter, the father says, "And the Lord commanded us to do all these statutes, to fear the Lord our God, for our good always, that he might preserve us alive, as we are this day" (Deut 6:24). Finally, Deuteronomy 26:16—19 is similar. Verse sixteen begins with the words, "This day the Lord your God commands you to do these statues and rules. You shall therefore be careful to do them with all your heart and with all your soul." After a statement of declaring fidelity to Yahweh (Deut 26:17), Moses immediately tells of the undeserved mercy that Yahweh has made Israel His treasure. In the midst of that declaration of favor, there is again the corresponding fruits of faith, "And the Lord has declared today that you are a people for his treasured possession, as he has promised you, and that you are to keep all his commandments...(Deut 26:18)." (See also Deut 5:6–21; 6:20–25; 7:7–11; 8:6–9; 10:14–16; 29:5–9).

Finally, Israel's entire wilderness experience mirrors what happens in sanctification. As noted, sanctification involves being connected to the death and resurrection of Christ in baptism. Christians die to sin but arise renewed in Christ. Because of their rebellion, the initial generation of Israelites died in the wilderness. By the mercy of Yahweh a new generation arose, which would inherit the Promised Land (Deut 1:34–40). Yahweh would renew His merciful covenant with them and give them life through the forgiveness given at the Tabernacle, the place where His name dwells (Deut 12:8–14, 14:24, 16:1–11). Admittedly, this illustration has a shortcoming. The new generation was still *peccator*, according to the Old Adam. Yet, the parallel of death and new life is noteworthy.

Law and Gospel

Proper distinguishing of Law and Gospel is a hallmark of Lutheranism. Grasping Law and Gospel is also vital to a proper understanding of the book of Deuteronomy. In Lutheran theology, God's Law includes the uses of a curb, mirror, and guide (**First, Second** and **Third Use of the Law**). These are all prevalent in Deuteronomy. This book is also replete with Gospel, as Deuteronomy speaks of Yahweh's great Old Testament acts of salvation. Such acts of rescue also point forward to the saving work of Christ.

The Law's use as a curb involves God's care to limit disorder in society. The Law coerces people to act in a civil manner with the threat of punishment and the promise of rewards. Civil authorities such as government, police, teachers, and parents actively serve as God's agents in this use of the Law. Deuteronomy includes this civil use of the Law. For example, a death penalty is threatened against any Israelite who kidnaps a person for slavery or profit (Deut 24:7). A judge may prescribe a beating proportional to the crime when one is found guilty in a dispute with one's neighbor (Deut 25:1–2). One accused of false testimony receives the detriment which he had schemed against his neighbor (Deut

19:15–21). There are civil fines involved for lying about a woman's virginity within the marriage context (Deut 22:19).

The second use of the Law, as a mirror, is its theological use. The Law shows us our sinfulness. It reveals our fallen, corrupted condition before God and others. Here the Law serves its most vital function of removing every hope of self-righteousness. It leads one to confession of sins (as in Deut 1:41). Thus, it prepares for the Gospel. Deuteronomy includes this second use of the Law. There are the statements about the Israelites as *peccator* as noted above (Deut 1:26, 32; 31:21b, 27a, etc.). Their human nature is set against Yahweh's will. The Law shows the Israelite habit of rebellion in Moses' summary of the golden calf event (Deut 9:18–29; see Exod 32). Moses specifically calls their action evil (Deut 9:18) and the calf sinful (Deut 9:21). An important aspect of this second use of the Law is the revelation of God's wrath against sin. God shows their action as evil by an appropriate punishment. If the Israelites forget Yahweh, they will perish, just as He made the other nations perish before Israel (Deut 8:18–20). If they do not obey, Yahweh's curse will fall upon them (Deut 28:15–68, esp. 28). Anyone who lives with a stubborn heart against Yahweh will not receive forgiveness. Rather, Yahweh will blot out his name from all remembrance (Deut 29:19–21). Even the other nations will wisely recognize the reason for the Israelites' destruction. Even they know that such occurs because the Israelites abandoned the covenant (Deut 29:22–29, esp. 25). As Yahweh tells Moses of his impending death, He also predicts that the people will forsake Him. In response, Yahweh will forsake them and allow them to be devoured (Deut 31:16–18, 29). In such examples the importance of the Law's second use becomes apparent in Deuteronomy.

For a Christian, the Law has a third function. While the Law still accuses a Christian, it also has a didactic use. It teaches and provides a guide for what is God pleasing. While the Law cannot motivate a Christian toward good works, the Law as a guide provides the content of God's will for life. This use is very prevalent in Deuteronomy. Certain passages speak generally about obeying the entirety of Yahweh's commands (Deut 5:32–33; 15:4–5). Others become quite specific. For example, Yahweh directs them not to conform to pagan practice, since they are His chosen people (Deut 14:1–2). They are to demonstrate a changed heart which shows justice for the needy and the sojourner among them (Deut 10:14–20). They should, for example, avoid marriage with pagans (Deut 7:3–4), avoid idolatry (Deut 7:5; Deut 12—13), cancel debts appropriately (Deut 15:1–11), not charge an Israelite interest (Deut 23:19), not deny justice to anyone (Deut 24:17), leave part of the harvest for the poor (Deut 24:19–22), free servants appropriately (Deut 15:12–18), and practice the Passover as God intended (Deut 16:5–8). Much of the legal code of Deuteronomy 12—26 involves the third use of the Law. One particular emphasis of Deuteronomy in this third use of the Law involves catechesis in the family. Parents are to teach their children about their merciful God and his instructions for right living. The proper time and place for this instruction is at any point in the regular day. As examples, Moses list times like "...when you sit in your house, when you walk by the way, and when you lie down, and when you rise" (Deut 6:7, see also 11:18–21). A parent should also be ready to answer questions when a child asks about Yahweh (Deut 6:20–25).

Gospel in its strict sense denotes Christ's gracious work of salvation by His life, death, and resurrection for a sinful world. Christ is indeed the center of Deuteronomy, although this message is often given in **types**. That is, persons, events, and institutions in Deuteronomy point forward to a greater fulfillment in Christ. The Gospel in Deuteronomy especially involves two categories (which are described more fully in the section on "God's Love for His People"). First, Yahweh graciously chooses Israel as His own (Deut 4:20, 7:6–7, 14:2, 26:18–19, 27:8–9). Thus, He grants them the identity of God's righteous people, just as Christians today receive such an identity in baptism. Second, Yahweh acts mercifully in the great rescue from Egypt (Deut 7:7–10, 19; 13:5, 29:2–4), preservation in the wilderness (Deut 2:7, 29:5–6), and the gift of the Promised Land (Deut 1:30, 3:12–20, 7:19–25, 20:16, 29:7, 33:29). All these gifts Yahweh gives to an undeserving people, who so blatantly demonstrate their sin. These events foreshadow the ultimate salvation in Christ. He rescued His people from the evil rule of sin and death, just as Israel was rescued from slavery to Pharaoh. He increases and preserves His Church in Word and Sacrament, having thus kept His covenant promise of numerous offspring. While the Church with its Word and Sacrament is our Promised Land in this life, Christians await the ultimate fulfillment of this salvation in our Promised Land in the resurrection of the body and life everlasting.

In these acts of salvation, Moses is a type of the coming Christ. First, Moses, as Christ, has the offices of prophet, priest, and ruler/king. Moses speaks the word of God in the role of prophet (Deut 34:10–12). He serves as priest to make a sacrifice of atonement (Exod 32:31–35), and he serves as a ruler of Israel (Deut 33:4–5). Christ is the great prophet in His revelation of God. He is the great high priest, in that He is both the one sacrificing as well as the one sacrificed once and for all. He is the king of the universe as well. Particular attention is due to 18:14–22. Moses speaks about a greater prophet to come. This text finds its fulfillment in Christ as the prophet (John 6:14; 7:40, Acts 3:22–26; 7:37). Second, Moses serves the role of mediator to still Yahweh's just wrath. In Deuteronomy 9:13–29 Moses recounts several instances of particularly heinous rebellions when the Israelites deserted Yahweh. In this context Moses retells how he lay prostrate before the Lord and prayed that His deserved anger would not fall upon the people. These acts of mediation to still God's wrath have their fulfillment in the ultimate mediator, Christ. By His life, death, and resurrection for us He stilled the justly deserved divine wrath against us.

In Deuteronomy many potential curses are mentioned for sins against unfaithfulness (see Deut 27—30). While the Israelites suffered some of these consequences, they did not receive them all. Christ receives the full justice and ultimate curse of God on the cross. Note here that Moses lay prostrate in mediation forty days and nights (Deut 9:18), symbolizing the span of Israel's punishment of wilderness wanderings for forty years. Moreover, Christ's temptation in the wildness has a vital connection here. His temptation lasted forty days and nights, just as the wilderness time and Moses' intercession (Matt 4:2; Mark 1:13; Luke 4:2). It is important that Christ quotes the book of Deuteronomy in response to the devil's temptation in the wilderness (Deut 8:3; 6:16; 6:13). These passages quoted from Deuteronomy indicate Israelites' sin. Jesus resisted similar temptation and, thus, made up for such sin by His perfect life.

In the Church, people receive the Gospel through Word and Sacrament. This is made possible by a Savior who became incarnate for us to work salvation. One should note that Yahweh often works through physical means to give His divine care to Israel. He guided and guarded them with the pillar of cloud by day and the pillar of fire by night. He spoke personally with Israel in the midst of the fire at Horeb (Deut 5:4). His divine presence was located with these physical things. The presence of His name associated with the Tabernacle is particularly important. Where He locates His name, there is Yahweh himself with His merciful forgiveness and blessing. Name theology was important in Numbers with the Aaronic benediction (Num 6:22–27). So also in Deuteronomy God connects His name with the Tabernacle where forgiveness takes place through the sacrificial system (Deut 12:11; 14:24; 16:5–6). The sacrifices pointed forward to the ultimate sacrifice of Christ. Similarly, the divine name associated with the physical Tabernacle foreshadows the incarnation as well as the Lord's Supper. The merciful presence of the name is reminiscent of baptismal grace where people are baptized into the name of the Triune God. In summary, God's manifests His gracious presence through the physical means of fire and cloud. While this demonstrates the habit of Yahweh to work through physical means, the presence of His name at the Tabernacle most poignantly foreshadows the incarnation and sacraments, since forgiveness is located there. There is Gospel.

The application of Law and Gospel is as vital as the definitions of these terms. Lutherans emphasize the proper distinction of Law and Gospel in application to one's life. Confusion of the two can lead either to self-righteousness or despair. Self-righteousness arises when Christians assume that they can sufficiently fulfill the Law to receive God's favor. Despair arises when the Law confronts a Christian with the perfect standard, which no one can fulfill. In Deuteronomy, certain passages may appear to confuse Law and Gospel. These passages promise God's favor and blessing in response to human action. For example, the review of the Ten Commandments includes the following words: "Honor your father and your mother, as the Lord your God commanded you, that your days may be long, and that it may go well with you in the land that the Lord your God is giving you" (Deut 5:16; see also 5:33; 6:3, 24–25, 7:12–16; 8:1; 15:10–11; 28:1–14). Certain passages very poignantly describe the conditional nature of rewards by stating that "if" they are faithful, "then" Yahweh will bless them.

> "For if you will be careful to do all this commandment that I command you to do, loving the Lord your God, walking in all his ways, and holding fast to him, then the Lord will drive out all these nations before you, and you will dispossess nations greater and mightier than yourselves" (Deut 11:22–23; see also 15:4–6; 30:1–3).

It is important to remember several truths when dealing with such passages. First, these texts indeed contain Law, since Gospel has no strings attached. Any conditions upon God's favor make it a Law statement. Second, as Law these passage can perform all functions of the Law. For example, as second use of the Law these portions of Scripture emphasize that any reward for human action is still an act of God's mercy. Third, there are indeed rewards in the area of civil righteousness. One passage above noted a benefit for obeying parents, an established authority in the civil realm. Yet, this civil righteousness does not earn salvation. It is not righteousness before God. Fourth, any good works which a Christian does are only reckoned as good because they are done in Christ. The forgiveness of Christ covers a Christian so that one's good works are pleasing, even though done by one who still has a sinful nature. Yet, again, these works done by a Christian do not merit eternal salvation, since Christ receives the credit for bringing them forth. Fifth, certain covenants of the Old Testament were Law covenants (for example: Gen 17, Exod 19—24, as well as many parts of Deuteronomy). Since humans are sinful and cannot fulfill God's Law, the Gospel covenants take priority (Gen 9:8–17; 15:9–21; Num 25:10–31; 2 Sam 7:5–16; Jer 31:31–34), particularly as they point forward to Christ. Only a Gospel covenant could truly save (See Galatians 3—5).

3. Overview of the book

The title *Deuteronomy* means *repetition of the Law*. This is a most appropriate title, since this book revisits the contents and themes of the Pentateuch. It highlights important theological points of Moses' previous four books. This title is appropriate also because Deuteronomy contains a renewal of the Mosaic covenant from Exodus 20. Since the old generation which heard the original covenant had passed away, Yahweh speaks the word again to the new generation about to enter the Promised Land. Although the title *Deuteronomy* describes the contents well, it is not the original title. The Greek Septuagint and subsequent Latin Vulgate assigned this title. Rather, the original Hebrew title is *Debarim* or *Words*. The Hebrew titles for the five books of Moses consist of the first word(s) of the respective book. Deuteronomy 1:1 proceeds: "These are the words that Moses spoke to all Israel..."

Deuteronomy consists of three sermons by Moses (Deut 1:1—4:43; 4:44—28:68; 29—33). Moses preaches these sermons at a pivotal time, since the people are about to inherit the land. In this land, many temptations from other nations might lead them astray. Also, this is a pivotal time, since Moses will soon die and relinquish the leadership to Joshua. In this historical context, Moses speaks heartfelt words, usually in the first person. Rather than the more dispassionate accounts of previous Pentateuchal books, Moses speaks in a very personal way. He reminds the people of Yahweh's gracious acts in the past and an appropriate response by this generation and following generations. He pleads with them to follow the Lord rather than rebel against Him. After the three sermons, Deuteronomy ends with the account of Moses' death.

The first sermon (Deut 1:1—4:43) describes Yahweh's gracious acts of the past, all the way from Sinai to Kadesh Barnea (Deut 1:6—2:1) and from Edom to the Plains of Moab. Emphases are upon the spies sent to Canaan, subsequent rebellion, wandering in the desert, and the defeat of Kings Sihon and Og. It also includes encouragement for obedience (Deut 4:1–40) and a description of the cities of refuge (Deut 4:41–43).

The second sermon (Deut 4:44—28:68) illustrates the way of life appropriate for God's people. Here Moses emphasizes the great commandment of absolute fidelity to Yahweh (Deut 4:44—11:32). Moses summarizes with the words, "You shall love the Lord your God with all your heart and with all your soul and with all your might" (Deut 6:5). Deuteronomy 12—26 portray how the relationship which Yahweh established applies in matters of daily life. Ceremonial issues appear in 12:1—16:17. Here Yahweh emphasizes that worship is only to occur where Yahweh allows His name to dwell. Additionally, the Israelites should follow no other gods and

Mt. Nebo

celebrate the annual feasts as Yahweh intends. This section also tells how to treat people in a dignified manner. Deuteronomy 16:18—21:23 concern the role of leaders such as judges, kings, priests and Levites. Deuteronomy then describes cities of refuge for those accused of taking another's life by accident (Deut 19:1–21). Thereafter, Moses illustrates appropriate practice in matters as warfare, a captive bride, and rights of a firstborn, among other issues. Deuteronomy 22:1—25:19 involves sanctity in matters of marriage, the purity of the Israelite congregation, and treatment of people in the legal system. Deuteronomy 26 emphasizes the Israelite confession of Yahweh as their God in the Israelite handling of firstfruits, tithes, and various other commands. Deuteronomy 27—28 denote the blessings of responding to Yahweh's covenant and the curses for rejecting it.

The third and final sermon begins with Deuteronomy 29, in which Moses summons the people and continues the covenant renewal. Thereafter, Deuteronomy 30 includes more blessings from faithfulness and encourages the people to choose life in Yahweh.

Deuteronomy 31—34 pertain to the succession of Israel's leadership. Deuteronomy 31:1–29 concerns the change in leadership from Moses to Joshua. Next follows the song of Moses in which he grandly describes Yahweh's faithfulness and the people's rebellion. Moses then blesses the twelve tribes (Deut 31:30—32:47). Finally, there is an account of Moses' death on Mount Nebo, followed by Joshua assuming full leadership (Deut 34:1–12).

View from Mount Nebo

Portraying Deuteronomy just as a compilation of sermons only illumines one facet of Deuteronomy. As mentioned, this book involves a renewal of the covenant. Recent scholarship has determined that the structure of Deuteronomy has great similarity to a suzerain/vassal type of covenant from the Ancient Near East. Here a **suzerain**, a great king, made a mutual covenant with a **vassal** king. The suzerain demanded loyalty and service from the vassal and promised protection in the event of danger. The vassal promised loyalty to the suzerain and reliance on his protection. The favor of the suzerain was contingent upon the vassal's compliance with the terms of the covenant. Such a covenant included a number of components. First, in a *preamble*, the covenant identifies and describes the suzerain. Second, in a *historical prologue* the suzerain recounts the gracious acts done in the past to the vassal. The suzerain directly addresses the vassal in this section, hoping to encourage obedience. Third are the *stipulations*, in which the suzerain articulates the obligations given to the vassal. Usually, the vassal must avoid relations with outside kingdoms. Fourth comes the *provision for the deposit of the document and its public reading*. Its public reading occurs, since the entire kingdom obligates itself to the covenant, not just the king. Fifth is the *list of witnesses* to the covenant. In the Ancient Near East this usually included gods or deified portions of nature. Finally, the covenant includes curses for breaking the covenant and blessings for following it. Deuteronomy follows this outline rather closely.

Preamble	1:1–5
Historical prologue	1:6—4:43
Stipulations of the covenant	4:44—26:19
Provision for deposit of the document and periodic public reading	31:9–13, 24–26
List of witnesses	30:19; 31:19–22
Curses and blessings	27—30

While the format of the covenant in Deuteronomy has much overlap with the suzerain/vassal covenant of the Ancient Near East, the content is not identical. Indeed, one can see the great parallel that Israel will have no other gods just as the vassal has no other alliances. Yet, Yahweh's relationship with Israel is much deeper than the political alliance of a secular treaty. He is their loving God, and they are His chosen, beloved people. The content of Deuteronomy emphasizes sin, grace, and a life of sanctification rather than political fidelity. Another striking difference occurs with the list of witnesses. Moses calls heaven and earth as witnesses against the people (Deut 30:19). He does not refer to nature as deified but rather as Yahweh's creation. Additionally, Yahweh commands the reading of Moses' song as a witness against the people regarding this covenant (Deut 31:19–22). In summary, Yahweh inspired Moses to employ a familiar format for the covenant. In this way, Yahweh uses this format for holy purposes. However, concerning content, the connection with a suzerain/vassal treaty is limited, since Deuteronomy speaks of the relationship between Yahweh and His Old Testament church.

Section 3
The Historical Books

9
Introduction to the Historical Books

It is said that a good driver spends about twenty-five percent of the time looking in the rearview mirror. It is important for drivers to know not only what is ahead of them, but also what is behind them. This is also true of life in general and has led humans throughout the centuries to write and study their history. Much of the Old Testament is written in historical narrative. It told the original readers what they, as Israelites, had experienced as a nation. This is already true in the Pentateuch. The next group of books that follow the Pentateuch in Christian Bibles is the historical books. These books continue the story of Israel from immediately after the death of Moses to life under the Persian Empire, a time span of about 1000 years.

1. The Contents of the Historical Books—*An Overview of the History of Israel from Moses to Nehemiah*
2. Telling Israel's Story as God's Chosen People—*Important Themes that Unite the Historical Books*

1. The Contents of the Historical Books

The one dozen books that comprise this section of the Old Testament (Joshua—Esther) tell a story that gives a continuous history of Israel ending about 430 years before Jesus' birth. The story begins with Joshua, Israel's leader following the death of Moses. The book that bears Joshua's name tells us of the initial conquest of the land of Canaan under Joshua's leadership. While Joshua's military campaigns overcame the primary resistance of the Canaanites, the book also tells us that according to God's instructions Joshua divided the land into twelve sections, one for each tribe of Israel. The individual tribes were to be responsible for subduing and occupying the territory allotted to them. Before his death Joshua urged the leaders of Israel to be faithful to God and pledged that he and his household would maintain their trust in the Lord, who had given them this land.

Judges continues with a short account of the failure of most of the tribes to remain faithful to God following the death of Joshua. For this reason, God did not allow them to drive the Canaanites out of the land, but left them among the Israelites to test them (Judg 2:20–23). Israel failed the test badly. Repeatedly the Israelites abandoned the worship of God for worship of the gods of their pagan neighbors, leading God to send foreign powers to oppress them. When the people would repent and again turn to God for help, he would raise up a "Judge" for them. These Judges were not primarily magistrates presiding over a courtroom. Instead, they were military leaders God raised up from time to time to deliver Israel from its enemies. This cycle repeats many times in Judges, emphasizing Israel's failure to live by the covenant God had so graciously given them.

The book of Ruth is set during the time of the Judges. Its story of some of God's people faithfully following God's laws reminds us that even though Israel as a nation strayed from God's commands, there remained some who clung to and practiced their faith. Since it also portrays the birth of an ancestor of David, it is also a pointer to things to come, including David's greater descendant, Jesus the Messiah.

The next two historical books, 1 and 2 Samuel, were originally written as a single composition. The book of Samuel tells of the transition of Israel from rule by God through Judges that he appointed to rule by kings. The opening section of Samuel relays the life of the prophet Samuel, who served as Israel's last Judge. During Samuel's lifetime the Philistines became a major threat to Israel, and the Israelites eventually became frustrated with relying on Judges that God would appoint. Therefore, they requested that Samuel ask God to appoint a king to rule over them.

This request for a king was more a rejection of God than it was a rejection of Samuel or the other Judges that preceded him (1 Sam 8:7). Nevertheless, God granted the people's request for a king. Samuel is instructed to give the people a king, and God arranges for a young man from the tribe of Benjamin, Saul, to become Israel's first king. Saul appears to be a good choice as a good-looking and impressive physical presence (1 Sam 9:2). However, Saul turned out to be a disappointment as king. From the beginning his major flaw was that he did not rely on God for guidance and victory in battle. Others around him, like his son Jonathan, demonstrated more confidence in God (1 Sam 14), and God blessed them in battle with victory. Eventually Samuel had to tell Saul that God had rejected him as king and would replace him with someone else. This is when we are introduced to a young man from Bethlehem in the tribe of Judah—David. God sent Samuel to Bethlehem to anoint David as the next king. However, Saul remained on the throne of Israel.

About half 1 Samuel traces David's rise to prominence and his eventual rivalry with Saul. David would become a general in Saul's army and even marry Saul's daughter Michal. However, Saul's jealousy of David's success would lead him to drive David out of his royal court and to repeated attempts by Saul to kill David. The writer of Samuel here contrasts God's blessings to his faithful servant David to the failure of Saul now that God had abandoned him. As 1 Samuel closes, Saul and his sons are in a final fierce battle with the Philistines.

God had predicted that Saul and his sons would die in the battle, and the Philistines celebrated their victory by desecrating the corpses of Saul and his sons.

2 Samuel traces David's rule as king over Israel for forty years. Following Saul's death, David's own tribe, Judah, publicly recognized David as king, and he began to rule them from the Judahite city of Hebron. However, the other tribes continued to recognize one of Saul's descendants as king. Yet, as the writer of Samuel tells us, God was with the faithful David, so that his house gained the upper hand in the struggle for rule over Israel (2 Sam 3:1). In a few years with the assassination of Saul's heir all of Israel came to acknowledge David as their God-approved monarch.

While David would become the outstanding example of a faithful Israelite king, David was not without his problems and sins. About half of the book of Samuel relates turmoil in David's house triggered primarily by David's most well-know sin: his adultery with Bathsheba, the wife of Uriah, one the foreign mercenaries serving in his army. Nevertheless, God did not take the kingdom away from David as he did from Saul. Here we are shown the difference between the two men: Unlike Saul, David genuinely repented of his sin. Although he was not sinless, David was a man of faith who always turned to God for forgiveness. Therefore, God blessed David and promised him that the ultimate king of Israel, the Messiah, would come from among his descendants to rule Israel eternally (2 Sam 7).

Like 1 and 2 Samuel, the next two historical books, 1 and 2 Kings, were originally composed as one book. The book of Kings tells about the kings of Israel who followed David, starting with his son Solomon. As David had become old and frail there began a power struggle among his sons to succeed him. However, both God and David had promised that David's son Solomon would succeed to the throne. To ensure this would happen, shortly before he died David had Solomon declared king. However, Solomon had to deal with his enemies immediately upon the death of his father.

Solomon then went to Gibeon to be recognized as king by all the tribes of Israel (1 Kgs 3). It is at Gibeon that God appeared to Solomon and granted Solomon a gift for which he is best known—wisdom. Solomon not only proved to be a wise king, he also was allowed by God to build a Temple in Jerusalem, a desire that David had but was prohibited by God from accomplishing. Solomon's reign saw Israel's greatest expansion and most prosperous era. However, Solomon was not the perfect king in God's eyes. He made many marriage alliances with the nations that surrounded Israel. Late in his life under the influence of his foreign wives he began to worship the gods of these nations in Jerusalem. This angered God. However, God had promised David a dynasty that would rule Israel, so instead of taking the kingdom away from Solomon, his prophet declared that after Solomon's death the kingdom would be divided and only part of it would be ruled by Solomon's son.

Upon Solomon's death his son Rehoboam sought to be recognized as king by all Israel. However, because he followed unwise advice from his court advisors instead of listening to the older advisors that had served Solomon, he alienated most of the tribes of Israel. They rebelled and placed Jeroboam, son of Nebat on the throne of Israel. Only the tribes of Judah and Benjamin remained faithful to David's line.

The rest of the book of Kings (1 Kgs 12—2 Kgs 24) traces the history of these two kingdoms. The northern ten tribes, known as the kingdom of Israel, quickly abandon God when their king Jeroboam set up gold calf idols at shrines in Dan and Bethel. He urged the people to worship these gods instead of going to Jerusalem to worship Yahweh. Jeroboam was afraid he would lose the loyalty of his people it they went to the annual worship festivals in Jerusalem, the capital of Rehoboam's kingdom. All of the subsequent kings of Israel followed Jeroboam's example, and many adopted the worship of other pagan gods. The book of kings records God's sending prophets like Elijah and Elisha to Israel to call them to repentance and faith in Yahweh, but the kingdom of Israel would never return to God. Kings tells us that God removed a number of kings from the throne of Israel, but none of the subsequent dynasties ever abandoned the corrupt practice of idolatry.

The southern two tribes, known as the kingdom of Judah, continued to be ruled by David's descendants throughout their history. Some of these kings such as Jehoshaphat, Hezekiah and Josiah were faithful to God like their ancestor David. However, many attempted to combine worship of Yahweh with worship of pagan gods of the nations surrounding Israel.

Kings tells us that although God was patient with these kingdoms, he eventually gave them into the power of foreign nations. Israel fell first. It was conquered by the Assyrian Empire in 722 BC, and the people were forced to leave the land God had given them and live in other parts of the empire. As they intermarried and assimilated to the culture of their new surroundings they eventually lost their identity as descendants of Israel.

Judah lasted longer, mainly because of God's love for the David and the few faithful kings that from time-to-time ruled Judah. However, the corruption of idolatry continued to grow in Judah and in 587 BC Jerusalem fell to the Babylonians who destroyed God's Temple and resettled the Judeans in the east around Babylon. With this Babylonian Captivity or Exile the book of Kings draws to a close.

The books of 1 and 2 Chronicles, like Samuel and Kings was originally one book. This book was written after the exile for Judeans who continued to believe in God. It traces much of the same history found in Samuel and Kings, but only follows the kings of Judah when the kingdom splits after Solomon's death. Chronicles actually begins with Adam and traces the origin of the people of Israel and their kingdom through genealogies preserved in 1 Chronicles 1—9. The establishment of the kingdom and most of Saul's reign is not discussed. Only Saul's death and David's ascent to the throne are considered important enough for the Chronicler to record. The rest of 1 Chronicles covers David's reign, while 2 Chronicles reports the reigns of the other kings of Judah and briefly tells of the exile and the Persian king Cyrus' permission for the Jews in his realm to return and rebuild Jerusalem.

While Chronicles covers much of the same material as Samuel and Kings, it adds its own perspective on the history of Israel and Judah. Chronicles emphasizes God's promise to David and the line of kings that came from David. It also emphasizes God's gift of the Temple in Jerusalem and worship that took place there. Since the writer was living in the time when Jews had returned to Jerusalem, he wanted to emphasize God's continued mercy to his people in preserving them and giving them access to him through worship in the Temple.

The last three historical books are set within the Persian Empire and relate God's work for his people when he allowed them to return to Jerusalem to rebuild the city and its Temple. The book of Ezra begins with the first return of Judean exiles from Babylon to Jerusalem in the early years of the Persian dominance of the Near East. Unlike the northern tribes, many of the exiles from the tribes of Judah and Benjamin did not lose their identity as the people of Yahweh when they were forcefully resettled in Babylon. Many of these organized a return to Jerusalem and began to rebuild the Temple there. The first half of Ezra relates their struggles over thirty years to rebuild the Temple and reinstitute full worship of God in Jerusalem. The second part of Ezra picks up the narrative some sixty years later with the work of Ezra, a priest and scribe who specialized in study of the Law of Moses. The Persian king Artaxerxes appointed Ezra to go to Jerusalem and ensure that the sacrifices in the Temple there were offered correctly according to the ancient commands of God through Moses. Artaxerxes even offered financial support for the worship in the Temple as long as the Jews would offer sacrifices for the king and his sons. The last half of Ezra then records the work of Ezra to establish once again respect for the Law of God given through Moses and to urge the people of Judah and Jerusalem to faithful living according to God's ancient covenant.

The book of Nehemiah is named after a contemporary of Ezra whom Artaxerxes appointed governor of Jerusalem. Nehemiah had held the important post of cupbearer to Artaxerxes. But because of Nehemiah's concern for Jerusalem, which despite having been resettled by Jews for almost a century, was not protected by defensive walls, Artaxerxes appointed him governor of the Persian province of Judah. As governor of Judah Nehemiah immediately organized the inhabitants of Jerusalem to rebuild its walls. He also worked with Ezra to ensure that the people would hear God's Word and be encouraged to live according to it.

The little book of Esther also takes place during the Persian period. Esther and her relative Mordecai, Jews living in the Persian city of Susa, are the subjects of this book. Esther relates how the young Jewish girl Esther became queen of the Persian Empire and, working with Mordecai, was able to save her fellow Jews from a plot to exterminate them throughout the Persian Empire.

These three little books from the Persian period together demonstrate that despite the favor that at times was shown to Jews in the empire, God's people continued to face challenges to their faith. Yet even as the Old Testament history closes, we are shown that God continued to watch over his people and reward those who faithfully sought to live holy lives according to his word and promise.

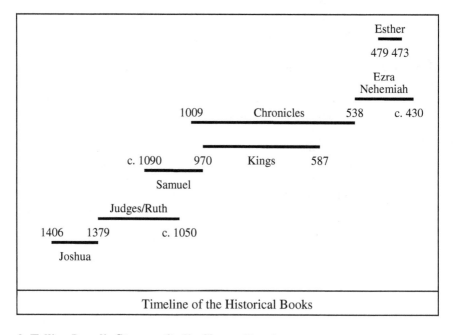

Timeline of the Historical Books

2. Telling Israel's Story as God's Chosen People

God's Faithfulness

One major theme that unites all of the historical books is God's faithfulness to his promises. The historical books begin with God keeping his promise to

Abraham, Isaac and Jacob to give their descendants the land of Canaan. Since this promise was always given in conjunction with the Messianic promise, the conquest of the land in the book of Joshua is a constant reminder of God's ultimate promise to send his Messiah to save his people.

Judges, Samuel, Kings and Chronicles continue the focus on God's faithfulness despite the repeated sins of Israel and its leaders. God is patient and merciful time and again. He forgave his people, sent them prophets to turn them from their sinful ways, and preserved their nation for over 900 years. Even when he allowed the Babylonians to take his people into captivity, he sustained them so that when the time was right, he would arrange the circumstances for their return to Jerusalem.

Ezra, Nehemiah and Esther demonstrate God's faithfulness to his promises as he guides his people through a new era where some return to the land of their ancestors, but others remain in other lands. No matter where they are, the Lord protected and strengthened them, gave them leaders who would defend them and lead them to follow his covenant with them.

Therefore, the historical books as a whole display God's grace and favor throughout centuries, and to this day they serve as a reminder of God's faithfulness to his promises. Readers throughout the millennia since these books were written have found comfort in knowing that God steadfastly keeps his promises and guides all events so that history serves his purposes and always runs its course in a way that is for the ultimate good of all who trust in him.

The Messianic Promise

A second theme that runs throughout the historical books is the Messianic promise. In the Pentateuch we are told that the Messiah was promised to Israel and would be a descendant of the tribe of Judah. As already noted above, the certainty of this promise was reinforced in Joshua when God gave the people the land of Canaan, another of his promises to Abraham, Isaac and Jacob that always accompanied the Messianic promise to the Patriarchs.

In the book of Judges we read of Israel constantly abandoning God. Does this mean that God will abandon his promise of the Messiah in response to Israel's unfaithfulness? No. Despite Israel's sins, God continued to be their God (see 2 Tim 2:13), a subtle but certain reminder that God had not forgotten his promise of a Savior from sin. Even when the people rejected God as their king and asked for a human king, God did not take back his promise. Instead, after the disappointing reign of Saul, God granted Israel an exemplary king—Jesse's son David. When the pious David received the promise that God would establish his kingdom forever through one of his descendants (2 Sam 7; 1 Chr 17), the Messianic promise was brought into the foreground once again. The Messiah would be the "Son of David" (Matt 9:27; 15;22; 20:30–31; 21:9; 22:42; Mark 10:47–48; 12:35; Luke 18:38–39). Even when the kings who followed David on the throne of Judah were unfaithful, God remembered his promise to David and spared his people, preserving them so that he could keep his promise to send the Messiah (2 Kgs 8:19; 2 Chr 21:7; Ps 132:17).

Ezra and Nehemiah reinforce this determination of God to send his Messiah as they relate God's raising up leaders among his people to rebuild the Temple and re-establish proper worship and piety among the Jews. In the centuries that would follow down to the birth of Jesus, the sacrifices in the Temple, the worship practices in accordance with the Law of Moses and the daily life of faithful Jews would be constant reminders of God's Messianic promise, just as God intended when he first gave the Law to Moses.

In Esther God used Esther and Mordecai as leaders among his people to preserve them from those who plotted to kill the Jews in the Persian Empire. In this way God preserved the Messianic hope of the Old Testament, since the Messiah would only come through the descendants of Abraham, Isaac and Jacob.

Therefore, although the historical books do not have a constant direct reference to the Messiah, taken as a whole, they demonstrate that the Messianic promise was of prime concern to God, and that he never deviated from his commitment first given to Adam and Eve that he would send a Savior to crush sin, Satan and death.

10
Joshua

Joshua and the book that bears his name provide an important second link in the history of God's people. Moses is the first link, providing history from the very beginning through the exodus from Egypt to the border of the Promised Land. Joshua, as the second link, was a witness to and participant in the Exodus. Joshua served as apprentice to Moses during the wilderness wanderings (Exod 17:9-14, 32:15-18). Joshua displayed the highest regard for the authority of Moses as God's servant (Num 11). Most importantly, Joshua demonstrated his faithfulness to the Lord by his desire to obey the Lord in the face of opposing forces. Joshua was one of only three adult men (Moses and Caleb were the others) who was prepared to enter the promised land the first time they approached it, according to the Lord's command (Num 13-14). He successfully led Israel into the Promised Land and defeated Jericho (Josh 3-6). He was appalled by the disobedience of Israelites (Josh 7). Joshua, like Moses, ended his life with solemn warnings and encouragement for the God's people. Thus, in many ways Joshua embodies the transition from Moses to the Judges.

1. Authorship and Date of Writing— *Is This an Autobiography by Joshua Himself?*
2. Date and Setting of the Events in the Book—*When in the World Did Joshua Lead Israel?*
3. Themes—*What Important Concepts Characterize the Book of Joshua?*
4. Overview of the Book—*From Moses to the Judges*
5. Important Passages—*Key Passages That Make the Purpose of the Book Clear*

1. Authorship and Date of Writing

The book of Joshua tells us that at least some of the book was written by Joshua himself, "Then Joshua wrote these words in the Book of the Law of God" (Josh 24:26). Joshua contains other history that took place after Joshua's death: the conquest of Hebron by Caleb, the conquest of Debir by Othniel, the conquest of Leshem by the Danites, and the account of the death of Joshua and Eleazar. A Jewish tradition suggests that Eleazar wrote the account of Joshua's death and that Phineas wrote the account of Eleazar's death. In any event, what was not written by Joshua was most likely written by an elder of Israel who was an eyewitness writing under divine inspiration. The idea that Joshua is the compilation of many sources, like the Pentateuch, is no more impressive here than there. The text presents itself as the writing of Joshua and the internal unity of the book confirms that assertion. Intimate biographical detail and use of archaic names for cities add further support for Joshua as author of many sections. Joshua lived from the mid-fifteenth to the mid-fourteenth century BC. Therefore, the core of the book would have been composed between 1400 and 1300 BC.

However, several passages indicate that the book in the form we have it today comes from a later editor. The frequent notice that some things mentioned in the book are still true "to this day" (Josh 4:9; 5:9; 6:25; 7:26; 8:28, 29; 9:27; 13:13; 14:14; 15:63; 16:10) point to a time later than Joshua's day. In addition, we are told that Joshua's prayer about the sun standing still in the sky is contained in the book of Jashar (Josh 10:13). Since this book also contained the poem written by David to mourn the death of Saul and Jonathan in 1009 BC, the final editor or author of Joshua had to live after that time. Therefore, the book of Joshua in its present form probably dates from sometime late in the reign of David (1009–970 BC) or in the reign of Solomon (970–931 BC).

2. Date and Setting of the Events in the Book

Conquest of Canaan		
1406 BC	1400 BC	c. 1389 BC
●	●	●
Crossing the Jordan	Caleb receives Hebron	Death of Joshua

Timeline of Joshua

This book is about Israel's conquest of the land of Canaan, a land which has a history that goes back at least to the time of Noah and his sons. Noah's son Ham and Ham's son, Canaan, showed gross disrespect to Noah and were cursed accordingly (Gen 9:20-27). Ham's descendents inhabited what became known as Egypt and Canaan's descendents lived in the land so named (Ps 105:23, 27). Abraham, Isaac, Jacob and his sons also sojourned in this land. God intended His chosen people to understand that as He provided for them physically in that land, so much more profoundly was He providing for them spiritually (Heb 11:8-22). Joshua witnessed God's great deliverance of Israel from the land of

Ham and would now conquer the land of Canaan. You may recall that shortly after the exodus, God brought the children of Israel to this land, as He had promised, but they refused to enter (Num 13). God led the Israelites in the desert forty years until all the adult males, who refused to enter according to the Word of the Lord, had died. Joshua and Caleb, who had originally urged Israel to trust God and enter according to His Word, remained to receive the promise they had trusted. The book of Joshua records the history of the conquest of the land of Canaan or the Promised Land, but it does more than that. Joshua contributes important support to major themes in the Old Testament. On the one hand, the children of those who originally refused to enter this land are no better than their parents. Israel continues to be plagued by disobedience to the Lord and by unbelief. The times of the Judges and Kings will underscore this reality. On the other hand, God is consistent and faithful in dealing with His people. He disciplines and corrects them so they might live and not die. He continues to provide for them, and especially for their eternal well being, because He is faithful in stark contrast to their faithlessness. We are just as bad as they were according to our human nature. We are just as well off as they were because God is faithful to His promises.

Summary of Joshua's Life		
c. 1499 BC	Joshua born	Josh 24:9; Judg 2:8
1446 BC	Joshua leads the Israelite army against the Amalekites	Exod 17
1446–1406 BC	Joshua serves as Moses' assistant	Exod 24:13; 33:11
1447 BC	Joshua is one of twelve Israelite spies sent into Canaan	Num 13—14
1406 BC	Joshua is consecrated as Moses' successor	Num 27:18–23; Deut 34:9
1406–1400 BC	Joshua leads the Israelite conquest of Canaan	Josh 14:10
c. 1389 BC	Joshua dies	Josh 24:29

3. Themes

God's Continuing Presence with His People

God's continuing presence with His people is evident in Joshua in four ways. First, in terms of a continuing presence the Lord says three times that He will be with Joshua as He was with Moses (Josh 1:5, 7, 3:7). There is a parallel to the Lord's appearance to Moses in the burning bush related in 5:13-15. While there is no burning bush, there is a flaming sword and the Lord commands Joshua to take off his sandals, as He had commanded Moses. Second, the presence of the Lord is evident though the nearness of His Word. A positive example is found in 8:27-35 where Joshua "read all the words of the law....There was not a word of all that Moses had commanded that Joshua did not read before all the congregation." Whenever Joshua leads the people according to the word of the Lord there is assurance that He is present with Joshua (Josh 3:7, 6:27).

A negative example is provided whenever the children of Israel disobey the Word of the Lord or fail to consult Him (Josh 7:1-13, 9:14-19). Thus, to the extent that Israel holds other words or counsel dear, the Word of the Lord, and therefore the Lord Himself, is distant.

Third, the presence of the Lord is evident in His knowledge and perception of the smallest and most secret details of Israel's activity. The Lord expected Israel to deal faithfully with Rahab and her family according to their promise. The Lord refused to be with Israel as they attacked Ai because of the sin of Achan. Finally, the presence of the Lord is evident in their victories, "...By this you shall know that the living God is among you and that He will without fail drive out from before you the Canaanites..."(Josh 3:10). This leads to our consideration of the other major theme in Joshua.

Victory Belongs to the Lord

There is no victory for Israel without the Lord and the victories that Israel realized were because of the Lord. Joshua makes this clear in a number of ways.

Jericho in the Distance

The failure of Israel in their first attempt to take Ai was due to the Lord's absence. On the other hand all successes were due to the presence of the Lord and Israel's obedience to His instructions. Sometimes the text simply expresses this truth, as at 1:2 where the Lord makes clear that He is the one who is giving Israel the land. Descriptions of God's activity in the conquest provide details; He will not fail to drive out the inhabitants (Josh 3:10ff), His actions melt the hearts of the enemy (Josh 5:1).

Besides simple comments the means of conquest also demonstrate divine action. Consider how peculiar and remarkable the fall of Jericho was, by actions that have no logical or physical force. Yet because these actions of shouting and marching were according to the Word of the Lord, the walls came tumbling down. Again when Israel was fighting the five kings of the Amorites (Josh 10:1-15), the Lord not only told Joshua that He would deliver them into Israel's hands, but the Lord Himself cast large hailstones upon them and caused the sun to stand still until a thorough end was made of the enemy. As God was with Moses to deliver Israel from her enemies by means which could only be attributed to Him, so God was also with Joshua by declaration and instruction, providing victory by similarly extraordinary means. God's victory over evil through Jesus is no less remarkable. As the incarnate Word of God, Jesus is the Lord and also demonstrates victory over all contrary powers by extraordinary means. The Lord remains clearly singular, as the One who grants victory over sin, death and the devil by His presence in a Christians' life through His Holy Word and Sacraments.

4. Overview of the Book

The book of Joshua is a bridge from the time of Moses to the time of the Judges. This bridge consists of four main sections; Joshua's initial words & preparation for conquest, conquest of the land, division of the land according to each tribe's inheritance, and Joshua's final words to Israel. A more detailed overview follows. Notice how the book begins and ends with Joshua's words to the people.

Joshua 1:1-5:15	Preparation for Conquest
1:1-9	God commissions Joshua
1:10-18	Preparations to cross the Jordan
2:1-24	Spying out the land with the help of Rahab
3:1-4:24	Crossing the Jordan
5:1-15	Circumcision at Gilgal
Joshua 6:1-12:24	Conquest of the Land
6:1-27	Capture of Jericho
7:1-8:29	Resistance at Ai, sin of Achan, Capture of Ai
8:30-35	Altar at Mount Ebal with Blessing and Cursing
9:1-27	Deception by the Gibeonites
10:1-43	Conquest of southern Canaan
11:1-15	Conquest of northern Canaan

11:16-12:24	Summary of Joshua's campaigns
Joshua 13:1- 21:45	**Division of Land**
13:1-7	Joshua's instructions for division
13:8-33	Division to Eastern Tribes
14:1-19:51	Division to Western Tribes
20:1-9	Cities of Refuge
21:1-45`	Cities for Levites
22:1-34	Eastern tribes dismissed
Joshua 22:1-24:33	**Joshua's Final Words to Israel**

11
The Period of the Judges
Judges and Ruth

Judges

Many of us think of a judge as someone who makes decisions in important cases or who is a magistrate in a courtroom. However, the Hebrew word translated *judge* can also signify an important political and military leader. This is how the term is used in the book of Judges. Therefore, the title of this Old Testament book is descriptive of the leadership which God provided for Israel between the time of Joshua and Israel's first king. The whole book reveals a pattern of increasing unfaithfulness among the Israelites. This pattern reflects an overall decline from the time of Joshua and his elders at the beginning of the book to the time of Samson and his tragic death. The book ends with a terse description of Israel's perilous condition in which "each one did what was right in his own eyes." But there is another pattern in this book, for all is not judgment and judges. God continually demonstrates His patience and compassion for His people coupled with His ability to save. Also remarkable is the way in which God works through the most unsuspecting of people. Most of the judges consider themselves unworthy and unable, as was the case also with Moses. God demonstrates His power by working in them mightily in contrast to those born with natural ability and stature who brought disaster by their own vanity and carelessness. Thus, the history of Israel during the time of the Judges points even more strikingly to the need for a Judge who will be faithful at all times and in every way.

1. Authorship and Date of Writing—*Who Compiled the History of the Judges of Israel?*
2. Date and Setting of the Events in the Book—*How Long Was Israel Ruled by the Judges*
3. Themes—*What Important Concepts Characterize the Book of Joshua?*
4. Overview of the Book—*Who was in Charge Between Joshua and King Saul?*
5. Important Passages—*Key Passages That Make the Purpose of the Book Clear*

1. Authorship and Date of Writing

The book of Judges offers no hints about who might have written it. However, the way in which the book measures Israel's history by the standard of faithfulness to the covenant suggests that it was written by a prophet. The unity of the composition is evident in the theme of Israel's dependence on her spiritual relationship with the Lord. This unity points to a single author. We may consider Samuel as a likely candidate for two reasons. First, Samuel was a prophet who embodied the perspective that is provided in the book. Second, Samuel was living at the right time. The date of writing would have been early in the monarchy of Israel (c. 1010 BC) for three reasons. First, Judges 1:21 reports that the Jebusites lived among the people of Benjamin "until this day." This probably had to be written before David's capture of Jerusalem (1002 BC; 2 Sam 5:6–10; 1 Chr 3:5–9). Second, Judges 1:29 reports that Canaanites dwelt in Gezer, which must refer to a time before Egypt conquered Gezer, and the King of Egypt gave it to Solomon as a dowry for his daughter (970 BC; 1 Kgs 9:16;). Third, Judges 18:1 and 19:1 describe the time as one in which "there was no king in Israel," giving a perspective from sometime during the reign of Saul looking back at Israel's past.

2. Date and Setting of the Events in the Book

The events of this book are easily dated by the lives of the Judges. The setting of the events of the book is well established by the book of Joshua. You may recall that much of Joshua records the lands that had been conquered by Israel and those which had not. Thus the setting of the book of Judges is the land to the East and West of the Jordan river, from the southern end of the Dead Sea as far North as Mt. Hermon. The dates of the history are as follows.

Judge	Oppressor	Years	Dates	Reference
Joshua/Elders			1399–1379	Judg 2:11
	Mesopotamia	8	1378–1371	Judg 3:9
Othniel		40	1371–1332	Judg 3:9–11
	Moab	18	1332–1315	Judg 3:12–14
Ehud		80	1315–	Judg 3:15–30
	Philistines			Judg 3:31
Shamgar			–1236	Judg 3:31
	Canaan	20	1236–1217	Judg 4:2–3
Deborah/Barak		40	1217–1178	Judg 4:4—5:31
	Midian	7	1178–1172	Judg 6:1
Gideon		40	1172–1133	Judg 6:11–35

	Amalek		1133–1131	
Tola		23	1131–1109	Judg 10:1–2
Jair		22	1109–1088	Judg 10:3–5
	Ammon	18	1088–1071	Judg 10:8
Jephthah		6	1088–1083	Judg 11:1—12:7
Ibzan		7	1083–1077	Judg 12:8–10
Elon		10	1077–1068	Judg 12:11–12
Abdon		8	1068–1061	Judg 12:13–15
	Philistines	40	1088–1049	Judg 13:1
Samson		20	c.1030–1049	Judg 13:2—16:31

3. Themes

Israel's Cycle of Unfaithfulness

The cycle of Israel's unfaithfulness is conveyed in a shorter and longer way in the book of Judges. This cycle can be seen *within* Judges 1, 2, 3, 10, and 21. In each of these chapters of Judges there is a record of Israel's conduct being more and more contrary to the Lord along with commentary about that. For example, Judges 1 cycles through six tribes of Israel, reporting that each had failed to drive out the inhabitants of the land. The last tribe mentioned, Dan, was kept out of its inheritance completely by the Ammorites.

The longer cycle of unfaithfulness is evident from chapter to chapter in Judges as Israel continues to adopt the idolatrous and wicked practices of her neighbors. The reader is meant to be astonished and shocked at the conduct of Israel on two counts. First, how can Israel keep turning to the wicked practices of the nations around them when they have already experienced the disaster of following those practices? Second, how can Israel show such contempt for God's deliverance through the judges by so quickly turning back into the very situation from which they were just delivered? This insanity is inherent in human nature since the fall and is described in Proverbs 26:11, "As a dog returns to his own vomit, so a fool repeats his folly." The apostle Paul addresses the insanity of repeated unfaithfulness throughout Romans 6, climaxing with this question, "What fruit did you have then in the things of which you are now ashamed? For the end of those things is death" (Romans 6:21). Thus, Jesus pressed the point to Nicodemus that human nature is helpless to break the cycle of unfaithfulness. Real deliverance comes only as God re-generates us by means of His Word and Spirit (John 3:1–8).

Israel's Increasing Corruption

The increasing aspect of Israel's corruption is made evident in a most remarkable way in the book of Judges. While the cycle of unfaithfulness is obvious, the increasing nature of Israel's corruption requires more careful observation. Note that in Judges 3:5–11 the pattern is established:

1. Israel is among the nations
2. Israel joins itself to the nations by marriage
3. Israel does evil
4. The Lord's anger burns
5. The Lord sells Israel into the hands of the nations to which it joined itself
6. Israel cries for help
7. The Lord has pity and provides a Judge
8. There is rest for the people.

This pattern is repeated through the rest of Judges, except that each time Israel repeats the pattern the corruption is worse, the consequences more tragic, and the text describing it is longer, as follows:

3:5–11	The Basic Pattern
3:12–30	Ehud
4:1—5:31	Deborah (the embarrassment of a timid male leader)
6:1—8:32	Gideon (no rest as Israel turns back into evil)
8:33—10:1	Abimilech (no rest)
10:2–18	A longer review of all that is wrong
11:1—12:4	Jephthah (shorter than Gideon, but no mention of rest)
13:1—16:31	Samson (tragic, but deliverance is still provided)
17:1—21:24	Micah (completely disastrous)

This same pattern of increasing corruption is evident in the history of Samuel and Kings where good kings continue to appear but not as good as the previous and less frequently over time.

Law and Gospel in Action

Gospel is the part of the cycle, and it stands in contrast to Israel's unfaithfulness. The mercy of God in the Gospel also increases in response to Israel's increasing corruption (Rom 5:20, "where sin abounded, grace abounded even more"). In spite of Israel's unfaithfulness, the Lord continued to be faithful to

His promises by preserving the people from whom the Savior would come. In spite of Israel's increasing corruption, the Lord continued to have pity upon them and sent judges (flawed as they were) to deliver them. Readers should remember that there was nothing wrong with the deliverance that the Lord provided. Israel suffered oppression again and again because they continually turned away from the Lord. The relationship between Law and Gospel evident in this history and is expressed in Psalms 104—107. Psalm 106:34–45 provides a clear example,

> They did not destroy the peoples, concerning whom the Lord had commanded them,
> but they mingled with the Gentiles and learned their works.
> They served their idols
> > ...Therefore the wrath of the Lord was kindled against His people
> > ...Many times He delivered them; but they rebelled against Him by their counsel
> > ...Nevertheless He regarded their affliction
> > ...and for their sake He remembered His covenant.

Notice then, that the gospel/grace of God is the backdrop or constant, against which the unfaithfulness of Israel's history is set. The remedy for fallen human nature does not come in a material kingdom nor a human judge. Real deliverance comes only in the Son of God who assumes human nature, not to judge, but to assume all judgments against humanity in His own life and death. His resurrection and faithfulness are the enduring answer of God's Gospel that alone delivers humanity from the tragedy of unfaithfulness and corruption.

4. Overview of the Book

The book of Judges presents its material in three distinct sections; an introduction, a series of examples, and a conclusion.

The introduction focuses on Joshua as a paradigm of faithfulness against which to warn Israel against unfaithfulness and then to contrast God's faithfulness to their unfaithfulness. Judges 1 begins with a sober acknowledgment of Joshua's death is followed by a series of descriptions of how the tribes of Israel failed to drive out all the inhabitants of their allotted lands. Judges 2 backs up to review the cause of Israel's failure: the Angel of the Lord will faithfully fight for Israel, but Israel has not obeyed the Lord. Therefore the Lord will not drive the nations out of Canaan. Judges 1 goes on to describe how Joshua wept over this situation, then exposes the cause of the trouble to come. Joshua, who had seen the great works of the Lord, was faithful, but the generation to come did not know the Lord. Judges 2 concludes with a paradigm that the rest of the book will demonstrate.

2:11–15	Israel did evil in the sight of the Lord	The Lord is against them
2:16–19	The Lord raises up judges	The people will not listen
2:20–23	The anger of the Lord burns	He leaves pagan nations to test Israel

The center and majority of the text of Judges provides the history of Israel's increasing unfaithfulness through a series of judges. Judges 3 gives a complete example of how accurate this paradigm is in describing Israel's unfaithfulness. Readers may note that the increasing unfaithfulness of each judge is exposed with a longer text, and there is less rest at the end of each subsequent judge's life.

The conclusion is very brief (one verse long) in order to make the point crystal clear and stinging: disaster of unimagined proportions follows when everyone does what is right in their own eyes (contrast this with Paul's exhortation that the Christian church be of one mind, Phil 1:27–2:5).

Ruth

The account of Ruth in the Old Testament and the inclusion of that history in the Old Testament canon is remarkable in many ways. First, women are not often mentioned in the narratives, since responsibility (for better or worse) rests with man, and the narrative is looking forward to the Son of Man, Jesus. Second, Ruth is a Moabite and therefore not highly esteemed among the children of Israel. She is thus set in contrast to men in general and Israelites in particular as a standard of faithfulness. Matthew uses such references to women in a very powerful way in his genealogy, mentioning Tamar, Rahab and Ruth (Matt 1:3, 5). Third, the book of Ruth demonstrates that God works out His plan of salvation in spite of all opposition, real or apparent. While Israel thought that God was for them and against their neighbors, God had intended to extend salvation to their neighbors through Israel. If Israel thought that foreigners were inherently excluded from God's favor and incapable of saving faith, Ruth exposes the error of their thinking. Thus, Ruth re-orients the reader to understand that God desires all people to be saved and come to the knowledge of the truth (1 Tim 2:4).

1. Authorship and Date of Writing—*Who Knew and Wrote down the History of Ruth?*
2. Date and Setting of the Events in the Book—*When was Ruth grafted into Israel?*
3. Themes—*What Important Witnesses to Faith does Ruth Provide?*
4. Overview of the Book—*How Ruth came from Moab to Israel*

1. Authorship and Date of Writing

On the one hand, the book of Ruth could not have been written before the time of David, since he is mentioned by name (Ruth 4:22). On the other hand, it would not have been written after the time of David since then the genealogy would surely have included Solomon. The Talmud identifies Samuel as the author. Samuel is a reasonable suggestion since his life parallels the purpose of Ruth. Just as Ruth provides a transition from the period of the Judges to the kingdom of David, so Samuel's life began in the period of the Judges and ended after he had anointed David king of Israel. Unfortunately, there is no way of proving that Samuel was the author.

Attempts have been made to date the book much later, in the post exilic period. These attempts are based on an interest in supporting unfounded hypotheses about late dating of the Old Testament books that precede Ruth. These hypotheses have been abandoned by many contemporary scholars, since they are without credible evidence and are, in fact, contradicted by the evidence that is available, such as the type of Hebrew used in the book.

2. Date and Setting of the Events in the Book

The events of this book took place during the period of the Judges, as the opening verse expressly states (Ruth 1:1). Boaz was the great-grandfather of David, thus placing the events of the book somewhere around 1100 BC. The events are set toward the end of the period of the judges but before Israel's first king. There is no indication that Israel is being oppressed at this time, on the contrary, Israelites apparently felt comfortable leaving home during the drought in order to seek relief in Moab.

3. Themes

The Faithfulness of God (Including the Kinsman-Redeemer)

The faithfulness of God is demonstrated through the account of Ruth in several ways. First, God demonstrates His faithfulness in dire straights. There is a famine but also a place to go for relief (Ruth 1:1). There is a time to return for "... the Lord had visited His people by giving them food" (Ruth 1:6). The Lord granted kind daughters-in-law, as Naomi recognized (Ruth 1:8). Best of all, the Lord inspired the devotion and care of Ruth for Naomi – and all this in spite of Naomi's bitter complaints (Ruth 1:13, 20–21). The faithfulness of God that benefited both Naomi and Ruth in this history bears similarities to Joseph's experience in Egypt, about which Joseph concluded, "... God meant it for good" (Gen 50:20). Paul expresses the same principle in Romans 8:23 "God makes all things work together for good to those who love Him."

Second, the faithfulness of God is seen in not-so-dire straights. The text reports that Ruth "happened to be" in the field of Boaz, but that is hardly an accident. While the general opportunity to **glean** fields was available (i.e., the right to pick up any stalks of grain that the harvesters dropped or left behind (Lev 19:9; 23:22), Ruth and Naomi are provided for more and more generously by Boaz, first in terms of food (Ruth 2:8, 14–16; 3:15), then by assuming all responsibility for their well-being (Ruth 3:11). The law of **kinsman-redeemer** is a simple yet profoundly effective means by which God provides for people (Lev 25). The principle and practice were clearly in place even before they were articulated in the Mosaic law. The kinsman-redeemer principle was at issue with Judah and his sons (Gen 38) though we have command of God for it until Deuteronomy 25:5–10. Thus God provided food for people by way of gleaning the fields and He provided for their other needs by way of a kinsman-redeemer.

Third, God's faithfulness is seen by looking at the particular events and details from the vantage point of His more comprehensive purposes. God provides family and children in time as a witness to His desire to make us His children and bind us together as His family eternally. God provides food for His people so that they might consider the more significant Bread that comes down from heaven, the Word of God that gives everlasting life (John 6). God works out His promise to Adam and Eve (Gen 3:15) to provide a seed that would save all people from their sin through many and various circumstances, culminating in the conception of Christ in the Virgin Mary.

God's People Reflect His Faithfulness

God's people reflect His faithfulness in at least four ways in Ruth. First, Naomi reflects God's faithfulness in spite of her complaints. She calls upon the Lord to deal kindly with Orpah and Ruth (Ruth 1:8–9), then she complains (Ruth 1:13, 20–21), then she confesses that the Lord has not forsaken His kindness (Ruth 2:20), then she counsels Ruth to submit herself to Boaz' care (Ruth 3:1–4, 18). Note how Naomi's last counsel to Ruth is that she "sit still," a theme that is very prevalent in Old Testament literature and in the Psalms especially (Ps 40). There is also a hint of faithfulness in Naomi as she expressed a desire to provide husbands for her daughters-in-law if only she could (Ruth 1:11).

Second, Ruth is the grand example of God's people reflecting His faithfulness. Her unwillingness to abandon Naomi seems squarely predicated on her absolute refusal to give up the God she has come to know by way of the witness of Elimelech and his family (Ruth 1:16–17). Her deep humility and selflessness reveal that faith in God makes self-interests unnecessary. In this way Ruth is paralleled in the New Testament by the Syro-Phoenician woman (Matt 15:21–28) in two significant ways. On the one hand, the simple faithfulness of a Gentile is contrasted with the lack of faithfulness demonstrated by those who were supposed to be the people of God. Even more significantly, the text urges us to consider that it is not nationality that makes on a child of God, but faith, as is the case with Abraham and his true descendants (Rom 2:28–29, Gal 3:29). The New Testament presents this same theme very dramatically as both Jesus (Matt 8) and Philip (Acts 8) minister to a series of people who would have been seen as increasingly outside of God's interest. These Gentiles or outsiders were not only within the care of God, but in fact display that they are more closely connected to God by faith than Israel ever was as a race or nation.

Third, greetings recorded reveal that the faithfulness of God was woven in the very fabric of daily life. Boaz greeted his reapers with "The Lord be with you" and they answered, "The Lord bless you" (Ruth 2:4). The people at the gate who witnessed Boaz' care for family blessed Ruth according to the faithfulness of God in giving Jacob children (Ruth 4:11).

Fourth, the faithfulness of God is reflected in Boaz, who provides for Ruth and Naomi. As the narrative unfolds Boaz continues to increase the care he provides, first in the fields as Ruth is gleaning (Ruth 2:8, 14–16) then as a kinsman-redeemer (Ruth 3). In the first instance Ruth takes advantage of the law that allowed poor people to glean in the fields. Boaz even commands his workers to purposely drop extra for Ruth (Ruth 2:16). In the second instance, Boaz keeps his word to follow the law of the kinsman-redeemer and to marry Ruth. Naomi highlights this faithfulness as she counsels Ruth, "Sit still … for the man will not rest until he has concluded the matter this day" (Ruth 3:18).

The Line of David and Christ

The book of Ruth ends with a genealogy recording only nine generations, from Perez to David. In this way the book of Ruth connects the end of Genesis (Perez is born in Gen 38) and Samuel (in which David becomes king). But is there more significance than this to the genealogy of Perez? Such significance is hinted at by reference to Perez in the blessing of the people upon Boaz, "May your house be like the house of Perez, whom Tamar bore to Judah, because of the offspring which the Lord will give you from this young woman" (Ruth 4:12). If we compare this text to the genealogy of Matthew we note that again, Tamar is mentioned along with Perez. What then is the significance of Perez and Tamar? Two points come to mind. First, Perez was technically not the first born but "broke through" in order to be born before his twin (Gen 38:27–30). Just as God often chose a son who was not the first-born to on the promised line of the Messiah, so God also chose people outside of Israel to carry out His purposes. Second, both Tamar and Ruth call to mind the principle of kinsman-redeemer. Perez was born to Judah and Tamar because Judah refused to give his youngest son to Tamar as her rightful husband. A contrast is thus also introduced, since Tamar had to pursue a relationship which was rightfully hers while Boaz eagerly pursued the same for Ruth. Matthew's genealogy mentions a third woman within this genealogy from Perez to David, that is Rahab (Matt 1:5). The passage of time from the conquest of Jericho until the birth of Boaz either means that the genealogy skips some generations or that this is the not same Rahab who harbored the spies of Israel. In either case, the name brings the faithfulness of a third woman to mind.

The history of humanity from its creation until its redemption by Jesus Christ is a messy business. Many of the men in the line from Eve to Mary were intensely faithful, like Noah and Abraham. Many judges were faithful as were many of the kings. On the other hand, many were scoundrels like Lamech (Gen 4:23–24) and Ham (Gen 9:21–27). Many judges and kings were also faithless. Nevertheless, the Lord continued to order history so that His promise of a Savior was fulfilled at just the right time (Gal 4:4). This history also demonstrates that God has those considered to be foreigners in mind, includes them in His purposes, and even uses them to remind us that faith, not physical descent, makes someone a child of God (John 1:11–14).

4. Overview of the Book

A reasonable overview of the book is provided by following the overall accomplishment recorded in the text: God draws Ruth into the fulfillment of His promises. Consider an outline under this heading: Ruth is Drawn into the Promises of God by Degrees

1. By marriage to the son of Elimelech (1:1–5)
2. By inspiration of God revealed in her devotion to Naomi (1:6–18)
3. By relocation to Bethlehem (1:19–22)
4. By daily labor and persistent devotion (2:1–7)
5. By invitation of Boaz (2:8–23)
6. By the counsel of Naomi (3:1–7)
7. By the counsel of Boaz (3:8–18)
8. By the counsel of Boaz to the elders in public forum at the gate of the city (4:1–12)
9. By marriage and childbirth (4:13–22)

The word of the Lord provides for a constant, general witness to His will that people should come into this life through conception (Gen 1:28; 9:1). Within that general witness God has provided a particular witness to a particular conception that will provide for the ultimate life and the ultimate remedy for death, the incarnation of His Son by the Holy Spirit in the Virgin Mary. The Word of the Lord provided for Ruth's faith in general and for her part in the fulfilling of God's promise to send His Son in particular.

12

Samuel

The early history of the Old Testament reports the ever-increasing distance between people and their creator. In the beginning, God walked with Adam in the garden. God appeared on several occasions to Abraham, Isaac, and Jacob. God looked after the children of Israel through Moses, the "man of God." The authority of Moses passed to Joshua then to the Judges of Israel. At that time the habit of people to "do whatever was right in their own eyes" (Judg 17:6; 21:25) became more prominent than ever, giving way to the people's desire to be "like the other nations." Samuel records the transition from the period of the judges to the time when Israel was governed by kings. The demand of Israel for a king highlights an even greater distance between God and His people, between God's prophets and the people's rulers. Samuel provides essential insight into the import of this change.

1. Authorship and Date of Writing—*Did Samuel Write Both Books That Bear His Name?*
2. Samuel Divided into Two Books—*Was the Book of Samuel Always Divided?*
3. Date and Setting of the Events of the Book—*What in the World Was Going on?*
4. Themes—*What Important Concepts Characterize the Book of Samuel?*
5. Overview of the Book—*Where Has It Come from and Where Is It Going?*
6. Important Passages—*Key Passages That Make the Purpose of the Book Clear*

1. Authorship and Date of Writing

The titles of books in the Bible often tell you who the author was. In some translations, the first five books of the Old Testament are called the "books of Moses." Prophet's names appear on books they wrote and many New Testament books are called by their author's names. While Samuel certainly could have written some of 1 Samuel, he could not have written all of it nor any of 2 Samuel since 1 Samuel 25:1 records his death. Since 1 Samuel 27:6 refers to the kings of Judah, it is clear that the books in their present form were not completed until after the division of the Northern and Southern kingdoms of Israel. We do know that Samuel and Nathan both wrote books (1 Chr 29:29). These books would have been placed together in their present form, most probably, by a prophet of Judah who lived shortly after the split between the Northern and Southern kingdoms (approximately 975 BC).

Modern scholars have theorized that the events of 1 and 2 Samuel are entirely fiction. Some scholars have argued that the entire content of these books is fiction, not history. These theories say that conquering nations like Babylon or the Greeks populated Palestine with a mixture of people in order to keep this important land of passage under control. These people realized that they had no history of their own, so they sat down and invented one! Such theories are problematic since they ignore archaeological evidence, the witness of the text itself (historical texts read very differently than fiction), and ultimately calls into question every historical witness. Moreover, the message of the Gospel is compromised by these theories, since they deny the inspiration and reliability of the Bible. If God did not act in history for his people as the book of Samuel says, then its witness to Christ, who came into history to save all people, is lost.

2. Samuel Divided into Two Books

The book of Samuel was divided into two when it was translated in Greek between 400 and 250 BC. These translators called these books the "First and Second Books of the Kingdoms." This made sense because the enduring issue of the books is the kingdom of Israel, rather than Samuel (though he had the unhappy task of inaugurating this form of rule by men).

3. Date and Setting of the Events of the Book

The whole Bible speaks to the inability of human beings in matters of life and living in contrast to the ability of God to act, especially in matters "impossible." How can there be life for us? Cain killed Abel and became a fugitive, but God gave Eve another son. Abraham and Sarah could not have children – how could the promise of God to send a Savior be fulfilled? God gave them Isaac. Through one circumstance after another, God is faithful in fulfilling his promise. As history unfolds, the book of Ruth sets the stage for Samuel. Ruth explains how the promise of a Messiah through the seed of a woman (Gen 3:15) was advanced in the line of Judah through this Moabite woman (see the genealogy, Ruth 1:18–22). Saul was anointed King in 1048 BC and ruled about forty years. 1 Samuel concludes with his death. David is anointed king already in 1 Samuel 16 but does not reign over all Israel until 2 Samuel 5. 2 Samuel ends with the intercession and restoration of David after his error in commanding a census, around 975 BC.

The collection of this history, compiled by Samuel and Nathan, responded to needs in their day and ours. On the one hand, the books of Samuel would have been used to correct the decline of Israel under its kings, especially after the kingdom was divided. Wicked behavior of kings and Israel is clearly condemned. The faithfulness of God is held high in order to inspire repentance and fidelity in God's people. The same correction applies to people in power today (in the church and in the world). The same truth of God's faithfulness inspires virtue and obedience.

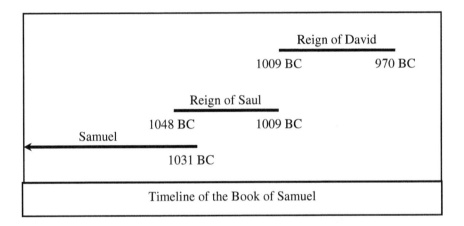

Timeline of the Book of Samuel

4. Themes

Office and Leadership

The books of Samuel focus on the combination of spiritual and civil leadership. The books also focus on the three well-known offices of the Old Testament; prophet, priest, and king. Interestingly, the main characters fulfill more than one office in their leadership. However, this leads to confusion of offices and is not always well received by the Lord. To begin with, Samuel was dedicated to the service of the Lord in the Tabernacle. But Samuel was also a prophet and at times a powerful source of civil leadership. Samuel's leadership on behalf of God (**theocracy**, that is, rule by God) very quickly collides with Israel's determination to have a king "like the other nations" (1 Sam 8:5). This determination is a climax of the rebellion of human nature demonstrated throughout the time of Moses, Joshua and the Judges. Saul was anointed as Israel's first king, in spite of God's warnings regarding the future and conduct of such kings. Though Saul prophesied once as witness to the power of God's Spirit among men, he was rejected as king when he was disobedient and presumed to do the work of a priest in offering sacrifices (1 Sam 13:9). David's early history, in contrast to Saul, is marked by simple faith and obedience that is blessed by God. While David remained faithful, the Lord blessed his service in all three offices. David's sin with Bathsheba marks the beginning of troubles in every area of leadership for him. Nevertheless, because of his contrition and faith, David remained the standard by which "good" kings were recognized.

The Messianic Promise

The promise of a savior was given first in Genesis 3:15 to Adam and Eve. That promise was repeated with more detail to Abraham (Gen 12:1–3) and his descendants. The prophet Nathan gives the clearest and most detailed promise of the Messiah to David in 2 Samuel 7. The account begins with David's desire to build a house for God. God responds by reminding David that the one true living God of Israel provides for His people, his people do not provide for Him. God would build an eternal dwelling place by means of a son who would be born of David's line. Much of the prophecy can be recognized as parallel to the reign of Solomon and subsequent kings. However, the prophesy is clearly speaking of the coming Messiah by David who says in response, "… You have also spoken of Your servant's house for a great while to come" (2 Sam 7:19). The significance of this prophecy is seen throughout the rest of Holy Scripture as the coming Messiah is called "the Son of David" in the New Testament.

Sin and Its Consequences

The books of Samuel have some of the greatest examples of virtue and faithfulness in the Bible. Hannah's prayer for a child and dedication of him, Samuel's faithfulness as a messenger of God, and David's slaying of Goliath are all remarkable. However, apart from God's intervention in the lives of people, we see fallen human nature at its worst. Eli raised two desperately wicked sons (1 Sam 2:27–36). Surprisingly, Samuel had the same trouble with his own sons (1 Sam 8:1–5). Saul disobeyed the Lord, rejected His Word and sought the counsel of a sorceress (1 Sam 15, 28). David committed adultery and murder (2 Sam 11). The text clearly demonstrates that even the best human beings refuse to hear God. Instead, they rebel with an incredible determination to contradict God's will.

The text of Samuel also leads the reader to recognize that contradicting God's will has consequences. Note that from the time Saul first disobeys the word of the Lord, he makes one bad decision after another. The consequences of those decisions cost the lives of many in Israel, and eventually led to the death of Saul and his sons. David also struggles with a host of bad consequences after his adultery with Bathsheba. Amnon, David's oldest son and heir to the throne, took advantage of his half sister Tamar (as David had taken advantage of Bathsheba). David's son Absalom took vengeance on Amnon and had him killed. As David had committed sexual sin and murder, so sexual sin and murder continued in his house. Notice how these examples of sin and their consequences contrast with the life of the promised Messiah. This Son of David was faithful in all things (Heb 3:3–6), sacrificing only His own life that everyone else might live (John 3:14–17).

5. Overview of the Book

In short, the two books of Samuel are the bridge between the time *before* kings to the time *of* the kings, from the time that God was so near that He ruled Israel Himself, to a time when God was so distant that he would no longer even speak to them (from Malachi to John the Baptist). The two main sections of this bridge are Saul and David. First Samuel describes the life of King Saul, Second Samuel describes the life of King David. Within each book, there is an overlap between main characters, each one offering comparisons and contrasts to the next. Samuel gives way to Saul, Saul give way to David, David gives way to his sons.

Samuel

1 Samuel 1—2	Hannah the faithful and her son Samuel / Eli the faithless and his sons
1 Samuel 3—4	Samuel the faithful – the beginning / the end of Eli and his sons
1 Samuel 5—7	The capture and return of the Ark of the Covenant with Samuel as judge

Saul

1 Samuel 8—11	Saul anointed king and serves faithfully
1 Samuel 12	Samuel's admonished Saul
1 Samuel 13—15	The faithlessness of Saul
1 Samuel 16—17	David anointed king, serves faithfully
1 Samuel 18—31	Saul's continual faithlessness and death

David

2 Samuel 1—5	David established as King over all Israel
2 Samuel 6—7	David brings the Ark to Jerusalem. Who will build God's house?
2 Samuel 8—10	David's kingdom grows stronger
2 Samuel 11—24	David's failures, end of his reign

13

Kings

The time of the Judges was plagued with the problem of "everyone doing what was right in their own eyes" (Judges 17:6). Samuel recorded the transition from that period to the time of the kings. Saul had demonstrated kingship at its worst and David at its best—though he was far from perfect. The two books of Kings provide the history of kingship in Israel from David's successor to the end of the period of kings at the Babylonian captivity. What can be learned from this history? First of all, "be careful what you ask for." Israel wanted a king who was human, a king they could manipulate according to their own devices, "like the nations" around them. The problem is that human kings are also manipulated by the evil desires of their own hearts, the world around them, and the devil. Second, even the best kings had their weaknesses and failings. This highlights the need for a King that will not fail, the King who was promised to David in 2 Samuel 7. Third, God continues to lead His people in spite of their folly and failures. Notice how deliverance comes when the king turns to the Lord for help. Notice also how quick God is to show mercy when a king repents. These lessons are important in our day as well if we are to serve God and neighbor as a *"royal priesthood"* (1 Peter 2:9)

1. Authorship and Date of Writing—*Who wrote about the kings and when did they write it?*
2. Kings Divided into Two Books—*Was the book of Kings always divided?*
3. Date and Setting of the Events of the Book—*What in the world was going on?*
4. Themes—*Important motifs that run throughout the book*
5. Overview of the Book—*Where has it come from and where is it going?*
6. Important Passages—*key passages that make the purpose of the book clear*

1, Authorship and Date of Writing

In contrast to Samuel, the title *Kings* seems to describe the subject matter rather than the author. Kings, like Samuel, makes use of written records. 1 Kings 11:41 mentions "The Book of the Words of Solomon." Many passages mention "The Book of the Chronicles of the Kings of Judah" (for example, 1 Kgs 14:29).

Similarly, the Kings of Israel were also chronicled (1 Kgs 14:19). The Jewish Talmud tractate entitled *Baba Bathra* reports that Jeremiah, the prophet, wrote his own book and the book of Kings. This proposition is inviting because of the resemblances between Jeremiah and Kings. On the other hand, this view is problematic because the account of Jehoiachin's deportation and imprisonment appears to have been written from Babylon, but Jeremiah was carried to Egypt (Jer 43:1–8). As with Samuel, Kings was probably compiled or written by a person who lived during the times described at the end of the books or shortly thereafter. This position is supported in 1 Kings 8:7–8 by a reference to the fact that the poles used to carry the ark were with the ark, as they should be, "to this day."

2. Kings Divided into Two Books

The book of Kings, like the book of Samuel, was divided into two when it was translated in Greek between 400 and 250 BC. These translators called these books the "Third and Fourth Books of the Kingdoms." This made sense because the content of these books continues the story of kingdoms in Israel, especially since the kingdom is divided after Solomon's reign.

3. Date and Setting of the Events of the Book

	━━━━━━━━━━━━━━━━━━━━━	
931 BC	Kingdom of Judah	587 BC
Solomon		
━━━━━━━━		
970 BC 931 BC		
	━━━━━━━━━━━━━━━	
931 BC	Kingdom of Israel	723 BC
	Timeline of the Book of Kings	

1 Kings begins with the issue of who will succeed David as king. This issue of who will rule over Israel has been prominent since Israel first demanded a king in 1 Samuel 8. If people reject God as their leader, then who will lead? At least two problems are highlighted. First, how will the selection of king be made? When Israel said they wanted a king like other nations (1 Samuel 8:5, 19) the emphasis was not on the fact that other nations had kings. Rather, the em-

phasis is on "like other nations," meaning that Israel wanted a king that they could control, like other nations had. The issue of selection and control becomes more prominent as the period of the monarchy continues. The early kingdom was always divided between Saul and David, to a large extent by the sentiment of the people. Absalom made use of the people's sentiment and attempted to usurp the reign from his father David (1 Sam 15:1–12). Now, at the conclusion of David's life (970 BC), the problem of who should rule appears again. This time the trouble is that David made certain promises regarding Solomon, yet by order of birth Adonijah would have been the next king. Though Solomon clearly becomes the king of all Israel, contention over ruling Israel surfaces again at his death with the division of kingdoms North and South. The book of Kings concludes with the Babylonian captivity of Judah (587 BC) during which time one of the last kings of Judah, Jehoiachin, is eventually released from prison (561 BC).

4. Themes

God's Promise to Israel

Since the beginning, God has made promises to His creation. Some of God's promises are unconditional some are conditional. Unconditional promises mean that God will do what He promised by His own determination without requiring anything from humans. For example, God promised Adam and Eve that from the seed of the woman would come a Savior, who would destroy the power of the Devil. That promise was repeated to Abraham, "In you and in your Seed shall all the nations of the earth be blessed" (Gen 12:3). God told David that one of his sons would rule forever (2 Sam 7:12–16). These promises would be fulfilled regardless of the conduct of Israel.

With conditional promises, in contrast to unconditional promises, God agrees to act for Israel as long as Israel fulfills the required condition. For example, just before Israel entered the Promised Land, Moses reminded them of the conditions of their life in that place (Deuteronomy 28). If Israel diligently obeyed the voice of the Lord, they would be blessed. If they did not obey the Lord, they would be cursed. The history of Kings reveals the relationship between these two types of promises. On the one hand, Israel continually fell into disobedience. As a result, they lost the blessings God had given them and experienced curses (Deut 28). Nevertheless, God did not utterly forsake Israel, because the unconditional promises He had made to their forefathers, including Adam, Abraham, Isaac, Jacob, and David.

God's Promise to David

"With God all things are possible" (Matt 19:26). A reading of Kings may leave the reader with the firm impression that there is no hope for the children of Israel. Will there ever be a king who is completely faithful? Though there were good kings among the bad, the overall trend through Israel's history is a downward spiral. In the end, even the kings that were somewhat faithful to God were plagued with weaknesses and failure. In stark contrast the writer of Kings highlighted the faithfulness of God and His promises. In spite of this downward spiral, Israel endures from one generation to the next, through rebellion, disaster, repentance, mercy and restoration. This enduring mercy of God rests on the unconditional promise that from David's line would come the King who would redeem Israel from all her iniquities. When kings were faithful, we have a glimpse of what this ultimate king will be like. When kings failed we see, by way of contrast, what the promised king will never do. Certainty of these promises would become all the more important as Israel continued to decline through captivity and subjection to foreign powers, even to the intertestamental period when the established promises of God were all the faithful people had.

Sin and its consequences

This topic was discussed earlier as part of the introduction to Samuel. The immediately preceding discussion also touches this topic by observations about the decline of Israel. The witness of Kings makes the reality of sin and its consequences undeniable. Sin is real. Sin is the contradiction of the design that exists in God's creation. There are serious consequences to contradicting God's design. These consequences are not trivial or arbitrary, but organic. We depend everyday on the certainty of God's laws in creation. We cannot live or thrive if the laws of nature are unstable or unpredictable. Therefore, any time a person would contradict the "law" that supports life, consequences must follow. Obedience to God is necessary, if Israel would live and thrive in the Promised Land under the blessing of God. The book of Kings provides generation after generation of evidence that consequences always follow the transgression of God's law. Every time Israel rejects God in order to act according to its own selfish thinking, like the surrounding nations, it experiences the consequences of that kind of thinking by the force of these nations. There is no alternative. If we cast off the care of a loving God, we fall under the abuse of self-serving idolatry. How is it that Israel is not entirely lost? The answer comes in the combination of God's promises, which are an expression of His longsuffering and mercy.

God's Longsuffering and Mercy

The period of Israel's history recorded in Kings is similar to that of Judges. Kings, like judges, come and go. Some kings are better, some are worse, but the God of Israel continues to be faithful to his unconditional promises to Abraham, Isaac and Jacob. If the children of Israel are faithless, He remains faithful, for He cannot deny Himself (2 Tim 2:13). The faithfulness and mercy of God stands in contrast to a steady decline in faithfulness and integrity among the kings. Consider the example of Elijah. Though Israel was being punished with a terrible drought, the Lord provided for Elijah by the Brook Cherith by means of ravens, who brought him bread and meat. After the brook dried up, the Lord sent Elijah to the widow of Zarephath, whose oil and floor never ran out while she provided for the prophet. (This remarkable sign of God's mercy is referred to by Jesus in the Synagogue, Luke 4:25–26.) Later during Ahab's persecution of the faithful, Elijah came to despair. At one point, Elijah claims to be the only believer left in all of Israel (1 Kgs 19:14). To this the Lord responds by saying that He has kept 7,000 people of Israel from committing idolatry to Baal. Besides these notable examples of mercy, God's longsuffering or patience is observable also. The number of years that pass and the number of opportunities that the Lord offers for Israel to repent is remarkable. This longsuffering is evidence of His mercy and consistent with it. The Lord is not slow, but longsuffering, not desiring that any should perish (2 Pet 3:9). The longsuffering and mercy of God are meant to act as dual forces; mercy creates saving faith, the longsuffering of God teaches us not to be careless with His mercy (Heb 2:1–4).

5. Overview of the Book

The book of Samuel establishes that Israel will have a king and that having a king other than God is nothing but trouble. The book of Kings records the history from the first king to follow David to the last king who reigned over the only two tribes of Israel that remained. This history continues to bear profound witness to the failings of human leadership, from Solomon's fall into idolatry to the division of the kingdom, to the loss of the Northern kingdom, and to the loss of Judah to Babylon. An overview of 1 and 2 Kings might look like this,

1 Kings ... from good to bad?	
1–2	Who will be king after David?
	Solomon is firmly established as successor to David.
3–4	How will Solomon rule?
	The Solomon of God: his prayer, wisdom and wealth.
5–6	Who will build God a house? Solomon's temple
7–10	Solomon's other buildings and accomplishments
11	How will Solomon endure?
	The Solomon of gods & foreign women: his downfall
12–14	Rehoboam of Judah versus Jeroboam of Israel a divided kingdom
15–22	Various kings—many are bad, but none as bad as Ahab of Israel
	Elijah the Prophet
2 Kings ... from bad to worse?	
	Elisha the Prophet
1–13	Various kings—none as good as David, many as bad as Ahab
14–16	Steady decline of Israel and Judah under their kings
17	Ten northern tribes of Israel fall to Assyria
18–20	The Godly Hezekiah
18–21	Steady decline of Judah despite Israel's fall
22–23	The Godly Josiah—a bright spot in Judah's history
24–25	Judah (and Benjamin) fall to Babylon

Solomon, like Moses before him, was aware of two things: he was not sufficient for the call he received, and God provided him with extra-ordinary gifts. God did miracles through Moses that surpassed human imagination. God gave Solomon wisdom that astounded the whole world. The potential for human leadership and human life experience is limitless while God is present. That is the key. On the other hand, life and leadership vanish in God's absence. This is the problem: abundance of physical blessings seems to displace faith in the God who provides the abundance. Moses let his human emotions lead him to overstep the word of the Lord. He indulged his human desire, took up his own cause and vented his frustration with Israel—for this he was prevented from entering the promised land (Num 20:7–13, Deut 4:21). Solomon followed the same pattern. Solomon was humble and expressed that in his prayer to God. God granted Solomon wisdom, yet Solomon's human nature lead him to ignore the warnings of wisdom (not to love foreign women) and pursue a multitude of foreign wives (remember how Samson also brought disaster on himself by his carelessness). This pattern of human nature is observable in the New Testament also, Peter being the prime example of one who often allows his sinful nature to override his godly intentions. The message remains the same and is essential for us: Beware of human nature's orientation toward self-destruction; be near to the Word of the Lord which brings and sustains life.

The abundance that Solomon's son, Rehoboam inherited confirms this pattern. Abundance and pride (nurtured by Rehoboam's young counselors) triggered the split of the ten northern tribes from Judah and Benjamin. Rehoboam's pride and self-serving methods resulted in his humiliation and were self-defeating in regard to the extent of what he considered his rightful kingdom.

The division of the kingdom into two marks the decline of Israel. From this point forward the text cycles back and forth between kings of Israel and kings of Judah, continually highlighting the presence of God to sustain them and their continued failures. Ahab rises as a primary example of leadership contrary to God, destined for destruction. He is contrasted to Elijah, the remarkable prophet of God. While Ahab murdered and stole (as in the case of Naboth's vineyard, 1 Kgs 21), Elijah fled into the wilderness and foreign countries for refuge. Yet Ahab died unsatisfied, while God provided for Elijah (by ravens in the wilderness and the widow in Zarephath), and did not die at all.

Elijah provides the transition from first to second Kings. Elisha picks up Elijah's mantle and his work as prophet at the beginning of 2 Kings. Elisha conveys the uninterrupted presence of God through his prophets; offering stability for the faithful and a reason for them to be faithful and maintain hope. The division of the kingdoms provides for the next great contrast between distance from or nearness to God. Israel continued to covet the ways of the unbelieving nations around them, and so was overcome by one of those nations, Assyria (2 Kgs 17:7–23; 722 BC). Judah, on the other hand, stood invulnerable to the Assyrian forces. How? Was it by human might or genius? No, by the power of God on behalf of those who depend on Him alone as Hezekiah did. There was no battle of Judah against Assyria, but God Himself fought and defended His people. Josiah, like Hezekiah, provided another bright spot at the end of this long decline of faithless kings. As a child, with faith like a child, Josiah is marked by simple obedience to and dependence upon the Word of God (2 Kgs 23:2–3). Sadly, neither Hezekiah nor Josiah nor many other prophets could prevent the remaining people from following the human determination of their relatives to the north. Judah was also intent on following the nations around them, so they were also overcome (2 Kgs 25:1–26).

By use of these contrasts, the book of Kings offered a profound warning to the remnant of Israel (Judah and Benjamin) as they considered the meaning of their captivity in Babylon. What did they have to show for abandoning the Lord to follow the worldly enticements around them? They are left to despair. On the other hand, examples of blessings that come to those who are faithful commend faith to them. At all times when Israel and her leaders were faithful, they enjoyed the richest blessings and protection. Although not every faithful person in the Bible received prosperity in this life, all of them received the blessing of eternal life.

The sum of those two essential truths points to the necessity of the promise of the Messiah—an eternal, faithful, leader who would be faithful on our behalf. The significance of this conclusion is supported by the number of prophets who were active in Israel during the period of Kings. Isaiah, Jeremiah, and nine of the twelve Minor Prophets held up warnings for the wayward people of God. More importantly, they proclaimed the graciousness of God, and the promise of His Messiah.

14

Chronicles

Samuel and Kings gave a historical perspective of Israel's history that was concerned with explaining why God's chosen people did not seem so chosen. Why was the kingdom divided? Why were the ten northern tribes overcome by the Assyrians and, therefore, lost? Why was Judah overcome by the Babylonians? What went wrong? The books of Chronicles have a different purpose and so a different perspective on Israel's history. Chronicles is explaining the history of Israel to people who are returning from exile. These people are wondering why some kings who were wicked had long reigns and others who were good had short reigns. These people were just as tempted as their ancestors to forget God and follow their own desires and the ways of the nations around them. Chronicles focuses on genealogy and worship to respond to these needs. Chronicles takes a comprehensive look at Israel's history, starting with Adam and ending with Israel's return from the Babylonian captivity. In spite of all the tragedies of that history, God continued to work out the fulfillment of His promise that a Savior would come through specific families: Adam, Abraham, Isaac, Jacob, Judah, David, and so forth. Chronicles also reminds the reader that the Temple and worship were the means by which Israel would stay close to the promises and blessings of the living God.

1. Authorship and Date of Writing – *Was the "Chronicler" a Single Person or Several?*
2. Sources Used by the Chronicler—*Where Did the Chronicler Get His Information?*
3. Chronicles Divided into Two Books – *Was the Book of Chronicles Always Divided?*
4. Date and Setting of the Events of the Book – *What Is Different from Samuel/Kings?*
5. Themes—*Motifs that Characterize Chronicles*
6. Overview of the Book – *From Where Has It Come and to Where Is it Going?*

1. Authorship and Date of Writing

Like Samuel and Kings, much of the data contained in Chronicles probably accumulated over the years. The book of Kings refers to the Chronicles of the kings of Israel (which is not a reference to our book of Chronicles), indicating that records were being kept throughout the history of Israel. The book of Esther (Esth 2:23, 6:1) mentions chronicles kept by the Persian Empire. But who put the records into the form we now know? An early Jewish source (*Baba Bathra* 15a) reports that Ezra (the priest—see the Old Testament book bearing his name) was the author of Chronicles. There are three good reasons to support this ancient witness.

First, Ezra was interested in this kind of thing. He was responsible for the remnant of Israel that came back to Palestine after the Babylonian captivity. He needed to re-connect them with their roots and warn them about their past.

Second, the opening verses of Ezra (Ezra 1:1–4) are very similar to 2 Chronicles 36:22–23. Careful research suggests that the Chronicles text came first, then Ezra—also suggesting that Ezra wrote one then the other.

Third, the Hebrew of Chronicles indicates that it came from the general period of Ezra. Thus, Ezra is the most likely person to have written Chronicles, although he never identifies himself as the author.

However, many scholars, noting that we cannot be certain whether or not Ezra wrote Chronicles, simply call the author of Chronicles "the Chronicler." While some who take this position deny that Ezra wrote Chronicles, others simply use this title for the author, because although Ezra could have written this book, we cannot be absolutely certain that he did. All things considered, Chronicles would have taken its present form as early as 450—425 BC.

2. Sources Used by the Chronicler

Speculation about sources for biblical books, while a constant topic for discussion among biblical scholars, is of little help to most Bible readers because it is often simply speculation. The text, as we have it, has authenticity demonstrated by the witness of people who recognized the text as authoritative and, therefore, defended and preserved it—often at the risk of their lives. The Lord Jesus Himself also authenticated the Old Testament by His references to it and its authors. The genealogies in Matthew and Luke as well as other references to the Old Testament by New Testament authors add further testimony. The Chronicler, however, does tell us about the sources he used. They can be listed as follows:

1. Many Old Testament books written before Chronicles were used as sources. Genealogies from Genesis as well as other lists referred to in Ezra and Nehemiah give abundant evidence to the lists and copies of letters that were kept in archives and consulted (Ezra 6:1).

2. The history of David was gathered from sources mentioned in 1 Chronicles 29:29: "The words of Samuel the seer, of Nathan the prophet, and of Gad the seer."

3. The history of Solomon was gathered from sources mentioned in 2 Chronicles 9:29, "The words of Nathan the prophet, the prophecy of Ahijah the Shilonite, and the visions of Iddo the seer against Jeroboam the son of Nebat."

4. The history of Judah and Israel was gathered from a source or sources variously described as
   a. "the book of the kingdoms of Judah and Israel" (2 Chr 16:11);
   b. "the book of the kings of Judah and Israel" (2 Chr 25:26);
   c. "the book of the kings of Israel and Judah" (2 Chr 27:7);
   d. "the book of the kings of Israel" (2 Chr 20:34);
   e. "the words of the kings of Israel" (2 Chr 33:18); and
   f. "the story of the book of the kings" (2 Chr 24:27).
   g. Though these all may be references to the same source, the fact remains that the Chronicler does list his sources, eliminating the need for speculation.

5. Other sources for the history of Judah are described as the work of:
   a. Isaiah the prophet (2 Chr 26:22)
   b. Shemaiah the prophet (2 Chr 12:15)
   c. Iddo the prophet (2 Chr 13:22)
   d. Jehu the son of Hanani (2 Chr 20:34)
   e. Hozai (2 Chr 33:19)

3. Chronicles Divided into Two Books

The book of Chronicles, like Kings and Samuel, was divided into two when it was translated in Greek between 400 and 250 BC. These translators called these books the "Things Omitted (or Passed Over)." Jerome suggested on the basis of the Hebrew title "Words of the Days" that the books should be called a "Chronicle" of the divine history. This made sense because the content of these books begins with creation and concludes with the present day circumstances of Israel at the time it was written/compiled. In Hebrew Bibles Chronicles comes very last, as it is a sort of review of the entire Old Testament. English Bibles place Chronicles after Samuel and Kings because it covers most of the same material in much the same way.

Kingdom of Judah		Kingdom of Israel	
King	*Reign*	*King*	*Reign*
Rehoboam	931-914	Jeroboam I	931-910
Abijah (Abijam)	914-912		
		Nadab	910-909
		Baasha	909-885
Asa	912-871	Elah	886-885
		Zimri (7 days)	885
		Tibni	885-880
		Omri	885-874
Jehoshaphat	873-848	Ahab	874-853
Jehoram (Joram)	854-841	Ahaziah	853-852
Ahaziah (Jehohaz)	841	Jehoram (Joram)	852-841
Athaliah (usurper)	841-835	Jehu	841-814
Jehoash (Joash)	835-796	Jehoahaz	814-798
Amaziah	798-780	Jehoash (Joash)	798-782
Uzziah (Azariah)	791-740	Jeroboam II	793-753
		Zechariah (6 months)	753-752
		Shallum (1 months)	752
Jotham	750-732	Menahem	752-742
		Pekahiah	742-740
		Pekah	752-732
Ahaz (Jehoahaz I)	735-716	Hoshea	732-723
		Fall to Assyria	723
Hezekiah	729 (?)-687		
Manasseh	697-643		
Amon	643-641		
Josiah	641-609		
Jehoahaz II (3 months)	609		
Jehoiakim	609-598		
Jehoiachin (3 months)	598		
Zedekiah	597-587		
Babylonian Captivity	605-538		
Cyrus' Edict	538		

4. Date and Setting of the Events of the Book

The events recorded in Chronicles, in contrast to Samuel/Kings, start from the very beginning with Adam and conclude with the end of the Babylonian captivity (this somewhat more comprehensive history of Israel explains in part why Chronicles is the last book in the Hebrew Bible). The book expresses a good part of its purpose as it closes with the words of Cyrus who calls upon the people of God to go up to Jerusalem and build God a house. An overview would be as follows:

1 Chronicles 1:1—9:44   Genealogies from Adam to Saul c. 4000—1009 BC
1 Chronicles 10:1—29:30 The reign of David   1009—970 BC
2 Chronicles 1:1—9:31   The reign of Solomon   970—931 BC
2 Chronicles 10:1—36:23 The history of Judah to its fall &
            the edict of their return by Cyrus, King of Persia 931—538 BC

5. Themes

Continuity of God's Work: Temple and Genealogies

This theme is evident from the emphasis given in Chronicles to the temple and genealogies. The overall view of Chronicles spans Adam to the return of the exiles from Babylon to the Promised Land. Chronicles thus intends to present a comprehensive history which takes the most important facts of Israel's history into account. Within that framework there is a pattern of observing problem and solution. The temple and genealogies help clarify where a good future is to be found for the children of Abraham who remain.

To begin with, consider the way in which the genealogies are presented. Most often the genealogies are arranged in a way that presents families from the least to most important. 1 Chronicles 1 records the sons of Noah in this order; Japheth, Ham, and Shem. Japheth is the least important for biblical history. Ham is important because from him descended the Egyptians and the Canaanites (Ps 105:23, 27). Shem is considered last because through his line the Christ will come. From Shem the text hurries to Abraham and then gives Isaac prominence by listing him first (1 Chr 1:28) before returning to the pattern by listing Ishmael's families first, then Isaac's. This pattern is evident again in 1 Chronicles 2:1–3 where Judah is listed fourth but whose genealogy is reported first and in a way that takes us to David quickly. The rest of Judah's family follows. 1 Chronicles 3 continues the pattern by moving through the genealogy quickly until we get to Solomon and the line of the kings (1 Chr 3:10–16). Now that the important lines are in place, the text fills out the history of Judah's descendants then moves on to the rest of the tribes of Israel, beginning with Reuben at 1 Chronicles 5:1.

The other family that receives emphasis in the genealogies is the Levites. Here is the connection between the continuity of God's work regarding His people (genealogies) and the means by which He preserved them in the faith (temple/Levites). Genealogical texts move rather quickly through all the other sons of Jacob except Levi. 1 Chronicles 6 provides many details about Levites in general, musicians among them (1 Chr 6:31–48), Aaron and the sacrifices (1 Chr 6:49–53), and the residences of the Levites (1 Chr 6:54–81). The relationship between problem and solution is presented more obviously in 1 Chronicles 9 where the text reports that Judah was carried to Babylon for its unfaithfulness but that the Levites were the first to inhabit their possessions in their cities. The rest of 1 Chronicles 9 provides great detail in lists of names and divisions of the Levites (priests 1 Chr 9:10–13, Levites 1 Chr 9:14–16, gatekeepers 1 Chr 9:17–21, etc.).

The history in Chronicles returns to a larger view of history in 1 Chronicles 10 just long enough to remind us that Saul died for his unfaithfulness, particularly that he did not inquire of the Lord through the priests but through a medium. The Chronicler punctuates the seriousness of this error by reporting that it was God who killed Saul for his mistake and put David in his place. Having reminded us of the big picture, again the text returns to the particulars of the solution. David, who is faithful in seeking the Lord alone, is victorious in battle with his armies, and this is recorded. But the real emphasis is on the ark and the Temple. The rest of 1 Chronicles devotes most of its time to issues of bringing the ark to Jerusalem, establishing regular worship, David's preparations for the Temple and his lengthy, detailed instructions to Solomon regarding the Temple and worship. In fact, the last seven chapters of 1 Chronicles are devoted to David's instructions regarding worship or the genealogies of the Levites according to their particular service in the worship of the Lord.

2 Chronicles does not provide such detailed nor lengthy information about genealogies or the Temple. This is due in part to the fact that 1 Chronicles covered the bulk of Israel's chronological history (from Adam to Solomon, 3000 years). By contrast, 2 Chronicles only covers the history from Solomon's construction of the Temple to promise of its reconstruction through Cyrus, king of Persia (500 years). Nevertheless, a pattern is evident in this singular genealogy of the kings of Judah: from true and faithful worship of the Lord to unfaithfulness and back again. In every case false worship brings dire consequences in the lives of the children of Judah and true worship brings blessing. Within this cycle the Levites continue to be mentioned in a prominent way. The Levites instituted reforms. The Levites taught the Kings and people and thus kept God's people connected with the source of their life and blessing. In spite of the uncertainty and lack of consistent faithfulness among the kings of Judah, God continued to fulfill His promises through two important families. David's line is preserved in order to provide for the human nature of Him who would be born king of the Jews. Levi's line is preserved in order to keep the Word of God present in the lives of His people until that Word would become flesh (John 1:14). The continuity of God's work in the history leading up to the first coming of Christ sup-

ports and is worthy of the confidence of God's people today who await His return.

God's Choices for his People:
Levites, David, Solomon, Jerusalem, the Temple and Worship

The words *choose* or *chosen* are used twenty-five times in Chronicles. In all but four cases, God is the one who is reported to have made the choice, primarily regarding the king, the priesthood, or Jerusalem and the resting place of the ark. The reader is to understand that the choices God makes for us are always good and worthy of our highest appreciation. Appreciating the choices God makes includes *recognizing* His wisdom, *availing* ourselves of the blessings His choices provide, and *adopting* a life that lives in conformity to and support of His ways. Consider a few primary examples:

The Chronicler put great emphasis on the tribe of Levi, as noted in the discussion above on genealogies. God's choice of the Levites is clearly suggested not only in the genealogy of 1 Chronicles 6:1–81, but also in the lengthy descriptions of their duties and their dwelling places. The Levites are also reported in terms of their relationship with God's chosen city, Jerusalem (1 Chr 9:2, 10–34). Next, the narrative impresses the reader with the essential function of the Levites through the account of moving the Ark. David's first attempt to bring the Ark was halted by the death of Uzzah who put out his hand to touch the ark. Two chapters later in 1 Chronicles, when David is ready to try again he expresses the importance of God's choice as he proclaims, "No one may carry the ark of God but the Levites for the Lord has chosen them to carry the ark and to minister before Him forever" (1 Chr 15:2). The later chapters of 1 Chronicles record David's appointment of Levites, orders for regular worship, and contain descriptions of their divisions. Levites are also demonstrated to be God's choice by their response to those who would reject God. Jeroboam chose to invent his own gods (golden calves) and his own worship. The Levites responded by leaving their common lands in Israel and congregating in Jerusalem. 2 Chronicles 13:9 records Abijah's rebuke of Jeroboam for casting out the priests. Finally, king Uzziah experienced dire consequences for presuming to take up the service God had chosen the Levites to provide.

David is clearly God's choice to serve as leader of His people. The genealogies move quickly to David (1 Chr 2:15, 3:1) while quickly dispensing with Saul (10:1-14). The Chronicler emphasizes David as God's choice by recording that "all Israel" came to Hebron to make David king (1 Chr 11:1). Records of David's success are provided as indisputable evidence that David is chosen and that no success exists apart from God's choices for his people. David was successful in taking Jerusalem (1 Chr 11:4), with mighty men and an army (1 Chr 11:10,

12:1), in his building programs (1 Chr 15:1–29), in establishing worship (1 Chr 16:1–6) and in the covenant (1 Chr 17:1–15). David himself punctuated the importance of being chosen by God in his last words, "Yet the Lord God of Israel chose me from all my father's house to be king over Israel for ever; for He chose Judah as leader, and in the house of Judah my father's house, and among my father's sons He took pleasure in me..." (1 Chr 28:4).

Like David, Solomon is clearly God's choice, and because of this the kingdom prospered under his rule. David appeals again and again to the fact that Solomon was the Lord's choice (1 Chr 28:5, 6, 10; 29:1). As the chosen king, Solomon also received lengthy instructions from David on how to fulfill the Lord's will for him. Like Israel's unanimous acceptance of David at Hebron, Solomon is also portrayed as having no competition for the throne. Chronicles "seamless" transition from David to Solomon, especially concerning the service of the Levites and the construction of the Temple inspire the reader to submit to, even long for, the ways that God chooses for us.

God's choice in terms of the Temple is not that one would be built, for God had reminded David that He, Himself would build a house for David (2 Sam 7:11, 1 Chr 17:10). Rather, God's choice had to do with how the Temple would be built, since men were determined to do so. God did not want a Temple any more than He wanted a human king for his people. Nevertheless, since the people were determined to have a king and build

Jerusalem's Temple Mount

a Temple, the Lord directed their activities. The text makes clear that the Lord did choose Solomon to build a Temple for the Lord (1 Chr 28:6-10) and that the Spirit of the Lord had provided the plans (1 Chr 28:12). The final and most absolute witness of God to the acceptance of the Temple is provided when He, himself fills the Temple at the dedication (2 Chr 7:1).

God's choice for his people in terms of worship has, along with David himself, the greatest attestation of all. Chronicles devotes chapter after chapter to recording the leaders of worship as well as those who support that worship musically and physically. The place of worship is also prescribed by God, though not entirely. Just as Israel wanted a "king like the other nations," and a Temple instead of a Tabernacle, so also David wanted the place of worship to be Jerusalem rather than Shiloh (see Ps 78:60 for an explanation of why God forsook the Tabernacle at Shiloh). Besides location and leaders, Chronicles devotes a fair amount of time to the system of worship and to restoration of that worship. The system of worship is carefully contrasted to the nations' idolatry as mentioned in

2 Chronicles 12:8, 11:13-14, 13:8-9, 14:2-5, 20:19 and 13:1-11. You may note that as time creates distance from David, idolatry becomes more and more of a problem. So restoration of proper worship or of the Temple is prevalent in almost every chapter in 2 Chronicles 15—35.

A few observations about God's choices for his people are essential. First, God's own choices for His people are always simple, clear and good. God is the King of Kings and his Tabernacle at Shiloh would have served Israel best. If God was Israel's king and his Tabernacle remained at Shiloh there would never have been a Jeroboam who set up altars in Bethel and Dan to compete with the Temple in Jerusalem. If the Tabernacle had been maintained, perhaps Israel would have remained a people of faith who looked for cities with heavenly foundations, as their father Abraham did (Heb 11:9-10). Though God guided the decisions that Israel was determined to make for itself, that determination continued to complicate and undermine their life. We find in Jesus the real king of God's choice (Matt 2:1-2) who worshipped the Father in perfect obedience (John 4:24, 34), and lived (or Tabernacled) among us as a sojourner (John 1:14, Matt 8:20).

The Law and the Prophets

The Law and the Prophets appear in Chronicles as the compliment to genealogies and the Temple. 1 Chronicles is almost entirely consumed with issues of genealogy and Temple but has hardly any references to Law and Prophets. That emphasis shifts in 2 Chronicles to Law and Prophets with very few references to genealogies or the Temple itself. More specifically, eighteen of twenty references to the Law occur in 2 Chronicles and ten of eleven references to Prophets occur in 2 Chronicles. How would we account for this shift? Remember that 1 Chronicles begins with Adam and hastens to David. The focus in 1 Chronicles is then to remember how Israel came to its golden age under David. David was established as king by God and remained devoted to God. Through David God established proper worship and the most magnificent of places for that worship. All Israel was united and prospered in this right relationship with the only true and living God. But establishing what is right is only half the battle. How can what is right be sustained among people with rebellious human natures? Sustaining what God established through David is the problem addressed in 2 Chronicles. This is the *exact* problem that has surfaced again now that the exiles of Israel have returned to the Promised Land (see Hag 1:1 – 2:23). The determination of human nature to turn away from God explains why the Law and Prophets are so prominent in 2 Chronicles.

The term "Law" occurs in two contexts in 2 Chronicles; some people keep the Law, some forsake it. Not surprisingly, kings who forsook the Law caused their life and reign to be short, endured and caused suffering during that short reign, and by their example fostered the same mistakes and subsequent disaster among the children of Israel. On the other hand, kings who kept the Law were established, blessed and prospered, and all the people prospered with them. To make this even more clear, Chronicles takes a different view of kings in order to make it clear that kings who enjoyed long reigns did so because they kept the Law (or because, at least, they were penitent). On the other hand, other kings had short reigns because they rejected the Law. Manasseh is the best example of this. In 2 Kings 20 – 24 Manasseh is depicted as the worst of all kings with absolutely no redeeming qualities, but he reigned fifty-five years! How would the Chronicler explain this to returning exiles who were themselves tempted to forsake the Law of God for their own interests? The Chronicler reports one essential moment in Manasseh's life—his repentance. 2 Chronicles 33:12–17 not only records Manasseh's humility and repentance but also describes how he repaired the Temple and restored worship. Josiah provides the contrasting example as a king who is among the best in 2 Kings 21—23 but is reported to have disobeyed God in 2 Chronicles 35:20–25 and so died after reigning only thirty-one years.

The other feature of the Law to note concerns who was responsible for promoting it. The text reports that the priests were the ones who taught the Law to the people (2 Chr 15:3, 17:9) and who were devoted to the Law (2 Chr 31:4). Note how the priests devotion to the Law here is paralleled by the apostles' and pastors' devotion to the Word of the Lord in the New Testament (Acts 6:2, 1 Tim 4:12-16). The king was responsible for the Law in terms of administration. As the Law and the priests teach, so the King was to uphold on behalf of God and enforce the Law for the well being of all (2 Chr 19:10, 25:4).

Just as the people's lives were affected for better or worse depending on their relationship to the Law, so were they in relation to the prophets. The evil and harm done by Ahab, king of Israel, is tied directly to the activity of the lying prophets (2 Chr 18:5, 9, 11, 21, 22) and his hatred and rejection of the one prophet who was known to speak the truth (2 Chr 18:12). The fall of Jerusalem to the Babylonians and the eternal condemnation of its leaders is also tied directly to the fact that they "mocked the messengers of God, despised His words, and scoffed at His prophets, until the wrath of the Lord arose against His people, until there was no remedy" (2 Chr 36:16). As rejecting the prophets is tied to disaster, so obedience to the prophet is strongly tied to success. Jehoshaphat's concern for faithful prophets and prophesy did not reverse mistakes he made but did reduce the damage he sustained (2 Chr 18:6–7, 19:3). When Judah was severely threatened by the vast army of Moab and Ammon, Jehoshaphat honored the Lord and His prophets before the people. This act is tied directly to the deliverance God provided without any action on Judah's part at all (2 Chr 20:20–24).

6. Overview of the Book

Chronicles reports the history of the people of Israel. This history of Israel begins at the very beginning with Adam and concludes with the command of Cyrus that the last remnant of Israel return from captivity to the Promised Land. The content of 1 and 2 Chronicles can be summarized in three parts:

The Rise of Israel: God's People	The Golden Age of Israel:	The Fall of Israel: Not God's People?
Genealogies from Adam—David	**David, Solomon** & **The Temple**	From Israel *turning* away from Judah — To Judah *returning* from Captivity
1................ 9	10 .... 29 1........ 9	10 36
1 Chronicles		**2 Chronicles**

15
Life Under Persian Rule
Ezra, Nehemiah, Esther

Ezra

"You can never go home again" is a saying that some have found to be true. When a person leaves home and lives for a long time in another place, the experience of going home for a visit or to live again is a strange one. Some things are the same, but other things may have changed quite dramatically in the intervening years. Imagine what the experience of returning to the Promised Land must have been like for the Jews who came back from the Babylonian exile. Only the oldest of them could remember what Jerusalem and its Temple were like before the exile. Most of the people who re-established the presence of God's people in Palestine had never lived there. They were going home to a land promised to them by God, but it was to a home that they had never seen. The book of Ezra tells us of some of their struggles and experience as they saw God's continued faithfulness to His promise to Abraham fulfilled in their work of resettling the land and rebuilding the Temple in Jerusalem.

1. Authorship and Date of Writing— *Did Ezra Write the Book That Bears His Name?*
2. Date and Setting of the Events of the Book — *Returning and Rebuilding under the Persian Empire*
3. Source Documents for Ezra — *What Documents Did the Writer Use As Sources for His Information?*
4. Overview of the Book — *What is Contained in Ezra?*

1. Authorship and Date of Writing

As already noted in Chapter 14, there is a close relationship between the books of Ezra and Chronicles. The last verses of Chronicles (2 Chr 36:22–23) are identical to the opening verses of Ezra (Ezra 1:1–3a). The language of Ezra and Chronicles is similar, and the concern for the role of the Levites and the place of worship in the life of Israel continues from Chronicles into Ezra. Many scholars assume that Ezra may not have been the author of his book or of Chronicles, but that both were written by an unknown author who is simply called "the

Chronicler." This view of the authorship of Ezra is reasonable and does not necessarily deny that the book could have been written by Ezra. Instead, it assumes that we cannot be certain whether or not Ezra was the Chronicler.

However, Ezra 7:27—9:15 is definitely from the hand Ezra, since it is written in the first person. Therefore, the most likely author of Ezra is probably Ezra himself. It appears as if he drew both upon official records for Ezra 1—6 (which probably took place before Ezra was born or when he was very young) and his own experience and memoirs for Ezra 7—10.

2. Date and Setting of the Events of the Book

The book of Ezra contains two distinct parts: the first return of Jewish exiles to Palestine and the rebuilding of the Temple (539–516 BC) and the return of more exiles under Ezra and his reforms in Jerusalem (458–457 BC). Ezra continued to live in Jerusalem after the last events in the book and is mentioned in the book of Nehemiah, which takes place after the events in the book of Ezra (Neh 8:1–2, 4–6, 9, 13; 12:1, 13, 26, 33, 36).

Persian King	Event	Reference
	March 538–March 537 Cyrus' first year (as king over the empire)	Ezra 1:1–4
	538 return under Sheshbazzar	Ezra 1:5–2:70
600–527 BC Cyrus	*537* Altar rebuilt	Ezra 3:1
	536 Temple building begun	Ezra 3:8
	536–530 Opposition to building the Temple	Ezra 4:1–5
	530–527 Work on the Temple stopped	Ezra 4:24
527–521 Cambyses	No work done on the Temple	Ezra 4:24
521–486 Darius Hystaspis	*520* Work on the Temple resumed	Ezra 5:2
	516 Temple completed	Ezra 6:15

486–465 Xerxes	Esther made queen	Esther
465–424 Artaxerxes Longimanus	*April 8, 458* Ezra leaves Babylon	Ezra 7:6–9
	August 4, 458 Ezra arrives in Jerusalem	Ezra 7:8–9
	December 19, 458 Ezra presides over a public assembly	Ezra 10:9
	December 29, 458– March 27, 459 Investigation into mixed marriages	Ezra 10:16–17
	April 445–April 444 20th year of Artaxerxes	Neh 1:1
	March–April 445 Nehemiah asks permission to go to Jerusalem	Neh 2:1
	Fall 445 Nehemiah arrives in Jerusalem	Neh 2:11
	October 2, 445 Walls of Jerusalem completed	Neh 6:15
	October 8–November 5, 445 Ezra presides over a public assembly	Neh 7:73–8:1
	October 22–28, 445 Feast of Tabernacles celebrated	Neh 8:14
	October 30, 445 Fast declared	Neh 9:1
	432 Nehemiah's term as governor ends; sometime later he returns to Jerusalem for a second time	Neh 5:14; 13:6

3. Source Documents for Ezra

Like Chronicles, the author of Ezra had to rely on source documents, especially for the events that happened before his lifetime. He often notes these source documents as he writes.

A. Documents from official sources:

    1.   list of items for use in the Temple (Ezra 1:9–11)
    2.   list of those who returned from exile (Ezra 2:1–70)
    3.   Ezra's genealogy (Ezra 7:1–5)
    4.   heads of Israelite clans (Ezra 8:1–14)
    5.   list of men in mixed marriages (Ezra 10:18–43)

B. Seven official documents and letters (the first in Hebrew, the other six in Aramaic):

    1.   the decree of Cyrus (Ezra 1:2–4)
    2.   letter from Rehum to Artaxerxes (Ezra 4:11–16)
    3.   letter from Artaxerxes to Rehum (Ezra 4:17–22)
    4.   report from Tattenai to Cyrus (Ezra 5:7-17)
    5.   memorandum: Cyrus' decree (Ezra 6:2b–5)
    6.   letter from Darius to Tattenai (Ezra 6:6–12)
    7.   authorization from Artaxerxes concerning Ezra (Ezra 7:12–26)

Extracts from Ezra's memoirs (Ezra 7:27—8:34)

4. Overview of the Book

Ezra

1.   The first Jewish exiles return during the reign of Cyrus (1:1—2:70)
        The decree of Cyrus (1:1–4)
        The return led by Sheshbazzar (1:5–11)
        A list of those who returned (2:1–70)
2.   Rebuilding the Temple and re-establishing worship in Jerusalem (3:1–13)
        The altar is constructed (3:1–3)
        The Feast of Tabernacles is celebrated (3:4–6)
        Rebuilding the Temple is begun (3:7–13)
3.   Opposition halts the rebuilding of the Temple during the reigns of Cyrus, Xerxes, Artaxerxes and Darius (4:1–24)
4.   The Temple is completed during the reign of Darius (5:1—6:22)
        The Temple completed with support of the prophets Haggai and Zechariah and with the permission of Darius (5:1—6:15)
        The Temple is dedicated (6:16–18)
        The Passover is celebrated (6:19–22)
5.   Ezra's return to Judah with other Jews (7:1—8:36)
6.   Ezra's reforms (9:1—10:44)
        Ezra discovers mixed marriages and calls the people to repentance (9:1–15)

The people repent (10:1–15)
The list of those who marriage foreign women (10:16–44)

Summary of the Events in Ezra

Ezra's first part (Ezra 1—6) records the return of the first exiles from Babylon to Jerusalem. This return is prompted by the decree of the Persian emperor Cyrus in 538 BC and reflects a general practice under Persian rulers: they allowed ethnic groups that had been exiled from their homelands by the Assyrians or the Babylonians to return. Ezra records how God used this policy to fulfill his promise to bring his people back to the Promise Land after seventy years of exile (Jer 25:11–12; 29:10). They immediately set out to rebuild the Temple, which had been destroyed when the Babylonians conquered Jerusalem.

This activity did not happen without opposition, however. Some of the residents of the land who lived in Israel since the Israelites had been deported from other lands under the Assyrians also wanted to help in rebuilding the Temple. These people had adopted the worship of the God of Israel, but in a way that combined pagan elements. They had intermarried with the few Israelites left in the land after the Assyrian conquest of Samaria. (2 Kgs 17:24–41). However, the Jews who had returned from Babylon were all too aware that God had sent them into exile because they had not been faithful to him, but had also combined the worship of Yahweh with the worship of other gods. Therefore, they rejected the offer of help. This led to opposition by the other people in the land, who had enough political influence to cause construction on the Temple to cease for ten years. However, when God sent the prophets Haggai and Zechariah to call the people to finish the Temple, they once again took up the task and completed the Temple in 516 BC.

The second part of Ezra (Ezra 7—10) begins fifty-eight years later in 458 BC. At the permission of the Persian emperor Artaxerxes, Ezra, a priest from the high priestly line of Zadok returned to Jerusalem to ensure that the Jews there were worshipping the God of Israel according to the Law of Moses. Ezra was a good choice for this, since we are told that he was "a scribe skilled in the Law of Moses that Yahweh the God of Israel had given." According to Artaxerxes' letter (Ezra 7:11–26), Ezra was to establish proper worship of God and to provide for sacrifices and prayers in the Temple for the Persian royal family. The letter states that the Persian government would underwrite the expenses for these sacrifices. Obviously, Artaxerxes wanted these sacrifices and prayers to be done in the proper way so that they would be favorably received by Israel's God. This was not only a religious act by the Artaxerxes, but also a shrewd political move, since by this practice he was attempting ensure the loyalty of his Jewish subjects. Once again, God was working through the acts of a Persian emperor to provide for His people.

However, shortly after Ezra arrived in Jerusalem he discovered an important threat to the Law of Moses: many of the Jews who had been living in the Promised Land had intermarried with pagans. This was a concern because this practice by their ancestors had led to idolatry and caused God to send them into exile in Babylon. Ezra immediately moved to put an end to this practice and purify the people from pagan influences. (Ezra 9—10).

Important Theological Themes in Ezra

The first part Ezra continues a major theme from Chronicles: worship. This theme is emphasized not only in the obvious account of the building of the Temple, but also in the prominent part that the Levites play in these chapters of Ezra. Moreover, with the dedication of the altar and the Temple, it is noted that feasts commanded in the Pentateuch were celebrated: the Feast of Tabernacles after the dedication of the altar and the Passover after the dedication of the Temple. This emphasis on worship continues Chronicles' emphasis on Temple and genealogy (see Chapter 14; note that Ezra's priestly genealogy is given in Ezra 7:1–5). The message is a continuation of Chronicle's message for a new era: the God who provided for his people before the exile is still providing for them. Through the worship at the Temple, which He authorized and through the ministry of the priests and Levites, God forgives sins and purifies His people. He enables them to rebuild the Temple so that they may come into His presence as His holy people and so that they may have hope in the Messiah who is prefigured in the Temple sacrifices.

This first part of this book also notes the opposition the Jews faced from others. This opposition even succeeded in stopping the work on the Temple for ten years. However, the Temple was completed. The message is clear, though not stated explicitly by the author: no human opposition can stand in the way of God's will for His people. Ezra looks back on these events and their completion despite human opposition to reassure his people that no human intervention can stop God's ultimate plan in the promised Messiah. Just as God provided the right time and circumstances so that the Temple could be completed (Hag 1:2–11; Zech 1:16), at the right time and into the right circumstances He would send His Son to redeem the world (Gal 4:4–5; Eph 1:9–10).

A second theme unites the two parts of Ezra and the book of Chronicles: the prophets. Just as God sent prophets to his people in Chronicles, so also in Ezra he sends them the prophets Haggai and Zechariah to preach his word (Ezra 5:1; 6:14). Just as in Chronicles he had given them the Law through his prophet Moses, so also he gives them Ezra, a scribe of the Law of Moses who calls them to repentance (Ezra 7:6, 11, 12, 21). God never leaves his people without His holy Word to guide them.

However, there is a startling difference between Chronicles and Ezra. Whereas before the exile many in Israel did not listen to the prophets or obey the Law of Moses, the Jews after the exile hear the prophets and the Law and they respond with repentance and faith. When Haggai and Zechariah encourage them to build the Temple, they respond by completing it. When Ezra warns them about the dangers of intermarriage with pagans, they repent and put away their foreign wives.

Thus, by its dual emphasis on God's grace in re-establishing worship in the Temple and God's grace in giving his Word to his people, the book of Ezra prepares the way for the coming of Christ. It demonstrates that God's Word is powerful and can turn the hearts of sinful people to repentance and faith in his promises.

Nehemiah

What is a city? Is it a place with a large concentration of people with large public buildings and a regular network of streets? Is it characterized as having its own local government and borders recognized as marking it off from the surrounding area? This is how we think of a city. However, in ancient times there was another important element to every city: the large defensive wall that surrounded the city and made the inhabitants inside feel safe from marauding thieves and invading armies. Without a wall a settlement was just a village. The story that occupies much of Nehemiah is the rebuilding of the walls of Jerusalem in 445 BC nearly a century and a half after they were destroyed by the Babylonians. This is a story that tells how God provided for his people through Nehemiah and the Persian government under which they lived. It is a reminder that as God used the faithful Nehemiah as a government servant to provide for his people, he still uses Christians in government service in our day.

1. Authorship and Date of Writing

The book of Nehemiah begins with the notice, 'The words of Nehemiah, son of Hacaliah." This indicates that the book is substantially the work of Nehemiah, and appears to be confirmed by Nehemiah's frequent use of the first person to refer to himself. However, this book could not have been written in its present form by Nehemiah, since it traces the line of high priests down to Jaddua, who was high priest under the last Persian king, Darius III Codommanus, who ruled 336–332 BC (Neh 12:11–12). This would have been about 100 years after the last event in Nehemiah (Nehemiah's second term as governor, which took place sometime after 432 BC, but certainly no later than 424 BC). Thus, it appears as if the book of Nehemiah as we have it is an edited version of Nehemiah's memoirs. Therefore, the main author is Nehemiah, whose work is supplemented by a later editor who completed the book around 335 BC.

Many scholars consider this later editor to be the Chronicler (see Chapter 14 on Chronicles and the discussion on the authorship of Ezra in this chapter), and assume that he wrote Chronicles, Ezra and Nehemiah very late in the Persian Empire or early in the reign of Alexander the Great. However, if the Chronicler wrote both Ezra and Nehemiah, the differences between the lists of exiles who returned to the Promised Land in Ezra 2 and Nehemiah 7 are not easily explained, since he would have to have been working with the same records for both. However, if Ezra was written earlier than Nehemiah by a different author, then the differences are easily explained: the two authors were working with different lists. (The differences can be seen as complementary, not contradictory). Therefore, it is most likely that the Chronicler (whether he was Ezra or someone else) wrote Chronicles and Ezra while a later editor compiled Nehemiah primarily using Nehemiah's memoirs.

At a very early time the books of Ezra and Nehemiah were considered one book. This was probably due to the fact that both were short and were often written on the same scroll. Since Ezra and Nehemiah relate events that were closely related in time and place, this joining of the books made sense. (It may even have been the editor of Nehemiah that first joined the books into one.) Often when ancient writers refer to the book of Ezra they mean the combined books of Ezra and Nehemiah. This is true for both the ancient Jewish historian Josephus (c. AD 37–100) and the Jewish rabbinic tradition preserved in the Babylonian Talmud (*Baba Bathra* 15a). The first person who is known to have distinguished between the two books is the Christian writer Origin (AD 185–253), who called them 1 Ezra and 2 Ezra. His approach was followed by Jerome when produced the Latin translation known as the Vulgate (AD 390–405).

2. Date and Setting of the Events of the Book

Like Ezra, the book of Nehemiah begins in a foreign land. We meet Nehemiah, who is cupbearer to the Persian king Artaxerxes (reigned 464–424 BC). This position was an important one, since the cupbearer was the one who tasted the king's wine before he drank it to ensure that it was not poisoned. Thus, Nehemiah was a trust official of Artaxerxes. However, Nehemiah requests to go to Jerusalem and repair its wall. Since he was a trusted member of the royal court, Artaxerxes appointed Nehemiah governor of Judah and Jerusalem. Nehemiah served two terms as governor, the first from 445–432 BC and the second sometime later, but certainly before the end of Artaxerxes' reign in 424 BC (13:6b–7). As the book indicates, Nehemiah was gone for some time between his first and second terms (13:6a).

	April 8, 458 Ezra leaves Babylon	Ezra 7:6–9
	August 4, 458 Ezra arrives in Jerusalem	Ezra 7:8–9
	December 19, 458 Ezra presides over a public assembly	Ezra 10:9
465–424 Artaxerxes Longimanus is Persian Ruler	*December 29, 458–* *March 27, 459* Investigation into mixed marriages	Ezra 10:16–17
	April 445–April 444 20th year of Artaxerxes	Neh 1:1
	March–April 445 Nehemiah asks permission to go to Jerusalem	Neh 2:1
	Fall 445 Nehemiah arrives in Jerusalem	Neh 2:11

October 2, 445 Walls of Jerusalem completed	Neh 6:15
October 8–November 5, 445 Ezra presides over a public assembly	Neh 7:73–8:1
October 22–28, 445 Feast of Tabernacles celebrated	Neh 8:14
October 30, 445 Fast declared	Neh 9:1
432 Nehemiah's term as governor ends; sometime later he returns to Jerusa- lem for a second time	Neh 5:14; 13:6

3. Overview of the Book

I. Nehemiah's first term a governor of Jerusalem (1:1—12:47)
    A. Nehemiah learns about Jerusalem's walls (1:1–11)
        1. Nehemiah receives word from Jerusalem (1:1–4)
        2. Nehemiah's prayer (1:5–11)
    B. Nehemiah begins his first term as governor (2:1–10)
        1. Nehemiah is appointed governor (2:1–8)
        2. The journey (2:9–10)
    C. Rebuilding the wall
        1. Nehemiah inspects the walls a night (2:11–16)
        2. Nehemiah encourages the people of Jerusalem to rebuild the wall (2:17–18)
        3. Opposition by Sanballat, Tobiah and Geshem (2:19–20)
        4. List of those who rebuilt the wall (3:1–32)
        5. Ridicule by Sanballat and Tobiah and Nehemiah's prayer in response (4:1–5)
        6. Threat of attack by Jerusalem's enemies (4:6–15)
        7. Guards are posted to protect those who rebuild the walls (4:16–23)
    D. Nehemiah deals with social and economic problems (5:1–19)
        1. Complaints by the poor that the rich are taking advantage of them (5:1–5)
        2. Nehemiah puts an end to usury and debt-slavery (5:6–13)
        3. Nehemiah sets an example as governor (5:14–19)
    E. Opposition to Nehemiah does not stop his work (6:1–19)
        1. Plots against Nehemiah are foiled (6:1—7:3)

2. The wall is completed (6:15–19)
3. Nehemiah appoints officials in Jerusalem (7:1–3)
F. List of the exiles who returned to Jerusalem (7:4–73a)
G. Ezra's reforms (7:73b—10:39)
    1. Ezra reads the Law of Moses (7:73b—8:12)
    2. The Feast of Tabernacles is celebrated (8:13–18)
    3. A day of fasting, confession and prayer leads to a binding covenant (9:1–38)
    4. A list of those who pledged to keep the covenant (10:1–27)
    5. The text of the covenant (10:28–39)
H. New residents for Jerusalem (11:1–43)
    1. New residents recruited for Jerusalem (11:1–24)
    2. Residents of the land of Judah (11:25–36)
I. Lists of Levites and priests (12:1–26)
J. Dedication of Jerusalem's wall (12:27–43)
K. Levites appointed for service in the Temple (12:44–47)
II. Nehemiah's second term a governor (13:1–30)
A. Abuses while he was gone (13:1–5)
    1. Mixed marriages (13:1–3)
    2. Tobiah occupies the Temple quarters (13:4–5)
B. Nehemiah's return (13:6-9)
    1. Nehemiah arrives in Jerusalem (13:6-7)
    2. Nehemiah expels Tobiah from the Temple (13:8–8)
C. Other Reforms (13:10–31)
    1. Ensuring that the Levites had provisions (13:10–14)
    2. Putting an end to work on the Sabbath (13:15–22)
    3. Mixed marriages (13:23–31)

Summary of the Events in Nehemiah

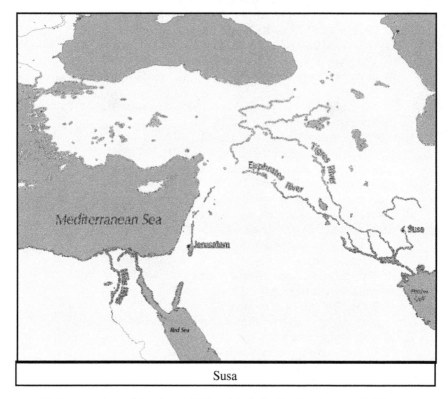

Susa

At the opening of the book Nehemiah is in the Persian capital Susa serv-ingas cupbearer to Artaxerxes. His brother Hanani, who had visited Jerusalem, reported to him that the Jewish inhabitants of Jerusalem are in dire straits and that Jerusalem's wall still lies in ruins.

Immediately Nehemiah fasted and prayed to God. One of his prayers is rec-orded in Nehemiah 1. It confesses the sin of Israel and asks God that he would be received with favor by the king. When Nehemiah next served the king, Arta-xerxes noticed Nehemiah's sadness and inquired about it. Nehemiah requested to return to Jerusalem to rebuild its walls. Not only did Artaxerxes appoint Ne-hemiah to this task, but he also gave him letters of safe conduct and authority to procure materials for his work.

Nehemiah knew that he would have opposition from some of the non-Jewish officials in Palestine, so he first inspected the walls of Jerusalem at night (2:11–16). After seeing the magnitude of the task, Nehemiah encouraged the inhabitants of Jerusalem to rebuild the walls and immediately is opposed by Tobiah (an Ammonite) and Geshum (an Arab), officials who do not want to see Jerusalem prosper. Nehemiah was not discouraged, however, and organized the rebuilding of the wall. Despite opposition and the threat of attack, the people followed Nehemiah's leadership.

However, Nehemiah's problems were not simply from outside the community in Jerusalem. He also heard complaints from the poor and needy in the community that those who were better-off were taking advantage of them (5:1–5). The abuse included the taking of interest on loans from one Israelite to another (known as *usury*) and selling debtors into slavery to serve non-Israelite masters. Both of these practices were forbidden in the Law of Moses (Exod 21:1–11; 22:25; Lev 25:36–43; Deut 23:19–20). Nehemiah not only put an end to these practices, but he also set an example for others by refusing to levy taxes on the people to pay for his expenses as governor (Neh 5:14–19).

The success that Nehemiah was having led to rumors of plots on his life. Because of Nehemiah's trust in God he did not allow these rumors to halt the work on the walls (Neh 6:11–13). The work on the wall was finished under his leadership in only fifty-two days (Neh 6:15).

However, Nehemiah was not simply interested in the walls of Jerusalem. He also wanted the city to prosper. So he consulted the records from almost 100 years earlier that listed those who had first returned to Jerusalem (Neh 7:4–73a). These records, which are very similar to those in Ezra 2:1–20, were used to recruit inhabitants from the descendants of the returnees to fill Jerusalem and make it a prosperous city with a sustainable population (Neh 11:1–24).

Nehemiah's work led to a renewed spirit among the people. They summoned Ezra to read the Torah to a sacred assembly, kept the Feast of Tabernacles, held a day of fasting and confession of sins and pledged to keep a new covenant that reaffirmed the Laws given by God through Moses (Neh 10:28–39).

At last the wall of Jerusalem was dedicated to God's glory with a festive worship service (Neh 12:15–19), and Nehemiah appointed Levites to care for the offerings that the people brought to the Temple.

The final chapter of Nehemiah is a brief account of Nehemiah's second term as governor. When he returned to Jerusalem after some time away, he found that both the people and the priests had begun to disregard God's Law. Eliashib, a priest who had been in charge of the Temple storerooms had allowed the Ammonite Tobiah to occupy one of these rooms. The people had once again neglected bringing sacrifices to the Temple and had begun to break the Sabbath law by doing work on that holy day. Some of them, including priests, had intermarried with non-Israelites. Nehemiah put an end to these practices, and once again ensured that the priests and the people kept the Law that God had given to Moses.

Important Theological Themes in Nehemiah

While there are some connections between Chronicles, Ezra and Nehemiah (e.g., the incorporation of official records into the narrative), the book of Nehemiah contains some important accents that set it apart from Ezra. One of these is the frequent prayers of Nehemiah (Neh 1:5–11; 4:4–5; 5:19; 6:9b, 14; 13:14, 22b, 29, 31b). In addition, the lengthy prayer led by some Levites when they led the people in confessing their sins is recorded (Neh 9:5b–37). While some of these prayers are introduced as prayer (e.g., Neh 1:4–5a), many are simply short interjections where Nehemiah seeks God's favor and mercy (e.g., Neh 13:14). Not only does this indicate that we are reading Nehemiah's private memoirs, but it also shows us that this great leader of God's people was a man of prayer. He knew his limitations and relied on God to strengthen him. He did not seek glory from humans or their praise, but sought God's favor, as he repeatedly begged God to remember the things he had done in His service. Nehemiah's prayers show us a man who trusted God to be a merciful and gracious God who wants to come to the aid of his people. These prayers relied on the unchanging God as a helper and aid in uncertain and changing times, and serve as a model of devotional life for those who seek to follow Nehemiah's example.

Another important theme in Nehemiah is that of the people's repentance and pledge to keep their obligations under the covenant God first gave to his people through Moses. This was preceded by the reading of the Law of Moses. Several times in its history Israel had similarly renewed the covenant that God had graciously made with them. Joshua had the words of Moses read to the people on Mount Gerizim and Mount Ebal, as Moses had commanded, thereby renewing the covenant with the first generation of Israel to live in Palestine (Josh 8:30–35; see Deut 11:29; 27:12). Before he died, Joshua again reminded Israel of God's gift of the Law given through Moses (Josh 23:6), and they renewed their pledge to honor God's covenant (Josh 24:1–27). In Josiah's day, when the Law was rediscovered in the Temple and read to the people, they renewed their pledge of faithfulness to the covenant (2 Kgs 23:1–3; 2 Chr 34:29–32). In each of these cases the presence of faithful leaders was instrumental in leading the people to repentance and renewal.

Nehemiah especially emphasizes the grace of God in his covenant. We are told that when the words of Moses were read and explained by Ezra, the people were moved to tears. Their sins were made known to them, and their consciences convicted them of their sins. However, God's covenant with his people is not simply about his Law. At the center of his covenant were the promises of the Gospel which brings comfort, joy and peace to troubled hearts. Nehemiah, Ezra and the Levites wanted the people to understand that God's covenant did not simply contain the demands of the Law, but that it was centered on God's grace in the Gospel (see their words in Neh 8:9). Nehemiah especially understood this as he encouraged the people to find the Gospel and its promises in the words of Moses, saying to them, "Do not be pained, because the joy of the Lord is your strength." (Neh 8:10) Therefore, the book of Nehemiah emphasizes that it is the Gospel and its promises that strengthened Nehemiah as he carried out his work. Because of his trust in God's promises Nehemiah was constantly in prayer. Since he knew the Gospel through the words of Moses' Law, he could be an encourager of his people as well as their leader.

Finally, the book of Nehemiah emphasizes that God can work through powers in this world even though they may not be established directly by Him as the kings of Israel were. They may not even acknowledge Him as the one true God. As Paul tells us in the New Testament, all earthly power is from God, and God expects his people to be subject to authorities (Rom 13:1–5). He works through the authorities of this world to accomplish His will. Nehemiah is an example of a godly attitude toward power and authority throughout the book. He is subject to Artaxerxes. He did not leave his post as cupbearer, but asked permission to go to Jerusalem (Neh 2:4). He returned to Artaxerxes' service, as he had pledged to do (Neh 13:6).

Moreover, as one in authority as governor, Nehemiah understood that he was given his position for the benefit of those he governed. His actions as governor show a keen awareness that his position was not given to him so that he could be served by those over whom he was placed, but so that he could serve those whom he governed.

Esther

What role does religion play in the everyday life of a child of God? Is it always evident to the world that someone believes in God from the way they live? If it is not, does that mean that their faith is shallow or a sham? These questions have been ones over which Christians have struggled throughout the centuries. In the book of Esther we encounter two Jews from the same family whose lives are quite different in this respect. One, Mordecai, is a Jew who is prominent in the court of the Persian king Xerxes. Mordecai's Jewish identity is well-known to others around him. At one point in the story Mordecai openly practices his faith as he dons sackcloth to mourn. The other Jew is Esther, Mordecai's younger cousin. Mordecai advised her *not* to reveal that she was Jewish (Esth 2:10). Esther follows this advice through most of the book, doing nothing that would reveal to others either her ethnic identity or her faith in God. Yet, as the book tells us, God worked through both of these believers to achieve his purposes for his people.

1. Authorship and Date of Writing—*Who Wrote Esther and When Was It Written?*
2. Date and Setting of the Events of the Book—*When Did Esther and Mordecai Save Their People?*

3. Important Themes in Esther—*Motifs that Make Esther Unique*
4. Overview of the Book—*The Contents of Esther*

1. Authorship and Date of Writing

Like most of the other historical books of the Old Testament, the author of Esther does not identify himself. However, given his knowledge of Jews and of Persian customs, his emphasis on the establishment of the feast of Purim, the setting of the story in the Persian city of Susa and the lack of any mention of Judah or Jerusalem, we can conclude that the author was a Jew living in Persia.

Since the events in Esther took place between 483 and 473 BC, Esther could not have been written before 473 BC. However, the book seems to indicate that the annual feast of Purim, first celebrated on February 28, 473 BC, had become a permanent custom among Jews and had been celebrated for some time before the book was written. Moreover, Esther 10 with its summary of the end of the reign of Xerxes and Mordecai's role as second-in-rank to the king, as well as the book's opening (Esth 1:1), implies that it was written after Xerxes' death (465 BC). On the other hand, the author does not appear to be influenced by Greek customs, which quickly spread across this part of the world when Alexander the Great conquered the Persian Empire (331 BC). Therefore, Esther was probably written sometime between 465 and 331 BC, with a date of about 460 BC being the most likely time of its composition.

2. Date and Setting of the Events of the Book

The book of Esther takes place during that middle of the reign of the Persian king Xerxes. Everything in the book centers on the city of Susa, one of four capital cities of the Persian kings. (The others were Ecbatana, Babylon and Persepolis.) Susa served as the winter home for the kings of Persia. Xerxes made extensive renovations on the palace in Susa, which was set on the city's acropolis or citadel (Esth 1:2). From the author's viewpoint all other events related in the book, even those that take place in the empire somewhere outside of Susa, are directly a result of events that happened in the capital city.

The Persian king Xerxes (called Ahashuerus in some English Bibles), was one of the most powerful men to rule the Persian Empire.[6] His attempts to conquer Greece from 482–479 BC were largely unsuccessful, yet his reign, like the reign of his father Darius, saw Persia at the height of its power.

Set in this city and in the court of this king, the book of Esther relates the roles played by Esther a Queen of Persia and her cousin Mordecai, who became Xerxes' most important official. The earliest event in Esther is Xerxes' lavish banquet that took place sometime in 483 or 482 BC (Esth 1). The latest event in the book is the celebration of the first Purim in February 473 BC (Esth 9).

Events in Esther		
Esth 1	Xerxes' feast	483–482
Esth 2:16	Xerxes marries Esther	479–478
Esth 3:7	Haman casts the Pur	April 5, 474
Esth 3:12	Haman issues edit concerning the Jews	April 17, 474
Esth 8:9	Mordecai issues edit concerning the defense of the Jews in the Empire	July 23, 474
Esth 3:13	Day to kills Jews according to Haman's edict	February 27, 473
Esth 8:12; 9:1	Jews defend themselves	February 27, 473
Esth 9:15	Jews defend themselves in Susa	February 28, 473
Esth 9:17	The first Purim	February 28, 473

3. Important Themes in Esther

The Jews Escape an Attempted Genocide

Esther is the account of how Esther and Mordecai worked together to save the Jewish people from being exterminated by the powerful Persian court official Haman. Circumstances that arise throughout the book enabled them to rise to the defense of God's chosen people.

Because of Xerxes' pride at being rebuffed by his queen Vashti (Esth 1), Esther was placed in position to become the new queen (Esth 2:1–18). Morde-

---

[6] Both the Greek form of this king's name (Xerxes) and the Hebrew form (Ahashuerus) are attempts to pronounce the Persian name *Khshayarshan*.

cai, as a powerfully placed Jew in the Persian capital gained knowledge of a plot to assassinate Xerxes, and, with Esther's help, foiled the plot (Esth 2:19–23).

However, Haman, the king's top official despised Mordecai, and, therefore, sought a way to destroy not only Mordecai, but also all of the Jews in the Persian Empire. He determined the best time to do this though choosing a day by casting lots, called *Pur* in Persian. When he determined the best day, he procured permission from Xerxes to have the Jews killed (Esth 3). Mordecai, upon learning of this plot to kill him and his people appealed to Esther to intervene with the king. Esther, who had not revealed her identity as a Jew to anyone in the palace, was reluctant to help but was eventually persuaded by Mordecai to reveal that she was a Jew and plead with Xerxes to save her and her people. (Esth 4—5).

In the meantime Haman had already made plans to execute Mordecai. However, despite Haman's plans, Mordecai continued to rise to prominence in the royal court as Xerxes decided to honor him for his role in saving his life (Esth 6). Finally, when Esther found the courage to reveal to Xerxes that she was a Jew, she also revealed Haman's plot to exterminate all the Jews in the empire. Filled with rage that Haman's plan has threatened the queen, and mistakenly thinking that Haman had attempted to molest Esther, Xerxes had Haman executed (Esth 7).

At this point the book quickly reverses Haman's plot. Mordecai is elevated to become Xerxes second-in-command and issues a decree allowing Jews to defend themselves on the day that Haman had planned to exterminate them (Esth 8). The Jews suddenly see a reversal in their status because of Mordecai's rank, and they easily overcome those who sought to harm them (Esth 9:1–17). In honor of their deliverance Mordecai commands that this deliverance be celebrated every year on the days that the Jews rose to their own defense. Ironically, this celebration was named *Purim*, from the lots that Haman had cast (Esth 9:18–32). The final chapter of Esther (Esth 10) quickly summarizes the remaining years of Xerxes' reign.

This remarkable little story of deliverance for God's people very obviously is a celebration of the averting of a genocide through the actions of Esther and Mordecai. To this day Purim is celebrated every year by Jews with the reading of the book of Esther and joyful festivity. Given the theme of this book, it is no accident that it has become one of the more prominent books of the Bible with reference to the German Holocaust of the 1940's. Unlike Esther, the Holocaust saw many Jewish lives lost. Nevertheless, it has been pointed out that the Jews have survived and even thrived despite the horrible atrocities committed by the Nazis, just as they survived and thrived in Persia and Babylon.

More importantly, Esther shows us God's continued commitment to his promise to bring the Savior into the world through the people of Israel. Jesus

could not have been born into a Jewish family in Palestine if Haman had succeeded in his plot to exterminate the Jewish people throughout the Persian Empire, including the Jews in Palestine. Yet, despite the determination of a powerful enemy, God's promise endured, and nothing, not even the power of the most
mighty kingdom of its day, could thwart God's plan and his promise of the Messiah.

Religion in the Background

One thing that most readers note about Esther is that God is never mentioned once! His promise is under attack but no one—the narrator, Mordecai or
Esther—ever speaks about God. In fact, religion seems to be in the background
throughout most of Esther. All of the important religious practices of the Jews—
worship, prayer, sacrifice—are also absent from the book. The author seems to
be avoiding religion altogether or to be completely oblivious to it. This has led
some to see little religious value in Esther.

However, religion does poke through at times in the book. Mordecai fasts
and dresses in sackcloth upon hearing Haman's decree. Fasting was always accompanied by repentance, meditation on God's Word and prayer. Moreover,
when Esther prepares to plead for her people before Xerxes, she requests that all
of the Jews in Susa fast for her for three days. By implication she is also request-
ing that they pray for her. Purim itself is a religious festival celebrated to this
day in synagogues.

But why did the author of Esther not explicitly mention any of these religious connections? The answer lies in his rhetorical strategy. Instead of mentioning how God arranged events to deliver his people, he more powerfully allows his readers to conclude that the Jews were delivered only because God was
in control of events even when he is not mentioned or acknowledged. There are
too many seeming coincidences in the book for them to be truly coincidental.
When we look at all of them together, we have to conclude that God is controlling the events even when humans do not acknowledge his control.

Consider these events in Esther: Vashti is deposed as queen, making way
for a Jewish girl to become queen of the most powerful nation on earth. Mordecai is in the right place at the right time to uncover the plot against Xerxes and to
foil it. Haman's use of lots to choose a day to exterminate the Jews ends up se-
lecting a day almost twelve months away, allowing plenty of time for his plot to
be undone. Xerxes has a sleepless night and requests that his attendants read to
him from the official records of his reign. They choose to read the account of the
foiling of the assassination plot against him, reminding him that he had not honored the man who saved his life. This brings Mordecai to the king's attention.

The king mistakes Haman's begging for his life with Esther as Haman's attempt to molest the queen, leading to the command to have him executed.

Are all these events simply an unlikely string of coincidences or are they something else? Without every one of them happening at the right time and in the right order, the Jews in the empire might well have perished. However, the reader who knows the rest of the Old Testament cannot escape the conclusion that the writer of Esther wants us to see the hidden but powerful hand of God moving throughout the narrative. Indeed, Mordecai himself hinted at this to Esther when she was reluctant to intervene with Xerxes for her people.

> Then Mordecai told them to reply to Esther, "Don't think to yourself that you will escape in the king's palace any more than all the other Jews. For if you keep silent at this time, *relief and deliverance will rise for the Jews from another place*, but you and your father's house will perish. *And who knows whether you have not come to the kingdom for such a time as this?*" (Esth 4:13–14)

By suggesting to Esther that she was made queen "for such a time as this," Mordecai was suggesting that someone—God himself—had seen to it that she became queen, and that she needed to acknowledge this by using her position for the benefit of God's people. Moreover, even if she did not do anything, Mordecai implied that God had other resources already in place so that help would come from "another place." Without directly saying it, the narrator of the events in Esther is powerfully telling us, "God will never break his promise to send the Messiah. He will rescue his people so that his promise to Abraham, Isaac and Jacob can be fulfilled."

Thus, while religion is in the background in Esther, we should not conclude that Esther is a non-religious, secular tale. Instead, it is a very powerful witness to the ability of God to arrange events in this world for the benefit of his people. By its subtle message it forcefully proclaims the Gospel of God's enduring love for all who trust in him.

In addition, Esther tells us that even when God's people pursue supposedly secular vocations without making a big show of their faith in God, they are nevertheless doing God's work. God uses his people in everyday circumstances, whether they are in positions of power or in what the world would consider lowly positions and occupations. When Christians go about their daily life and even when they are not trying to be outwardly religious, as they seek to do things that serve their neighbor's good, they are God's instruments to help others just as Esther and Mordecai were.

Feasts and Celebrations

Another striking feature of Esther is the large number of parties and celebrations packed into ten short chapters. In fact, the book could be outlined around the feasts in the book:

Xerxes' feasts (Esth 1—2)	1. Party leading to Vashti's removal as queen 2. Party celebrating Esther's becoming queen
Esther's feasts (Esth 3—7)	3. First dinner party—Haman made bolder 4. Second dinner party—Haman executed
The Feast of Purim (Esther 8—10)	5. The first day of Purim—Jews in the Provinces 6. The second day of Purim—Jews in Susa

The many parties and celebrations in Esther serve to temporarily take the reader's eyes off of the solemn and serious events in the book. Yet, they also serve to point to God's work. Even when Xerxes or Haman, Esther or Mordecai seem to be enjoying themselves, it does not mean that God is not present and active. Even at such profane times as the drunken revelry of Xerxes' first feast (Esth 1), God is guiding the events and using them to the best advantage of his people. Thus, Esther teaches us that no matter how secular or profane society may become, it is still under the control of the holy God who never abandons his people.

Israel Versus the Amalekites

Another theme that the author of Esther has skillfully and subtly woven throughout his book is the continued rivalry between Israel and the Amalekites. Israel first encountered the Amalekites after the Exodus from Egypt when they attacked and sought to prevent Israel from journeying toward the Promised Land (Exod 17:8–16). Following their defeat, Moses prophesied that "The Lord will be at war with the Amalekites from generation to generation." Later, God used Gideon to defeat Amalek when it joined with the Midianites to oppress Israel (Judg 7). Still later, God commanded Saul to attack and defeat the Amalekites, though Samuel had to finish the job by executing the Amalekite king Agag (1 Sam 15).

When we first meet Haman, the writer of Esther tells us that he was "the son of Hammedatha, the *Agagite*." That is, Haman was a descendant of Agag, the Amalekite king. This little bit of information explains to readers who know the previous books of the Old Testament why Haman had such a hatred of Mordecai and the Jews. His hatred was part an age-old feud dating back to the days of Moses. Moreover, Mordecai was especially hated because he was a descendant of Saul's father Kish (1 Sam 9:1) through Shimei, a member of "Saul's house" (2 Sam 16:5; see Esth 2:5)! Haman's hatred ran deep, and his resources as Xerxes most trusted official were great. Yet, once again the writer of Esther shows us that God kept his promise. He made war again on the Amalekites and defended his people, just as Moses had pledged in his prophecy.

Therefore, all the major themes that run throughout Esther emphasize God's unswerving commitment to his promises. They also demonstrate that God always controls events among humans so that in the end his people will be blessed. This most seemingly secular book of the Old Testament is, therefore, actually a testimony to a deep faith in God.

4. Overview of the Book

The book of Esther is a short book of ten chapters. The following outline is based on the six feasts mentioned in the book.

    I. Xerxes' feasts (1:1—2:18)
        A. The first feast—Vashti is deposed as queen (1:1—2:18)
        B. The second feast—Esther becomes queen (2:1–18)
    II. Esther's feasts (2:19—7:10)
        A. Mordecai uncovers the assassination plot (2:19–23)
        B. Haman's plot to exterminate Mordecai and the Jews (3:1–15)
        C. Mordecai calls on Esther's help (4:1–17)
        D. Esther's first feast—Haman made bold (5:1–8)
        E. Xerxes' sleepless night leads to Mordecai being honored (5:9—6:14)
        F. Esther's second feast—Haman executed (7:1–10)
    III. The Feast of Purim (8:1—10:3)
        A.   An edict in favor of the Jews (8:1–17)
        B.   The institution of the Feast of Purim (9:1–32)
        C.   Mordecai and Xerxes' second-in-command (10:1–3)

Section 4
Poetry and Wisdom

16
Introduction to Hebrew Poetry and Biblical Wisdom

In many contemporary English Bibles the poetic sections are easily recognized because the editors have set the poetry in verse form instead of the simple paragraph form used for prose. Therefore, many readers can easily recognize that a given section of the Bible is poetry, but that does not help them understand what features characterize poetry in the Bible.

In a similar manner, many readers of the Bible are aware that the books of Job, Proverbs, Ecclesiastes and Song of Songs are considered to be wisdom literature, but they do not know which concepts mark a book as wisdom. In this chapter we will explore some key characteristics of poetry and wisdom in the Old Testament to help us to understand these features better. Although we normally think of five books as poetry and wisdom (Job, Psalms, Proverbs, Ecclesiastes and Song of Songs), both wisdom and poetry can be found in other parts of the Old Testament and even in the New Testament. Therefore, it is helpful to be able to recognize and understand the characteristics of that mark poetry and wisdom wherever they are found in the Bible.

1. Understanding Hebrew Poetry—*What Are the Major Features of Poetry in the Old Testament?*
2. Understanding the Concept of Wisdom in the Old Testament—*What Important Features Define Wisdom?*

1. Understanding Hebrew Poetry

A number of features of poetry in the English language are familiar to many people. Poetry may make use of meter, rhyme, and plays on word sounds such as alliteration, assonance, dissonance and paronomasia. Because of the nature of the Hebrew language, rhyme is very simple to produce. Therefore, since rhyme does not need a poet's skill, rhyme is a fairly rare phenomenon in Hebrew poetry (although there are occasional rhyming couplets; e.g., Judg 14:14, 18; 16:24). Hebrew poetry does not exhibit the classical meter that we associate with much poetry in English. (The issue of whether or how the Hebrew poets used meter in the composition of their poems is controversial among biblical scholars.) However, Israelite poets did make much use of plays on word sounds. Unfortunately, in most instances translators cannot reproduce these in English.

Parallelism

Thankfully, the most important feature of Israelite poetry is largely able to survive translation from one language to another. This feature, called **parallelism**, involves the deliberate matching, contrasting or comparing of features from two or more adjacent lines of poetry. Parallelism may occur in prose (as, for instance, in John Kennedy's famous line from his inaugural speech, "Ask not what your country can do for you, ask what you can do for your country"). However, Hebrew poetry, unlike prose, is marked by the constant and consistent use of parallelism.

Parallelism may involve the *syntax* of two or more lines of poetry. In this case the grammatical features of the lines of poetry are used to complement one another. Since word order in Hebrew is much more flexible than word order in English, Hebrew poets could place different parts of a sentence (subject, verb, direct object, etc.) in different orders to produce identical or contrasting grammatical patterns in adjacent lines of poetry. While translators may at times be able to reproduce this syntactic parallelism in English, it is not always possible to preserve this feature in English translations.

More importantly, parallelism in Hebrew poetry makes use of the meaning of two or more adjacent lines. This *semantic* (meaning based) *parallelism* is the most outstanding feature used by ancient Israelites (and other peoples in the ancient Near East) in their poetry. Since the first and most important task for all translators is to reflect accurately the meaning of the words they are translating, semantic parallelism can be observed in the Bible's poetry after it has been translated into English. This means that although we cannot see and appreciate the entire range of the poets' artistry when we read Old Testament poetic books in English, we can see and understand the most important poetic device they used. Indeed, to understand and appreciate most fully Old Testament poets' message we must be aware of their use of parallelism.

Parallelism is not the only feature that we can observe in the Bible's poems, however. Often in conjunction with parallelism poets used **focusing**. Since semantic parallelism opposes the meaning of words in one line of poetry to the meaning of the words in another line, it can become boring to simply compare or contrast similar words. To alleviate this problem, poets often narrowed or focused the meaning of a word or phrase by use of similar but more specific word or phrase in subsequent lines. This focusing enabled the poets to work with similar meanings in adjacent lines while also introducing new concepts in the later lines. Thus, simply by expert use of parallelism and focusing in conjunction with one another a skilled poet could employ a wide palette of meanings to paint a picture in the mind's eye of his readers.

Synonymous Parallelism

A common type of parallelism is **synonymous parallelism**. In this type of parallelism two or more adjacent lines express the same basic thought. For example,

> Pride precedes destruction,
> and an arrogant attitude precedes a fall. (Prov 16:18)

In this proverb *pride* and *arrogant attitude* are essentially the same and *precedes* occurs in both lines. *Destruction* and *fall* both denote a disaster. However, in the second line the poet has focused the disaster with the word *fall* which not only speaks of the destruction to come but also of the way in which it will happen.

Another example is:

> Give her the fruit of her hands,
> and let her achievements praise her in the city gates. (Prov 31:31)

In this verse a good wife is to be given the fruit or reward of what she has done. Once again the poet has focused the thought in the second line by using *praise in the city gates* to define *fruit*.

Antithetical Parallelism

When two or more lines of poetry deal with contrasting ideas the poet is using **antithetical parallelism.** One example is:

> The lips of a righteous person know good will,
> but the mouths of wicked people know perverted things. (Prov 10:32)

In this verse *righteous* and *good will* stand in contrast to *wicked* and *perverted things*. The major elements are contrasting concepts. However, it should be noted that not every element in these two lines form a contrast. *Lips* and *mouths* are not contrasting but are, instead, near synonyms. Nevertheless, this verse is in antithetical parallelism because its purpose is to contrast two different types of people and their behavior.

Another example of antithetical parallelism is:

> A lazy person craves food and there is none,
> but the appetite of hard-working people is satisfied. (Prov 13:4)

The contrasts in this verse are *lazy* versus *hard-working* and *none* versus *satisfied.* Once again, not every element of the two lines are contrasting, however, since *craves* and *appetite* imply similar desires.

A third example of antithetical parallelism is:

> A wise son makes his father happy,
> but a foolish child despises its mother. (Prov 15:20)

In this verse the obvious contrast is between *wise* and *foolish.* Another contrast is between parental happiness with a child and the implied parental heartache that comes from being despised by one's own flesh and blood. There is another contrasting pair in these two lines of poetry: *father* and *mother.* However, these do not fit well with the other contrasts in this verse. In this case the poet has chosen two gender opposites to heighten the contrast between the two lines. However, the poet has not used this gender contrast to imply anything about fathers or mothers in particular. He is not implying that only fathers (not mothers) are happy when a son is wise. Nor is he implying the foolish children never despise their fathers. Instead, he chose *mother* and *father* to help make the contrast between the lines sharper. Thus, when examining parallel lines in poetry we must always distinguish between the essential message of the lines and other supporting elements that may be used by the poet.

Synthetic Parallelism

While synonymous and antithetical parallelism are the most common types of parallelism, poets often wanted to express their thoughts in ways that these two types of parallelism would not allow. Therefore, like contemporary poets, the ancient Israelite poets made use of other types of complementing thoughts in parallel structure. These are generally grouped together as **synthetic parallelism.** A few modes of thought that can be found in this type of parallelism are:

Comparison:

> A whip is for the horse,
>   a bridle is for the donkey
>   and a rod is for the backs of fools. (Prov 26:3)

> Like vinegar to the teeth,
>   like smoke to the eyes,
>   so is the lazy person to those who send him on a mission.
>   (Prov 10:26)

Conclusion (the second line draws a conclusion from the statement in the first line):

Stay away from a fool,
because you will not receive knowledge from his lips. (Prov 14:7)

Entrust your efforts to Yahweh,
and your plans will succeed. (Prov 16:3)

Stairlike parallelism contains a number of adjacent lines giving the impression of building to a climax (like ascending a flight of stairs) or the impression of descending to an anticlimax (like going down a flight of stairs). This is also called climactic, step or chain parallelism:

The proverbs of Solomon, David's son who was king of Israel, given
to grasp wisdom and discipline,
to understand deep thoughts,
to acquire the discipline of wise behavior...
to give insight to gullible people,
to give knowledge and foresight to the young...
to understand a proverb and a clever saying,
the words of wise people and their riddles. (Prov 1:1–6)

These examples do not exhaust a list of various modes of synthetic parallelism. Indeed, since the poets were often very creative, it is not possible to classify every type of parallelism. They may combine types or even create totally new types to fit the message of their poem

External Parallelism

At times poets not only used parallelism among adjacent lines of poetry, but they also used it between two or more groups of adjacent lines, creating **external parallelism**. The first psalm is a masterpiece of external parallelism. The first verse is synonymous stairlike parallelism that describes what a person who is blessed by God does not do. The second verse is also synonymous parallelism, describing what this person does. The first two verses stand in antithetical parallelism to one another. They create the first example of external parallelism in this psalm. Verse three is synthetic parallelism (stairlike comparison) that compares the blessed person with a tree. Verse four is synthetic parallelism (comparison) that describes a wicked person. Therefore, verses three and four create another external antithetical parallelism. Verse five is synonymous parallelism that states the doom of the wicked person. It creates another external parallelism with verse four. This time it is synthetic (conclusion). Finally, verse six is antithetical parallelism that contrasts the righteous and the wicked. It creates the final external parallelism with the first five verses as a whole (synthetic parallelism: conclusion).

Other Poetic Devices

Several other important ways in which poets organized the thoughts in their poems can often been seen in English translation. These are devices that affected the overall structure of a poem or of several verses.

Acrostics

An **acrostic** poem is one that is based upon the alphabet. In Hebrew acrostic poems the psalmist typically arranges the beginning of the lines of a poem to begin with the letters of the Hebrew alphabet from the first line (or verse or section) beginning with first letter to the last line (or verse or section) beginning with the last letter. Since there are twenty-two letters in the Hebrew alphabet, acrostics usually involve twenty-two lines, sections or verses of a poem. The simple acrostics in the Old Testament are:

Psalm 37 (twenty-two sections over forty verses)
Psalm 111 (twenty-two lines over ten verses)
Psalm 112 (twenty-two lines over ten verses)
Proverbs 30:10-31 (twenty-two verses)
Lamentations 1 (twenty-two verses)
Lamentations 2 (twenty-two verses; with *'ayin* and *peh*, the sixteenth and seventeenth letters reversed, reflecting an alternate order for the Hebrew alphabet)
Lamentations 4 (twenty-two verses; with *'ayin* and *peh*, the sixteenth and seventeenth letters reversed, reflecting an alternate order for the Hebrew alphabet)

In addition, poets sometimes innovated on this simple acrostic structure. One innovation was to omit a few letters of the alphabet. Several of these incomplete acrostics are found among the psalms:

Psalm 25 (twenty-one acrostic verses with a non-acrostic concluding verse; missing *waw* and *qoph*, the sixth and nineteenth letters, and repeating resh, the twentieth letter)

Psalm 34 (twenty-one acrostic verses with a non-acrostic concluding verse;
   missing *waw*, the sixth letter)
Psalm 145 (twenty-one verses, missing *nun*, the fourteenth letter)

Another variation was to repeat the beginning letter over several verses before
continuing to the next letter of the alphabet. There are two of these multiple
acrostics in the Old Testament:

Psalm 119 (one hundred seventy-two verses; eight verses per letter)
Lamentations 3 (sixty-six verses; three verses per letter with *'ayin* and *peh*,
   the sixteenth and seventeenth letters reversed, reflecting an alternate
   order for the Hebrew alphabet)

Unfortunately, it is often impossible to reflect the acrostic structure of these
poems in English. Many Bibles do not note that a poem is an acrostic, with the
exception of Psalm 119. Many Bibles divide this psalm into eight-verse sections,
indicating its acrostic nature. In addition, many Bible also place the name of the
Hebrew letter or the Hebrew letter itself above each section of Psalm 119, indicating that each verse begins with the letter listed above this section.

Chiasm

Chiasm is the deliberate reversal of the order of items in the second half of
a literary unit. Thus, it produces patterns in the forms such as ABBA or
ABCCBA or ABCDDCBA. Chiasm takes it name from the Greek letter *chi*,
which is formed like the English letter X. (One half of an X is an inversion of
the other half.)

Chiasm is a widespread phenomenon in Hebrew literature and can be found
in individual verses, sections of a literary work or an entire poem or work of literature. Nor is chiasm confined to poetry, though it finds its most frequent use in
poetry. An example of chiasm within one verse are the first six words (in Hebrew) of Genesis 9:6:

Whoever sheds *blood* **of a human,** **by humans** *his blood* will be shed.

Chiasm serves to unite a sentence, paragraph, poem or larger unit and make it
memorable. Chiasm can be signaled by the repetition of specific words or by the
repeating of themes. Thus, it can often (but not always) be discerned in English
Bibles. Some psalms have a chiastic structure. Daniel 2—7 form a chiasm in
which the theme of Daniel 2 matches the theme of Daniel 7, while Daniel 3
matches Daniel 6, and Daniel 4 matches Daniel 5.

Inclusio or "Envelope Structure"

Closely related to chiasm is **inclusio** or **envelope structure**. An inclusio is formed when the end of a section or poem repeats the words or the theme of the opening. This device serves to emphasize the unity of a section or a poem or to reinforce its theme. Psalm 8 offers a classic example of an inclusio, since it begins and ends with the same words:

O Lord, our Lord, how majestic is your name in all the earth! (Ps 8:1a, 9)

While we can read, understand and appreciate the poetic sections of the Bible without being aware of literary features such as chiasm and inclusio, being aware of their use not only deepens our understanding of the poets' craft, but also enables us to understand their message more fully.

2. Understanding the Concept of Wisdom in the Old Testament

Wisdom is often thought to be a practical virtue. Someone who is wise has insight into the world and into other people. A wise person can offer good advice and help others who need to know how to handle a difficult situation. All these things are also true of wisdom in the Old Testament. However, wisdom is more than these things according to the biblical sages. For the biblical writers wisdom was a theological category. It centered on God and his ways. A wise person according to this view, therefore, is more than a person who understands people and society. A wise person understands his own relationship to God and understands how to apply the principles that God has revealed in his Word to the problems of the world.

Wisdom As a Theological Category

Biblical wisdom is marked by a number of basic assumptions. These include:

1. Wisdom is divine. It is taught by God through authorities such as the head of the family or the king as they apply Law and Gospel to specific situations.
2. Unlike prophecy, wisdom does not often address society as a whole in order to transform it, but it addresses individuals, who will then have an effect on society.
3. Wisdom most often addresses practical knowledge instead of theoretical knowledge. It emphasizes what to do, how to do it and what the conse-

quences will be. This takes precedence over the greater principles reflected in living wisely. Though this is clearly the focus of the Bible's wisdom literature, wisdom writings do contain passages that set the forth the principles of wisdom. Moreover, biblical wisdom emphasizes personal character over simple outward actions. It is the wise person's individual moral character, formed by God through his Word, that leads to proper decisions and actions.

Biblical wisdom is first and foremost an attribute of God. All true wisdom is godly wisdom, and any wisdom that people possess is a result of his gift of wisdom. This, however, often can only be perceived by understanding that it is the assumption lying behind the Old Testament wisdom literature's teaching on wisdom. Rarely does the Bible make explicit statements about God's wisdom. Instead, it assumes that God is all-wise and that the person who wants wisdom needs to receive it from him.

Perhaps the clearest statement on wisdom as God's possession is found at Proverbs 3:19:

> Yahweh founded the earth by wisdom. He established the heavens by understanding.

Wisdom here is not a human attribute, because it predates humans. Wisdom is Yahweh's to use and to grant.

> …Yahweh gives wisdom. From his mouth come knowledge and understanding.
> (Prov 2:6)

Only when we understand that wisdom is God's alone and that real human wisdom is a gift of God, do the biblical wisdom writings come into clear focus and offer us further chances to grow wise.

Wisdom literature in the Old Testament employs terms we might naturally associate with wisdom such as *wise, foolish, knowledge, understanding, insight, discipline, guidance* and *advice*. However, since wisdom also is theological, it employs a number of terms that many people would not associate with wisdom such as *righteous* and its opposites *evil* and *wicked*. This link of righteousness and wisdom runs throughout the wisdom books of the Old Testament, but is most clearly stated at Proverbs 9:8–10 where a wise person and a righteous person are equated:

> Do not warn a mocker, or he will hate you.
> Warn a *wise person*, and he will love you.
> Give advice to a *wise person*, and he will become *wiser*.

> Teach a *righteous* person, and he will add to his learning
> *The fear of Yahweh* is the beginning of *wisdom*.
> The knowledge of the Holy One is *understanding*,

Throughout the wisdom books this fundamental connection between wisdom and righteousness is assumed, although it is seldom discussed. Only the righteous, those who through faith have received God's righteousness, can have access to divine wisdom. The righteous alone have a relationship with him based on the Gospel. While reading wisdom literature in the Old Testament it is important to keep this in mind. If these books are read as only practical advice for tinkering with everyday situations, they will fall far short of the expectations readers place upon them. The advice they present does not always lead to an easy life, and in fact, can lead to decisions that make life more difficult (Prov 29:10). Biblical wisdom is not intended to make life easier and more comfortable, to be practical from a worldly point of view. Instead, it is intended to make life more godly, to reinforce the relationship the righteous have with Yahweh through his grace which they receive in his Word as it comes to them in Scripture and in the wisdom of others who trust in Yahweh. At times this may make their life better, but when this happens it is a secondary benefit.

Law and Gospel in Wisdom Literature

Biblical wisdom assumes a Law and Gospel dynamic as its basis. The wise person certainly understands God's Law with its prescriptions and prohibitions and its threat of punishment. However, these in themselves do not make one wise according to the biblical sages. After all, everyone has some understanding of right and wrong and fears punishment, but not everyone is wise. The wise person also understands the Gospel and knows God as a God who forgives penitent sinners and saves them from their sins. Thus, the book of Job tells us of Job's own confidence that God forgives sins and that he provides a redeemer (Job 14:13–17; 19:23–27). While the Gospel may not always be explicitly stated in every passage in the Bible's wisdom literature, it is always the center of the wise person's relationship with God.

The Fear of the Lord

An important concept in wisdom literature is the fear of Yahweh. Though found most often in wisdom literature, the concept of fearing God is also mentioned elsewhere in the Old Testament.

The **fear of Yahweh** can denote fear of God's wrath (Prov 24:21). More often, however, it denotes a positive, trusting-child-to-loving-father relationship between a wise person and God that causes a person to want to please the Heavenly Father (Prov 8:13). God initiates this positive relationship when he bestows blessings for temporal and eternal life and leads to wisdom. This relationship with God is established by Christ, the Wisdom of God (1 Cor 1:24; Prov 8:1–36). Thus, the fear of Yahweh is first and foremost a loving relationship initiated by God when he reckons sinners as righteous through faith (Gen 15:6). They can then have a positive relationship with God who has forgiven them and made them his children.

Proverbs most often speaks about this relationship with God by using the phrase *the fear of Yahweh*. In other books *fear* is used as a verb, and people are urged to fear Yahweh. It was God who established this relationship with his people when he called their ancestor Abraham (Gen 17:7; Deut 29:13) and when he delivered them from Egypt and graciously promised to be their God (Ex 6:7; Lev 11:45, 22:33, 25:38; Num 15:41; Jer 11:4). Therefore, the guiding principle behind the fear of Yahweh is not terror inspired by God's law, but trust built upon the Gospel, initiated by God and sustained by him. This Gospel relationship to Yahweh is encapsulated in the phrase *the fear of Yahweh*. In biblical thought all wisdom obtained by humans comes through this relationship.

Wisdom and Sanctification

Finally, we should note that wisdom is intended to help one live a life pleasing to God. Thus, its main goal is the sanctified life of a believer. This does not mean that it has little practical application. On the contrary, wisdom speaks about all types of life situations and offers guidance in coping with them. However, that guidance is not a human wisdom that judges the correctness of a decision by whether things appear to turn out good in this world. Rather, it offers guidance in how to behave in a way that both pleases God and leads to the wise believer's ultimate prosperity. This biblical wisdom takes into account the consequences for one's actions on two levels: the consequences for one's future in this life as well as the consequences for one's relationship with God. The wise person learns from biblical wisdom how to behave so that one has the best outcome in this life without sacrificing one's relationship with God by disregarding his Law (Prov 3:4; 28:9; Eccl 2:24; 8:12–13; 12:13–14).

17
Job

When adversity and troubles strike God's people, it can challenge their faith and cause them to question their relationship with God. Job faced such challenges as he lost his wealth, family, and health. Although his friends came to comfort him, they turned out to be his severest critics, accusing him bringing his own troubles upon himself because of his sin. Job sought answers to his problems and begged for God to explain the reason for his misery. God did appear to Job, but instead of explaining life's mysteries to him, led him to repentance. Ultimately, Job learned again to rely on God's grace and forgiveness.

1. Authorship and Date of Writing

The author of Job is unknown. He never identifies himself, nor does he offer any information about when or where he wrote this book. However, the book does contain a few clues that scholars have used to propose several theories about the author and his times. The author was most likely an Israelite. As narrator of the book he consistently calls God by his covenant name Yahweh. The only other person in the book to do this is Job, and he only uses God's name a few times (Job 1:21; 12:9). Early Jewish tradition named Moses as the author. While this is an unlikely possibility, we cannot rule out anyone from Moses through Jeremiah.

The author's account of Job's conversations with his friends and, later, with God himself, shows that he was well-versed in the wisdom literature of his day. He records proverbs, rhetorical questions and riddles. He shows extensive knowledge of plant and animal life and of a number of ancient Near Eastern cultures. In short, the author of Job was probably an upper class Israelite who studied and knew wisdom traditions from Israel and other cultures.

When the author lived and wrote is as uncertain as his identity. Job shares a number of phrases and metaphors with other books of the Bible, including Psalms, Proverbs, Lamentations and Isaiah. Unfortunately, it is impossible to determine whether Job was written before or after any of these books. Possible dates include the reign of Solomon in the tenth century or the reign of Hezekiah in the late eighth or early seventh century, since both of these kings showed interest in wisdom (Prov 25:1). By Ezekiel's day during the early Babylonian captivity, Job had been classified with Noah and Daniel as outstanding men of righteousness (Ezek 14:14, 20). However, any date from Solomon's day up to Judah's exile to Babylon would be possible. Since the book contains a number of references to Canaanite religious practices, a date during or after the Babylonian exile seems unlikely.

2. Date and Setting of the Events of the Book

A number of features in Job point toward a date in the early-to-mid second millennium shortly after the time of Israel's patriarchs for the historical setting of the events related in this book. Like Abraham, Isaac and Jacob, Job lived more than 100 years (Job 42:16). Job received money from his friends in the form of a *kesitah*, a measure of silver that is mentioned elsewhere in the Old Testament only in connection with Jacob (Gen 33:19; Josh 24:32). His wealth is measured in cattle. He served as his family's priest, offering sacrifices for his children, a practice that would have been illicit once the Aaronic priesthood had been established by God under Moses. The people mentioned in Job also point to this period of time: Job's friends included Eliphaz, a descendant of Teman, Esau's grandson and Bildad, a descendant of Shuah, Abraham's son by his wife Keturah. In Job we also meet Elihu, a descendant of Buz, the son of Abram's brother Nahor (Gen 22:21).

Job lived in the land of Uz (Job 1:1). Places by this name are mentioned twice elsewhere in the Old Testament (Jer 25:20; Lam 4:21). In Lamentations the land of Uz is said to be in Edom. Apparently, this portion of Edom was named after Uz, the son of Dishan, a descendant of Esau (Gen 36:28; 1 Chr 1:42). This location is confirmed by that fact that one of Job's friends, Eliphaz, was from Teman, a region in southern Edom named after one of Esau's grandsons (Gen 36:11, 15, 42). We can conclude that Job appears to be a wealthy Edomite who lived more than two generations after his ancestor Esau, Jacob's

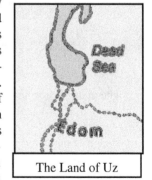

The Land of Uz

brother. Thus, Job must have lived sometime between the eighteenth and fifteenth centuries, during the time that the people of Israel were in Egypt.

3. Overview of the Book

Content

Job

Introduction (1:1—2:13)
    Job's life as a prosperous and godly man
    Satan and God discuss Job's integrity and faith
    Job's prosperity is taken
    Satan and God again discuss Job's integrity and faith
    Job's health is taken
Job and his friends debate the reason for his sufferings (3:1—27:23)
    Job states his complaints
    Job and his friends take turns debating his sufferings
    Job's final reply to his friends
Job's poem about wisdom (28:1–28)
Job restates his complaint (29:1—31:40)
Elihu confronts Job (32:1—37:24)
God confronts Job (38:1—41:34)
Job repents (42:1–6)
Conclusion: Job's health and prosperity restored (42:7–17)

Job is mostly a poetical book of wisdom. However, the opening chapters of Job and the epilogue (Job 1:1–2:13; 42:7–17) are prose. In the opening Job 1—2 we meet Job, a rich worshipper of God who is a man known for this integrity. The scene quickly shifts, however, to heaven when Satan comes before God, who points out Job and his faithfulness. Satan challenges God, stating that Job may deny God if his comfortable lifestyle is taken from him. God gives Satan permission to do this, but not to harm Job himself. Immediately we read of a series of disasters that strike Job so that he loses his possessions and his children. Nevertheless, Job refuses to lose his faith in God. Instead, he says,

"Naked I came from my mother's womb, and naked I will return there.
    Yahweh gave, and Yahweh has taken.
    May the name of Yahweh be blessed." (Job 1:21)

When Satan appears before God a second time, God continues to point to Job as a faithful man, Satan complains that God has not given him the chance to perform the ultimate test: to strike Job himself. God once again gives Satan permission, this time to strike Job, but not to kill him. Satan afflicts Job with painful sores, so that even his wife tells him now to curse God. Job still refuses, saying,

"Should we accept good from God and not accept bad?" (Job 2:10)

Because the news of Job's problems spreads, three of his friends, Eliphaz, Bildad and Zophar come to comfort him. The book now moves into the wisdom poetry that will deal with Job's struggle to understand his misery and its causes, his relationship with God and God's mercy.

Beginning with the Job 3, Job and his friends begin to debate the reason for the calamities that have befallen him. Job starts by bemoaning his life and wishing he had never been born (Job 3). Then Eliphaz, Bildad and Zophar in turn begin to accuse Job of harboring some unrepented sin that has brought him disaster and disease at the hands of an angry God. Job replies to each one, and the debate goes back and forth between Job and his friends until Job 27. Job's friends insist that his problem is sin. Job insists that, though he is a sinner, his problem does not stem from God's punishment on an unrepentant sinner. This debate drags on for chapter after chapter with speeches by Job and his friends until they completely exhaust every argument on both sides. In addition, Job from time to time calls out to God. He begs for God to appear to him and explain to him his problems. He claims that God appears to be unfair and capricious in dealing with him. However, Job never loses his faith in God, nor does he stop seeking a relationship with the Almighty who has allowed him to suffer both physically and emotionally.

With Job's final reply to his friends (Job 26—27), they fall silent. In Job 28 we meet a turning point in the book. As Job contemplates true wisdom, he concludes:

"The fear of Yahweh—that is wisdom,
and to turn from evil is understanding." (Job 28:28)

This conclusion signals that Job is now ready to move beyond demanding an answer from God. He is prepared at last to "fear Yahweh," that is, trust in him without knowing a reason for everything God does.

Yet, Job has to struggle further with his faith before he can realize the full meaning of his words. In Job 29—31 Job bemoans his life, this time noting how far he has fallen from his former position of wealth, power and respect in his community. He calls on God to confront him, for he knows of no sin that he has committed that would cause God to punish him.

Before God can answer, however, a young man named Elihu steps forward to challenge Job. Elihu had kept silent up to this point out of respect for his elders. Now, however, he feels compelled to speak, because Job's friends had allowed Job to assert that he was more righteous than God and had not properly refuted him (Job 32:2–3). Elihu's words move the argument forward by defending God against the accusation that he had dealt with Job unjustly. He challenges Job to accept God's ways as beyond human understanding, even the understanding of the wisest humans.

Immediately after Elihu speaks God appears to Job in a storm and challenges Job's words. Pointing to example after example from creation—from the stars in the sky to animals that roam the earth—God asks Job whether he was wise and knowledgeable enough to make and sustain the universe. When God finishes his challenge to Job, all Job can do is repent and confess that he spoke out of ignorance.

The book quickly moves to its conclusion. God rebukes Job's friends for speaking incorrectly about him. He blesses Job. Although Job had spoken out of ignorance, he had not lost his faith in God. Then God restores Job's fortune with twice as much as he had previously. More children are born to him, and he lives long enough to see his great-grandchildren.

Important Topics in Job

Through the drama of Job's suffering we are led to grapple with a number of themes that are still in the minds of people today.

Theodicy

The concern of **theodicy** permeates the book of Job. Theodicy, from the Greek words for *God* and *justice*, is the discussion of how God is a just and righteous God despite the suffering and injustices that beset human existence in a sinful world. Job and his friends debate theodicy, and offer three approaches to explaining God's justice:

1. *Legalism*: Job's friends, in arguing that God is punishing Job for some unrepented sin, explain God's justice through legalism: If one suffers, God is measuring out punishment for sin. If one is prosperous, God is rewarding good behavior. While it is often tempting to blame the poor and the suffering for causing their own misery (John 9:2), we know from experience that people often suffer even though we cannot connect their suffering to a specific sin. Job's friends sought to make God into a being who works through mechanical and predictable retribution. This offered a solution for the ques-

tion of theodicy, but viewed God only as a God of law and not a God of mercy.

2. *Rationalism*: Job often called on God to explain his actions. At times it appears as if Job thought that he could understand God's execution of justice if it were only made plain to him. This also offers a solution for the question of theodicy, but at the risk of making God answerable to humans and God's wisdom and knowledge no greater than that of humans.

3. *Mysticism*: At times Job sought to simply experience God. This ultimate experience of God, he hoped, would give him intuitive insight into God's ways. Like mystics throughout the ages, Job hoped he could sense God's justice from simply being in direct communion with God. Mysticism, the search for direct communion with God, offers a solution to theodicy, but it does this by equating the limited human spirit with God's infinite nature.

Ultimately God does appear to Job. However, God not only refutes the legalism of Job's friends, he shatters the notion that humans can grasp his wisdom and knowledge and explain his justice in terms that will satisfy all of their questions. Even though Job sees God in the storm, his experience does not grant him mystical insight into God's justice. While theodicy is a topic of discussion throughout Job, ultimately neither Job nor the readers (who, unlike Job and his friends, know of God's decision in heaven) ever find a complete answer to *how* God is just. Instead, they are directed to other concerns.

Faith and Integrity

More important than theodicy is the drama of Job's faith and integrity. From the beginning of the book God asserts that Job is an outstanding example of one of his faithful servants. Satan, his attacks and even Job's friends work to undermine his faith and challenge his integrity. Although Job's faith is tested to the limit, it survives. Job clings to his faith in God and refuses to compromise his integrity. In the end this is more important than the question of theodicy. God asserted that Job was a man of faith. Satan challenged God's assertion. God proved to be correct. But why? Was it simply because Job was a stronger-willed person than Satan imagined? No, it was because God, who grants and sustains faith, guided Job through his crisis, even when Job was not conscious of God's help. God implies as much when he reminds Job that he cares for mountain goats, wild donkeys and oxen, ostriches, horses, hawks and eagles (Job 39). Surely, God takes care of humans, too (Matt 6:26)! Job's faith endures because God, who grants, sustains and nourishes faith remains faithful to Job, even when Job questions and doubts God. Therefore, the message of this book is that more important than knowing God's ways with justice is knowing God's work in our life to bring us to faith and preserve us as his children.

God's Love and Mercy

This leads us to one more important theme in Job: God's love and mercy. Though in his misery Job often feels that God is a God of punishment, readers know from the beginning that God is merciful to Job. Satan admits as much when he says that God has provided for Job (Job 1:10–11). God shows us his mercy when he will not allow Satan to kill Job (Job 2:6). Job, though his faith wavers, ultimately clings to his belief that God loves and forgives him (Job 10:12). Elihu reminds Job of God's love and mercy (Job 33:23–29; 36:15–16; 37:13). Ultimately, the book of Job tells us that God's love and mercy toward us provide the only hope for humans, whether they are rich or poor, healthy or diseased, in anguish or in comfort.

18

Psalms

Called *Praises* in Hebrew and *Psalms* in English, the most beloved book of the Old Testament is an ancient hymnal that still speaks across the centuries to Christians today. Its name comes from the Greek word *psalmos*, which originally indicated a composition sung to the accompaniment of a harp. Five centuries ago Luther wrote in his introduction to this book:

> The Psalter ought to be a precious and beloved book, if for no other reason than this: it promises Christ's death and resurrection so clearly—and pictures his kingdom and the condition and nature of all Christendom—that it might well be called a little Bible. In it is comprehended most beautifully and briefly everything that is in the entire Bible. It is really a fine enchiridion or handbook. In fact, I have a notion that the Holy Spirit wanted to take the trouble himself to compile a short Bible and book of examples of all Christendom or all saints, so that anyone who could not read the whole Bible would here have anyway almost an entire summary of it, comprised in one little book.[7]

Luther's observations about the psalms reveal why this has been a beloved book for Christians for both personal devotional life and for corporate worship. It covers the entire range of life experiences and lays out the Bible's central teachings in 150 hymns of God's people.

1. Authorship of the Psalms — *Poems from Several Authors*
2. Organization of the Psalms — *Five Books and the Editorial Shaping of a Collection*
3. Psalm superscriptions — *Information about the Psalms and Their Original Setting*
4. Types of Psalms — *Songs That Cover a Range of Human Emotions and Situations*
5. A Few Important Psalms — *Exploring the Rich Tapestry of Israel's Ancient Hymnbook*

---

[7] Martin Luther, *Luther's Works* (Philadelphia: Fortress, 1960) 35:254.

1. Authorship of the Psalms

From the earliest times the book of Psalms has been associated with David, "the sweet psalmist of Israel" (2 Sam 23:1). When one looks at the psalms' **superscriptions**, the short notices that appear before many of the psalms, this seems to be confirmed: Almost half of the psalms are attributed to David. While many have tried to understand these attributions of authorship as something else (such as indication of a dedication to the memory of a person or as an indication of style, such as "in David's style"), a number of these superscriptions are clearly indicating authorship, for instance, the superscription on Psalm 3 reads:

A psalm of David, when he fled from Absalom, his son.

This is most certainly claiming that this psalm was written by David during Absalom's rebellion (2 Sam 15–18).

However, this book is not the product of one author. Instead, it is the collection of compositions by some of Israel's most skilled musicians and poets. The psalms span the history of Israel, from Moses, who wrote Psalm 90 to the descendants of Korah, Levites who were singers in the temple (2 Chr 20:19) and even to the exile and beyond (Ps 137). One third of the psalms have no known author. The other two-thirds are from seven different authors or groups of authors:

David: 73 psalms
Asaph, one of the leaders of the choir in the temple (1 Chr 6:39): 12 psalms
The descendants of Korah: 11 psalms
Solomon: 2 psalms
Moses: 1 psalm
Ethan the Ezrahite (i.e., a descendant of Zerah, Judah's son): 1 psalm
Heman the Ezrahite: 1 psalm (written with the descendants of Korah)

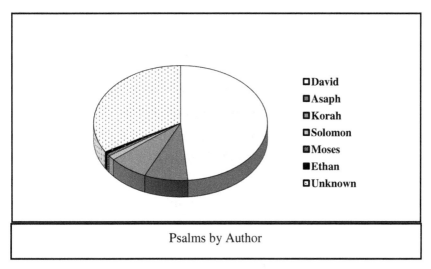

Psalms by Author

The authors of the psalms at times borrowed material from one another. The first three verses of Psalm 73 are borrowed from Psalm 31, a psalm of David. Psalm 135:15–20 is nearly identical to Psalm 115:4–11. David himself reused Psalm 40:13–17 in Psalm 70:1–5 and combined Psalm 57:7–11 and 60:5–12 and added a closing verse to create Psalm 108. In addition, Psalms 14 and 53 appear to be two nearly identical versions of a psalm of David, and Psalm 18 is another version of David's song of thanksgiving for being saved from Saul (2 Sam 22:1–51).

2. Organization of the Psalms

This collection of hymns is not simply a random assortment of Israel's hymns. Rather, it is a carefully arranged collection. This can be seen from its organization into five books in imitation of the Pentateuch:

Five Books of Psalms

Book 1	Psalms 1—41
Book 2	Psalms 42—72
Book 3	Psalms 73—89
Book 4	Psalms 90—106
Book 5	Psalms 107—150

This organization is an ancient one, and is indicated by the blessing and praise of God that concludes the first four books:

Blessed be Yahweh, the God of Israel, from everlasting to everlasting. Amen and Amen. (Ps 41:14)

Blessed be the name of his glory forever. May his glory fill all the earth. Amen and Amen. The prayers of David, son of Jesse, are ended. (Ps 72:19–20)

Blessed be Yahweh forever. Amen and Amen (Ps 89:53)

Blessed be Yahweh, the God of Israel, from everlasting to everlasting. And all the people said, "Amen." Hallelujah. (Ps 106:48)

Within each book there are also signs of editorial activity. For instance, in Book 1 God's name *Yahweh* is used about six times as often as the generic word for God. In Book 2, just the opposite is true: the word for God occurs about six times as frequently as does God's name. Other patterns can also be discerned:

Groups of Psalms

Psalms by David	Psalms 3—41; 51—72; 138—145
Psalms by Korahites	Psalms 42—49; 84—85; 87—88
Psalms by Asaph	Psalms 73—83
Psalms about God as King	Psalms 93—100
Psalms of Praise	Psalms 103—107
Hallelujah Psalms (beginning or ending with *Hallelujah*)	Psalms 111—118; 146—150
Songs of Ascents (perhaps songs sung by pilgrims ascending to the Temple)	Psalms 120—134

3. Psalm superscriptions

The superscriptions of the psalms often preserve a number of interesting notices relating to the psalms' composition and use. While some scholars have doubted the accuracy of these notices, we should keep in mind that they are part of the ancient Hebrew text of the psalms. Although they are often printed in English Bibles in smaller type and are not given verse numbers, in Hebrew Bibles they are counted as verses and are treated no differently than the rest of the psalms they introduce. The types of information we find in these superscriptions include:

Author

Occasion for writing (e.g., "A psalm of David when he fled from his son Absolam," Ps 3)

Occasion for performance (e.g., "A psalm: a song for the Sabbath day," Ps 92)

The word *Hallelujah*

Musical directions, including:

> Instrumentation (e.g., "with stringed instruments," several psalms; "with flutes," Ps 5)
>
> Type of Song, including psalm, song, prayer and the little understood Hebrew words *mitkam*, *maskil* and *shiggaion*;
>
> Unknown terms, such as *sheminith* (perhaps meaning *octave*) and *gittith*
>
> Tune title; this may include "Lilies" (four psalms), "The Doe of the Morning" (Ps 22) and "A Dove on Distant Oaks" (Ps 56)

The notice "For the choir director"

These superscriptions testify to the wide range of human experience from which the psalms were composed. They tell us of the importance of music in Israel's worship. Moreover, they also point us to a wide range of situations in our lives which the psalms address.

4. Types of Psalms

There seems to be some ancient classification of psalms. Many of them are called *psalms*, indicating they were to be sung to the accompaniment of stringed instruments. More than thirty psalms are called *songs*. Five psalms are called *prayers,* one a *shiggaion*, six a *miktam* and thirteen a *maskil*. Psalms 38 and 70 are characterized as *petitions*. Psalm 145 is called *praise*.

These ancient classifications, however, do not help us compare the content of psalms. For this reason modern studies often look at psalms that have similar themes and literary structures. While scholars do not agree on how all psalms should be classified, there are a few basic categories that are widely accepted.

Lament or Complaint

Many psalms feature a desperate cry to God for help in times of trouble. Out of distress the psalm writer turns to the only one who can help at all times—God. These psalms not only show us how God's people in the past relied on him, but they also remind us of our only hope in time of need. **Lament** psalms often follow a pattern that consists of the following parts:

1. Invocation: the psalmist prays to God
2. Complaint: a description of the troubles that the psalmist faces
3. Petition: the psalmist pleads with God for help
4. Conclusion: this may include various elements such as confidence that God will hear the prayer, praise of God or a vow to worship God when he answers the prayer

Many complaint psalms are in books one and two. A typical example of a complaint of an individual is Psalm 13. The complaint of Israel as a whole can also be the subject of psalms. Psalm 44 is an example of such community laments.

Praise and Thanksgiving

Given that the entire book of Psalms is called *Praises* in Hebrew, it comes as no surprise that quite a few psalms offer praise to God or thank him for what he has done either for an individual or for all of God's people. Thanksgiving psalms often begin with a call to praise or thank God or with the psalmist's stated intent to thank him. In the body of these psalms one often finds an account of God's works on behalf of his people that give rise to the occasion for thanking him. The end of these psalms often returns to the praise and thanksgiving theme. An example of the thanksgiving of an individual for God is Psalm 138. Some psalms are the community's expression of thanksgiving. One example is Psalm 136, with its thanksgiving for God's protection and deliverance of Israel throughout its history.

Closely related to thanksgiving psalms are praise psalms. These psalms begin with a call to praise God. The main body of the psalm, which can be quite lengthy, gives a reason why God should be praised. Among these reasons are God's wonderful acts of creation (Ps 19), God's work in history (Ps 105), God's reign as king (Ps 96) and God's presence among his people in the Temple on Mount Zion (Ps 84). Praise psalms often end as they began, with a renewed call to praise God.

Both the praise and thanksgiving psalms remind us that worship focuses on the great acts of God for his people's salvation. This was as true in the Old Testament as it is today. It is no wonder, then, that the psalms have inspired Christian hymn writers to write such hymns as "Praise God from Whom All Blessings Flow" or "Praise to the Lord, the Almighty, the King of Creation."

Wisdom

A number of psalms incorporate themes commonly found in the wisdom books of the Old Testament. These psalms encourage meditation on the Word of

God and have a devotional quality to them. Among the wisdom themes found in these psalms are:

Contrast between a righteous person and a wicked person (Ps 1)
Wisdom contrasted with foolishness (Ps 49)
Fear of the Lord (Ps 112)
Meditation on God's Word (his *torah*, "law/instruction"; Ps 119)

These poems are a source of instruction for the people of God. They warn us of foolish attitudes and behavior:

The complete fool said in his heart, "There is no God" (Ps 14:1; 53:1)

They also tell of the blessing of wise behavior:

Blessed is the person who fears Yahweh, who greatly delights in his commands (Ps 112:1)

Messianic

While many scholars would not consider psalms about God's Messiah to be a separate category of psalm, it is important to note that since New Testament times Christians have understood certain psalms as prophecies of Christ. (For example, see the use of Ps 2 at Acts 13:33, Heb 1:5; 5:5 and Rev 19:5 or the use of Ps 110 at Matt 22:44, Mark 12:36, Luke 20:42–43, Acts 2:34–35; 1 Cor 15:25 and Heb 1:3, 13.) Luther affirmed this reading of the psalms when he noted that this book "promises Christ's death and resurrection so clearly, and pictures his kingdom...." These psalms portray the Messiah in two basic ways: as king (e.g., Pss 2, 45 and 110) or as suffering servant (e.g., Ps 21). Some depict both his servanthood and his dominion (e.g., Ps 8).

The presence of messianic psalms among the hymns used by God's ancient people remind us that they, like us, found their hope and comfort in God's deliverance through the work of his chosen savior. While we look back in time to see these psalms fulfilled in Christ, they looked forward in confidence to the one who would fulfill the promise of God to save his people from their sins.

19

Proverbs

Virtually every society and culture has made use of proverbs, familiar short sayings that convey general truth and advice, such as, "Don't count your chickens before they're hatched." Much of the book of Proverbs seems to contain this type of saying. However, Proverbs is more than simply a book of wise sayings that grew out of hard, practical experience. While this book of wisdom is designed to give advice and guidance for living, it is part of Scripture because its wisdom arises out of God's revealed wisdom, not humanly devised guidance.

1. Authorship and Growth of the Book of Proverbs — *How Did Proverbs Come to Be?*
2. Theme — *The Fear of the Lord and Related Principles*
3. Overview of the Book — *What Is Proverbs All About?*
4. Law and Gospel in Proverbs — *Understanding How Proverbs Shows Us God and His Message for Us*
5. Applying Proverbs: Know the Situation — *Understanding and Applying Individual Proverbs*

1, Authorship and Growth of the Book of Proverbs

As one might suspect of a book of the Bible that presents itself as God's revealed wisdom, Proverbs is often associated with Solomon. King David's son was known for receiving wisdom from God (1 Kgs 3:4–28; 4:29–34). In addition, Solomon spoke three thousand proverbs (1 Kgs 4:32). However, although large parts of the book of Proverbs come from Solomon, he did not compose all of the sayings in this book. In fact, when one pays close attention to the notices in the book itself, it is apparent that this collection of wise saying grew over time. The book's origin and growth most likely took place in the following way:

The first stage of the assembling of Proverbs involves the composition and editorial activity of Solomon himself. This first stage includes Proverbs 1—24, and is subdivided into several parts. The first part is Proverbs 1:1—9:18, an introduction to wisdom, which is characterized as "The proverbs of Solomon son of David, king of Israel...." (Prov 1:1) This introduction is not primarily made up of the short sayings we associate with Proverbs, but with longer discourses on what wisdom is, what its benefits are, how to find it and how to use it.

The second part of Solomon's work on Proverbs is Proverbs 10:1—22:16. This long section, that is called "The Proverbs of Solomon," (Prov 10:1) consists of short sayings of one verse each, in keeping with what we know as proverbs. A third part of Solomon's work, Proverbs 22:17—24:22 is a compiling of sayings of other wise people. This section begins, "Pay attention and listen to the words of wise people..." (Prov 22:17) and is apparently a compilation of wise sayings that Solomon made and appended to his own sayings. With the discovery of an Egyptian document known as *The Wisdom of Amenemope* over one hundred years ago, scholars now believe that a number of the sayings in Proverbs 22 were adapted from this Egyptian work. This should not be surprising, since Solomon had many contacts with Egypt, married an Egyptian wife (1 Kgs 3:1), and his wisdom was compared to that of the Egyptian wise men as well as others throughout the Ancient Near East (1 Kgs 4:30–31). Finally, Solomon added a second, shorter collection of wise sayings from others (Prov 24:23-34), of which we are told, "These also are from wise people...."

The second stage of the growth of Proverbs is represented by Proverbs 25—29. "These also are the proverbs of Solomon transcribed by the men of King Hezekiah of Judah" according to Proverbs 25:1. A few of these sayings are repetitions of proverbs that also appear in Proverbs 10:1—22:16, but most of them are unique to this collection and were probably handed down in the court of the Judean kings from Solomon's time. Who the "men of King Hezekiah" were, is unknown, but the most likely candidates are Hezekiah's secretary Shebnah and his recorder Joah son of Asaph (2 Kgs 18:18, 37).

The final stage of growth of this anthology of wisdom produced Proverbs 30 and 31. Proverbs 30 is the composition of Agur (Prov 30:1), of whom we know nothing except his name. While we cannot be certain when Agur wrote Proverbs 30, based on its content and vocabulary, it is likely that he wrote it around the time of King Hezekiah. The first nine verses of Proverbs 31 are characterized as "The words of Lemuel, a king. A prophetic revelation that his mother used to discipline him." (Prov 31:1) No king by this name is known from the Bible, so once again we cannot be certain of the date of this composition. However, given the language and content of Proverbs 31, it is likely that Lemuel is another name for a righteous king of Israel, perhaps Hezekiah or Josiah. The final twenty-two verses of Proverbs 31 are an acrostic poem about a good wife (see Understanding Hebrew Poetry in Chapter 16 for a discussion of acrostic poems in Hebrew). No author is given for this work, and its time of composition cannot be determined with any accuracy. It probably is no older than Hezekiah's day, but no younger than the early Persian period, the time of the composition of the last books of the Old Testament. It is likely that this poem comes from the final compiler/editor of Proverbs who assembled the sections of the book as we have them today.

Growth of the Book of Proverbs

Stage One c. 950 BC	Solomon writes and compiles 1—24 a. Introduction 1—9 b. Solomon's Proverbs 10:1—22:16 c. Sayings of Wise People 22:17—24:22 d. More Sayings of Wise People 24:23–34
Stage Two c. 700 BC	Solomon's Proverbs Compiled by Hezekiah's Men 25—29
Stage Three c. 650 BC (?)	Other Compositions Added by the Final Editor 30—31 a. Agur's words (30; c. 700 BC) b. Advice from Lemuel's Mother (31:1–9; 7th century BC) c. Poem: A Good Wife (31:10–31; perhaps 7th century BC)

2. Theme

Solomon sets forth the theme of this book in the very beginning of his introduction. He tells us that these proverbs are:

> …intended to teach knowledge of wisdom and discipline,
> to give knowledge of knowledgeable words
> to acquire discipline for wise judgment: righteousness, justice and fairness
> to allow gullible people to acquire insight
> to give a young man knowledge and foresight
> > (A wise person will listen to these proverbs and continue to learn,
> > and a knowledgeable person will acquire guidance.)
> to give knowledge of a proverb and a clever saying,
> > the words of wise people and their riddles.
> The fear of Yahweh is the beginning of knowledge.
> Stubborn fools despise wisdom and discipline. (Prov 1:1–7)

In short, Proverbs seeks to impart wisdom that leads to *the fear of the Lord* (see Understanding Wisdom Literature in Chapter 16 for a full discussion of this term). This attitude of trust in God that is both Gospel oriented in that it comes from knowing the promises of a gracious God, and guided by the Law, since those who have the fear of the Lord do not want to do anything to harm their relationship with the heavenly Father.

A number of key concepts that support this theme are mentioned here and throughout the book of Proverbs. *Discipline* is necessary for the person who has the fear of the Lord. While this may begin early in life as discipline administered by parents and others in the form of regulation and punishment, Proverbs seeks to impart to every reader a mature self-discipline that does not require constant oversight by others or the threat of punishment.

Judgment, righteousness, justice, insight and *foresight* are also important qualities of a person with the fear of the Lord. While these can be useful in the everyday world, they are not meant to be concepts that are only humanly devised. Justice and righteousness are defined by God's concept of right and wrong, as many of the sayings of the book remind us. While humans may establish an imitation of God's justice with laws and courts, the person with the fear of the Lord seeks to do what God considers just, whether or not human powers would sanction or encourage such justice. Judgment, insight and foresight may be good things to have when making a business deal or choosing friends or a spouse, but in Proverbs these concepts are most concerned with spiritual discernment: knowing and trusting the promises of God and recognizing the consequences of both faith and unbelief.

Thus, the theme of Proverbs points the reader to God, who gives all good things, and encourages the reader to learn God's ways. Those who understand this theme and implement it in their lives may not always be prosperous in this life, but they look forward to a prosperity promised by God and granted by him. Therefore, they seek to align their lives with God's will.

3. Overview of the Book

Solomon	Introduction (1—9)
	The Proverbs of Solomon (10:1—22:16)
	The Words of Wise People (22:17—24:22)
	Additional Words of Wise People (24:23–34)
Hezekiah's Men	The Proverbs of Solomon (25—29)
Agur	The Words of Agur (30)
Lemuel's Mother	The Words of Lemuel (31:1–9)
Unknown	Acrostic Poem: A Good Wife (31:10–31)

As we have already noted, the book of Proverbs is divided into several sections. The introduction (Prov 1—9) contains longer discourses on wisdom. Solomon is preparing the reader for the task of reading and understanding the short sayings that begin in Proverbs 10. He wants us to understand that true wisdom that comes from God is different in its outlook and goals from worldly, human wisdom. True wisdom does not guarantee success in this life, but, as Solomon emphasizes over and over in these chapters of Proverbs, it is a gift from God that brings us closer to him and guides us in living our lives. Since Solomon addresses these introductory discourses to young, maturing men (*son* or *sons* is used twenty-one times in Prov 1—9), he often depicts wisdom as a lovely and wise woman who has much to offer them. In addition, he warns his readers of the dangers of straying from God's ways and the ultimate destruction that awaits those who ignore or scorn God's wisdom. For Christians, perhaps the most important chapter in this section is Proverbs 8, which many have understood to be a depiction of Christ (Matt 12:42; Luke 11:31; Matt 11:19; Luke 7:34–35; 1 Cor 1:24,30; 2:7–8; Col 2:2–3), the true source of wisdom, in the guise of Woman Wisdom. Proverbs 9 is a transition to Solomon's sayings. It is a contrast between two women: Wisdom and Foolishness. Wisdom imparts life and God's blessing, whereas Foolishness leads to destruction and death.

Solomon's proverbs in Proverbs 10:1—22:16 are short, pithy sayings. Each is one verse. While these can be read as merely a string of sayings, there is a loose arrangement in the order of these proverbs. For instance, many of the early proverbs in this collection emphasize the contrast between wisdom and foolishness or the contrast between righteousness and wickedness. Read together, these seem to indicate that wisdom and righteousness complement one another, while foolishness and wickedness are two sides of the same coin. These sayings cover all areas of life: family relationships, friendship, how to behave in society, the value of work, business and economics, government and many other topics.

The Words of Wise People (Prov 22:17—24:22) and the Additional Words of Wise People (Prov 24:23–34) are similar in theme and form to Solomon's Proverbs, though many of them are longer than one verse. These serve not only to reinforce the themes in Solomon's Proverbs, but also show that godly wisdom from God's Law (which is written on the hearts of all people; Rom 2:14–16) can sometimes be found among unbelievers.

The proverbs from Solomon preserved by Hezekiah's men (Prov 25—29) contain many sayings that are not found in Proverbs 10:1—24:16, though a few are duplicates or near-duplicates of earlier proverbs. This collection of sayings appears to be arranged as advice for kings and those who serve them, since a good number of them mention kings and their duties.

Agur's words divide into two main sections. The first part (Prov 30:1–10) contains prayers to God and advice to Agur's readers. The second part (Prov 30:11–33) consists of sayings that form lists of things (often, but not always, with the formula "…three things…four things…"). These lists of sayings climax in a surprise ending in the final item listed. For instance:

> Four things are small on the earth, yet they are wiser than the wisest people:
> Ants are a species without strength, but they store their food in summer.
> Rock badgers are a species without power, but they make their home in a cliff.
> Locusts have no king, but they advance together in ranks.

A lizard can be held in one's hands, but it is in a king's palace. (Prov 30:24–27)

This saying is a list of four creatures that seem small and have little power. The final creature is the most powerful of all, because even though he seems powerless, the lizard can gain access to the most powerful man in the kingdom, whereas most commoners cannot.

The sayings taught by Lemuel's mother (Prov 31:1–9) form a short instruction about the proper behavior for kings and others in authority. The final section, the acrostic poem about a good wife is intended not only to help a young man pick out a godly, wise wife, but also intended to remind readers of the woman Wisdom at the beginning of the book. Thus, the final note in the book brings us back to the very beginning, showing us what is truly wise, from A to Z.

4. Law and Gospel in Proverbs

Many of the Proverbs offer advice. They indicate what the reader should do. Thus, Proverbs contains much explicit Law. For this reason, Proverbs is often seen as a book with little or no Gospel. It is true that Proverbs has few passages that are nothing but Gospel, but it is not true that Proverbs is without the Gospel. In fact, all of Proverbs presupposes the Gospel. This can be seen by its use of the Law, which focuses on two goals: to keep readers from sinning and harming themselves (**first use of the Law**) and to guide the person with the fear of the Lord who wishes to do God's will (**third use of the Law**). The predominance of these two uses of the Law match Proverbs' view of humans as wise or foolish, righteous or wicked. Fools can be restrained from their sinful ways only through the first use of the Law (threat of punishment that tends to keep them from sinning). The Law also guides righteous people (third use). The Law is seldom used in Proverbs to directly convict readers of their sins (**second use of the Law**; though it is always present since the law always reminds us of our failure to keep it.) This relative lack of passages that convict readers of their sins also points us to the primary intended audience of Proverbs: it is written to speak to God's people, those who have a relationship with him through his promise. In Old Testament terms, it was intended for the instruction of young men who had been incorporated into God's people through the promise connected with their circumcision. It is not primarily intended for the unbeliever, and therefore, does not often explicitly seek to move readers to repentance by condemning their sins. In New Testament terms, it speaks to the baptized people of God who have been brought into God's kingdom and who have been brought to repentance and faith. Thus, few passages in Proverbs speak the Law while seeking to apply it in its theological use (i.e., the second use). However, since human nature is fallen and even in the regenerate people of God sin persists in this life, the law in Proverbs will always remind them of their sin and drive them to daily repentance.

The use of the Law to restrain sin is especially employed to combat the foolish behavior typical of sinful human nature. This is often found in threats of punishment and suffering:

> They would not accept my advice,
> and they despised all my warning.
> They will eat the fruit of their way,
> and their appetite will be satisfied with their own advice.
> Gullible people kill themselves because of their own turning away,
>> and by complacency fools destroy themselves. (Prov 1:30–32)

The first use of the law is also evident in promised benefits to those who follow the Law (see Smalcald Articles, Part III, Article 2, paragraph 1):

> Like the coldness of snow on a harvest day is a trustworthy messenger to one
> who sends him.
>> He revives his masters' soul. (Prov 25:13)

> Without wood a fire goes out,
> and without gossip a quarrel dies down. (Prov 26:20)

Some proverbs use both threat of punishment and promised benefits:

> A kind man benefits himself,
>> but a cruel man brings trouble on himself (Prov 11:17)

> A person who is greedy for ill-gotten gain troubles his own household,
>> but the person who hates bribes will live (Prov 15:27)

This use of the Law to discourage sin and encourage civil righteousness is needed even by the people of God, since they remain sinful as long as they are in this life. For this reason, the proverbs contain some of the Scripture's sharpest images of the punishment that God can meet out to those who fail to keep his Law.

The Law as a guide for the person who by faith knows God and wants to please him is found throughout Proverbs. For instance, those who have been made God's children are encouraged to keep the Third Commandment by praying to him:

> Yahweh is far away from wicked people,
>> but he hears the prayer of righteous people. (Prov 15:29)

Often Proverbs assumes that readers are among God's people when it presents the Law's precepts:

> Honor Yahweh with your wealth and the first part of your harvest. (Prov 3:9)

> Do not despise Yahweh's discipline, my son,
> and do not resent his warning,
>> because Yahweh warns the one he loves,
>> and is like a father who is pleased with a son. (Prov 3:11–12)

In many cases God's promises are used to encourage his people to do good:

> The person who spreads blessing will prosper,
> and the person who refreshes others will be refreshed. (Prov 11:25)

Proverbs, therefore, often assumes that its readers are children of God, presupposing the Gospel has brought them into his kingdom and that they understand their adoption into the family of God. Its sayings are intended to encourage them to good works even though the sinful world may weigh heavily upon them. It seeks to provide guidance in the way of God's holy Law as they live their lives.

While Proverbs does not have a large number of well-known Gospel passages, nevertheless, the Gospel makes Proverbs both powerful and comforting. The forgiveness of God and the righteousness he credits to his people form the basis for many of the Proverbs that assume readers have a positive relationship with him. Most notable of the passages with much Gospel content are the discourses of Solomon about Wisdom found in the first part of the book (Prov 1:20–33; 8:1–36; 9:1–18) as well as Solomon's second address to his Son (Prov 2:1–22). In addition, scattered throughout Proverbs are a number Gospel proverbs that point to God's work in the lives of his people:

> Whoever places his trust in his wealth will fall,
>> *but righteous people will sprout like foliage.* (Prov 11:28)

> In the path of righteousness there is life,
>> *and the way of that pathway is not death.* (Prov 12:28)

In Proverbs sayings that apply the Law are far more frequent than sayings that bring the comfort of the Gospel. Yet the Gospel predominates in this book, because it alone brings comfort for those who have fallen short of God's expectations. It empowers them to live as God's forgiven and reconciled people and, therefore, grow in wisdom and righteous living.

5. Applying Proverbs: Know the Situation

Many Christians have turned to Proverbs for answers to questions that their lives have posed to them. They want to know the correct way to live and the correct moral and ethical decisions to make. However, the sayings in this book seldom give direct answers to life's questions. Instead, they require contemplation and growth in wisdom so that one can learn to apply them properly. Therefore, one needs not only the proverbs themselves, but also the insight that allows one to know the situation to which each proverb applies. For instance, Proverbs 23:4–5 advises:

> Do not wear yourself out getting rich.
> Have the insight to know when to stop.
>> Will your eyes glimpse it before it is gone?
>> It will quickly make wings for itself.
>> Like an eagle it will fly into the sky.

The principle of this proverb is easy to understand: do not seek riches far in excess of what can be used. However, the application of this proverb is difficult. When does one reach the point where money is no longer needed? For the desperately poor this point may never come. For the fabulously wealthy, this point has long passed. Their decisions are easy. Those somewhere in-between are the persons who need the wisdom to assess their situation and know when to pursue other interests.

Another example of needing to know the situation one is in so that one can properly apply a proverb is the case of the twin proverbs at Proverbs 26:4–5:

> Do not answer a fool according to his stupidity
>> Otherwise, you, too, will be like him.
> Answer a fool according to his stupidity.
>> Otherwise, he will consider himself wise.

In any given situation does one answer a fool or not? Only the God-given wisdom and insight that Proverbs commends can guide a person who seeks to implement this advice. The same is true of most of the proverbs. One simply cannot expect them to be a simple, follow-the-instructions textbook to life. Instead, they are designed to help the reader grow in wisdom and learn how to use

them through a life that increases in the knowledge of the Gospel that alone
brings fallen sinners to God and empowers them to live according to his will.

Since the book of Proverbs is often read for advice and guidance in life, it is
important to realize that these sayings offer different amounts of advice. Some
offer no guidance. Others imply what one is to do without stating it directly. Still
others flatly tell the reader what to do or avoid.

The Observation of Life

Some sayings simply observe the way life is. They are not meant to offer
advice as much as to inform the reader of the realities of life in the fallen, sinful
world of humans.

> A rich person's wealth is his strong city.
>> Poverty ruins poor people. (Prov 10:15)

> One person pretends to be rich, but has nothing,
>> another person pretends to be poor, but has great wealth. (Prov 13:7)

Neither of these proverbs gives any guidance. They tell what life is like
without recommending or even implying a course of action. It is important when
encountering these proverbs not to read them as advising a certain course of action.

The Observation and Conclusion

Some proverbs not only observe life, they also offer a conclusion about
what has been observed. These sayings *imply* that a wise person will take a certain a course of action without directly commending that course of action. For
some sayings the implication is gentle:

> A fulfilled desire is sweet to the soul,
>> and turning from evil is a disgusting thing to fools. (Prov 13:19)

Some have a stronger implication as to the correct mode of behavior that a godly
person will have:

> Insolence only produces quarrels,
>> but wisdom is with those who take advice. (Prov 13:10)

Still others come close to recommending a course of action without actually recommending it:

The person who walks with wise people becomes wise,
>but a companion of fools will be harmed. (Prov 13:20)

The majority of the sayings in Proverbs fall into this category of observation and conclusion.

Command and Prohibition

A number of sayings in proverbs commend certain actions. Other sayings forbid some actions. In many cases these are found in the same proverbs:

Discipline your son while there is hope,
and do not make yourself responsible for his death. (Prov 19:20)

Do not love sleep, or you will become poor.
Keep you eyes open, and you will have enough to eat. (Prov 20:13)

However, some sayings contain only one:

Commit your efforts to Yahweh,
>and your plans will be firm (Prov 16:3)

Occasionally a command or prohibition will also include the reason for the advice that is given:

Do not rob a poor person because he is poor,
and do not crush an oppressed person in the city gate,
>because Yahweh will defend their cause
>and deprive those who deprive them of life. (Prov 22:22–23)

Do not befriend a hot-tempered person,
and do not associate with a hothead,
>otherwise you will learn his path,
>>and set a trap for yourself. (Prov 22:24–25)

The Spectrum of Advice

All of these differing levels of advice in Proverbs are meant to help the reader ponder God's wisdom as it is revealed in the book. Each saying must be understood in its own right as falling somewhere on a spectrum of advice that offers some amount of guidance and leaves some amount of choice to the reader as to how and when to implement the advice. The spectrum could be diagrammed as:

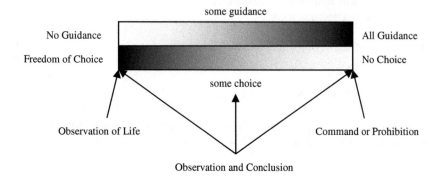

20
Ecclesiastes

What is the point of life? Where can a person find ultimate meaning for life? These questions have occupied humans in every generation and continue to be at the core of great philosophical debates. The writer of Ecclesiastes was also interested in these questions, but pursued them from a unique perspective. He sought to know whether humans could discover any lasting purpose and meaning for life by their own efforts and through their own search for that meaning without any help from God. His search and his conclusion ultimately led him back to God.

1. Authorship — *Several Theories of Authorship*
2. Theme — *Life from a Human Perspective Is Like a Vapor*
3. Law and Gospel in Ecclesiastes — *Understanding God's Promises Give Meaning to Life in a Sinful World*
4. Overview of the Book — *What is Ecclesiastes All About?*

1. Authorship

Ecclesiastes comes from "Qoheleth, son of David, king in Jerusalem" (Eccl 1:1). The unusual word *Qoheleth* derives from the Hebrew root *qhl*, which signifies an action of assembling or collecting. The meaning of this word is debated, but most English versions, following Luther's German version, translate this word as *preacher*, assuming it means someone who speaks to an assembly of people. Others offer *teacher* or simply use the Hebrew word *Qoheleth*. The ancient Greek translation was *ecclesiastes,* which means a member of a regularly summoned assembly. This Greek translation has given the book its name in English.

While we may not know exactly what Qoheleth signifies, the designation of the book's source as a son of David and king in Jerusalem narrows the field to only the kings from Solomon to Zedekiah (since the Hebrew word for *son* can signify any male descendant). However, this is designation is later narrowed to "king over Israel in Jerusalem" (Eccl 1:12). The only person who could claim to be both son of David and king of Israel (and not simply king over Judah) was Solomon. Therefore, Ecclesiastes was traditionally viewed as the work of Solomon.

Yet, for several reasons many scholars have argued that the author could not have been Solomon. First, they point to the unusual Hebrew grammar and vocabulary of the book, which is usually taken as an indication that the book was written much later than Solomon's day. However, the Hebrew used in Ecclesiastes does not share the characteristics of Hebrew that mark other documents in any era before 200 BC with the exception of Songs of Songs, which is also difficult to date and also traditionally attributed to Solomon. (200 BC is the latest possible date for the writing of Ecclesiastes, since Ecclesiastes is mentioned in Ben Sira, which was written about 200 BC) Thus, the unusual Hebrew is no guide to the date of the composition of Ecclesiastes.

Secondly, they note several words used in Ecclesiastes may be loan words from ancient Persian, such as *pardēs*, park (Eccl 2:5), a word that is used only in Song of Songs (4:13) and the Persian era book Nehemiah (Neh 2:8) and *pitgām*, edict, decree (Eccl 8:11), a word that is used elsewhere only in books set in the Persian era: Esther (Esth 1:20), Ezra (Ezra 4:17, 5:7, 11; 6:11; all in Aramaic) and Daniel (Dan 3:16; 4:14; both in Aramaic). If these are loan words from Persian, they could indicate that Ecclesiastes was written during the Persian era or later. However, these words may come from India into both Persian and Hebrew, and, therefore may serve as no reliable guide as to the date of the book. Since Solomon imported goods from many far away countries, he may well have had contact with India.

Finally, these scholars note that outside of Ecclesiastes 1 and 2, Qoheleth's description of himself does not seem to match Solomon. Most often it is noted that statements later in the book are critical of kings or seem to advise others as to their behavior before kings:

> A poor and wise youth is better than an old and foolish king who does not know how to take advice anymore. (Eccl 4:13)

> If the anger of the ruler rises against you, do not resign your position, because calmness will lay great errors to rest. (Eccl 10:4)

Yet none of these or similar statements in Ecclesiastes absolutely prove that Solomon was not the author. He may well have been king and yet, because of his God-given wisdom, also may have been critical of kings in general and offered advice as to how to deal with them.

If, according to this view, Solomon did not write Ecclesiastes, who did? One answer often given is that it was written by someone in the Persian era or later. This person was not claiming to be Solomon, but in the first two chapters of Ecclesiastes adopted Solomon's persona for the purpose of exploring wisdom in the name of the wise king. This persona was then abandoned for the rest of the book. Thus, it is claimed that no deception was involved on the part of the author. The problem with this view is that the author claims to have been king and gives no indication that he is merely assuming a persona in order to engage in philosophical exploration.

Another view notes that several passages in Ecclesiastes speak about Qoheleth as if the writer is writing about another person, in contrast to the first person pronoun *I*, which is used throughout most of the book:

> "Completely vaporous!" *said Qoheleth*, "Completely vaporous! Everything is vapor!" (Eccl 1:2)

> "Look, this is what I have found," *said Qoheleth*, "Adding one thing to another to find a meaning." (Eccl 7:27)

> "Completely vaporous!" *said the Qoheleth*, "Everything is vapor!" *Not only was Qoheleth wise, but he also taught the people knowledge and heard and searched and arranged many proverbs. Qoheleth sought to find pleasant words; correct things were written—words of truth.* (Eccl 12:8–10)

These passages may imply that the bulk of the words in Ecclesiastes originated with Solomon, but that they were recorded and arranged by some later editor. If this is the case, one could speak in some sense of Solomon as the author of Ecclesiastes, since the bulk of the book comes from him. At the same time, we can perhaps speak of a later editor who brought together Solomon's thoughts and added a few comments, most especially the final advice in the book (Eccl 12:8–14).

Theories on the Authorship of Ecclesiastes

Author	*Evidence*
Solomon	Ecclesiastes 1:1, 12
Solomon + a later editor	Ecclesiastes 1:1, 12 + Ecclesiastes 1:2; 7:27; 12:8–10
Someone in the Persian era or later	Unusual Hebrew grammar; possible loan words from Persian; some statements considered not appropriate for Solomon to make

2. Theme

At the beginning and end of Ecclesiastes we find nearly identical statements:

"Completely vaporous!" said Qoheleth, "Completely vaporous! Everything is vapor!" (Eccl 1:2)

"Completely vaporous!" said Qoheleth, "Everything is vapor!" (Eccl 12:8)

These verses are often said to present Qoheleth's theme. The word *vapor* is often translated *vanity* to signify futility of human existence that Qoheleth sees. Qoheleth uses the Hebrew word for vapor thirty-eight times to express his frustration with human existence in the world. Since life is like a vapor, humans often are frustrated that there seems to be nothing that is permanent that one can grasp and hold and that will never disappoint (Eccl 1:14). Also, life's accomplishments seem as transient as vapors that can vanish into thin air as quickly as they appeared (Eccl 2:1, 11). Some experiences of life are disgusting, like a foul-smelling vapor (Eccl 4:8). Moreover, as nothing can be done to control a vapor, and it eventually disperses into the air, so also death eventually brings all people to the same end, and nothing can be done about it (Eccl 2:15).

However, these two verses do not present the entire theme of Ecclesiastes. When Qoheleth says that everything is vapor, he does not mean everything in heaven and earth. This can be seen by the qualifying phrases *under the sun* which occurs twenty-nine times and *striving after the wind* which occurs seven times in Ecclesiastes. Qoheleth is saying, in effect, that all human effort (striving) in the realm of human existence (under the sun) is like a vapor. This is the key to understanding Qoheleth's message. Throughout the book he explores the human condition. He seeks to find meaning and permanence through human wisdom, through work and professional life, through joy and pleasure, through riches and wealth. Yet, each of these fails and proves once again that human life *from a strictly human perspective* is like a vapor.

This leads to another important accent in Ecclesiastes: only God can give meaning in life because God, who does not change, is permanent and unchanging, unlike the vapor of human existence. Note some of the passages in which God alone gives things that are worthwhile to humans or does things which cannot be undone:

There is nothing better for a person than that he should eat and drink and make his life good in his labor. This, also, I saw was from the hand of God. (Eccl 2:24)

> I saw that everything that God has done endures forever. Nothing can be added to it and nothing can be taken away. God has done it so that they will fear him. (Eccl 3:14)

> Consider the work of God, because who is able to straighten what he has bent? (Eccl 7:13)

> Though a sinner does evil a hundred times and prolongs his life, yet I also know that it will be well for those who fear God because they fear him. (Eccl 8:12)

> But all this I took to heart, clarifying all of this, that the righteous and the wise and their deeds are in the hand of God. Whether it is love or hate, a person does not know all that is before him. (Eccl 9:1)

Therefore, the book ends by advising:

> The end of the matter: all has been heard. Fear God and keep his commands, for this is all humans have. (Eccl 12:13)

Thus, we can conclude that the theme of Ecclesiastes is that life from a human perspective is like a vapor, and only a relationship with God ("fearing God") can give meaning and purpose to life.

3. Law and Gospel in Ecclesiastes

Once the theme of Ecclesiastes is understood, the dynamics of God's Law and his Gospel are easily seen. Qoheleth uses the Law primarily to force humans to see the futility of their situation apart from God. This is the classic theological ("second use") of the Law. A few examples are:

> The wise person has his eyes in his head, but the fool walks in darkness. Yet I know that one fate befalls all of them (Eccl 2:14)

> I praised the dead who are already dead above the living who are still alive. But better than both is the person who has never been. He has not seen the evil deeds done under the sun. (Eccl 4:2–3)

> Indeed, there is no righteous man on earth who does good and never sins. (Eccl 7:20)

> This is an evil in all that is done under the sun, because there is one fate for all.
> Also, the heart of the children of Adam is full of evil, and madness is in their
> hearts during their lives. Afterwards they go to the dead. (Eccl 9:3)

Over and over again throughout Ecclesiastes everything that Qoheleth examines
in his wisdom leads him to the same conclusion: all people are sinners and all
meet the same end: death.

This is not to say that other uses of the Law are absent. In a number of cases
Qoheleth used the Law to curb evil behavior by warning of the consequences of
sin (first use of the Law):

> When a sentence against an evil deed is not carried out quickly, then the heart
> of the children of Adam is encouraged to do evil. (Eccl 8:11)

> Because of laziness the rafters sag, and because of negligent hands the house
> leaks. (Eccl 10:18)

On occasion the Law is also a guide for those who seek to please God (third
use of the Law):

> Guard your feet when you go to the house of God and go near to listen rather
> than offer the sacrifices that fools bring, because they do not know that they are
> doing evil. (Eccl 4:17)

Thus, through all of Qoheleth's wisdom and examination of the human situation the Law leads him to the conclusion that without God humans will see
misery and death. This does not mean that they should willfully sin, because
God judges (Eccl 3:17; 5:5), and he also reaches out to his creatures who fear
him and watches over them (Eccl 8:12).

This leads to the Gospel in Ecclesiastes: it is God who grants humans good
things and gives meaning to life. They are unable to find good, but God brings
them to good things and blesses them physically and spiritually (Eccl 2:24; 5:18,
20; 8:15; 9:1, 7; 12:7). Indeed, Qoheleth emphasizes that

> I saw that everything that God has done endures forever. Nothing can be added
> to it and nothing can be taken away. God has done it so that they will fear him.
> (Eccl 3:14)

And Ecclesiastes notes that all true wisdom comes from God, who is a Shepherd, guarding his flock (Eccl 12:11).

While these Gospel passages are few in Ecclesiastes, they stand out in bold
relief to the constant threat of the Law. Through the hammer of the Law both

Qoheleth and his readers are driven to God and his promises. It is in these brief glimpses of God's blessing and mercy that comfort is found. Thus, the Gospel becomes the only sure refuge and hope for human drowning in a sea of the Law's condemnation throughout Ecclesiastes.

4. Overview of the Book

Ecclesiastes

Title (1:1)
Thematic observations: Reasons life is like a vapor (1:2–11)
Qoheleth the king discovers that life is like a vapor (1:12—2:26)
      Wisdom fails to give meaning to life
      Pleasures fail to give meaning to life
      Both the wise man and the fool will die
      Work fails to give meaning to life
God has determined a time for everything (3:1–22)
      Examples of a time for everything
      Exploring what God does among humans
Disappointments in life (4:1–16)
      Oppression
      Labor
      Greed
      Popularity
Advice (5:1–20)
      Honor God
      The futility of jealousy and greed
God gives wealth, but humans cannot keep their wealth (6:1–12)
Wise observations and advice about life (7:1—11:6)
Youth and old age (11:7—12:7)
Thematic observation restated (12:8)
Qoheleth's wisdom is recommended to the reader (12:9–12)
The conclusion: fear God and keep his commands (12:13–14)

Ecclesiastes is difficult to outline, since Qoheleth's thoughts do not move in a linear, logical progression. Instead, his method is to move from one topic to the next, sometimes allowing the reader to see connections between topics, other times digressing to expand upon previously discussed topics, and still other times having no obvious logical connection between topics. In this way the organization of the book itself illustrates that life is like vapor: it cannot be grasped, it is elusive, and it is frustrating. In the end, one's only hope is to trust and rely on God ("fear God").

21
Song of Songs

Love between a man and a woman in marriage, including its sexual dimension, was part of God's design for humans and preceeded the fall into sin (Gen 2:20–25). Despite the corruption that sin brings to marriage and sexuality (a corruption evidenced not only in modern society, but also in the pages of Scripture), these remain gifts of God in which God's people can rejoice. The Song of Songs shows us this marvelous gift of God as the two main characters in the book rejoice in their love and desire for emotional and physical intimacy with each other. At the same time, as God's people read this book it also raises another question: Is the love and closeness that a man and woman might experience a reflection of God's love and closeness to his people?

1. Authorship — *Several Theories of Authorship*
2. Theme — *Human Love/Divine Love*
3. Approaches to Interpreting Song of Songs — *Which Is in View: God's Love for His People or Love Between a Man and a Woman?*
4. Overview of the Book — *What is Contained in Song of Songs?*

1. Authorship

This book begins, "The song of songs which is Solomon's" (Song 1:1). Already in ancient times this was understood to name Solomon as the author, and is the most natural reading of the book's opening. Solomon in his wisdom was associated with song writing (1 Kgs 4:32). However, in more recent times this opening has been interpreted to mean several things including:

Subject matter: the book is about (but not written by) Solomon; (Song 3:7, 9, 11; 8:11, 12)
Dedication: the book is dedicated to Solomon
Tradition: the book is written in the wisdom tradition of Solomon

The reason for these other interpretations is doubt over whether Solomon could have written Song of Songs. Some argue that the unusual language of the Song indicates a late date (see the discussion of the authorship of Ecclesiastes in Chapter 20 for a similar approach). Others question whether Solomon, known for having many wives, would have been an appropriate author for a book about marriage and fidelity. Still others note the minimal role that Solomon plays in the book, being mentioned in only three passages (Song 1:5; 3:7–11; 8:11–12).

None of these arguments is decisive against Solomonic authorship. Arguments on the basis of language are difficult to prove, especially for ancient Hebrew. Moreover, it should be noted that the closest parallel in Hebrew grammar and language to Song is Ecclesiastes, another book long associated with Solomon. While it is true that Solomon had many wives, this does not automatically disqualify him from writing about human fidelity, especially if the book was written early in his life before his many marriages and before his foreign wives led him into idolatry (1 Kgs 11:4). While Solomon plays a small role in this book, it does not imply that he did not write Song of Songs. Indeed, many authors do not include themselves in their books at all.

Other features of Song appear to point to Solomon as the author. Jerusalem is mentioned throughout the book. In addition, many other places in and around both Israel and Judah are mentioned: Kedar, En Gedi, Sharon, Lebanon, Gilead, Amana, Senir, Mount Hermon, Tirzah, Shulam, Heshbon, Bath Rabbim, Damascus, Mount Carmel and Baal Hamon. Such a broad range of places is most appropriate given the cosmopolitan nature of Solomon's kingdom. The mention of many spices in the book may point to a time of great international trade appropriate to Solomon's day. The large variety of plants mentioned in the book coincides with Solomon's interest in botany (1 Kgs 4:33).

Given all of the evidence, there is no compelling reason to eliminate Solomon as the author of this wisdom book. This makes the most likely date of its composition sometime during Solomon's reign in the early tenth century BC.

2. Theme

"Let him kiss me with the kisses of his mouth, for your love is better than wine," begins the first poem in the Song of Songs. Very clearly this book contains rich imagery of human love including its most intimate physical manifestations. The comparison of the enjoyment of love between a man and a woman to many sensual delights (e.g., "better than wine") heightens this effect. Nor does the book shy away from sexual imagery. At one point the man says of his beloved,

> How beautiful and how pleasant you are, My Love, with all your delights!
> Your stature is like a palm tree,
> and your breasts like its clusters,
> I said, "Let me climb the palm tree
> and take hold of its fruit."

Your breasts are like clusters of the vine,
and the fragrance of your breath is like apples;
the roof of your mouth is like the best wine,
flowing smoothly for my beloved,
gliding over the lips of those who sleep. (Song 7:6–10)

However, it would be a mistake to state that this book is about the mutual love of a woman and a man and leave it at that. The book takes great pains to set this relationship in the context of marriage. Throughout the book the two lovers long for their wedding day, and seek to express their love within the confines of this God-ordained relationship. This is seen by the refrain "do not awaken or arouse love until it pleases." (Song 2:7; 3:5; 8:4) This refrain reminds the reader that there is a God-pleasing institution for sexual intimacy. This is made even more explicit in the final chapter of Song of Songs, where the young woman's brothers speak and she responds:

"We have a little sister, and she has no breasts.
What shall we do for our sister on the day she is spoken for?
If she is a wall, we will build a barricade of silver on her,
but if she is a door, we will bind on her cedar planks."
"I am a wall, and my breasts are like towers;

Then, in his eyes I was like one who finds peace.

Solomon had a vineyard in Baal Hamon.
He gave the vineyard to caretakers.
Each was to bring to him one thousand silver shekels for its fruit.
My vineyard, which is mine, is before me,
The thousand shekels are yours, Solomon,
and two hundred for the caretakers of its fruit." (Song 8:8–12)

These highly metaphorical lines speak of the brother's wish to guard their sister's chastity until she is married. She, in turn, speaks of her chastity and promises her love to Solomon. Therefore, Song of Songs speaks of love between a man and a woman properly expressed in marriage.

However, there is still more to its message. We are also told near the end of the book:

Set me as a seal upon your heart,
like a seal on your arm,
because love is as strong as death,
passion is as severe as the grave.

Its flames are flames of fire,
a blazing flame of Yah(weh). (Song 8:6)

As this passage indicates, the love in this book is a love given and sustained by Yahweh. God, who created humans male and female and blessed them (Gen 1:27–28), is the one who gives them the ability to love one another in marriage. Thus, we could conclude that the theme developed throughout Song of Songs is God's gift of love between a man and a woman and all that it entails is properly expressed in fidelity to one's partner in marriage.

3. Approaches to Interpreting Song of Songs

Although the theme of Song of Songs seems clear on its surface, there have always been questions about how to properly interpret the book. Three basic approaches have been taken to understanding Song of Songs.

The Allegorical Interpretation

Early Jewish and Christian interpreters often understood Song of Songs as an allegory. That is, though on the surface it speaks of human love, the real message of the book is God's love for his people. Since Song is viewed as an allegory, virtually every detail of the book is said to symbolize a spiritual truth. Thus, writing around A.D. 200, the church father Hippolytus understood the woman's two breasts (Song 4:5) as the Old and New Testaments.

The problem with the allegorical interpretation is immediately obvious to those who study any of the ancient and medieval interpreters who followed this approach. One can claim that the various details of Song of Songs illustrate specific spiritual truths, but one cannot demonstrate that the identifications made by any interpreter are what were intended by the author. There is no way to prove one allegorical interpretation to be superior to another. The allegorical method degenerates into guesswork and private opinion. For this reason few interpreters today would endorse this approach.

Why then, was the allegorical method so popular for so long among Christians and Jews? One reason was the embarrassment many felt over the frank and open discussion of sexuality in Song of Songs. Many simply felt that this was out of place among the books of Scripture. When this was coupled with the medieval Christian emphasis on celibacy as a higher calling than marriage, there was a strong reason to deny that the surface meaning of Song of Songs was the meaning intended by its author.

Moreover, since Song of Songs mentions God only at one point (Song 8:6), many felt pressure to justify it as a holy book with a truly scriptural message.

Since the Scriptures as several points speak of God's relationship to his people under the metaphor of a marriage relationship (e.g., Hosea), the allegorical approach appealed to this perceived need to justify it as a holy book worthy of inclusion in the canon of Scripture.

The Natural or Literal Interpretation

With the rejection of the allegorical approach, many interpreters have favored reading Song of Songs according to its surface meaning. It is simply a wisdom book dedicated to celebrating human love as a gift of God to be enjoyed within the institution of marriage. Many Christian interpreters see the Song of Songs as endorsing a proper relationship of husband and wife in a marriage characterized by companionship, mutual support and sexuality expressed according to the will of God. The Song is then interpreted according to a number of schemes that seek to divide the book into several sections. Several popular approaches are:

A Love Story Involving Two Main Characters

This approach, which is at least as old as the church father Theodore of Mopsuestia (c. 350–428), sees Song of Songs as a series of connected poems that narrate a story about two lovers who anticipate their wedding day. The two are Solomon and a young Shulammite woman. The several poems climax in the last scene, where the marriage covenant is ratified in the Shulammite's home (Song 8:5–14). While taking seriously the book's message on love between a man and a woman in marriage, a weakness with this approach is that there is no clear indication of a narrative that runs throughout the book and connects all of its parts into a coherent story.

A Love Story Involving Three Main Characters

This approach, which is at least as old as the Jewish scholar Ibn Ezra (c. 1089–1164), is similar to the previous one, but sees two men involved in seeking the Shulammite as a bride. In this interpretation the Shulammite's beauty has caught the attention of King Solomon, but she loves and is loved by a simple country shepherd. The Song's message is one of the superiority of true love over a legally arranged marriage. This approach, like the two-character interpretation, cannot point to a clear narrative thread that runs throughout Song of Songs.

A Series of Love Poems

Finally, many contemporary scholars view Song of Songs as simply an anthology of love poems. This approach has been popularized most recently by Marcia Falk in her influential English translation and notes on Song of Songs. Often these love songs are seen as songs originally sung for a bride or a bridal party in preparation for a wedding. The major problem confronting this approach to reading the Song of Songs is that the book is very difficult to divide into distinct poems. Often within Song of Songs there are no clearly defined boundaries that would indicate where one poem ends and another begins.

The Analogical Interpretation

This interpretation understands Song of Songs according to its surface meaning: it encourages human love as a gift of God to be enjoyed within the institution of marriage. However, at the same time, it views the book as also intended to allow readers to understand more fully God's relationship with his people. Unlike the allegorical interpretation, this approach does not seek to find a spiritual interpretation of every detail of the book. Instead, much like Paul's approach to understanding marriage in Ephesians 5:21–33, the relationship between the lovers in Song of Songs is not only intended to teach about the proper expression of the love, but also is intended to remind God's people of his relationship with them through an extended analogy that compares marriage to the relationship between God (the husband) and his people (the bride). Thus, this interpretation helps the reader not only understand God's intention that men and women express their love for each other within marriage, but also helps them apply this to their relationship with God through an analogy used elsewhere in Scripture (e.g., Jer 31:32).

4. Overview of the Book

Although the Song of Songs is difficult to divide into sections, the following is one of a number of possible outlines and serves only to offer a guide to the book's contents. The speeches of the woman and the man can be distinguished not only by indicators that are obvious in English translations but also are indicated in Hebrew, which has different words for *you* in the feminine and masculine genders.

Superscription (1:1)

The Shulammite yearns for her beloved (1:2–4)

The Shulammite modestly describes her appearance (1:5–6)

The Shulammite and her beloved seek to meet one another (1:7–8)

The king admires his beloved's beauty (1:9–11)

The Shulammite anticipates intimacy with the king (1:12–14)

The lovers rejoice in each others beauty (1:15–17)

The lovers seek to share each others' love (2:1–7)

The Shulammite sees her beloved coming and anticipates their union (2:8–17)

The Shulammite seeks her beloved, finds him and brings him to her mother's home (3:1–5)

Solomon's wedding procession (3:6–11)

The king describes his beloved's appearance (4:1–7)

The bride and groom go away together to a garden feast (4:8—5:1)

The Shulammite dreams of her beloved's arrival, but he is to be found in the garden (5:2–6:3)

The king describes his beloved's appearance (6:4–10)

The Shulammite in the nut grove is called to return (6:11–13)

The king describes his beloved's appearance (7:1–9)

The Shulammite invites her beloved to share an intimate relationship (7:10—8:4)

The power of love (8:5–7)

The Shulammite's brothers seek to guard her virtue, and she declares her virtue (8:8–12)

The king and the Shulammite seek each other's love (8:13–14)

Section 5
The Prophets

22

Introduction to the Prophets

Most people, when asked to define what a prophet is would probably reply that it is a person who speaks about the future with words of warning, hoping to change people's behavior in the present. This description of a prophet would fit the biblical prophets, but would fall short of accurately describing their message and mission. The prophets of the Bible were individuals chosen directly by God to be his spokesmen. Though they often pointed to the future, their message was not simply one of doom and warning. The prophets also brought messages of hope and comfort because they declared the entire word of God, both Law and Gospel. God raised up prophets to call his people to repentance for their sins, so the prophets were indeed messengers who came with warnings of the failure to repent. However, for those who repented and turned to God they were also messengers of hope and forgiveness and spokesmen for the hope of salvation through the Messiah.

1. The Prophets and Their Ministry—*What Made a Person a Prophet and What Was Their Message?*
2. A Chronology of the Prophets—*When Did the Prophets Minister to Israel?*
3. The Prophets As a Collection—*Why Are These Books Arranged This Way?*
4. Important Concepts in the Prophets—*What Themes and Motifs Do the Prophets Share with Each Other?*

1. The Prophets and Their Ministry

The Prophets and Their Call

While the seventeen books gathered together to form the section of the Old Testament that Christians call the Prophetic Books present several centuries of prophetic activity, they do not represent all of the prophets God sent to Israel. The Old Testament tells us of other men whom God raised up to be prophets such as Samuel, Gad, Iddo, Elijah and Elisha as well as women like Deborah and Huldah. What set these servants of God apart as prophets? The answer is that the prophets had a call from God. In most cases this was an **immediate call**, that is, the Lord called them to be prophets directly, without any person or persons used by God as an intermediary to place them into the prophetic office. The first such calling or choosing of a prophet is the account of Moses at the burning bush in Exodus 3. Several other prophets also describe their call as coming from God, often in a vision. Such accounts are given by the prophets Isaiah (Isa 6), Jeremiah (Jer 1), Ezekiel (Ezek 1–3) and Amos (Amos 7). An exception to this pattern of prophets receiving immediate calls is the prophet Elisha, whom God called through a **mediate call**, a call that came through another person, in this case, Elijah (1 Kgs 19). In contrast to prophets, priests in the Old Testament and pastors in the church today receive their office only through mediate calls. But whether the call for a prophet was directly from God or came from God through someone else, prophets were chosen by God as his spokesmen.

This is why at times the Old Testament distinguished true prophets of God from false prophets. Anyone could claim to have a call from God, but God desired that his people listen only to those whose claim to have a call from him was true. Only prophets who had been called by God could preach an absolutely trustworthy message. This is why Moses warned the people of Israel about false prophets and instructed them so that they could distinguish between true prophets of God and those whose claim to the prophetic office was false (Deut 18:15–22). On the other hand, God expected his people to listen and respond to the preaching of his prophets. Failure to listen to a prophet was failure to listen to and obey God himself, since he had sent the prophet.

At times Israel did not want to hear the word of God. Instead, the people wanted to believe the words of a false prophet, because the false prophet would tell them what they wanted to hear instead of calling them to repent of sins. The confrontation between Jeremiah and Hananiah was a confrontation between God's prophet who spoke words the people did not want to hear and a false prophet who gave the people false comfort by preaching a message that they were prepared to accept, even if it was false (Jer 28).

The Message of the Prophets

As God's spokesmen, the prophets declared God's word to particular circumstances faced by Israel at particular times. Since they were speaking God's word, their message consisted of both Law and Gospel applied to Israel's specific problems and challenges. The prophets often spoke stern words of judgment because Israel had strayed from God's Law and placed their faith in the gods of the nations. They called the people to repent of their sins. But the prophets also frequently spoke of God's love for Israel, his offer of forgiveness and life for those who turned back to Yahweh in repentance and faith.

Therefore, the prophets were messengers of God's promises to his people. At times these promises were **conditional promises**. Such promises of God would only come to the people if they met conditions that God required. God's promise of victory to Israel's king Joash given through the prophet Elisha (2 Kgs 13:14–19) was a conditional promise. The promise of long life in the land connected to the fourth commandment is another example of a conditional promise (Exod 20:12; Deut 5:16). However, the most important promises of God preached by the prophets were **unconditional promises**. These promises required nothing of God's people and were purely gifts of God that his people neither earned nor deserved. The promise of God's abiding love for Israel and his promise of the Messiah were unconditional promises. Conditional promises were sometimes given to Israel, mainly to encourage them to trust in God for earthly blessings he wanted to give them. However, the Gospel was the most important message preached by all of the prophets and it is based on the unconditional promises of God. Therefore, the prophets' goal was to preach so that Israel came to trust in God's promises of eternal life which would be won for them through the Messiah. The prophets did not preach the Gospel in the abstract, however. God sent them to apply the Gospel to the immediate circumstances that his people faced. The prophets were his instruments to move the people to trust God for their immediate needs and then to lift their eyes beyond their immediate situation so that they would trust God for all things, including eternal life.

Studying the Prophets' Recorded Works

While the Old Testament tells us of many prophets that God sent to his people, besides Moses only sixteen of these prophets contributed a record of the words they preached as books in the Old Testament. The first of these literary prophets were from the eighth century BC, and the last were from the fifth century. During these four hundred years God inspired his prophets not only to preach and minister to his people, but also to record their words for future generations. Their books, along with Lamentations, comprise the fourth major section of the Old Testament. However, the books of the prophets are not arranged in chronological order in modern Bibles. So a study of these prophets is best done by rearranging them and studying them in roughly chronological sequence. When this is done, a number of connections and themes emerge and allow us to see the prophets in their own context. In this way the message of a particular prophet can be compared to the message of other contemporary prophets. Additional comparisons with prophets who came before or after them can also be made more easily if we follow a chronological arrangement. Therefore, unlike our study of the other sections of the Old Testament, in the next chapters we will follow the prophets era-by-era in order to better understand their words.

2. A Chronology of the Prophets

Modern books are often easy to date. Due to desires of authors and publishers to protect copyrights, almost every book has a date on its opening pages. Due to historical records, it is often possible to have an accurate idea of when books were written even before copyright notices began to be used. However, in antiquity many authors did not date their works. Others tell us only of the general historical setting of their composition. Therefore, scholars often study ancient works to determine when they were written. In the case of the prophets, some are easily dated, since these prophets tell us who was king when they prophesied. Some even tell us the year, month and day when they prophesied. Other prophets refer in their prophecy to contemporary events that give us a good idea of the historical setting of their ministry. However, a few of the prophets give us few reliable clues as to their exact historical situation. Thus, the dates for the prophets range from approximations to exact dates. In the case of two prophetic books—Obadiah and Joel—scholars are unable to definitively state when they were written. In fact, both of these books have led scholars to propose several dates as to when they were written. In the following chapters the date of composition of each prophetic book will be discussed. Below is a general summary of the dates or possible range of dates of the ministry of the prophets and their books.

Jonah	c. 790 BC
Joel	c. 790 BC??
Amos	c. 791—c. 753 BC
Hosea	c. 752—c. 715 BC
Micah	c. 750—c. 715 BC
Isaiah	740—c. 701 BC
Nahum	c. 663—c. 612 BC
Zephaniah	c. 640—c. 609 BC
Habakkuk	c. 605 BC
Jeremiah	628—587 BC
Daniel	605—536 BC
Ezekiel	593—573 BC
Obadiah	580 BC??
Haggai	520 BC
Zechariah	520—c. 480 BC
Malachi	c. 430 BC

3. The Prophets As a Collection

Obviously, the Prophetic books are not arranged in strictly chronological order. What, then, is the logic behind arrangement of the Prophetic Books? A quick glance at a Bible will reveal that the longer books of the prophets precede the much shorter books. The first four prophets (Isaiah, Jeremiah, Ezekiel and Daniel) are often called the **Major Prophets** because these books are longer than the remaining twelve prophetic books, called the **Minor Prophets**. These labels do not reflect a judgment on the importance of the message of these books, but is only a characterization of the length of the prophet's book.

The Major Prophets are arranged from longest to shortest (with Lamentations following Jeremiah as a companion work). This arrangement also places them in roughly chronological order.[8]

The Minor Prophets are arranged in groups in a sort of chronological order. The first six books are four prophets from the eighth century (Hosea, Amos, Jonah, Micah) plus Joel and Obadiah, both of whom may have prophesied even earlier during the ninth century, although dating for either prophet is uncertain. The next three books (Nahum, Habakkuk, Zephaniah) are prophets of the seventh century. The final three books (Haggai, Zechariah, Malachi) are prophets of the post-exilic period in the sixth and fifth centuries.

Because the Minor Prophets are so short, it became customary in ancient times to collect them together and write them on one scroll. For this reason in the Jewish reckoning of the canon they are one book, the Book of the Twelve Prophets. This collection is mentioned already in the apocryphal book of Ben Sira (second century BC) and is probably mentioned as a collection by Stephen in the book of Acts (Acts 7:42).

4. Important Concepts in the Prophets

While each prophet's message was unique in its own right and tailored to speak directly to the lives of his hearers, there are several themes and recurring motifs that run throughout the prophets. We will now consider several of the more important of these.

The Legal Complaint as a Rhetorical Device

One rhetorical device that is used by several of the prophets is the legal complaint, often called by its Hebrew name the *rib* (pronounced *reeve*). This de-

---

[8] Although the first events in Daniel predate the call of Ezekiel, Daniel prophesied after Ezekiel had ceased his ministry, and his book was written after Ezekiel was completed.

vice was one of the ways the prophets would call Israel's attention to God's indictment of them for their sins. It enabled the prophets to persuade their hearers to look at the issue from the perspective of an impartial third party. In the case of the legal complaint that third party was made up of those who were addressed as judge and jury. (In ancient Israel there was often no distinction; one could act both as judge and jury.) The legal complaint includes a direct address to the judges and a complaint or indictment claiming that a wrong has been committed.

For instance, Isaiah used the legal complaint as a device to explain the meaning of the parable in his Song of the Vineyard (Isa 5:1–7). Although the vineyard represented the people of Judah, he also called on them to be judges of the vineyard:

> And now, Inhabitants of Jerusalem and Men of Judah, judge between me and my vineyard. What more was there to do for my vineyard that I have not done for it? When I looked for it to yield grapes, why did it yield wild grapes? (Isa 5:3–4)

In a similar manner Jeremiah appeals to the heavens as his jury as he indicts Judah for its sins. He appeals to the jury's emotional reaction, calling on them to be shocked by Judah's idolatry:

> "Be appalled at this, Heavens. Be shocked! Be utterly desolate," declares Yahweh, "because my people have committed two evils: They have forsaken me, the Fountain of Living Waters, and they have cut out cisterns for themselves, broken cisterns that cannot hold water." (Jer 2:12–13)

This fairly common rhetorical device used by many of the prophets drove home an important point to God's people about their sin: They had willingly entered into the covenant that God had graciously granted them at Mount Sinai. They wanted all the benefits of God's grace, but they often broke the Law by which God expected them to live. By depicting God as initiating a legal proceeding against a party that broke its solemn commitment to him, the prophets were emphasizing the grave importance of Israel's sins. At the same time, they were helping Israel to view those sins from a different perspective. Instead of viewing their sins from the perspective of a selfish, stiff-necked people who were intent following on their own self-destructive ways, the prophet's audience was invited to step outside their own perspective and view their sins as an impartial observer might view them. This was a powerful way to make Israel aware of its sins so that the prophet could follow his indictment with further prophecies pointing to God's offer of forgiveness and life to those who confessed their crimes against the Lord.

The Day of the Lord

Another way that the prophets drew attention to God's judgment on Israel was through the concept of the "Day of the Lord." This phrase is used in Isaiah, Jeremiah, Ezekiel, Joel, Amos, Obadiah, Zephaniah and Malachi. However, the concept of the day of the Lord can also be found in other prophetic books. This day is a reference to a time when God will execute judgment on his enemies (Jer 46:10), but will defend his faithful people (Joel 2:18). At times the day of the Lord refers to an event in the near future in when God will use the might of earthly kingdoms and powers to bring judgment (Zeph 1:7–13). However, such "days of the Lord" are only a preview of the ultimate judgment of God in the "great day of the Lord" (Zeph 1:14; Mal 4:5). This great day of the Lord is the final, **eschatological** judgment of God upon all people. The judgment not only can lead to the pouring out of God's wrath upon sinners, but can also be a judgment in favor of God's faithful people. Therefore, the day of the Lord has aspects of both Law and Gospel as it points to both punishment for sinners and deliverance for those who repent and trust in God.

By reminding their audience that the day of the Lord is coming and that it is inescapable, the prophets seek to drive their hearers to admit their sin and turn to God who alone can deliver them from the coming wrath. Everyone, no matter what nation they claim, must stand before God to be judged (Ezek 3:30; Joel 3:14). For those who have sinned and turned their backs on God, that judgment is a frightening and terrible prospect (Isa 13:6; Joel 2:1–2; Amos 5:18, 20). However, for those who have repented of their sins and turned to God with faith in his mercy, it is a day that they do not have to fear, because it is the day of their deliverance.

Unfortunately, there were those in Israel who assumed that deliverance on the day of the Lord was their right by birth, and they assumed they did not have to fear the day of the Lord, even though they had abandoned Yahweh and his covenant with them. The prophet Amos warned such people that although they longed for the day of the Lord, it would not be a pleasant day for them unless they repented:

> Woe to you who desire the day of Yahweh! Why do you want to have the day of Yahweh? It is darkness, and not light, as if a man fled from a lion, and a bear met him, or went into a house and leaned his hand against the wall, and a serpent bit him. Isn't the day of Yahweh darkness, and not light, and gloom with no brightness in it? (Amos 5:18–20)

Therefore, the prophets warned their hearers and us that no one can take God's love and mercy for granted. Their preaching about the day of the Lord was designed to stir those who heard their message out of their complacency and ease that they felt with their sins so that they would daily learn to rely on God, repenting of their sins and relying instead on God's mercy and eternal kindness.

Oracles to Gentile Nations

A number of the prophetic books contain the prophets' preaching about God's judgment on non-Israelite nations for their sins. For instance, Isaiah devotes no less than eleven chapters to eleven different oracles against Gentile nations (Isa 13—23). Except for the preaching of Jonah in Nineveh, all of these oracles to the nations were delivered to Israelites. What would be the point of preaching about God's punishment on the nations, if the nations themselves never heard them? The prophets were emphasizing three important truths.

First, by demonstrating that God would judge all nations, the prophets were proclaiming that Israel's God was different from the gods of the nations. The nations worshipped gods who were largely linked to their nation alone. Yahweh, however, claimed to be the God who created all nations and, therefore, had a claim upon everyone. When Israelites were tempted to worship the gods of the nations around them, the oracles against the nations reminded them that they were abandoning Yahweh for lesser gods who could not even keep their own nations' people safe from Yahweh's wrath. Moreover, these oracles also warned them that they could not escape judgment by Yahweh by seeking refuge with the nations and their gods.

Secondly, the oracles against the nations demonstrated that God was absolutely just and impartial in His judgment. He did not simply punish Israel for its sins while the nations would go unpunished for their transgressions. Instead, Yahweh was a God whose judgment condemned all sin, whether committed by a member of the chosen nation of Israel or by someone from a Gentile nation.

Finally, the oracles against the nations proclaimed God's love of His people as He promised to judge the nations who attacked and mistreated Israel. On the day of the Lord the nations would have to answer for their mistreatment of God's people. Faithful Israelites who trusted God's promise of love, forgiveness, mercy and eternal life, were encouraged beause His defense of His people would come when He punished the nations for their sins and deliver His people from those who oppressed them.

Therefore, the Gentile oracles were an important part of the prophets' declaration of both Law and Gospel. As Law they threatened punishment on sinners. As Gospel they pointed to God's deliverance from his people's enemies, ultimately assuring faithful Israelites that Yahweh would not only deliver his people from their enemies among human nations, but also serving as a reminder of His greater deliverance from the ancient spiritual enemies of God's people: sin, death and Satan. Of course, this deliverance would come through the long-promised Messiah.

Repentance

As already emphasized, one of the prophets' most important goals for their message was to produce repentance among Israel. Their preaching was not designed simply to amaze their hearers that God had inspired them with astoundingly insightful predictions about the future. Nor was it simply to alert them to the sinfulness of their behavior, making them feel bad about their acts of rebellion against God. Instead, the prophets desired to move God's people to repentance. That is, they sought to produce in their hearers true sorrow over their sins that had offended God and harmed their neighbors. Moreover, they sought to move their hearers from sorrow and hopelessness that their sins had condemned them before God to joy that God had promised them forgiveness and life as they were led to turn to God for mercy.

Therefore, the prophets continually reminded Israel that only God could save them, that "in Yahweh our God is the salvation of Israel" (Jer 3:23). This meant that the prophets also preached joy, the good new or Gospel, that in abandoning all hope of saving oneself by one's own works and trusting in God's surpassing power to save his people, they could find the joy of being freed from sin and death. They would be able to say, "I will trust, and will not be afraid, for the Lord is my strength and my song, and he has become my salvation" (Isa 12:2). They would express the joy of the forgiven people of God by saying "I will rejoice in the God of my salvation" (Hab 3:18).

Of course, this salvation would come as a result of God being willing to pay the price for his people's sin. The call to repentance was also a call to look again at the promise of the Messiah, who would bear the punishment that should have been poured out on humankind (Isa 52:13—53:12) so that all who repented and believed in him could find the joy of the Gospel of forgiveness and life.

Messianic Hope

While all of these other themes in the prophets are important, they all lead to the most important theme in the prophets and in the Old Testament as a whole: the Messianic promise, the true hope of God's people. The Pentateuch and the Historical Books traced this Messianic promise from the time it was first given to Adam and Eve (Gen 3:15) through Abraham, Isaac, Jacob and Judah until it was finally promised to David that the Messiah would come from his line (2 Sam 7:1–17; 1 Chr 17:1–15). The prophets continue this attention to God's great promise, often connecting the Messiah to the line of David. Thus, Isaiah calls him the "shoot from the stump of Jesse" or the "root of Jesse" (Isa 11:1, 10; Jesse was David's father). Amos tells of God's promise to raise up "the fallen booth of David" (Amos 9:11). Micah describes him as coming from David's ancestral town, Bethlehem (Mic 5:2). Ezekiel even depicts God describing the Messiah as "my servant David" (Ezek 34: 23, 24; 37: 24, 25).

However, the prophets also use many other descriptions of the Messiah. He will be Immanuel, "God with us" (Isa 7:14), the "Son of Man" (Dan 7:13), "the messenger of the covenant" (Mal 3:1) and "the Sun of Righteousness with healing in his wings" (Mal 4:2). To miss the messianic hope that runs throughout the prophet's preaching is to miss the point of their message. The prophets were sent by God to call Israel to repentance and give them hope. Without the Messiah to free God's people from their sins, there is no point to repentance. Without the Messiah who would suffer for God's people but also rise to rule them as the great king from the line of David, there is no hope for Israel or for the world. However, the prophets, while preaching about a wide variety of subjects, never lose sight of God's salvation. Their message continually returns to God's first promise to humankind after the fall—to send a Savior into the world through Israel so that all nations could be blessed (Gen 18:18; 22:18; 26:4; Ps 72:17; Mal 3:12).

23

Two Hard-to-Date Prophecies
Obadiah and Joel

Obadiah

Rivalries often become bitter when they are between people or groups who share a close connection. Sports rivalries between two high schools in the same town or neighboring towns or two colleges in the same state or neighboring states often lead to hard-fought contests. Rivalry between siblings dates back to the very beginning of humanity, as the story of Cain and Abel in Genesis 4 tells us. The Bible knows of other such rivalries, including that between Israel and her neighbor to the southeast, Edom. Not only were Israel and Edom close neighbors. They also shared a common ancestry and history of rivalry from the beginning, since Israel was descended from Jacob, and Edom was descended from Jacob's brother Esau. Obadiah's prophecy is a condemnation of Edom and a prophecy of Edom's coming destruction at the hands of the Babylonians. Obadiah is not simply a prophecy of revenge, however. Edom's hostility to Israel led it to aid others in attacking Jerusalem. Esau's descendants helped the invader commit atrocities against Judah's people, and God's prophet declared that God would hold Edom responsible for its role in helping the invader.

> 1. Authorship and Date—*Who Was Obadiah and When Did He Prophesy?*
> 2. Theme—*What Is Obadiah About?*
> 3. Overview of the Book—*The Contents of Obadiah*
> 4. Important Verse—*Obadiah 21*

1. Authorship and Date

Obadiah gives no direct indication of the date of his prophecy. Since there are eleven men in the Old Testament with this name (which means "servant of Yahweh"), even the prophet's name is of little help. However, based on Obadiah's description of Edom's role in aiding invaders who sacked Jerusalem (Obad 11–14),[9] scholars have proposed two dates for him and his prophecy:

1.   Jerusalem was attacked by the Philistines and Arabs during the reign of Jehoram (854–841 BC; 2 Kgs 8:20–22; 2 Chr 21:8–20). This would make the prophet a contemporary of Elisha, and date his prophecy sometime between 850 and 830 BC.
2.   The Babylonians attacked Judah and Jerusalem several times between 605 and 587 BC. This would make Obadiah a contemporary of Jeremiah and place his prophecy sometime between 605 and 533 BC, when Obadiah's prophecy of Edom's fall was fulfilled by Babylon's total subjugation of Edom.

While there is no way to be certain which of these dates may be correct, the later date seems more likely, given the close connection between Obadiah 1–7 and several verses in Jeremiah. This means that one-third of Obadiah is parallel in some way to Jeremiah.

Connections between Obadiah and Jeremiah		
Obad 1–4	Jer 49:14–16	Close parallels
Obad 5–7	Jer 49:9–10	Common phrases
Obad 7b	Jer 38:22a	Exact match

We know nothing about the author of this book besides his name (Obad 1:1). Whether he is the same person as one of the eleven men with this name mentioned elsewhere in the Old Testament or whether he is a twelfth Obadiah cannot be determined.

2. Theme

The theme that occupies the twenty-one short verses of Obadiah is the judgment on Edom for her sins against Judah. Edom's cruelty was inexcusable, because it betrayed a sinful antagonism against God's chosen people, a "brother nation" (Obad 12). For fourteen verses the prophet describes Edom's sinful behavior and prophecies that Edom's allies will turn on her and destroy her.

---

[9] Since Obadiah has only one chapter, usually only verse numbers are given when referring to specific passages.

However, Edom's doom and judgment serves as a backdrop to a greater judgment—the day of the Lord for all nations (Obad 15). Here the prophet first introduces the Gospel as he promises:

> But on Mount Zion there will be deliverance, and it shall be holy, and the house of Jacob shall possess its inheritance. (Obad 17)

The judgment on the nations not only brings doom, but it also brings blessing for God's people, Israel (Obad 20). The climax of the day of the Lord comes in Obadiah's final verse when "the kingdom will be the Lord's" (Obad 21).

3. Overview of the Book

Obadiah's twenty-one verses divide into three major sections:

I.   Introduction—The Lord's call to the nations to attack Edom (Obad 1)
II. Judgment on Edom (Obad 2–14)
III. The Day of the Lord (Obad 15–21)
    A.   The nations judged and Zion delivered (Obad 15–18)
    B.   The Lord's kingdom is established (Obad 18–21)

Joel

If you had to depict the great day of God's judgment, what would you use to describe or portray the wrath of the Almighty? Modern motion pictures have produced a number frightening depictions of the day of judgment, always with the intent to shock and horrify, but with little attempt to offer a way for viewers to find sure and certain escape or refuge from God's wrath. When Joel prophesied about the Day of the Lord, he chose an interesting analogy to make the wrath of God understandable to his audience: Joel chose to compare the execution of God's judgment on humans to a plague of locusts. These voracious insects periodically infest parts of Africa and the Near East. A single cloud of locusts can strip a tree bare in only a few hours. They can consume large plots of crops in only a few days. Their ability to reduce agricultural land to stubble make them feared as bringers of natural disasters of epic proportions. For Joel's original audience the choice of locusts as a picture of God's wrath was appropriate and produced a powerful picture, since many would have seen at least one locust plague in their lifetime.

1. Authorship and Date

Little is known about Joel other than the name of his father, Pethuel (Joel 1:1). His name is a common one that he shared with six other men in the Old Testament.

Since Joel gives no hint of historical events surrounding his prophecy, he is probably the most difficult prophet to assign a date. Scholars have proposed dates for his work as early as 800 BC or as late as 450 BC. Since Joel has literary connections to Amos, Obadiah, Micah, Zephaniah, Jeremiah and Ezekiel, it is not possible to use his style or language as an indication of date. The most likely time of his ministry seems to be an early date, perhaps during the reign of Uzziah (791–740 BC). This would make him a contemporary of Amos and slightly older than Isaiah and Micah.

Joel most likely was a prophet to Judah and lived in or near Jerusalem, since he frequently mentions both the nation and the city and is concerned about the land, its people, the holy mountain of Zion and the Temple (Joel 1:14; 2:1, 15, 23, 32; 3:1, 6, 8, 12, 16, 17, 18, 19, 20, 21).

2. Theme

Joel's great concern is to call the people of Judah to repentance before the "great and dreadful day of the Lord" (Joel 2:31). To expand this theme, Joel uses both Law and Gospel. The Law is most vividly seen in Joel's use of the plague of locusts that will devour the land (Joel 1:2–12; 2:1–11). He calls on all of the land of Judah, both people and priests, to mourn and fast because of their sins (Joel 1:6–14). The prophet urges his hearers to repent while they can, since the day of the Lord is a day of "darkness and gloom, clouds and blackness."

Joel does not want his people merely to put on an outward display of repentance with tearing of their clothes, dressing in sackcloth and fasting. Instead, he seeks to use his vision of the devouring locusts to move the inhabitants of Judah to genuine sorrow over their sins. He urges them:

"Even now," declares Yahweh, "return to me with all your heart, with fasting, with weeping, and with mourning; and rend your hearts, not your garments." Return to Yahweh, your God, for he is gracious and merciful, slow to anger, and abounding in steadfast love, and he relents over disaster. Who knows whether he will not turn and relent, and leave a blessing behind him, a grain offering and a drink offering for Yahweh your God? (Joel 2:12–14)

Therefore, Joel is not only a masterful preacher of God's wrath, but he is also a skillful prophet of the Gospel, who summons Judah to turn to God for escape from punishment. Those who trust in God's mercy can also look for him to bless them.

For this reason we should not think of Joel as simply a prophet of gloom and doom, but instead, as a prophet with the heart of a true pastor. He wants to turn his people from their sins and restore them to faith in God who alone can save them on the day of the Lord.

3. Overview of the Book

Joel's three short chapters cover two related topics: the day of the Lord and salvation that is found only in God.

I.   Superscription: the prophecy of Joel (1:1)

II. The plague of locusts as a foretaste of the day of the Lord (1:2—2:17)
- A. The locusts as a picture of God's wrath (1:2–12)
- B. A call for repentance (1:13–20)
- C. A second picture of the locusts as messengers of God's wrath (2:1–11)
- D. A second call for repentance (2:12–17)

III. God's salvation on the day of the Lord for all who repent and trust in Him (Joel 2:18–3:21)
- A. The Lord will bless his people and their land (2:18–27)
- B. The Lord will pour out his Spirit on his people (2:28–32)
- C. The Lord will judge the nations, but be a refuge for his people (3:1–16)
- D. The Lord will bless the land and bring forgiveness to his people (3:17–21)

24
Prophecy to Israel in the Eighth Century
Jonah, Amos and Hosea

Jonah

Some of the most fascinating and attention-grabbing books and movies depend on characters that do something unexpected or have something unexpected happen to them. The out-of-the-ordinary experience fascinates us and makes a story's plot interesting. Most people are familiar with Jonah because of its report of an out-of-the-ordinary event: a man who survives after being swallowed by a sea creature. However, there is another even more important and unexpected event in Jonah: the repentance of the people in the Assyrian city of Nineveh. It is this event that reveals the central theme of the book.

> 1. Authorship and Date—*Who Was Jonah and When Did He Prophesy?*
> 2. Theme—*What Is Jonah About?*
> 3. Overview of the Book—*The Contents of Jonah*

1. Authorship and Date

The book of Jonah is unique among the prophets in that it is entirely written in a narrative telling about Jonah's ministry to Nineveh. None of his preaching except "Forty more days and Nineveh will be overthrown" (Jonah 3:4) is recorded. Instead, the book is primarily about the experiences of the prophet.

Jonah was the son of Amittai and lived in the Israelite town of Gath Hepher in the territory of the tribe of Zebulun (Jonah 1:1; 2 Kgs 14:25). He prophesied during the time of the Israelite king Jeroboam II (793–753 BC).

The book that bears Jonah's name does not identify its author. Traditionally, Jonah has been considered the author of the book. However, because of the book depicts Jonah's preaching to the Gentiles and because of the account of Jonah in the belly of the sea creature, many higher-critical scholars claim the book was written after the Babylonian exile when Jews were living among the Gentiles. This argument fails on several counts, however. First, it assumes that the events in the book are fictional, and are only designed to give readers an object lesson about God's mercy toward all people, including the Gentiles. Secondly, it assumes that ministry to the Gentiles did not take place until after the exile.

The first assumption flows from the anti-supernatural bias of higher critical studies. Miracles, such as Jonah being swallowed by a fish and living to tell about it, are deemed impossible. However, it should be noted that Jesus tied his resurrection to the historicity of Jonah:

> But he [Jesus] answered them, "An evil and adulterous generation seeks a sign, but no sign will be given to it except the sign of the prophet Jonah. For just as Jonah was in the belly of the great fish three days and three nights, so the Son of Man will be three days and three nights in the heart of the earth. The men of Nineveh will rise up at the judgment with this generation and condemn it, because they repented at the preaching of Jonah. And, behold, something greater than Jonah is here." (Matt 12:39–41; see Matt 16:4; Luke 11:29–32)

Clearly, Jesus taught that Jonah was in the belly of the sea creature and that Jonah did indeed preach to the people of Nineveh. If these things did not happen, then Jesus did not rise from the dead. Therefore, Christians cannot be consistent in their faith if they reject the historicity of the events in Jonah while believing that Jesus rose from the dead.

The second assumption is invalidated by the Old Testament itself. During the eighth century there were several prophets who were concerned about Gentile nations, including Elijah and Elisha (1 Kgs 17:7–24; 2 Kgs 8:7–17) and Amos (Amos 1:3—2:16; 9:7, 12). Jonah's ministry to Nineveh is completely at home in the eighth century and does not need to be shifted into the post-exilic period because of its content.

While the book does not specifically identify Jonah as the author, he is the only one who would have known about many of the events depicted in the book (e.g., Jonah 1:17—3:2; 4:1–11). Therefore, it is best to understand the author to be Jonah or some other prophet who worked closely with him and to whom Jonah related the events of his ministry to Nineveh. Since the book prophesies the fall of Nineveh and God's lifting of his decree that Nineveh would fall within forty days of Jonah's preaching (Jonah 3:4, 10), it is unlikely that the book would have been written after the fall of Nineveh to the Medes and Babylonians in 612 BC. Instead, the book most likely was written by Jonah during his lifetime.

2. Theme

Every chapter of the book of Jonah emphasizes that God is a merciful God who hears those who call to him. Jonah brought danger to Gentiles sailors as he tried to avoid preaching to Nineveh. Instead, he went to Joppa and boarded a ship for Tarshish (probably ancient Tartessus on the coast of Spain). God sent a storm on the sea to stop Jonah. Eventually, Jonah is forced to admit to the sailors on the ship that he is the reason for the storm, since Yahweh, the God who made both land and sea, had sent the storm (Jonah 1:9). Jonah even advised them to throw him overboard, but the sailors were not willing to send Jonah to his death in the sea. When the sailors on the ship finally decided that they must throw Jonah overboard to save themselves, they prayed to Yahweh "please do not let us die for taking this man's life" (Jonah 1:14), we see God's mercy in action. They throw Jonah into the sea, and the sea became calm. In response to God's mercy the sailors offer sacrifices and vows to him.

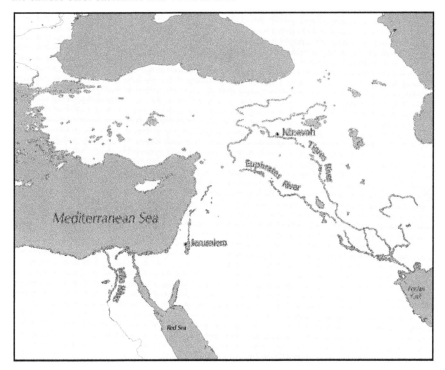

Jonah is also a recipient of God's mercy when he is in the belly of the sea creature. Jonah 2:2–9 records Jonah's prayer to God for mercy and deliverance. Based on a number of verses from the psalms, this prayer is an acknowledgment of sin and plea for mercy. Jonah received that mercy when God commanded the fish to vomit Jonah onto dry land (Jonah 2:10).

After Jonah preached his message of God's judgment to Nineveh, the king and people of that city repented and called on God for mercy. They fasted and wore sackcloth, both signs of the seriousness of their repentance. Once again, God showed mercy to repentant sinners, and he did not bring destruction upon Nineveh (Jonah 3:10).

God's mercy actually becomes the topic of discussion between God and Jonah in Jonah 4. Jonah resented God's mercy toward Nineveh. This great Assyrian city was responsible for much of the misery that had been afflicted by foreign armies on the kingdom of Israel. Jonah wanted them punished, not pardoned. In fact, when God did not bring destruction on the city of Nineveh, Jonah told God that this is why he did not want to go to Nineveh in the first place:

> And he prayed to Yahweh and said, "Yahweh, is this not what I said when I was yet in my country? That is why I hurriedly fled to Tarshish, because I knew that you are a gracious and merciful God, slow to anger and abounding in steadfast love, and relenting from disaster." (Jonah 4:2; see Exod 34:6; Num

---

Nineveh

14:18)

As Jonah sat in a shelter he made outside of Nineveh waiting for its destruction, God provided a plant to grow and provide shade for the prophet. The next day when God also provided a worm that ate and killed the plant, Jonah in his bitterness over God's mercy to Nineveh, wanted to die. It is at this point that God told Jonah that if Jonah had concern about the vine, it was certainly more important that God was concerned about the people of Nineveh. This is where the book ends, with an ironic twist: Jonah, who had received God's mercy when he repented, did not want God to show the same mercy to others who repented.

With this powerful ironic end to the book, the contrast between human attitudes and God's mercy is highlighted. God is willing to pardon all who truly repent and come to him for forgiveness. The irony is heightened because Jonah was an Israelite who knew Yahweh as a gracious and forgiving God and was part of God's special people and a recipient of the promise to Abraham, Isaac and Jacob. Yet he did not respect God's command to preach to Nineveh or his decision to pardon the city. In contrast, the sailors on the ship and the people of Nineveh, who did not know Yahweh and were not part of the people God had chosen, repented when confronted with their sins. The Gentiles who did not know God were godlier than the Israelites who had known him for generations!

Therefore, Jonah sends a special message about God's mercy: it is for all who repent and trust in him. While Yahweh may have chosen Israel as his special people, he is God of all people, and he desires that all repent and be saved (2 Pet 3:9). Those who would deny mercy to others as Jonah did demonstrate that they do not understand God's mercy toward them. God's mercy is shown to all who repent, since God does not show partiality to anyone (Acts 10:34; Rom 2:11; Gal 2:6; Eph 6:9).

3. Overview of the Book

The book of Jonah's four short chapters easily divides into two main parts.

I. Jonah flees from Yahweh (1:1—2:10)
    A. Jonah called to preach, but he flees to Tarshish (1:1–3)
    B. A storm on the sea causes the pagan sailors to cry out to their gods (1:4–6)
    C. Jonah must admit his disobedience to God's command (1:7–10)
    D. Jonah thrown into the sea and swallowed by a large sea creature (1:11–17)
    E. Jonah prays for mercy from the belly of the sea creature (2:1–10)
II. Jonah preaches for Yahweh (3:1–4:11)
    A. Jonah goes to Nineveh and preaches (3:1–4)
    B. Nineveh repents and calls on Yahweh for mercy (3:5–10)
    C. Jonah and God discuss Jonah's bitterness and God's mercy (4:1–11)

Amos

Criticism is often hard to accept. It is even more difficult to accept it from someone who is considered an outsider, since outsiders are often perceived as poking into business that does not concern them and having a perspective that is not sensitive to the context that an insider could appreciate. Amos was viewed as an outsider by the people to whom God sent him to preach. He was from Judah, but the Lord sent him to Israel to call them to repentance. For this reason Amos's ministry is an interesting contrast to that of Jonah, another eighth century outsider prophet. While the people of Nineveh listened to Jonah, the people of

Israel, who claimed to be Yahweh's people, refused to listen to his prophet Amos.

> 1. Authorship and Date—*Who Was Amos and When Did He Prophesy?*
> 2. Themes—*What Important Messages Does Amos Contain?*
> 3. Overview of the Book—*The Contents of Amos*
> 4. Important Passages—*Two Passages in Amos*

1. Authorship and Date

Amos was a shepherd and tender of sycamore-fig trees from Tekoa, a small town in Judah some six miles south of Bethlehem or about eleven miles from Jerusalem (Amos 1:1; 7:14–15). Judging from his skillful use of words and his broad knowledge of history and of the world in general, Amos was not a simply peasant farmer, but may have had a measure of education and stature in his community. Since the book of Amos appears to be a carefully arranged series of prophecies, it is likely that Amos, who obviously possessed good communication skills, wrote and organized his own book.

In the book's superscription (1:1), Amos tells us that he prophesied during the prosperous reigns of Uzziah of Judah (791–740 BC) and Jeroboam II of Israel (793–753 BC). This would mean that his ministry began no earlier than 791 BC and ended no later than 753 BC.

2. Theme

Amos clearly states the theme of his book:

> But let justice roll down like waters, and righteousness like an ever-flowing stream. (Amos 5:24)

Throughout his prophecy Amos calls for social justice. He decries the various practices that allowed the rich to take advantage of the poor, the powerful to mistreat the weak. He pointed out many in the upper classes in Israel live in luxury, but they do not share their wealth with the poor of the land and are not concerned about their suffering. He condemned the leaders and even their wives (Amos 4:1) as complicit in oppressing the poor and needy in Israel.

For Amos, a concern for social justice demonstrates true piety. The person who believes in Yahweh, the God who had compassion on Israel when it was weak and oppressed in Egypt, will reflect that compassion by concern for the weak and the oppressed. Moreover, Amos points out that even the worship of Israel had become corrupted, with worshippers thinking that merely going through the outward motions of the rituals was enough to please God. This was true whether they worshipped at Israel's shrines in Bethel, Gilgal and Dan or even at Judah's shrine at Beersheba.

Shrine Cities Condemed by Amos

Therefore, Amos pronounced God's harsh judgment on Israel. The northern kingdom would fall to a pagan kingdom that would uproot the people and carry them into captivity. God's judgment would be harsh, because the people had totally abandoned his word and rejected the call of prophets like Amos. The prophet quotes God as threatening:

> "If they dig into Sheol, my hand will take them from there. If they climb up to heaven, I will bring them down from there. If they hide themselves on the top of Mount Carmel, I will search them out and take them from there. And if they hide from my sight at the bottom of the sea, I will command the serpent there, and it will bite them. If they go into captivity in front of their enemies, I will command the sword there, and it will kill them. I will fix my eyes upon them for evil and not for good." (Amos 9:2–4)

However, Amos was not simply a prophet of destruction and the wrath of God. He was also a prophet who invited his hearers to repent and receive the mercy of God:

> Seek good, and not evil, that you may live. Then Yahweh, the God of Armies, will be with you, as you have said. Hate evil, and love good, and establish justice in the gate. It may be that Yahweh, the God of Armies, will be gracious to the remnant of Joseph.

In fact, Amos ends his prophecy on a note of compassion and hope as he prophesies that God will "raise up the fallen booth of David" (Amos 9:11), a clear reference to the promised coming of the Messiah. As a result of his coming there will be an abundance of spiritual blessings for God's people, which Amos pictures in high metaphor as a superabundant harvest as God will restore his people from exile (Amos 9:13–15).

Therefore, like all of the prophets, Amos skillfully uses the Law to condemn sins. But he also uses the Gospel to draw sinners who acknowledge their sins to God. He points them to the Messiah who will bring blessings that shower the forgiven children of God with prosperity that outshines the most prosperous and affluent days of Israel under Jeroboam II.

3. Overview of the Book

Amos has grouped similar prophecies together in his book. It is not possible to determine the original order of these prophecies, but it is clear that Amos has grouped and ordered his messages to emphasize his message of God's displeasure with Israel for social inequities, and yet to end on a note of the Gospel.

I.   Superscription (1:1)
II. Amos's Message of Wrath (1:2)
III. Judgment on nations in the land of Canaan for their sins against humanity (1:3—2:16)
   A.   Aram (1:3–5)
   B.   Philistia (1:6–8)
   C.   Phoenicia (1:9–10)
   D.   Edom (1:11–12)
   E.   Ammon (1:13–15)
   F.   Moab (2:1–3)
   G.   Judah (2:4–5)
   H.   Israel (2:6–16)
IV. Oracles of condemnation for Israel (3:1—5:17)
   A.   Judgment on Israel for forsaking God (3:1–15)
   B.   Judgment on Israel for stubborn lack of repentance (4:1–13)
   C.   Judgment on Israel for its lack of justice and compassion (5:1–17)
V.   The exile announced (5:18—6:14)
   A.   Judgment because of distorted religious practices (5:18–27)
   B.   Judgment because of complacency and callousness toward the needy (6:1–7)
   C.   Judgment because of arrogant pride (6:8–14)
VI. Five visions of God's judgment (7:1—9:10)

   A. A swarm of locusts (7:1–3)
   B. A consuming fire (7:4–6)
   C. A plumb line (7:7–17)
   D. A basket of ripe fruit (8:1–14)
   E. The Lord strikes the altar (9:1–10)
VII. A Vision of the Gospel (9:11–15)
   A. Raising the fallen booth of David (9:11–12)
   B. Israel's future blessings depicted as return and blessings in the land (9:13–15)

Hosea

Marriage provides one of the closest and most intimate relationships that many people ever experience. As a part of God's plan in creation (Gen 2), marriage is a great gift of God to humanity and was designed by the Lord to provide a special relationship of love and companionship. However, sinful humans have often corrupted the institution of marriage. Perhaps the greatest harm against this gift of God is caused by unfaithfulness to one's wedding vows. The prophet Hosea experienced the hurt caused by an unfaithful spouse. In fact, when God commanded the prophet to marry, he told Hosea that his wife would be unfaithful. God used the prophet's experience of an unfaithful spouse as a way to tell Israel how hurtful its unfaithfulness to him was. God compared himself to a husband and Israel to his wife. Yet, despite Israel's unfaithfulness, God continued to love Israel and forgive her, just as Hosea was told to forgive his wife and take her back.

   1. Authorship and Date—*Who Was Hosea and When Did He Prophesy?*
   2. Theme—*What Is Hosea about?*
   3. Overview of the Book—*The Contents of Hosea*
   4. Important Passages—*Three Passages in Hosea*

1. Authorship and Date

We know little about Hosea's background except that he was an Israelite and that his father's name was Beeri. Hosea tells us that he prophesied during the reigns of four kings of Judah: Uzziah, Jotham, Ahaz and Hezekiah (Hos 1:1).

This would mean that he began his ministry no later than about 752 BC and continued to prophesy until at least 715 BC when Hezekiah became sole ruler of Judah. This would make Hosea a younger contemporary of Amos. Like Amos, Hosea predicted the fall of Israel to the Assyrians. However, whereas Amos did not name the nation that would conquer Israel and take it into captivity, Hosea declared that it would be the Assyrians (Hos 9:3; 10:6; 11:5).

Since there are a number of references to Judah in the book (Hos 1:1, 7, 11; 4:15; 5:5, 10, 12-14; 6:4, 11; 8:14; 10:11; 11:12; 12:2), since Hosea primarily marks his ministry by references to kings of Judah (Hos 1:1), and since Hosea prophesied into the reign of Hezekiah, the book in its present form was probably composed in Judah by Hosea or an associate of his sometime after the fall of Israel to the Assyrians in 722 BC.

2. Theme

From beginning to end Hosea is about God's relationship to unfaithful Israel. The first three chapters of Hosea concentrate on Hosea's family and marriage and use it as a metaphor for understanding God's relationship with Israel. God instructed the prophet to take a wife, knowing that she would be unfaithful (Hos 1:2). This marriage produced children (Hos 1:3–11), all of which were given names that signified some aspect of God's relationship with Israel. Hosea 2 explains Israel's punishment for its unfaithfulness to God, but it is immediately followed by Hosea 3, where God commands Hosea to continue to love his wife, even though she has committed adultery. God promises to do the same for Israel. Israel will be brought back to God just as it was brought out of Egypt and made to be God's nation, a theme that runs throughout the book (Hos 1:11; 2:14-23; 3:5; 11:10–11; 14:4–7).

Starting with the Hosea 4 Hosea's marriage and family fades from view, and the prophet concentrates on exposing Israel's continual fascination with pagan Canaanite religion. Over and over the prophet demonstrates that God loves Israel (Hos 11:1–4). Israel's pursuit of the Canaanite god Baal was nothing short of spiritual adultery. God would judge the unfaithful Israelites, but ultimately God's love is an abiding love that never gives up on his faithless people and is always ready to forgive them. That forgiveness was shown not only by his calling Israel out of Egypt, but ultimately by his calling Jesus out of Egypt to save his people (Hos 11:1–4; Matt 2:15).

3. Overview of the Book

Although Hosea is divided into fourteen chapters, it is a short book. Only one of its chapters has more than twenty verses, while a few have less than ten.

I.   Superscription (1:1)
II. An Unfaithful Wife and a Faithful Husband—Hosea's family as a metaphor for God's relationship to Israel (1:2—3:5)
     A. Hosea's marriage and his children as signs to Israel (1:2—2:1)
     B. Israel condemned as God's unfaithful wife (2:2–23)
     C. The faithful husband takes his wife back (3:1–5)
III. God remains faithful even when Israel is unfaithful (4:1—14:9)
     A. God's charges against unfaithful Israel (4:1—7:16)
     B. God's punishment for Israel because of her unfaithfulness (8:1—10:15)
     C. Despite his anger over Israel's unfaithfulness, God will love her and offer forgiveness to all who repent (11:1—14:9)

25
Prophecy to Judah in the Eighth Century
Micah and Isaiah

Micah

Sometimes a very talented person is overshadowed by an even more talented contemporary. This could lead many to overlook an important contribution
made by the lesser of two great lights. This is often the case with Micah. His
contemporary Isaiah is one of the greatest prophets in the Old Testament, so it is
easy to overlook Micah's prophecy. Micah's style is similar to that of Isaiah,
and like Isaiah, his prophecies of God's grace are some of the most comforting
in the Bible.

1. Authorship and Date—*Who Was Micah and
   When Did He Prophesy?*
2. Theme—*What Is Micah About?*
3. Overview of the Book—*The Contents of Micah*
4. Important Passages—*Three Passages from Joel*

1. Authorship and Date

Little is known about Micah other than what we read in the superscription
to his book (Mic 1:1). He was from Moresheth, probably the Moresheth Gath in
southern Judah mentioned at Micah 1:14. He prophesied during the reigns of
Jotham, Ahaz and Hezekiah of Judah. This means that he began his ministry
sometime between 750–732 BC. Since he seems to have no knowledge of Hezekiah's religious reforms, his ministry probably ended before 715 BC when Hezekiah assumed sole control of the throne of Judah. This would make Micah a
contemporary of both Hosea and Isaiah.

Micah is one of the few prophets mentioned by name in another prophetic
book. Jeremiah tells us that Micah spoke the prophecy of Micah 3:12 during the
reign of Hezekiah, which would make Micah 3 one of the last of his prophecies
(Jer 26:18). Since Micah, like Hosea, predicted the downfall of Samaria at the
hands of the Assyrians (Micah 1:5–7), we can date the prophecy of 1:3–16 to
sometime before 722 BC. The rest of his prophecies cannot be dated with certainty, and they are not necessarily in chronological order. Instead, Micah seems

to have arranged them in alternating oracles of God's judgment and God's grace.

2. Theme

It is difficult to speak of a single theme uniting the entire book of Micah. Instead the prophet emphasizes two distinct actions by God: judgment for Israel and Judah because of their sins and deliverance by God for the penitent. Thus, Micah emphasizes that God hates idolatry, rebellion, injustice and worship that is only outward action and not heartfelt devotion. At the same time, Micah also emphasizes that God finds joy in pardoning those who repent of their sins. Because of this, he looks forward to a great, glorious day for Jerusalem and Mount Zion when God will establish David's kingdom forever through the Messiah.

3. Overview of the Book

As mentioned earlier, Micah seems to have arranged his prophecies in alternating oracles of God's judgment and God's grace.

I. Superscription (1:1)
II. God's judgment on Judah and Israel (1:2—3:12)
    A. Announcement of Judgment (1:2)
    B. Judgment on Samaria and Jerusalem (1:3–7)
    C. Weeping and Mourning (1:8–16)
    D. Judgment on those who plan to do evil (2:1–5)
    E. Judgment on false prophets (2:6–11)
    F. Deliverance for Jacob (2:12–13)
    G. Judgment on leaders and prophets (3:1–12)
III. Deliverance for Judah and Israel (4:1—5:15)
    A. The coming kingdom in Zion (4:1–13)
    B. The coming ruler from Bethlehem (5:1–5a)
    C. Deliverance for Jacob from the Assyrian threat (5:5b–15)
IV. Yahweh's legal complaint against Israel (6:1–16)
    A. The accusation (6:1–8)
    B. The coming punishment (6:9–16)
V. God turns despair into hope (7:1–20)
    A. Micah's despair over sin in Judah, but his hope in God (7:1–13)
    B. A prayer to God: He protects and pardons his people (7:14–20)

Isaiah

Suppose something happened to you that changed completely how you looked at everything else in the world and inside yourself. How could you describe that difference to someone else? This is what happened to the man named Isaiah. He was caught up in a vision of God and God's grace, and then spent the rest of his life trying to communicate the importance of this to his fellow citizens. He came to understand both the horror of human sin, and the power of God's redeeming love. He devoted his entire life to creating the most powerful and compelling presentations he could of the truths of God's judgment and God's grace. Isaiah is especially famous for his predictions of the New King that God would send to rescue His people, who could not redeem themselves.

1. Authorship and Date—*Exploring the Possibilities*
2. Major Themes—*Isaiah as "The Old Testament Evangelist"*
3. Important Passages—*Isaiah Points Us to Christ*

Authorship and Date

What We Learn from Isaiah's Writings

We know very little about Isaiah himself, even though the book of Isaiah is quite large. The times in which he lived are well-described in the books of Kings and Chronicles (both of which mention Isaiah by name), and the man had a long ministry of preaching to Judah. He is repeatedly identified as "the son of Amoz," but we have no other information about Amoz, and there is no connection to any Biblical genealogy. (Amoz is not to be confused with the other prophet Amos—the names look very similar in English, but are distinct in Hebrew.) It is common for scholars to offer the opinion that Isaiah was related either to the royal family, or else to the priestly family. These connections are suggested because Isaiah seems to have had easy access to the royal Davidic household, and he was very concerned about "holy" things, which were the concern of the priests. But as far as access to the royal family, Isaiah did hardly anything more than was done by John the Baptist in rebuking the Herodian family, and John was not related to the Herods. Moreover, there is no reason why Isaiah would have to be of priestly descent to care about the holy things, since all of God's people were to be holy (Lev 11:45). If anything, the fact that Isaiah's ancestral history is left simply as "son of Amoz" might be taken to indicate a distinction from any royal or priestly family lines.

We know that Isaiah was married and that he had at least two, or possibly three, sons. The firstborn was Shear-Yashuv ("A Remnant Shall Return"), the last was Maher-Shalal-Hash-Baz ("Hasten to the Booty, Hurry to the Prey"), and some scholars think that in between these two the child Immanuel ("God is With Us") was also Isaiah's son (see more on this below). The mother of Maher-Shalal-Hash-Baz is referred to as "the prophetess." This title could be given to her because of her role in the birth of this symbolic son, or it might be an honorific title because she was married to Isaiah, or perhaps she was indeed a prophetess of God in her own right. The last possibility raises interesting speculations about this family, reminiscent of Miriam being a prophetess alongside her brothers Moses and Aaron; but again we have no further information on this matter. It is assumed that this family lived in Jerusalem, since so many dramatic scenes in Isaiah's ministry took place in that city. However, it is never explicitly said that Isaiah was from Jerusalem, unlike the information supplied about the home town of many of the other prophets, so this cannot be certain. Many of the dramatic episodes in his life were at times when much of the region near Jerusalem would have sought shelter within the city.

We are given very little information about any actions of Isaiah. He intercepted wicked King Ahaz on a road, he visited good King Hezekiah at the palace, he visited the priests on at least one occasion, and he spent one three-year period walking around nude or nearly nude to symbolize the coming defeat and stripping of Egypt. If Isaiah 6 describes his call to the prophetic ministry, that would date to 740 BC, and one verse of Isaiah 37 provides information that took place in 681 BC. Good King Hezekiah reigned until 687 BC, when he was followed by wicked king Manasseh. Isaiah 1:1 does not list Manasseh as one of the kings during whose reign Isaiah preached. There is a late Jewish tradition that says that Manasseh put Isaiah to death by having the old man stuffed into a hollow log and then ordering the log to be sawn in half (some speculate that Heb 11:37 refers to this). There is no way to know if this tradition had a basis in fact or not. The difference in beginning and ending dates means that Isaiah served as a preacher for fifty-four or more years.

The one thing that we do know about Isaiah was that he was well-educated and very productive. According to Chronicles he wrote a biography of good King Uzziah and also of Hezekiah, and the book of his sermons is one of the largest books in the Old Testament, with the largest vocabulary of different words (2186) of any book of the Old Testament. His poetry is universally regarded as magnificent, and the archaeological discoveries of the past century have also made it clear that Isaiah had a detailed knowledge of the religions and cultures of the neighboring nations.

If Isaiah began his ministry of preaching in 740 BC at perhaps age twenty-five, he would have lived to about the age of eighty. In his early years Judah enjoyed peace and prosperity, but that was upset with the rise of Assyria and the poor decisions of wicked King Ahaz. As the years rolled on Isaiah saw the complete destruction and deportation of his northern brother tribes, the nation of Israel. He saw the good reformation of King Hezekiah, but also saw the horrible effect of Hezekiah's one disobedience, when the Assyrian Sennacharib conquered all of Judah and besieged Jerusalem in 701 BC. Isaiah experienced God's marvelous rescue of Jerusalem from destruction at that event, but had to deliver the message that it was only a matter of time until another Mesopotamian power, Babylon, would similarly destroy Jerusalem and deport the people of Judah. Equipped with the revelation that God would both deport his people and later bring them back (a revelation delivered in common with his contemporary prophets Amos, Hosea, and Micah), Isaiah probably used his considerable poetic skills during the last decade of his life to look ahead in time and write of the great release from Babylon that he knew would take place someday in the future. While the inhabitants of Judah suffered under Assyrian taxation, Isaiah wrote of greater sufferings, and even greater blessings and rescue, to come after his time.

Critical Theories on the Authorship of Isaiah

As with many of the books of the writing prophets, the matter of authorship is complicated by the possibility that the prophet may have composed the material in various stages over the course of his ministry, but someone else may have compiled and arranged the book that collects the words of the prophet. Certain sections of the book of Isaiah have a clear first-person voice. For example, Isaiah 6 ("I saw ... I said") and Isaiah 8 ("The Lord said to me, ... Here am I and the children the Lord has given me"). These sections certainly suggest that they were written by the prophet Isaiah himself. But other sections refer to the man Isaiah in the third-person. For example, Isaiah 7 ("The Lord said to Isaiah ... Then Isaiah said") interrupts Isaiah 6 and 8. Isaiah 20 has a prose reference to Isaiah in third-person again, and Isaiah 36—39 are closely related to the parallel accounts in Kings and Chronicles and use the third-person to refer to Isaiah. These sections suggest that somebody later was writing about Isaiah. In three places headings are placed in the text to identify the material as coming from Isaiah (Isa 1:1; 2:1; 13:1). The second and third of these seem unnecessary if this book was the direct product of Isaiah. Their inclusion suggests that different collections of sermons by Isaiah were assembled at some point later in time. Most of the book consists of the direct address of the prophet to his audience (the people of Judah or other locations), and in many cases the prophet speaks as the mouthpiece of God. These sections usually provide no information useful for determining who arranged and published this material.

But alongside this evidence for different people being involved in assembling this book, there is also evidence pointing in the direction of one rather unique author. The book as a whole has a certain logical flow to it. It begins with the problems of Israel and Judah in the early years of Isaiah, leading to the crisis of the Assyrian siege of Jerusalem in 701 BC. In connection with this crisis it describes the visit of the Babylonian ambassadors in Isaiah 39 and Isaiah's prediction of the Babylonian exile. It then continues with the account of the future rescue from Babylonian enslavement in the latter chapters of Isaiah. Several subsections of the book clearly depend on each other, such as the relationship of Isaiah 7 and 8. It is widely acknowledged that Isaiah 40—55 constitute some sort of united composition (though there are disagreements about which chapters belong to the unified composition), and many of the themes of that section continue in the subsequent chapters of Isaiah. It has recently been argued that Isaiah 2—12 are arranged in an overarching poetic symmetry that links that entire set of sermons together, even though pieces of these chapters clearly come from different dates in the life of the prophet Isaiah. These indications of intentional large-scale structuring of the book force one to consider who would have both the talent and the temerity to arrange and present Isaiah's material in this fashion. The simplest answer would be Isaiah himself, who is widely regarded as the most talented poetic writer in the Biblical collection.

The issue of authorship is further complicated by many theories that suggest the material comes from not one prophet named Isaiah, but from two or more different men living in different centuries and thus in different conditions.

The book of Isaiah is unusual in that it contains material addressing two different times in the history of God's people, one during the lifetime of Isaiah and one long after his lifetime. In most of the material in Isaiah 1—39 the Judeans are considered to be in their own land, the great threat is the nation of Assyria, and the message delivered by Isaiah is the warning that God is angry at the behavior of his people and that they need to repent. Many historical figures are mentioned by name, such as King Hezekiah and the Assyrian King Sennacharib in 701 BC. Beginning with Isaiah 40 the situation pictured is quite different. The Judeans are pictured as captives in Babylon, and are informed that it is time to be set free. The foe is the nation of Babylon (which did not become an empire until about 620 BC), whose overthrow is predicted as imminent. The major message delivered by Isaiah is one of comfort, release, and salvation by God. In Isaiah 44:28 and 45:1 the name *Cyrus* is mentioned. This is the great king of the Medes and Persians who overthrew the Babylonian empire in 539 BC, and authorized the Jews to return to Judea. There is no parallel for any other book of the Bible addressing two such different historical situations, at least not on this scale.

The traditional view is that Isaiah of Jerusalem not only delivered all of God's messages warning the people about God's use of Assyria to punish his disobedient people, but also forecast the eventual conquest of Judah by the Babylonians, and then delivered in advance the content of the chapters of Isaiah that look forward to the day when God set the Jews free from Babylon.

The rise of modern critical scholarship of the last couple of centuries assumed as one of its fundamental starting points the concept that the Bible was a book of ordinary human propaganda, consisting mostly of religious opinions and distorted truths and subject to a long history of re-editing and re-arranging to serve new purposes. With this premise in the background, many scholars refused to believe that the second portion of the book of Isaiah was written by the same man. Many alternative theories were proposed to explain the authorship of the various parts of the book of Isaiah, all with the assumption that during the intertestamental period the Jews somehow combined all of these different works into the one book named for Isaiah.

The most basic form of alternative theory is that there were two prophets: Isaiah of Jerusalem in the eighth century BC and some anonymous poetic prophet two centuries later who predicted and lived through the release from Babylon in the sixth century BC. The book of Isaiah was divided roughly into two halves, Isaiah 1—39 and 40—66. These parts of the book came to be known as **First Isaiah and Second Isaiah**, and these labels are often used today to refer to the sections of the book of Isaiah even by conservative scholars who hold to a single author. But other scholars suggested refinements on the basic theory, with many dividing out a portion called **Third Isaiah**, consisting of Isaiah 56—66, separate from Second Isaiah, which was then only Isaiah 40—55. Third Isaiah was thought to be the work of another prophet, living after the second prophet. While the second man had lived in Babylon and predicted the release from Babylon (c. 540 BC), the third man lived in the area of Jerusalem in Judea in the post-exilic era, either just before or around the same time as the prophets Haggai and Zechariah (c. 520 BC).

Critical Theories on the Multiple Authorship of Isaiah

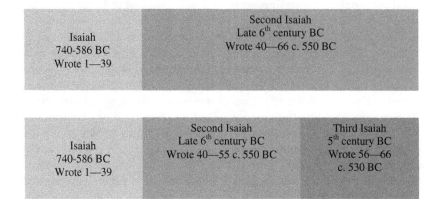

One of the questions that these theories create is the identity of these great post-exilic prophets. The man known as Second Isaiah is sometimes considered to be the greatest poet of the Bible. Why would we have the works of such great poets, and no trace of their names or other personal history? The sections of prophecy left behind are of considerable size. If we divide the book of Isaiah into these three portions, the shortest, Third Isaiah, is about the same length as the longest of the books of the Minor Prophets, Hosea or Zechariah. If even small books such as Obadiah and Haggai still have names attached to them, why are these larger works (Second and Third Isaiah) preserved with total loss of memory of the specific prophets? The simplest solution to this riddle would be to suppose that these later writers were also, by coincidence, named "Isaiah," and that the later Jews somehow mistook the identity of name for identity of persons. But that requires the intertestamental Jews, even their textual scholars, to misunderstand their own recent history when compiling their sacred texts, and this seems unlikely.

Another solution is preferred by most critical scholars: these sections were the work of prophetic groups, rather than individual men. These groups or schools of prophets, perhaps continuing their work over several decades, admired and continued to use the material of First Isaiah in their preaching. Gradually they added some of their own sermons to the material, probably conceiving of this work as simply an expansion and updating of the genuine Isaiah material. In this way they did not think of their work as the product of another new prophet, but as the living continuation of the preaching of the original Isaiah. A second question raised by this theory is then at what time and for what reason this expansion ceased, and the book was considered "closed"? This is difficult to answer.

The issue of the divisions and sources of the book of Isaiah becomes further complicated when many scholars point out that much material inside the chapters assigned to First Isaiah contain information and themes that seem to fit well with the presumed setting of Second Isaiah or Third Isaiah. Isaiah 35, for example, is very similar to material in Isaiah 40—55, and Isaiah 13 and 14 promise God's retribution upon Babylon for the most part, rather than Assyria. Isaiah 24—27 expand the vision of God's judgment to encompass the entire world, including references in Isaiah 25 and 26 to the resurrection of the dead. Many (but not all) critical scholars consider the idea of the resurrection of the dead to be a religious idea borrowed from Persian religion by Judaism during the time of the Persian empire, that is, after the exile period. In that case even First Isaiah is already stuffed with additions from later writers. The result of this thinking is that the entire book of Isaiah is not the work of an eighth century BC prophet, but the result of some early fifth century BC committee. It becomes a matter of judgment of each individual scholar as to which phrases and which ideas originated at what time.

There is no way to prove the question of authorship or the divisions of the book of Isaiah one way or the other, unless in the future some significant new documents were to be found by archaeologists. Some people believe that the New Testament settles this matter because the New Testament contains quotations from all the different sections of the book of Isaiah with only simple attribution to Isaiah. But others believe this merely reflects the common reference to the book at that time, and does not genuinely speak to the question of historical authorship. Either the works of two (or more) men from different times have been combined into one book, for which there is no real parallel elsewhere in Scripture, or else one prophet was guided by the Holy Spirit to deliver information that applied to two widely different times and situations.

Two further things must be said, however. First, one of the main themes of Second Isaiah is the ability of the God of Israel to predict the future and guarantee the accomplishment of his prediction. If it is assumed that such successful prediction as the fall of Babylon and the conquest by Cyrus the Persian must have been written after the fact, this material loses much of its force and much of its value. It would seem to have little power to convince the people, and little value to guide people unless it had been delivered in advance of the events predicted. If it is assumed that it was delivered in advance of the fulfillment, that the future, including the rise and success of Cyrus, was successfully forecast significantly before the events took place, then this miracle of prediction can be assigned a date any time before about 550 BC (Cyrus became a major political figure and potential threat to Babylon about 550). But if it is a genuine prediction, then there is little reason not to assign it to the famous historical prophet of the eighth century, Isaiah of Jerusalem, who is a known figure rather than an "anonymous genius," and to whom the material is attributed by virtue of inclusion in this book.

Moreover, Isaiah's contemporary prophets are also forecasting the exile and the return, though not in the detail that Isaiah gives. Hosea 11 is about this same event, the exile and return. Amos predicts the possibility of exile over and over again, but in Amos 9 he too predicts a day when God brings back and rebuilds his exiled people. Even Micah specifically mentions exile in Babylon and return (Mic 4:10). The account of Isaiah 39 narrates that Isaiah had specific information about the exile in Babylon as early as 701 BC. Given that he is the most productive and most visionary of the prophets of his time, it is not at all beyond reason that he should be led to ponder and discuss at length the future time of salvation as well. It has been pointed out that the material called Second Isaiah contains a detailed knowledge of the geography of Canaan, but reveals nothing about the geography of the area around Babylon. This is consistent with a source located in Canaan, rather than in Babylon (contrast the book of Ezekiel, which contains specific information about Babylonian geography).

Second, the material of Second and Third Isaiah, combined with material extracted from First Isaiah, is taken by many critical scholars as the definitive information for what conditions and ideas were like during the exile and early post-exile period. Assuming that these materials come from that period, they study these materials to deduce what that period was like, and from that they derive criteria to decide which other passages need to be assigned to similar dates. One must note the circular process of reasoning involved here. If the chapters of Isaiah are all dated back to ca. 690 BC, then they provide no historical information about the exile and post-exilic period. In that case much of the critical scholarship of the past century about the post-exilic period collapses into meaninglessness because of lack of data. One should be aware of how much of these critical scholars' view of the exile and beyond depends on this issue of the division and dating of the chapters of Isaiah.

2. Major themes

Law and Gospel

Naturally, a book as big as Isaiah has several significant themes which run through it. But without question the largest of the major themes in Isaiah is what Lutherans call Law and Gospel. Isaiah not only contains strong and explicit expressions of God's Law, condemning the sin of God's people and pointing them toward a better direction, but he also contains some of the most clear and encouraging expressions of the Gospel, the promise of salvation by God's grace, found throughout the entire Bible. Isaiah's expression of the Gospel is so clear that he has often been set alongside Matthew, Mark, Luke, and John and called "the Evangelist of the Old Testament."

What is the difference between the Law and the Gospel?	
The Law:	The Gospel:
– teaches us what we are to do and not to do;	– teaches us what God has done, and still does, for our salvation;
– shows us our sin and the wrath of God;	– shows us our Savior and the grace of God;
– must be preached to all people, but especially to impenitent sinners.	– must be preached to sinners who are troubled in their minds because of their sins.

The Law-Gospel theme can be easily perceived in the larger structure of Isaiah. Isaiah 1 opens with God's call for judgment upon the sin and unfaithfulness of his people, and the material of First Isaiah hammers at this sinful status continually. But Second Isaiah opens with the words "Comfort, comfort my people", and announces that "sin has been paid for" and salvation is at hand. Nevertheless, both "halves" of the book express both Law and Gospel, and it would be difficult for anyone to choose whether the "best" expression of Law or Gospel occurs in either section. (Is the Law aspect of Isa 53 stronger or clearer than that of Isa 1 or Isa 5? Is the Gospel of Isa 53 clearer or stronger than Isa 1:18; 9:2–7, or Isa 11?)

Isaiah 1:10–17 contains dramatic condemnation of the sinful behavior of God's people. They are identified as the spiritual equivalent of the "rulers of Sodom" and the "people of Gomorrah." Although the people are outwardly very religious, they are revealed to be selfish sinners on the inside. God condemns the "multitude of [their] sacrifices" and their "many prayers." Their deeds are identified as "evil;" they should "stop doing wrong, learn to do right!" They need to change their behavior in order to "seek justice" instead of selfishness. Isaiah 1:18 follows with one of the sweetest and clearest expressions of the good news of God's love and saving grace: "Though your sins are like scarlet, they shall be as white as snow; though they are as red as crimson, they shall be like wool."

This is followed in Isaiah 1:19–20 with the summary statements of the promises of both Law and Gospel, in inverted order: "If you are willing and obedient, you will eat the best from the land; but if you resist and rebel, you will be devoured by the sword." For those who repent and believe the Gospel of God's forgiveness, there is promised God's abundant care and blessing. But for those who hear the Gospel offer and persist in their sin, who refuse to repent, there is only the repeated threat of death and destruction.

Isaiah 2 opens with the vision of the success of the Gospel message—that it will result in world-wide repentance and peace. "Many peoples" and "nations" will turn to Israel's God to learn truth and to trust in his word. But this chapter of Isaiah moves swiftly into revealing that at the present time, even God's people who currently have his word of truth and salvation are rejecting it and turning to other things. God's people are "full of superstitions" and "their land is full of idols." Therefore the Law must be pronounced, the sin and pride of man must be condemned. "The eyes of the arrogant will be humbled, and the pride of men brought low; the Lord alone will be exalted in that day."

Isaiah 3:16—4:6 contains the dramatic reversal that will come to the women of Jerusalem who take pride in their outward appearance and what it can get for them. But beginning at Isaiah 4:2 this is again reversed with the Gospel promise of God's cleansing and God's restoration of his presence among them. Isaiah 6 contains the wonderful account of the forgiveness of Isaiah through the touch of the burning coal. "See, this has touched your lips; your guilt is taken away and your sin atoned for." But it goes on to predict for Isaiah a ministry of preaching that will be without effect. The condemnation of God's Law will have its effect where the promise of the Gospel of grace is ignored.

The saving grace of God is received through faith alone, without any contributing effort on the part of humans. This Gospel truth of the New Testament is already revealed explicitly in Isaiah. Isaiah 28:16 testifies that God will "lay a stone in Zion," and "the one who trusts will never be dismayed." Isaiah 30:15 explains that "in repentance and rest is your salvation, in quietness and trust [in God] is your strength," rather than in trusting the ideas and plans of mankind.

Isaiah 34 and 35 are juxtaposed against each other in a way that illustrates this balance of Law and Gospel in Isaiah. Isaiah 34 predicts the judgment of God upon the nations, with the effect that civilized nations such as Edom will become desolate wildernesses inhabited only by wild creatures. But Isaiah 35 announces the reversal of this curse upon the land. "The desert will be glad...will rejoice, and blossom" for "the burning sand will be come a pool, the thirsty ground [will become] bubbling springs." The coming of God's salvation will result in blessings both for God's people and for God's created world. There will be cures for the "blind... deaf... lame...(and) mute." God will create a highway of holiness that will be protected against any threat by any dangerous beast. "Only the redeemed will walk there," and it will lead them straight to God and all his blessings.

Isaiah 40 opens, as noted above, with the promise of comfort. This Gospel comfort is needed because of the effect upon Jerusalem of "all her sins." Over and over this section of Isaiah balances the proclamation of Law and Gospel. The Lord comes with salvation because "all mankind is [merely] grass." The messenger should shout the good tidings of the coming of God to rescue Zion because nothing else is the equal of God. The savior of God's people is no one less than the Creator of the universe, not some prince or earthly nation or man-made idol. The people of Israel are rebuked for complaining about God's behavior, that it does not meet their desires for earthly pleasure, but God's wisdom and plan are much greater than they can understand, and "those who hope in the Lord will renew their strength."

Isaiah 53 (see more on this chapter of Isaiah below) identifies sinful humans as the problem, and God's agent of salvation as the solution. "We all, like sheep, have gone astray…and the Lord has laid on him the iniquity of us all." "He bore the sin of many, and made intercession for the transgressors," and "the punishment that brought us peace was upon him."

Isaiah 59 reveals to God's people that "your iniquities have separated you from your God." Therefore "justice is far from us, and righteousness does not reach us. We look for light, but all is darkness." But "the Lord looked…and was appalled that there was no one to intervene; so his own arm worked salvation for him." Isaiah 60 continues with the exhortation that God's people should "Arise, shine, for your light has come, and the glory of the Lord rises upon you." This alternation between words of Law and words of Gospel is constant throughout the book of Isaiah.

Holiness

A second important theme in Isaiah is the concept of sanctity or holiness. One of the favorite titles Isaiah uses for God is "the Holy One of Israel." He uses this title twenty-six times, twelve times in "First Isaiah" and fourteen times in "Second Isaiah." This title is only used six other times in the entire Old Testament, and at least half of those are either quotations or allusions to passages in the book of Isaiah. Thus the title is distinct to Isaiah.

What does it mean to be holy? Some interpreters have tried to link this concept to God's righteousness, that God is holy in the sense of being perfectly just and moral. A better way of viewing this is the other way around: that God is perfectly righteous because he is so holy. God's holiness points to both his power and his mysteriousness. God is different, special, set apart. He is not fully known or understood by humans. There is a mysterious power there that we do not know how to use or to predict. God is awesome. He is fantastic. He is even frightening. God is the "other," the contact from the other realm that is outside human experience. God is *super*-natural, involving power that is above and beyond this world. Human beings do not normally have contact or access with this power. But when things are connected with God, they take on a share of this holiness. Thus the temple of God becomes a holy house, the place where God reveals himself becomes holy ground, and the people used by God become holy, such as the high priest. The meat used in the animal sacrifice ceremonies becomes holy food.

Unfortunately, this label was also used in both Canaanite and Israelite culture for those males and females who worked at the various temples as cult prostitutes: they were called the "holy ones." This title did not at all speak about whether this behavior was considered righteous, just that it was considered by many to be connected with God.

But for the biblical God, the fact of his holiness meant that He was greater than any human being in every characteristic, including His moral sense. Thus because God was holy, He was more righteous than any human being. His ability to know and do what was correct in any situation, even when He was inflamed by emotion, was superior to that of humans. Thus for the biblical God, one aspect of holiness was perfectly righteous behavior. And the only way for defective human beings to try to measure up to God's standards of righteousness was for them to have access to divine holy power. But if they had this contact with the divine, then they were under obligation to reflect this connection in their entire lives: "Be holy, because I, the Lord your God, am holy" (Lev 19:1).

Let us look at some examples of this theme. In Isaiah 1 the Israelites are described as disobedient children who do not understand what they are doing. They "have spurned the Holy One of Israel and turned their backs on him." They do not realize how dangerous and how inappropriate their behavior is in abusing this contact with the Holy One. In Isaiah 4 it is only the survivors of God's purging of the people who will be called holy, those who are cleansed by the power of God from their stains. In Isaiah 10:17 the Holy One will become a flame that will destroy Assyria: the mysterious power will be unleashed against the foreign nation that does not respect Israel's God. In Isaiah 6 the song of the angels identifies God as "Holy, holy, holy," more mysterious and powerful than even the supernatural angels can comprehend. At the end of Isaiah 6 the "holy seed" will be those left over after God's judgment, who by the mighty mysterious power of God will be rebuilt into the new community of God. In Isaiah 11:9 the new Eden is called the "holy mountain" because it is the place where everyone and everything has contact with and knowledge of God. In Isaiah 29:23 it is when the redeemed see the work of God that the wicked are repaid and the humble are rescued, that "they will keep my name holy; they will acknowledge the holiness of the Holy One of Jacob, and will stand in awe of the God of Israel." In Isaiah 35:8 the special highway that God will create for the redeemed is connected to his sacredness: "it will be called the Way of Holiness." Isaiah 40 asks: "'To whom will you compare me? Or who is my equal?' says the Holy One." In Isaiah 52:20 "The Lord will lay bare his holy arm," unleashing this mysterious power in front of all people. In Isaiah 63:11 it is the "holy" spirit of God that unleashed the saving power that rescued ancient Israel from Egypt, and in Isaiah 63:10 it is this same "holy" spirit that reacted in a negative way: "Yet they rebelled and grieved his Holy Spirit. So he turned and became their enemy and he himself fought against them." For Isaiah, pointing to the holiness of God was pointing to the truth of who and what he was and all that meant for Israel.

The counterpoint to the holiness of God, or His hidden majesty, was His glory, which can be understood as His revealed majesty. Thus the glory of God often appears or is revealed to humans. The word *glory* comes from a root with a sense of weightiness: the unveiling of God's glory has a force, a weight, that has an effect upon people. In Isaiah 6:3 we read in the song of the angels both the praise of God's holiness, or hidden majesty, and his glory, or revealed majesty, which is identified with the fullness of creation. Everything God has done and created reveals a part of Him, who is nevertheless greater and more mysterious than all creation.

Second Exodus

Another theme that is especially prevalent in Isaiah 34—66, but which also occurs in the 1—33, is the Second Exodus. The primary topic in Isaiah 34—66 is the prediction of the release from the Babylonian exile. Isaiah delivers this prediction using the images of the story of the Exodus from Egypt. He understands the release from Babylon to be the equivalent of, and a repetition of, the Exodus from Egypt. The Exodus story is the foundation of Israel's faith, and sets the understanding of Israel's God and his actions. As God came to save the Israelites from bondage to the foreign power of Egypt, so God will come again to save the Israelites from bondage to the foreign power of Babylon (and Assyria). Note the parallels listed in the chart below.

EVENTS IN THE FIRST EXODUS FROM EGYPT	PARALLEL EVENTS IN THE SECOND EXODUS FROM BABYLON/ASSYRIA Isaiah 1—33	PARALLEL EVENTS IN THE SECOND EXODUS FROM BABYLON Isaiah 34—66
Moses = God's Agent	The Messiah will be God's Agent of salvation 9:6–7; 11:1–10	The Servant = God's Agent 42:1–7; 49:1–7; (50:4–9); 52:13—53:12; 61:1–7
God controlled Pharaoh for His purposes	God will control Assyria for His purposes 7:18–25; 10:5–6	God will control Cyrus for His purposes 44:24—45:7, 13
God defeated Pharaoh and the gods of Egypt	God will defeat Assyria and Babylon and Egypt 10:5–19; 24—34; 13:1—14:23; 19:1–25	God will defeat Babylon and its gods 46:1–2; 47:1–15; 48:14,20; 52:4–5, 11–12; 52:4–5, 11–12
God forecast each of the Ten Plagues and the Exodus	God forecasts His actions of salvation 7:11—8:10	God forecasts the victory of Cyrus and the release of Israel 40:12–26; 41:1–16, 21–29, 42:8–9; 43:1–13; 44:6–8; 44:24–28; 45:18–25; 46:1–13, 47:12–15; 48:3–16; 55:10–11
God led the Is-raelites in tri-umph across the sea	God will lead the Israelites in triumph and safety through the waters and defeat the water forces of Egypt, Assyria, and mythology 11:15–16; 19:5–10, 27:1	God will lead the Israelites in triumph across the waters 43:2, 16–21; 51:9–11
God brought water out of the rock	God will bring water into the desert 32:15–20	God will bring water into the desert 35:1–7; 41:18–19; 43:16–21; 44:3–4; 48:21; 49:9–10; 51:3
God led the Is-raelites on the path to Ca-naan, the Promised Land	God will lead the Israelites (and foreigners) out of trou-ble on a path to Canaan 2:2–5; 4:5–6; 11:10–16; 27:12–13	God will lead the Israelites on a holy highway back to Canaan 35:8–10; 40:3–5,9–11; 42:1–17; 43:2, 5–8; 19–21; 49:8–12. 22–23; 51:11; 52:7–12; 55:12–13; 57:14; 62:10–12; 63:1–6

Of course, the ultimate exodus of God's people is the one that Jesus leads from sin and death. Therefore, Isaiah not only points Israel forward to simple exodus from captivity in foreign lands, but uses this second exodus theme to continue to point forward to the coming Messiah, who would lead his people into the New Jerusalem (Rev 3:12; 21:2).

Power of Prediction

An important theme of Second Isaiah, which also occurs in First Isaiah, is the role of prediction for God's prophets. In Isaiah 40—55, particularly 41—49, God announces through Isaiah, "See, the former things have taken place, and new things I declare; before they spring into being I announce them to you" (Isa 42:9). The coming salvation from the power of Babylon is compared to the ancient salvation from the power of Egypt. As the power of God stood behind the words of Moses in the ancient days, so the power of God stands behind the new predictions of Isaiah in his day. Note this emphasis in Isaiah 43:18–19, "Forget the former things; do not dwell on the past. See, I am doing a new thing! Now it springs up; do you not perceive it?" This theme becomes an important challenge to the validity of any other religious view. The God of Israel challenges all other supernatural powers to see if any are his equal (Isa 44:6–8):

> Who then is like me? Let him proclaim it.
> Let him declare and lay out before me
> what has happened since I established my ancient people,
> and what is yet to come—
> yes, let him foretell what will come.
> Do not tremble, do not be afraid.
> Did I not proclaim this and foretell it long ago?
> You are my witnesses. Is there any God besides me?
> No, there is no other Rock; I know not one."

Indeed, this is the special significance of the announcement of the Persian conqueror Cyrus, that the God of Israel predicts him ahead of time (Isa 44:24–28):

> I am the Lord, ...
> who foils the signs of false prophets
> and makes fools of diviners,
> who overthrows the learning of the wise
> and turns it into nonsense,
> who carries out the words of his servants
> and fulfills the predictions of his messengers,
> who says of Jerusalem, 'It shall be inhabited,'

of the towns of Judah, 'They shall be built,'
and of their ruins, 'I will restore them,'
who says to the watery deep, 'Be dry,
and I will dry up your streams,'
who says of Cyrus, 'He is my shepherd
and will accomplish all that I please;
he will say of Jerusalem, "Let it be rebuilt,"
and of the Temple, "Let its foundations be laid."'

This emphasis, that the Biblical God should be trusted because he has a demonstrated history of predicting and controlling the future, also plays a significant role in the material of the first half of the book. In Isaiah 38 (which is in the second half of the book but is traditionally considered part of First Isaiah) King Hezekiah becomes ill and Isaiah delivers the message that God has chosen to end Hezekiah's life. But Hezekiah prays to God asking that God would change his mind, and Isaiah is sent back to announce that God has responded to this prayer and will add fifteen years to Hezekiah's life. Hezekiah is then given a miraculous sign to assure him that these words are true: the sun's shadow reverses itself in direction. Likewise, in Isaiah 7—8 Isaiah delivers a message of encouragement to King Ahaz, and offers him the ability to pick whatever miraculous sign he wants to be sure of this encouragement. But wicked King Ahaz refuses to cooperate with this event. Therefore the baby Immanuel is predicted as a sign that Isaiah's words will come true, that the country and the royal family will be protected, and that God is truly with this nation, watching over them. Even though Ahaz will not cooperate, God will save the nation and the royal family, and it will all take place on schedule before Immanuel is old enough to know right from wrong.

Messianic Agent

This leads to one more important theme in the book of Isaiah: the role of God's agent. Isaiah is perhaps most famous for his explicit promises of a New King to come in the Davidic royal family line, which Christians recognize as fulfilled in Jesus of Nazareth. Isaiah 9 and 11 contain the clearest promises that God will cause to be born a new child of the Davidic family that will serve God's purposes and rescue all the people through his blessed rule. In the second half of the book Isaiah is envisioning the far-off future, when the Jews are living in the exile under the control of Babylon. In this part Isaiah continues these predictions of a human agent to come who will be used by God to rescue all his people. But in these chapters of Isaiah he is merely called the "servant" of God, and nothing is explicitly said about his being a royal figure. Indeed, the title of "Messiah" or anointed one is transferred to the Persian King Cyrus, who will be

God's agent and do his will, even though Cyrus himself does not know or worship Yahweh. But the "servant" of God will know him, and will serve God's purposes in rescuing his people. In both the first half of the book and the second half of the book the agent of God will be endowed by the Holy Spirit and will exercise governmental function by bringing justice to both the people of Israel and to foreign nations. Jesus and his apostles apply these Messianic passages to himself, making Isaiah one of the most-quoted Old Testament books in the New Testament.

Overview of the book

I. Law and Gospel in Light of Judah/Israel's Rebellion and the Assyrian Threat (1:1—33:24)
   A. Introduction to Words and Themes of Isaiah (1:1–31)
   B. Law and Gospel for Judah: The sin of God's people Israel/Judah brings His wrath, but His love also brings His salvation (2:1—12:5)
       1. Woe to Israel and Judah for sin (Six woes in Isa 5; 2:1—5:30)
       2. The Exile is forecast at the call of Isaiah (Isa 6:1–13)
       3. Children signify God's coming punishment upon the nation of the current disobedient King of Judah, and also signify His coming salvation to the nation through the birth of the perfect king, the Messiah (7:1—12:5)
   C. Law and Gospel for Specific Nations and for the Entire Earth (Isa 24—27 is called The Isaiah Apocalypse; 13:1—27:13)
   D. Law and Gospel for God's Nations Judah and Israel (Six Woes; 28:1—33:24)
II. Law and Gospel in Light of the Babylonian Exile (34:1—66:24)
   A. God's word of salvation for His people Judah is also His word of judgment against the nations of this world, exemplified in Israel's brother nation, Edom (34:1—35:10)
   B. Salvation for Judah is also defeat for Assyria; but condemnation for Judah is also victory for Babylon: Historical interlude setting the stage for the need for a future release from Babylon (36:1—39:8)
   C. Salvation for Judah is defeat for Babylon and victory for Cyrus; and humiliation for God's "Servant" will become victory for God's "Servant" (40:1—62:12)
   D. Separation of the "servants" of God: One brother is doomed (Edom), but one brother is saved (the True Israel; 63:1—66:24)

The outline disregards the traditional higher-critical division between First and Second Isaiah in favor of other evidence that perhaps better reflects the organization of the book as a whole. The actual midpoint of the book occurs to-

ward the end of Isaiah 33. Isaiah 35 is better associated with Isaiah 40 and following, and Isaiah 34 is better associated with Isaiah 35 and 63. Isaiah 36—39
fit with the comfort theme that begins in Isaiah 40, and the fact that they are
prose balance with the prose material of Isaiah 7—8 in the first half of the book.
There are other parallels between some of the corresponding sections of the two
halves of the book.

26

Prophecy to Judah in the Seventh Century
Nahum, Habakkuk, Zephaniah

Nahum

The world in our day has become very small as events in one part of the world quickly become international concerns. Threats to the stability of one region have the potential to plunge the entire community of nations into turmoil, and disasters that affect one nation can send shock waves throughout the world. For much of the seventh century BC actions by one particular nation sent waves throughout the entire Near East. That nation was Assyria with its capital at Nineveh. It dominated the entire Fertile Crescent and its armies terrorized nations wherever it waged war. One of those nations was Judah. However, God offered comfort for Judah as it sought to survive the attacks of the cruel empire that dominated its world. The prophet Nahum, whose name means *comfort*, prophesied that God would defend his people and judge the Assyrians. His short prophecy describes Assyria's impending fall in 612 BC in order to comfort the people of Judah.

1. Authorship and Date—*Who Was Nahum and When Did He Prophesy?*
2. Theme—*What Is Nahum About?*
3. Overview of the Book—*The Contents of Nahum*

1. Authorship and Date

Little is known about Nahum. He tells us that he was from Elkosh (Nah 1:1), but the location of that village in Judah is unknown. Nahum prophesied sometime in the mid-to-late seventh century BC. He speaks about the fall of the Egyptian city of Thebes as a past event (Nah 3:8–10). Since Thebes fell to the Assyrians in 663 BC, his ministry cannot have been earlier than this. Nahum prophesies that Nineveh will fall to an invader. Since Nineveh was conquered by the Medes and Babylonians in 612 BC, he had to have been active before that date. Most probably Nahum prophesied during the reign of Josiah (641–609 BC), since he depicts the fall of Nineveh as on the horizon. This would make him a contemporary of Zephaniah and somewhat older than Jeremiah.

2. Theme

Nahum is occupied with a single theme: God will judge Nineveh. In fact, he calls this short book "an oracle concerning Nineveh" (Nah 1:1). Nahum begins with an address to Judah noting some characteristics of God that enable him to execute his judgment throughout creation (Nah 1:4–6):

> Yahweh is a jealous and avenging God.
> Yahweh is avenging and wrathful.
>> Yahweh takes vengeance on his adversaries
>> and keeps wrath for his enemies.
> Yahweh is slow to anger and great in power.
> Yahweh will by no means clear the guilty.
>> His way is in whirlwind and storm,
>> and the clouds are the dust of his feet. (Nah 1:2–3)

But these attributes of God that execute the demands of his Law are not the only ones that Nahum knows. He also knew that

> Yahweh is good,
> a stronghold in the day of trouble.
>> He knows those who take refuge in him. (Nah 1:7)

Both of these sets of attributes of God are used by Nahum to comfort the people of Judah, since he will pour out his wrath on Assyria (Nah 1:12), but in an echo of Isaiah 52:7, will send the feet of a messenger to bring good news to Judah that Assyria will no longer invade her.

The rest of Nahum is a description of Nineveh's fall, addressed as if the prophet were speaking directly to the Assyrian capital city. With sharp language and stern judgment the prophet announces what awaits Nineveh because of its sins. While Nineveh had repented in Jonah's day, it very quickly forgot the threatened judgment of God, so Nahum ends his prophesy with condemnation and doom:

> There is no easing your hurt.
> Your wound is fatal.
>> All who hear the news about you clap their hands over you.
>>> For upon whom has your unceasing evil not come? (Nah 3:19)

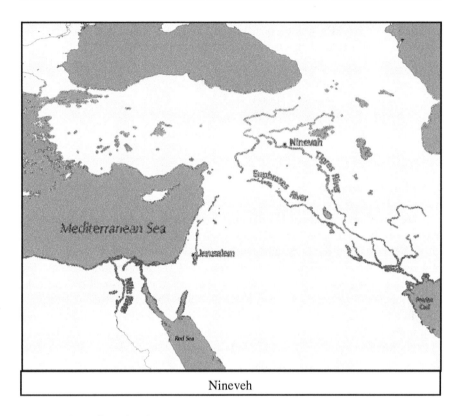

Nineveh

3. Overview of the Book

This short book of only forty-seven verses divides easily into two major sections: an address to Judah and an address to Nineveh.

   I.   Superscription (1:1)

  II. Address to Judah: God will judge Nineveh (1:2–15)

 III. Address to Nineveh: Assyria's fall will be fierce (2:1—3:18)

Habakkuk

Injustice and corruption have plagued human society since humans first fell into sin. The very existence of widespread injustice has raised concerns among many over God's role in the world. If God is a just God, why does he allow this disease to fester? Why does he allow some to suffer under the unjust and corrupt acts of others? These concerns also bothered the prophet Habakkuk as he looked at Judah in his day. He was supposed to be living in a nation that God chose as his people. How could such corruption exist even among the people of God?

1. Authorship and Date—*Who Was Habakkuk and When Did He Prophesy?*
2. Theme—*What Is Habakkuk About?*
3. Overview of the Book—*Contents of Habakkuk*

1. Authorship and Date

We know nothing about Habakkuk's background, since he reveals nothing about himself in his book. Since Habakkuk foresaw the invasion of the Babylonians, he must have lived in Judah and prophesied late in Josiah's reign (641–609 BC) or early in Jehoiakim's reign (609–598 BC). Most scholars date his prophecy a few years before or after the battle of Carchemish in 605 BC. At Carchemish on the Orontes River in Syria the Babylonian army routed the Egyptians in a battle that would signal the irreversibility of Babylon's rise as a dominant power in the Near East. The Babylonians pursued the Egyptians all the way to the border of Egypt. They would soon dismantle what was left of the Assyrian Empire and establish their own Empire that would dominate the Fertile Crescent for almost seventy years.

2. Theme

Habakkuk's prophecy is unique in that the prophet revealed to Judah and to us a dialogue he had with God. This dialogue concerned Habakkuk's cry to God to stop the injustice that he saw in Judahite society in his day. Thus, like Job, Habakkuk explores the topic of **theodicy**, the discussion of how God is a just God in a world where injustice flourishes. This is the question he raises at the outset:

> Yahweh, how long will I cry for help, and you will not hear?
> Or cry to you "Violence!" and you will not save?
>> Why do you make me see wickedness,
>> and why do you idly look at wrong?
>>> Destruction and violence are before me.
>>> Strife and contention arise.
>>>> So the law is paralyzed,
>>>> and justice never goes forth.
>>>>> The wicked surround the righteous,

so justice is perverted. (Hab 1:2–4)

The prophet does not understand how God can allow wrong to continue without immediately punishing the wrongdoers. Habakkuk knows that God is a righteous God who cannot tolerate sin. So why does God not stop those who sin and turn justice into injustice? Why are they allowed to continue to do these things and even to prosper?

God's answer is dramatic. He tells Habakkuk to look to the events among the nations, because he is raising the Babylonians to be his fierce instrument to judge the people of Judah (Hab 1:5–17). In this way God indicated to the prophet that he had not been ignoring the sins and injustices within Judah. Through geopolitical events that Habakkuk himself could see, he had been putting his plan into action all along.

However, God's answer raised an even more perplexing question. The Babylonians were a wicked and ruthless nation, more wicked than Judah. How could God use such a wicked nation to punish Judah? After all, Habakkuk knew that God could not tolerate evil:

> Your eyes are too pure to look on evil
> You cannot tolerate wrong.
>> Why then do you tolerate the treacherous?
>> Why are you silent while the wicked swallow up those more righteous
>> than themselves? (Hab 1:13)

How could God allow the Babylonians to destroy other nations without mercy? (Hab 1:17). The prophet did not know the answer, but he was confident that God had an answer. He made himself ready to receive the answer (Hab 2:1).

When God's answer comes to Habakkuk, he is commanded to write down what God reveals (Hab 2:2), and is promised that God's answer to evil will take place (Hab 2:3). Since God commanded the prophet to write his words down for others to read, it is certain that Habakkuk's conversation with God was not simply a private conversation. It was intended as the prophet's divinely revealed oracle for the enlightenment of God's people (Hab 1:1).

God's answer to Habakkuk has two important components: God will punish those who do evil, but in his own time and in his own way. Meanwhile, "the righteous person will live by his faith" (Hab 2:4). God reinforced a principle at the heart of the Gospel: Through faith the child of God receives forgiveness and life from God. Otherwise, no person could stand before God's judgment. This statement in Habakkuk is quoted several times in the New Testament (Rom 1:17; Gal 3:11; Heb 10:38; see Rom 4:14; 2 Cor 5:7; Gal 2:19–20). It is central to Paul's argument that Christians are not saved by keeping God's Law, but by God's forgiveness in the Gospel, which is received by faith.

God then emphasizes that he will not overlook sin, pronouncing woes for several types of corruption:

> Woe to the one who piles up stolen goods and becomes wealthy by extortion...
> Woe to the one who builds his realm by unjust gain...
> Who to the one who builds a city with bloodshed and establishes a town by crime...
> Woe to the one who gives drink to his neighbors...in order to gaze on their naked bodies...
> Woe to the one who says to wood, "Come to life!" or to lifeless stone, "Wake up!"... (Hab 2:6, 9, 12, 15, 19)

However, these threats are not designed simply to condemn Judah's corrupt rulers and people. They are a warning intended to move hearers to repentance and faith. Therefore, Habakkuk closes God's reply with the conclusion:

> But Yahweh is in his holy temple.
> Let all the earth be silent before him. (Hab 2:20)

Habakkuk concludes his prophecy with a prayer that indicates that he accepted and understood God's answer. The prayer is in the form of a psalm. In fact, it employs musical or liturgical terms, such as *selah,* that are found primarily in the book of Psalms.

The key statement in Habakkuk's prayer is "in wrath remember mercy" (Hab 3:2). The prophet had come to realize that he would not receive an explanation for every instance of God's use of events in history to punish sin and repair injustice. However, he came to trust that God does control history and will execute his judgment on sinners who do not repent. Instead, he now begged God to remember his mercy toward his people as he uses events to bring his wrath on evildoers.

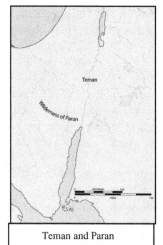

Teman and Paran

The prophet then pictures God marching from Teman and Mount Paran in his glory. All creation is at his control and cringes as he passes through it (Hab 3:3–11). This activity of God was not merely to demonstrate his power, however. Instead,

You went out for the salvation of your people,
for the salvation of your anointed one. (Hab 3:13a)

The prophet now not only realized that God does indeed punish wickedness but also that he does it in a way that protects and saves his people. That salvation is seen through his saving of his "anointed one." In Habakkuk's day the king was often considered God's anointed leader, and in the past Yahweh had preserved the royal line of David through the time of the Assyrian threat, thereby saving his people and their homeland. However, Habakkuk's reference is not simply to the kings of Judah, since Habakkuk has already been told that the Babylonians would punish Judah, and Isaiah and Micah had already foretold the Babylonian captivity, which would bring the Davidic monarchy to an end. Therefore, the reference to an anointed one is to the great anointed one, the Messiah. The heavenly Father defends his Messiah, thereby saving his people. Habakkuk now understood that he will never know why God allows certain wicked acts in this life to appear to go unpunished. However, he had confidence that through the Messiah God will save his people and punish all wickedness.

This confidence allowed the prophet to look beyond the immediate evil of the Babylonians and to "…wait quietly for the day of distress to come on the nation invading us." (Hab 3:16). This confidence leads to the conclusion of Habakkuk's hymn, where he no longer ponders questions of theodicy. Instead of needing answers to questions that are beyond his capacity to understand, the prophet has learned to rejoice even when it appears as if disaster has struck God's people.

Though the fig tree should not blossom,
nor fruit be on the vines;
the produce of the olive fail,
and the fields yield no food;
the flock be cut off from the pen
and there be no herd in the stalls,
    yet I will rejoice in Yahweh.
I will take joy in the God of my salvation.
      Yahweh, my Lord, is my strength.
        He makes my feet like deer's feet.
        He makes me tread on my high places. (Hab 3:17–19a)

3. Overview of the Book

Habakkuk's prophecy is most easily divided into a dialogue between God and the prophet ending with Habakkuk's prayer.

I.   Superscription (1:1)
II. Habakkuk's first question to God: "Why does evil flourish in Judah?" (1:2–4)
III. God's Answer: "I will punish Judah with the Babylonians." (1:5–11)
IV. Habakkuk's second question to God: "How can you use the evil Babylonians to punish your people?" (1:12—2:1)
V.   God's Answer: "Babylon will be punished, and the righteous person will live by faith." (2:2–20)
VI. Habakkuk's Prayer: A plea for God's mercy even as he executes his wrath, since no one could stand before the righteous God without receiving mercy. (3:1–19)

Zephaniah

When a verdict is handed down, who gets judged more severely? Across the centuries one of the criticisms of judgments of courts is that the rich and well-connected often are able to use their money and influence to get a different kind of judgment than the average defendant. They hire the best lawyers to defend them, giving them a better chance at acquittal or a less-severe sentence when punishment is imposed by the court. In some circumstances they may even be able to use their influence to have the charges dropped. In contrast, Zephaniah pictures a different kind of justice when God is holding court. This prophet depicts God's judgment on several nations, but reserves his harshest words for God's people in Judah. Their position as God's ancient people does not win them favors before God's judicial bar. Instead, Yahweh holds them more accountable for their sin than he does the nations, since "everyone to whom much was given, from him much will be required, and from him to whom they entrusted much, they will demand more" (Luke 12:48).

1. Authorship and Date—*Who Was Zephaniah and When Did He Prophesy?*
2. Theme—*What Is Zephaniah About?*
3. Overview of the Book—*The Contents of Zephaniah*

1. Authorship and Date

Zephaniah came from a well-connected family. He was a great-grandson of Judah's righteous king Hezekiah (715–686 BC; Zeph 1:1). Many of Zephaniah's statements reveal that he was familiar with the royal court and the political issues of his day.

Zephaniah's ministry was during the reign of Josiah (641–609 BC). He prophesied the destruction of Nineveh (Zeph 2:12), so his ministry must have ended before 612 BC at the very latest. Since the description of Nineveh at Zephaniah 2:15 depicts the city as powerful and secure, Zephaniah was most probably active sometime before the death of the powerful Assyrian king Ashurbanipal (627 BC). Moreover, he has a scathing condemnation of widespread idolatry in Judah and Jerusalem (Zeph 1:4–9). This would mean that he prophesied before Josiah began his reform in 629 BC (2 Chr 34:2) and before Jeremiah was called to be a prophet (628 BC; Jer 1:2). His ministry would have overlapped Nahum's and preceded Habakkuk's by about a quarter of a century.

2. Theme

Zephaniah's prophecy is occupied with God's judgment on the day of the Lord (see the discussion of this concept in Chapter 22). He begins with a general statement by God about that day:

> "I will completely sweep away everything from the face of the earth,"
>> declares Yahweh.
> "I will sweep away human and beast.
> I will sweep away the birds of the heavens
>> the fish of the sea,
>>> and the rubble with the wicked.
> I will remove humans from the face of the earth,"
>> declares Yahweh. (Zeph 1:2–3)

The prophet then shifts to a much more specific description of God's judgment of Judah for the idolatry that is taking place there (Zeph 1:4–13). He appears to be prophesying the fall of Jerusalem to the Babylonians as he predicts:

> Their goods shall be plundered,
> and their houses laid waste.
>> Although they build houses,
>>> they shall not inhabit them.
>> Although they plant vineyards,
>>> they shall not drink wine from them. (Zeph 1:13)

Yet the coming destruction of Jerusalem by the Babylonians is only a foretaste of the ultimate day of the Lord, as Zephaniah quickly announces that "the great day of Yahweh is near" (Zeph 1:14). This day is described in grim terms of distress, anguish, darkness, gloom, clouds and blackness, a theme adopted by Jesus in the New Testament (Matt 24:29). Moreover, no amount of status or influence can save sinful humans from the coming judgment:

> Neither their silver nor their gold will be able to deliver them on the day of the
>   wrath of Yahweh.
> In the fire of his jealousy all the earth will be consumed.
> For he will make a full and sudden end to all the inhabitants of the earth.
>   (Zeph 1:18)

But there is a way to escape God's wrath:

> Seek Yahweh, all you humble of the land,
>   who do his just commands.
>   Seek righteousness.
>   Seek humility.
> Perhaps you may be hidden on the day of the anger of Yahweh. (Zeph 2:3)

Humans will not be able to save themselves from God's wrath, but God himself can save them. The prophet urges his audience to seek Yahweh and find righteousness and humility in him. Then, although they cannot hide themselves from his anger, they will be hidden under his protection from the day of his wrath.

Zephaniah then prophesies about God's judgment on specific nations, including the Philistines, Moab and Ammon, Cush and Assyria. Next he returns to condemn Jerusalem, "the city of oppressors" (Zeph 3:1). All these nations and more will feel God's wrath on the day of judgment:

> "Therefore wait for me," declares Yahweh,
> "for the day when I rise up to seize the prey.
>   For my decision is to gather nations,
>   to assemble kingdoms,
>   to pour out upon them my indignation,
>   all my burning anger.
> For all the earth will be consumed in the fire of my jealousy." (Zeph 3:8)

But, once again the prophet notes that God has a plan of escape for those who trust in him no matter what people they come from. He will enable them to repent and call on him:

> For at that time I will purify the lips of the peoples, that all of them may call
> upon the name of Yahweh and serve him with one accord. (Zeph 3:9)

These people with pure lips will be gathered from everywhere they are scattered (Zeph 3:10), and within Jerusalem will be only those who trust in Yahweh (Zeph 3:12). They will become the "remnant of Israel" (Zeph 3:13). Zephaniah closes out his short prophecy with a lavish description of what God will do to restore his people and save them from the day of wrath (Zeph 3:14–20). He promises:

> Yahweh your God is in your midst,
>> a mighty one who will save.
>>> He will rejoice over you with gladness.
>>> He will quiet you with his love.
>>> He will delight over you with loud singing. (Zeph 3:17)

Therefore, Zephaniah points forward to the Messianic era and the salvation from sin and death that comes from God alone. This is the only hope for humans as they look toward the day of the Lord.

3. Overview of the Book

Zephaniah's prophecy is only three chapters long. These fifty-three verses may have been a single prophecy.

I.   Superscription (1:1)
II. Warning about the coming wrath of God (1:2–3)
III. Judgment on Judah because of its idolatry (1:4–13)
IV. The great day of God's wrath (1:14—2:3)
V. God's judgment on the nations (2:4—3:8)
    A. Philistia (2:4–7)
    B. Moab and Ammon (2:8–11)
    C. Cush (2:12)
    D. Assyria (2:13–15)
    E. Jerusalem (3:1–8)
VI. Redemption of God's people (3:9–13)

27

Prophecy of the Fall of Judah and the Exile
Jeremiah, Lamentations, Ezekiel and Daniel

Jeremiah

Jesus once asked his disciples, "Who do people say the Son of Man is?" (Matt 16:13). The disciples listed several rumors circulating through the community, one of which was that Jesus was the reincarnation of "Jeremiah the Prophet." Why should the people identify Jesus with Jeremiah? Was it the strong zeal for God and for righteousness that both these preachers exhibited? Was it the way both were rejected by the authorities in spite of the evidence that the power of God was with them? Was it the personal intimacy and honesty with God exhibited in both their prayer lives? Was it the fact that they both condemned the leadership of Jerusalem and predicted the city's destruction? Jeremiah's courageous and clear preaching and his revelation of some of his intimate prayers have made this prophet a favorite of many readers. In one real sense he offered the people nothing new, he simply held them accountable to the terms of the Sinai Covenant delivered by Moses. But because he delivered this clear conviction of human sin, he also delivered the promise that God would save his people through the Messiah. Therefore, Jeremiah is known as the prophet of the New Covenant that would be established when the Messiah came.

1. Authorship and Date—*The Persecuted, Unpopular, Suffering Prophet*
2. Major Themes—*Doom and Hope*
3. Overview of the book—*Jeremiah Confronts Jerusalem*
4. Important Passages—*The Promises of God are Trustworthy*

1. Authorship and Date

The prophetic ministry of the prophet Jeremiah began in 626 BC, forty years before the conquest of Jerusalem and continued past the destruction of Jerusalem in 586 BC. The prophecy described in Jeremiah 44 was the last recorded word of Jeremiah, and it is suggested that it be dated about 580 BC, after the

Jewish refugees had had time to settle in Egypt. This would indicate a preaching ministry of at least forty and perhaps as many as forty-six years.

But the book of Jeremiah is another thing. Although great parts of the book quote Jeremiah speaking in the first person, and it includes several personal prayers of Jeremiah, after Jeremiah 24 the messages of Jeremiah are each framed in narrative described by some editor. At the end of Jeremiah 51 we read "The words of Jeremiah end here." The following chapter, Jeremiah 52, provides a historical review of the fall of Jerusalem and the exile of the population, including mention of a deportation that took place in 581 BC. The final paragraph describes the release of the hostage King Jehoiachin from Babylonian prison in 561 BC, and comments on the comfort of the remaining years of this exiled king until he died in Babylon. Thus the final form of the book appears to be the work of an editor who collected, annotated, and published the sermons of Jeremiah. Since we read that Jeremiah used Baruch son of Neriah as a secretary to record as least part of his preaching (Jer 32; 36, also mentioned in 43), it is a reasonable supposition that Baruch may have been the editor that produced the final form of the book.

This impression is reinforced when we note Jeremiah 45. The story of Jeremiah and his sermons about Judah end in Jeremiah 44, and Jeremiah 46—51 contains a collection of his sermons against foreign nations with only the briefest of editorial dating information. In between these sections the very short Jeremiah 45 contains a personal prophecy delivered from Jeremiah to Baruch. Though Baruch apparently had a brother named Seraiah who was a government official (Jer 51:59), and Baruch himself was accused of political scheming (Jer 43:3), God spoke to Baruch to urge him not to focus on traditional goals of worldly success and comfort, and God promised that he would preserve Baruch alive through all the disasters he was going to witness. This is very reminiscent of the way St. John allowed brief attention to himself as the author of his Gospel, especially in his last chapter.

Other questions about the structure of the book of Jeremiah are raised for scholars when one turns to the Greek Septuagint, in which the book of Jeremiah is significantly shorter than that in the Hebrew Masoretic Text, and which has a different arrangement of chapters. (Jeremiah is the longest book of the Hebrew Old Testament by word count.) This is somewhat the opposite situation from the book of Daniel, where the Greek version is considerably longer than the Hebrew version. In the Greek version of Jeremiah the oracles about foreign nations contained in Jeremiah 45—51 are placed not at the end of the book, but after Jeremiah 25:13. They are thus the third quarter of the book in the Greek version instead of the fourth quarter as in the Hebrew text. Document fragments from Qumran seem to attest to the existence of both versions in Hebrew. Although this information is tantalizing for scholars who want to speculate on the history of the transmission of the text, it has little other value.

Jeremiah himself was probably born about 646 BC. We are told that he was quite young when he was called to be a prophet in 626 BC, so we must guess at his age at that call (perhaps twenty years old) and his birth year prior to that. He is descended from the line of priests, but these are described as "the priests of Anathoth." Anathoth in Benjamin is the home town to which Abiathar retired when Solomon removed him from functioning as High Priest (1 Kings 2:26). Thus Jeremiah is most likely descended from the family of High Priest Eli in the book of 1 Samuel. Eli was promised punishment for his failure to discipline his sons, and his branch of the priestly family was eventually permanently removed from functioning as priests. Jeremiah appears in Jerusalem about 350 years later. It may well be that the contemporary priests, descendents of the line of Zadok, viewed Jeremiah as a religious rival, and their sense of rivalry contributed to the fact that Jeremiah never enjoyed political favor and was often persecuted throughout his ministry. It is interesting to note that both Jeremiah and Ezekiel, who was descended from the line of Zadok, lived at the same time and preached essentially the same message (predicting the fall of Jerusalem and the later return from exile). Both used many action prophecies, but in different locations. Jeremiah preached in Jerusalem, while Ezekiel was taken captive to Babylon and carried out his ministry there, thus also never being allowed to function as a priest. It is highly likely that there was communication of the messages of these men between the Jewish groups in Babylon and in Jerusalem (see Jer 29), but neither book mentions the other man in any way.

When Jeremiah was a young boy, there was an abrupt change of government in Jerusalem. The young boy-king Josiah (age eight) was placed on the throne after his father was assassinated in an attempted coup. Jeremiah would have grown up at the same time this boy-king finished growing. Josiah was a good, religious king. Jeremiah was called to become God's prophet in Josiah's thirteenth year of rule, which would be 626 BC. Five years later King Josiah ordered repairs made on the Temple, and during the process the priests found something called "the Book of the Law of Moses." When this book was read to King Josiah, he was so impressed that he led the entire country in a thorough reformation of their religion (see 2 Kgs 22—23). He tried hard to guide the nation back to faithfulness to the Lord. As part of this process he deliberately consulted the prophets in Jerusalem for guidance. We read of interaction with a prophetess named Huldah (2 Kgs 22:14), but we never read of any contact with Jeremiah, who had then been prophesying for five years. This may be some indication of the fact that Jeremiah was constantly held at arm's length from the government and the official religious establishment.

Nevertheless, some of the government officials respected Jeremiah, and protected and aided him. We learn of the family of Shaphan son of Azaliah (2 Kgs 22), who served as Secretary in Josiah's government. He was the one who brought the newly found book to the attention of the King, and he was among those sent to consult Huldah. Three generations of this family served in government and each gave support to Jeremiah, in spite of his political ostracism. Shaphan's sons Ahikam (2 Kgs 34:20; Jer 26:24), Gemariah (Jer 36), and Elasah (Jer 29:1–3), and Ahikam's sons Micaiah (Jer 36:11–13) and Gedaliah (Jer 39—43) supported Jeremiah (Shaphan's son Jaazaniah seems to have not maintained the same faith, Ezek 8:11).

But the excitement and devotion of King Josiah's reformation came to an end with his untimely death in 609 BC, when Jeremiah would have been between the ages of 35 and 40. We do not know whether or not Josiah had an agreement with the Babylonians, but he fought to frustrate the purposes of Egypt and died in battle. His son Jehoahaz became king, but was quickly taken prisoner by Pharaoh Necho and died in Egypt. The next son of Josiah was Jehoiakim, who served Egypt until Babylon defeated Egypt and became the master of Judah. Jehoiakim then plotted with Egypt to rebel against Babylon. Nebuchadnezzar of Babylon came to punish this rebellion, and Jehoiakim died while Jerusalem was under siege. Jehoiakim's son Jehoiachin was put on the throne, but the city surrendered and Jehoiachin was carried hostage to Babylon. Josiah's next son Zedekiah was put on the throne of Jerusalem, but he too plotted with Egypt to rebel against Babylon. In 586 BC Nebuchadnezzar punished Jerusalem with destruction and exile.

None of these rulers after Josiah were praised by the Biblical writers. Jeremiah often preached against this reliance on Egypt, and called for honest allegiance to the treaty made with Babylon. No doubt this continued to increase his political ostracism. King Jehoiakim tried to arrest and kill Jeremiah (Jer 36), and King Zedekiah imprisoned Jeremiah. Zedekiah sometimes consulted Jeremiah while he had him in prison (Jer 37:17–21; 38:1–28), though he also sometimes insisted on secrecy (Jer 38:24–27). He protected Jeremiah against threats from other officials (Jer 37:21) though once he agreed to a plan to kill Jeremiah (Jer 38:5ff), but was convinced to reverse his decision before it was too late.

So Jeremiah's life was one of opposition, frustration, and suffering. Not only did he have political foes, but he also had religious foes. Priests and other prophets (identified as false prophets) worked against him. He was arrested and beaten (Jer 20:2), banned from the Temple (Jer 36:5), and opposed by other preachers (Jer 28:1–17; 29:26). Even his own relatives from Anathoth opposed him (Jer 11). The Law of Moses stated that anyone proven to be a false prophet should be put to death, so many of his opponents hoped that they could catch Jeremiah in just one unfulfilled prophecy, and use that to have him condemned (compare Jer 20:10). God took over Jeremiah's entire life to use him as a tool for warning the people of Jerusalem about the approaching doom. Jeremiah was forbidden by God to marry, or even to attend weddings, and forbidden to attend funerals (Jer 16). All of this would have been unusual behavior, and would have caused talk. But that kind of talk was to be used as a cue for Jeremiah to proclaim his message. Whenever someone asked why he didn't marry or attend weddings, he was to respond that this was no longer a time to celebrate weddings and new families, since doom was coming to Jerusalem. Whenever someone asked him why he didn't attend a funeral, he was to respond that this was no longer a time to celebrate the end of life and make a proper burial, because Jerusalem would be destroyed by war, and the bodies would not be properly buried or properly mourned by their families. These kind of constant grim reminders of doom no doubt contributed to Jeremiah's lack of popularity with most people.

When Jeremiah's prophecies about the destruction of Jerusalem finally came to pass in 586 BC, he was at first rounded up with the survivors and placed in a group to be marched as prisoners to Babylon. Even though Jeremiah was unpopular, he had apparently developed a reputation, and this reputation had become known even to the Babylonian officials. Since Jeremiah had constantly preached against rebellion, and had prophesied that the exiles should settle down in Babylon and be good citizens and raise families, he was perceived by these Babylonian officials as pro-Babylon. Therefore after the city fell orders were given to locate this supposed Babylonian supporter and give him his liberty. Jeremiah was offered the choice to relocate to Babylon and live in comfort, or to remain in Judah as a free man in the care of the new governor of the province of Judah. The Babylonians had appointed Gedaliah, grandson of Shaphan, to be the new governor, since they had removed the royal family of David from power. Jeremiah chose to stay with Gedaliah.

Unfortunately, this was not the end of trouble for Jeremiah. Gedaliah was assassinated by a descendent of the Davidic family who had plotted together with the King of Ammon. The assassin tried to take the rest of the leadership captive to Ammon, but another Jewish official named Johanan combined with the army officers to stop him. The captives were rescued and taken back to the vicinity of Bethlehem. Johanan and the other military leaders feared that Nebuchadnezzar would punish the Jews for the murder of the governor, so they decided to flee for sanctuary to Egypt. They asked Jeremiah to consult God for instructions. Jeremiah received an answer from God that they would be safe if they stayed in the land of Judah. Although they had sworn an oath to follow Jeremiah's words, they did not trust this prophecy, and forced everyone to move to Egypt for sanctuary, including Jeremiah and Baruch. In Egypt Jeremiah complained about the disobedience of the people—particularly the worship of the goddess "the Queen of Heaven" (probably Astarte). He predicted God's wrath upon these rebellious Jews and God's plan to deliver Egypt to the control of Babylon. Once again, the people rejected Jeremiah's prophecies and chose their own way. In summary, no matter how many prophecies of Jeremiah came true, God's people of Judah continued to reject his words and not trust in what he said.

One of the special aspects of the book of Jeremiah is that it contains several personal prayers of Jeremiah (Jer 10:23–25; 11:18—12:6; 15:10–21; 17:9–11; 14–18; 18:18–23; 20:7–18), which illustrate his emotional struggle and suffering. These prayers often appeal to God to punish those wicked people who were causing Jeremiah's suffering and to rescue his servant. The fact that the prophet made these appeals shows us how difficult these disobedient sinners made life for Jeremiah. (For more on these prayers, see below in Major Themes: True and False Prophecy, and also in Important Passages: Jer 20.)

2. Major Themes

The content of the book of Jeremiah can be efficiently collected in three major themes: Jerusalem is Doomed; the Old Covenant and New Covenant; and True and False Prophecy and True and False Religion.

Jerusalem is Doomed

The overarching theme of Jeremiah is that Jerusalem and Judah are doomed because of their sin, specifically their unfaithfulness to Yahweh and to the Sinai Covenant. Although many of Jeremiah's prophecies offer or imply the possibility of avoiding doom if the population repents, it is clear that God did not expect that to happen, and so the book forecasts the doom as inevitable, and describes its fulfillment within Jeremiah's lifetime.

Jeremiah 24 can be viewed as a perfect summary of this historical prediction. In this chapter God gives Jeremiah a vision of two baskets of figs, one containing good figs and the other containing rotten figs. The good figs represent the people of Judah and Jerusalem that have been carried away into exile in Babylon. They are the good ones that God has harvested and taken away to keep safe. The bad figs represent the people left behind in Jerusalem. Although they believe that they are the favored ones who have been saved by God by not being carried away, they are in fact those that have been left behind as rotten. They are the figs that have been left too long on the plant and which have gone bad. They are useless for any human purpose, and God will throw them away.

Jeremiah 7 and Jeremiah 26 are usually understood to be an account of the same event in the life of Jeremiah (though it is possible that they represent two separate but similar sermons of Jeremiah). Jeremiah 26 is a prose account of the events that happened, with a brief recount of the sermon, while Jeremiah 7 is the longer sermon that was preached, linked in that chapter to other sermons from Jeremiah's early years. In these two passages Jeremiah went to the Temple and compared Jerusalem to the ancient city of Shiloh. Shiloh was the location of the Tabernacle sanctuary and of the Ark of the Covenant in the days of the High Priest Eli, when Samuel received his call to be a prophet (see 1 Sam 1—6). At that time God announced his anger against Israel and against the priestly family of Eli, and declared his intention to punish them. The Israelites were defeated in a war against the Philistines, members of the priestly family were killed, the Ark was captured, and High Priest Eli died when he learned this information. Although the Bible does not explicitly describe what happened to Shiloh, the implication of Jeremiah's sermon is that the Philistines subsequently overran the city since it served as the headquarters of leadership in Israel. When the Ark was eventually returned to the Israelites, it was placed in Kiriath-Jearim instead of Shiloh. This seems to imply that the old site of Shiloh was no longer an option. The point that Jeremiah made by referring to this city and these old events was that even though Shiloh had the Tabernacle, it was no guarantee of safety if the God who was to be worshipped at the Tabernacle was angry at the Israelites. Even the Ark of His Presence was no guarantee. People should not try to manipulate these manifestations of God's presence as if they somehow forced some control over God. So in Jeremiah's day the fact that Jerusalem contained the Temple built by Solomon was no guarantee that God would automatically defend the city. God was again angry at the behavior of his people, and the Temple in Jerusalem was no defense when it was God who was behind the attack.

Since Jeremiah was descended from the line of Eli, this historical event concerning Shiloh would have been well known to his clan, for it greatly affected the later history of their family line. However, this prophecy may also have been interpreted by the current priests of the Temple, descended from the line of Zadok, as offensive just because it came from a priest who was a descendent of Eli.

It appears that a tradition had arisen in Judah that Jerusalem would never fall. According to this tradition the presence of God in his Temple there and the presence of the Davidic line of kings there, guaranteed that God would always protect this city. Jerusalem was the City of David, the seat of David's government and the throne on which his descendents ruled, and God had promised David that he would never lack a descendent sitting upon the throne. This promise to forever protect David's dynasty was thought to extend to forever protecting David's city. A century earlier, in the time of the great prophet Isaiah, the Assyrians had conquered everything else in Israel and Judah, and besieged the city of Jerusalem, but God had rescued the city. This was taken as proof that God would always protect Jerusalem. So the people believed they simply needed to have faith in this doctrine. But Jeremiah pointed out that God's protection depended upon the obedience of the people to God, not simply on their location, as evidenced by the past history of Shiloh. Faith in God's promises, when not accompanied by a life of discipleship, was a dead or empty faith and would not result in any divine salvation (compare Jas 2).

The Old Covenant and New Covenant

Jeremiah is famous for his prediction of a new covenant that would replace the Sinai Covenant (Jer 31:31–34), but this is best understood when it is realized that a great portion of Jeremiah's preaching rests on the foundation of the Sinai Covenant. Beginning with the first sermon in Jeremiah 2 Jeremiah bases his rebuke of Judah upon their special relationship with God established at the event of the Exodus from Egypt. Though the people of Israel had contracted to show God devotion (Jer 2:3) and to follow him, they had in fact forsaken him (Jer 2:13), and so God has concluded that the time has come to bring charges against them (Jer 2:9). Modern religious readers are often so indoctrinated with the concepts that no one is perfect and all humans sin that they almost take for granted that the Israelites would sin against God, and see that as normal human behavior. Jeremiah reminds us of how unusual and shocking these charges are in Jeremiah 2:10–12 when he points out that cultures do not usually abandon their religion and change their gods.

> "Cross over to the coasts of Kittim and look, send to Kedar and observe closely; see if there has ever been anything like this: Has a nation ever changed its gods? (Yet they are not gods at all.) But my people have exchanged their Glory for worthless idols. Be appalled at this, O heavens, and shudder with great horror," declares the Lord.

Cultures are usually open to a change in religion when the old religion no longer works, when the culture is being overwhelmed by new outside forces and the old religion no longer seems satisfactory. But Israel experienced success and blessing under the religion of Yahweh, from the time of the Exodus, through Joshua's conquest, through the time of David's empire, on down through the blessings that came to Judah in the reign of King Hezekiah. The prophetic history declares that the only times things did not go well with the Israelites are those times when they became indifferent about their religion. So it should be with some shock that we realize that it was at the times of peak success, wealth, and blessing that the Israelites fell prey to the temptation to follow other some religion, usually the religious ideas and gods of Canaan.

Further references to the Sinai Covenant by way of mention of the Exodus, the "Law," or the covenant occur in Jeremiah 3:16; 6:19; 7:22; 8:8; 9:13; 11:2; 14:21; 16:11,14; 18:18; 19:5; 22:9; 23:7; 26:4; 32:20; 34:13; 34:13; and 44:10, 23.

In Jeremiah 30—33 the prophet offers words of hope for the future. He predicts a time of reconciliation and rebuilding, a time of salvation by God. These promises of future blessing are further guaranteed by God when he compares his new promises to his decrees of creation. In Jeremiah 31:35–37 and again in Jeremiah 33:19–26 God emphasizes that his future promises are as certain as his establishment of heaven and earth, day and night. While Jeremiah 33 focuses on God's guarantee of his promise to David that his descendents would rule, Jeremiah 31 focuses on the existence of Israel as a nation and on their special relationship with God. "'Only if the heavens above can be measured and the foundations of the earth below be searched out will I reject all the descendants of Israel because of all they have done,' declares the Lord" (Jer 31:37). These passages make it clear that the future blessings are a result of God's past promises. Even though Israel had sinned and deserved to be cursed, God on His part will not forsake the relationship He had established. He will discipline Israel as He sees appropriate, but He will not break off the relationship or break His past promises. It is in this context that we encounter the famous passage Jeremiah 31:31–34, which is read at every celebration of the Lutheran Reformation. God will make a "new covenant" with Israel and Judah, one different from the Sinai Covenant that was made when "I took them by the hand to lead them out of Egypt." This covenant will be different in two ways: it will be based on complete forgiveness (Jer 31:34), and it will involve a spiritual change in the people so that they truly know and follow God (Jer 31:33–34). Although various passages in Isaiah and Ezekiel refer to the new things God will do in the future and sometimes seem to imply a change in covenant to something new, this passage in Jeremiah is the only passage that explicitly promises a new and different covenant. Therefore this must be to what Jesus refers when, at the institution of ritual we call the Lord's Supper, he said: "This cup is the new covenant in my blood, which is poured out for you" (Luke 22:20; see also Matt 26:27; 1 Cor 11:25). Jesus sets up a new ritual, involving a sacred meal with God, to replace the rituals of the sacrifice meals with God commanded by the Sinai Covenant. With the new ritual comes a new covenant, a new contract, a new relationship between God and his people. But while we cannot overemphasize the importance of the New Covenant, neither should we neglect to realize that throughout his prophecies Jeremiah makes it clear that the New Covenant is founded on the Sinai Covenant. The Old Covenant is obsolete because it is replaced by something better. But the something better is a continuation of the promises and blessings of God. The New Covenant does not throw away the Old Covenant or Old Testament, but in replacing the Old the New fulfills the Old, improves on the Old, extends the beneficial effects of the Covenant to a wider range of people, and includes greater divine gifts. Some things change, notably the ritual aspects. Some things remain constant, such as the call to love God, love our neighbor, and to be holy as God is holy. It is given to Jeremiah to forecast a new covenant with changes because it is also given to him to apply the demands and the condemnations of the Sinai Covenant in all their severity. Because Jeremiah is led to understand that the children of Adam are hopelessly corrupted by their sin, he can understand that the future relationship with God must involve God creating some special changes (compare St. Paul's statements in Rom 3):

> "Judah's sin is engraved with an iron tool, inscribed with a flint point, on the tablets of their hearts" (Jer 17:1)

> "Can the Ethiopian change his skin or the leopard its spots? Neither can you do good who are accustomed to doing evil" (Jer 13:23)

> "I will make a new covenant ... I will put my law in their minds and write it on their hearts ... and [I] will remember their sins no more" (Jer 31:31–34).

True and False Prophecy and True and False Religion

The third theme that plays out in the book of Jeremiah is the contrast between true and false prophecy—and along with that comes a distinction between true and false religion. Jeremiah found himself in conflict with other Judahite prophets and with other religious officials. More so than in any other book we learn of the struggle this type of conflict created among God's people, and we also learn of Jeremiah's personal and inner struggles that he experienced while involved in this conflict.

Deuteronomy 13 and 18 lay out the rules for judging and handling conflicting prophecies and prophets. The true prophet must speak in the name of Yahweh, the God of the Exodus, and thus must be consistent with everything previously revealed in the Torah of Yahweh. Whatever a prophet speaking in the name of Yahweh predicts must in fact come to pass. If it does not, the Israelites were to recognize him as a false prophet and dispose of him. Predictions regarding the long-range future obviously could not be judged by this criterion, since the community had to wait decades or sometimes longer to see if this took place. But the prophet himself could be judged by the success of his short-range predictions, and thus the community had some grounds for deciding which speaker of long-range predictions should be believed. In connection with this it is worthwhile to note how Biblical prophets such as Isaiah and Jeremiah sometimes attached specific time spans to their predictions, so that the community could easily judge whether or not their predictions came true within the predicted time frame (2 Kgs 22:28; Isa 7—8; Jer 28:15-17; 25:11-12; 29:10).

Jeremiah condemns false prophets repeatedly throughout the entire book, but certain chapters illustrate this struggle in vivid detail. Jeremiah 27—28 tell us the story of Jeremiah's conflict with another prophet named Hananiah. Several international officials had come to Jerusalem to discuss a secret plan to join in rebellion against Babylon. Jeremiah was commanded by God to make a model of a yoke, such as one would use to hitch up oxen to a wagon or a plow, but fit to wear on himself. He was to wear this model as a symbol of God's command that Judah and the other nations should be faithful to their treaties to be in allegiance to Babylon, to serve Babylon, and not rebel against her. Even though Judah and its rulers were so engrossed in sin and rebellion against God, he was still trying to guide them in the safest course of action that would be good for them. But Hananiah deliberately contradicted Jeremiah and predicted that Babylon's government would collapse, and that the Jewish captives would be set free to return to Jerusalem within two years. Jeremiah warned him that this prediction would be tested by seeing if it came true. Hananiah then yanked the model yoke off of Jeremiah's shoulders and broke it, and repeated his prediction of the quick end of Babylon's power. We infer from this account that Hananiah was more popular and his prediction won the approval of the crowd at the Temple. But Jeremiah was later sent to deliver a private message to Hananiah: because he had succeeded in misleading the community with his false prophecy, God condemned him to death within the current year. Hananiah died two months later. The two years predicted by Hananiah came and went (the fourth to sixth years of the reign of Zedekiah), and Babylon remained firmly in control of its empire. This is an example of how Jeremiah's short-term prophecies always came to pass, and still the community refused to trust his words or follow his directions for repentance.

Jeremiah 29 follows this story with an account of an earlier incident involving Jewish prophets in Babylon. God directed Jeremiah to write a letter to the Jewish exiles informing them that their sojourn would last seventy years, and directing them to pray for the prosperity of Babylon. He specifically instructed them not to listen to prophecies contradicting this message, and condemned two prophets by name. Nevertheless, a third prophet named Shemaiah wrote to the High Priest in Jerusalem demanding that Jeremiah be imprisoned for publicizing what Shemaiah labeled as Jeremiah's "false prophecy." The High Priest read the letter of Shemaiah to Jeremiah, who then delivered a promise from God that Shemaiah and all his descendants would perish.

Jeremiah 26 relates an even earlier incident, the account of the Temple sermon about Shiloh mentioned above. In this account both the priests and the other prophets working at the Temple in Jerusalem condemn Jeremiah for his prediction that the Temple and Jerusalem will fall. Jeremiah was in serious danger of being lynched, but fortunately several government officials intervened and arranged to spare Jeremiah's life. However, this chapter concludes with the sad story of another prophet, named Uriah, who was pursued by the government of King Jehoiakim and who was put to death for preaching the same predictions of doom for Jerusalem that Jeremiah was preaching.

These incidents give us a vivid context in which to understand the bitter prophecies of condemnation of false prophets that occur in Jeremiah 14 and 23. Apparently there was an abundance of prophets who were preaching a message of blessing to Judah and Jerusalem. Though God had sent Jeremiah to predict the doom of Jerusalem for her disobedience, these preachers offered a different message:

> From the least to the greatest, all are greedy for gain; prophets and priests alike, all practice deceit. They dress the wound of my people as though it were not serious. `Peace, peace,' they say, when there is no peace (Jer 6:13–14).

This conflict with other prophets also affected Jeremiah personally. Because his message was so unpopular, the prophet was unpopular, and there were many people who desired to do away with Jeremiah (as indicated in the incidents above). The so-called confessions of Jeremiah (Jer 11:18–23; 12:1–17; 15:10–21; 17:12–18; 18:18–23; 20:7–18) are a set of private prayers in which Jeremiah poured out his frustrations, his loneliness, and his fears in the face of all this struggle and opposition. In these passages we learn that even his own kinsmen from his hometown of Anathoth were conspiring against him (Jer 11:18–23; 12:6), and his friends and associates were tempted to join in such schemes (Jer 18:18; 20:10). They constantly challenged his prophecies:

> They keep saying to me, "Where is the word of the Lord? Let it now be fulfilled!" (Jer 17:15)

> "Report him! Let's report him!" All my friends are waiting for me to slip, saying, "Perhaps he will be deceived; then we will prevail over him and take our revenge on him." (Jer 20:10)

Often approaching despair at his lonely situation, Jeremiah complains:

> O Lord, you deceived me, and I was deceived; you overpowered me and prevailed. I am ridiculed all day long; everyone mocks me. Whenever I speak, I cry out proclaiming violence and destruction. So the word of the Lord has brought me insult and reproach all day long. (Jer 20:7–8)

In these prayers Jeremiah provides a good example of how each Christian must turn to God alone as his personal Savior. Along with the Psalms, they are an example of how we can be honest in our conversation with God, grappling with the full range of our human emotions in our earthly existence. Jeremiah speaks some strong words calling for God's vengeance upon his persecutors. These words need to be placed alongside Jesus' instructions for Christians to "love your enemies and pray for those who persecute you" (Matt 5:44). In one sense it is correct for Jeremiah to hate the enemies of God, who are opposing God and opposing God's servants (compare Ps 139:19–24). In the New Testament both Jesus and his servant St. Paul speak words of condemnation at some point against those set on opposing them, and a major part of Jeremiah's mission was to deliver God's words of condemnation to his countrymen. In another sense, it must be remembered that Jeremiah's book represents God's earnest effort to warn the people of Judah and to give them a chance to escape their doom. So Christians today must learn to identify sin, condemn it and oppose it, and yet still seek in love to bring the sinner to repentance. Perhaps the most instructive thing about these private prayers is that Jeremiah steadfastly leaves the matter of vengeance to God. He does not act himself against his false friends, even in some verbal tirade of spite, but pours out his feelings in his prayers and asks for God to set things right.

Related to this conflict between true and false prophecy is the matter of true and false religion. Jeremiah's opponents include many from among the prophets, priests, government officials, and common people of God's kingdom of Judah. All of these people were outwardly religious. All of these people claimed faith in God and allegiance to Yahweh. But their actions were not consistent with their claims. Jeremiah 2 contains several examples of the people acting in defiance of God's instructions, and then still claiming to be disciples of Yahweh (2:5–9, 20–25, 27, 31–36). The sermon in Jeremiah 7, where Jeremiah compares Jerusalem to Shiloh, is a good example of the contrast between the actions of those who sincerely follow God and those who only claim to do so. Jeremiah 34 relates an outstanding example of the difference. While Jerusalem was under attack by the Babylonians, King Zedekiah led an act of reformation in which all the leaders of the community gave emancipation to their Jewish slaves. This brought the community back into conformance with the Torah laws which prevented Israelites from reducing their countrymen to slavery (they could only be forced into service for their debts for a maximum of seven years). The officials even swore a formal covenant at the Temple to follow this practice from then on. But as soon as the Babylonian army withdrew – temporarily to deal with the Egyptian army, and then they returned to Jerusalem! —King Zedekiah and all the officials abrogated the emancipation and re-enslaved the victims. God had nothing but condemnation for such two-faced behavior.

Jeremiah 43 is yet another example of the difference between outward religious statements and actual deeds. After the assassination of Governor Gedaliah, the leaders of the community demanded that "Jeremiah the Prophet" consult God and bring back instructions as to how they should avoid falling under the wrath of Babylon for the assassination. Jeremiah brought back a word from God that they should remain in Judah, and they would be safe. But the leaders accused Jeremiah of lying and delivering a false prophecy, and against Jeremiah's advice they forced the entire community to flee for refuge in Egypt, as if they were all guilty of the political assassination. A few verses from Jeremiah 5 will serve to complete the illustration of this theme:

> Go up and down the streets of Jerusalem, look around and consider, search through her squares. If you can find but one person who deals honestly and seeks the truth, I will forgive this city. Although they say, "As surely as the Lord lives," still they are swearing falsely. (Jer 5:1–2)

> I thought, "These are only the poor; they are foolish, for they do not know the way of the Lord, the requirements of their God. So I will go to the leaders and speak to them; surely they know the way of the Lord, the requirements of their God." But with one accord they too had broken off the yoke and torn off the bonds. (Jer 5:4–5)

> A horrible and shocking thing has happened in the land: The prophets prophesy lies, the priests rule by their own authority, and my people love it this way. But what will you do in the end? (Jer 5:30–31).

3. Overview of the Book

There is no clear method governing the structure of the book of Jeremiah. The first twenty chapters are in the first person, and have no dating information, but the later chapters are mixed between first person and third person accounts, and the dates provided jump all around the latter part of the lifetime of Jeremiah. As a result, all any scholar can do is offer an outline by selected topics to help guide the reader. The outline below calls attention to some major features and also to a few minor features that suggest some pattern. But even so, it obscures the fact that, for example, significant passages about evil rulers and false prophets occur in Jeremiah 22—23, and not only in Jeremiah 26—29.

I. Introduction: God calls Jeremiah to be a prophet (1)
II. Jeremiah's words of prophecy and prayer (2—25)

Includes Jeremiah's personal prayers (the six prayers in Jer 11—20. are often labeled Jeremiah's personal "confessions") (10:23–25; 11:18–23; 12:1–17; 15:10–21; 17:12–18; 18:18–23; 20:7–18)

Includes private condemnation of Pashhur (20:1–6)

III. Opposition to Jeremiah from priests, prophets and rulers (26—29)

Includes private condemnation of Hananiah (28:15–17) and of Shemaiah (29:24–32)

IV. Words of future consolation (30—33)

V. Examples of obedience and disobedience (34—36)

Includes private promise to Recabites (35:18–19)

VI. The story of the end of Jerusalem and the last years of Jeremiah's ministry (37—45)

Includes private promise to Ebed-Melech (39:15–18) and to Baruch (45)

VII. Jeremiah's oracles against Foreign Nations (46—51)

(Jer 51:64 states "the words of Jeremiah end here.")

VIII. Historical appendix on the fall of Jerusalem and the Exile (52)

Lamentations

The unexpected loss of an important public person, institution or building is often an occasion for public mourning and anguish. The destruction of the World Trade Center buildings in New York in 2001 brought forth a time or mourning for the people who died in the attack by terrorists as well as plans for a memorial on the site. In the history of ancient Israel only one event of destruction directly led to the production of a book of the Bible. That event was the destruction of the Temple in Jerusalem by the Babylonian armies in 587 BC. The book of Lamentations contains five poems that mourn or lament the loss of the Temple and all that it represented. What would Israel do without a place to offer sacrifices to God? Had God abandoned them? Had He rejected Israel? Where could they turn for help in the face of the destruction of the holy city and the Babylonian captivity? These are the questions the people of Judah and the writer of Lamentations faced. As the poet who wrote Lamentations offered answers to these questions to his people, he also continues to speak to us about dealing with devastating loss and sorrow by focusing us on the mercy and love of God.

1. Authorship and Date— *Who Wrote these Five Poems?*
2. Themes — *Mourning the Loss of the Temple, Finding Hope in God*
3. Overview of the Book — *What is Contained in Lamentations?*

1. Authorship and Date

In Christian Bibles Lamentations immediately follows Jeremiah's prophecies. Since Jeremiah was the prophet who saw the fall and captivity of Jerusalem, this arrangement is logical. In fact, since ancient times Lamentations has been connected to Jeremiah. Probably based on 2 Chronicles 35:25 and Jeremiah 7:29; 8:21; 9:1, 10, 20, ancient Jewish and Christian attributed the book's composition to Jeremiah. However, the book as it stands is anonymous. We cannot be certain that Jeremiah wrote it (although in some Bibles it is called "The Lamentations of Jeremiah"). Nevertheless, Jeremiah is a likely choice for the author of the book. There are a number of similarities in content and style between Jeremiah and Lamentations:

Sins of prophets and priests	Jer 5:30–31; 14:13–14; Lam 2:14; 4:13
Fear and terror all around	Jer 6:25; 46:5; Lam 2:22
Appeal to God for vengeance	Jer 11:20; Lam 3:64–66
Eyes flow with tears	Jer 9:1; 13: 17; 14:17; Lam 1:16
"Virgin daughter of Zion" in shame and misery	Jer 14:17; Lam 1:15; 2:13
Appeal for God's judgment on nations who rejoiced over Jerusalem's destruction	Jer 49:2; Lam 4:21

Therefore, it is entirely possible that Jeremiah wrote Lamentations, even though we cannot be certain that this is the case.

Since the book cannot have been written before the fall of Jerusalem, the earliest possible date for its composition is 586 BC. Since it is a cry not only of mourning but a cry for help from God, it was probably written before the first hint of God's continuing love for his people in the captivity was given with Jehoiachin's release from prison in 561 BC (2 Kgs 25:27; Jer 52:31).

While Lamentations is placed after Jeremiah in Christian Bibles, in the Jewish canon it is grouped with four other short books that are reserved for special yearly festivals. In synagogues Lamentations is read each year on the anniversary of the fall of Jerusalem (in late July or early August; the anniversary remembers both that fall to Babylon in 587 BC and the later fall to the Romans in AD 70.)

2. Themes

Three major themes are woven together throughout Lamentations. The first is the repeated admission that the people of Judah and Jerusalem have received just and proper punishment from God. The people had abandoned God and turned to idols. They refused to listen to the prophets who had declared God's word. Ultimately God brought his judgment on them, and they had no excuse. The poet declares:

Jerusalem sinned grievously; therefore she became filthy.
Everyone who had honored her despises her,
    because they have seen her nakedness.
She herself groans and turns her face away. (Lam 1:8)

The second theme builds on this: God has brought about the punishment that the people experienced. Since nothing happens without God's hand being in it, the prophet is convinced that this is God's doing, and his people need to acknowledge and accept this. He quotes the city of Jerusalem as saying:

"The Lord rejected all my mighty warriors in my midst.
He summoned an assembly against me to crush my young men.
The Lord has trampled the virgin daughter of Judah as in a winepress."
(Lam 1:15)

However, this does not mean that God is simply angry with his people. As is true throughout the Scriptures, God is a merciful God who is always willing to forgive his repentant people. Here the writer of Lamentations finds hope:

For the Lord will not cast off forever.
Although he causes grief,
he will have compassion according to the abundance of his steadfast love,
    because he does not willingly afflict or grieve the children of men.
(Lam 3:31–33)

This is the important third theme of Lamentations. God does not use his Law simply to punish. Instead, the Law drives people to sorrow over their sins. God then offers his repentant people forgiveness and life. This is what the poet longs for:

> Restore us to yourself, Lord, that we may be restored!
> Renew our days as of old! (Lam 5:21).

In this way Lamentations points to the mercies of God that are ultimately fulfilled in Christ. God would restore his people to Jerusalem seventy years later when Babylon fell to the Persians. More importantly, God permanently restored his people to himself in the cross of Christ and made them citizens of the New Jerusalem (Rev 3:12; 21:1).

3. Overview of the Book

Lamentations is a collection five poems that mourn or lament the fall of Jerusalem to the Babylonians. The first, second and fourth poem each begin with the exclamation "How...!" (The Hebrew word for *how* is *'eykah*, which supplies the title of the book in Hebrew.)

Each of the first four poems is an acrostic written in the order of the twenty-two letter Hebrew alphabet (see Chapter 16). (The order of the sixteenth and seventeenth letter is reversed in the second, third and fourth poems.) The first poem has twenty-two verses of three lines each. The first lines of each verse begin with a successive letter of the Hebrew alphabet, using all twenty-two letters. The second poem has the same structure. The third poem, however, is different. It has sixty-six verses arranged in stanzas of three verses each. The beginning letter of each verse in a stanza is the same Hebrew letter, with the stanzas arranged in alphabetical order. The Lamentations 4 has twenty-two verses of two lines each. The first lines of each verse begin with a successive letter of the Hebrew alphabet, using all twenty-two letters. Lamentations 5, while divided into twenty-two verses, is not an acrostic poem.

Clearly, Lamentations is not simply the emotional outpouring of a bereaved inhabitant of Jerusalem in the face of the Babylonian destruction of the city. Instead, it is a carefully crafted set of five poems. The acrostic structure shared by the first four poems is discarded in the fifth poem. This breakdown of the acrostic structure is a visual reminder to the reader of the fall of Jerusalem and the breaking down of its walls and buildings.

The five poems move from the devastation of the city and its people to hope in God alone, since in his mercy he forgives repentant sinners.

Poem	Theme
1	Jerusalem's sins led to devastation
2	God's anger poured out on his people
3	God's anger against sin, but mercy toward sinners
4	Contrast between Zion's glorious past and miserable present
5	An appeal to God for mercy and forgiveness.

Ezekiel

Jesus told the Samaritan woman at the well that the time was coming when those who worship God "will worship the Father in spirit and truth," and the old forms of worship in Jerusalem and Samaria would become obsolete. Six hundred years prior to Jesus, Ezekiel was assigned the task of criticizing the improper worship that had been conducted in Jerusalem and in the territory of Israel north of Jerusalem (later known as Samaria), and forecasting the perfect worship that would exist when God sent His Messiah and redeemed his people from all their sinfulness. Ezekiel is known for his prophecy of the New Temple that God would create, which foreshadows John's vision of the New Jerusalem coming down out of heaven.

1. Authorship and Date—*Not Priest but Prophet*
2. Major Themes—*Ezekiel As the New Moses, The Holy Presence of God, God Is the Judge*
3. Overview of the book—*Everything in Perfect Order*
4. Important Passages in Ezekiel—*Ezekiel Reminds Us of God's Power*

1. Authorship and Date

Ezekiel was born into a priestly family in Judah in 623 BC. Everything we know about Ezekiel we learn from this book alone, and we have no further genealogical connection than his immediate father's name, Buzi. As Ezekiel grew up he prepared to serve as a priest at the Temple in Jerusalem. From the fact that the census in the book of Numbers (Num 4) counts only those Levites between the ages of thirty and fifty, we infer that one became a full-fledged Temple worker only after reaching the age of thirty. There may have been a five-year-long apprentice period before this. Ezekiel's childhood years would have included the exciting period following the religious reformation by good King Josiah (622 BC), which may have inspired his desire to serve as a proper priest in the only legitimate worship center, that is, Jerusalem. But with Josiah's untimely death (609 BC), Judah came under the control of first Egypt, and later Babylonia (605 BC). Judah's King Jehoiakim was not a particularly good ruler, and when his rebellion against Babylon was crushed in 598/597 BC, his successor King Jehoiachin and many of the leading citizens of Judah were transported by Nebuchadnezzar to Babylon as hostages to ensure the loyal conduct of the rest of their countrymen. Included in this group was Ezekiel, who had finally reached the age of 25 and was ready to begin his temple service training. Thus Ezekiel had his desired career ripped away from him just as it was about to begin. All the study of the Pentateuch he had done to prepare to become a priest seemed futile: he would never see Jerusalem and the divine Temple again. But in 593 BC, when Ezekiel had reached his thirtieth year, his God Yahweh appeared with all his glory in the vicinity of Babylon, and ordered Ezekiel to serve him as his prophet to the exiles in Babylon.

For the next seven years Ezekiel carried out this role as prophet among the exiles. Like Jeremiah, Ezekiel is famous for his action prophecies: symbolic activities that he had to act out in front of the crowd. The grown man Ezekiel had to draw a model of Jerusalem on clay and make war against it – imagine a grown man playing in the city street with toy soldiers and catapults! He had to tie himself up, lie on his side and eat only siege rations to symbolize the coming siege and punishment of Jerusalem. After that period he had to cut off his hair and symbolically destroy it or disperse it to signify the death and exile that was coming to Jerusalem. On another day he had to pack up all his possessions and carry them out through a hole he dug in his house to symbolize the coming exile and the attempt at escape that would be made by the king of Jerusalem. Beyond this, at the end of this period Yahweh informed Ezekiel that his wife, whom he loved dearly, would die, as a further sign that the Judeans were about to lose their beloved city Jerusalem. Ezekiel was ordered by God to act in public as if nothing had happened, and to mourn only in private, to symbolize that the Judeans who lived as citizens of Babylon would have to rejoice outwardly that their government, Babylon, had defeated the rebel Jerusalem, and only mourn in private the loss of their traditional capitol and history. During these seven years God also removed Ezekiel's ability to participate in normal conversation: Ezekiel could not speak, except when he had a message from God to deliver. He also found that his prophetic actions often aroused hostility from his fellow Judeans, and some of them considered him mad and in need of confinement.

After Jerusalem was destroyed, God returned to Ezekiel his ability to speak normally. He continued to serve as a prophet, but the content of his messages changed. For fifteen more years, from 586 until 571 BC, he delivered oracles of promise and hope for the future of the Judeans. With the loss of Jerusalem the exiles had no hope of ever returning to their old situation, and they felt their story and their sense of community were coming to an end. But Ezekiel emphasized that God still had his plans, and that he was not abandoning the promises he had made to Abraham, Moses, and David. There would be a return to the promised land, and there would be a new Messiah. Sometimes these oracles of hope still reminded the people of their previous sin that had caused their captivity, and sometimes these oracles promised help for Israel by way of promising destruction to their enemies. His longest vision and message came in his fiftieth year, 573 BC (Ezek 40—48). In this vision Ezekiel forecast the re-creation of the Temple and city of Jerusalem, along with the perfect worship and the perfect divine blessings that would be connected with the New Temple. His latest oracle in the book is dated two years after that, in 571 BC. In that year Nebuchadnezzar finally conquered Tyre, as Ezekiel had previously predicted (Ezek 26), and God promised that he would also allow Nebuchadnezzar to conquer Egypt.

It is interesting to note the similarities between Ezekiel and Jeremiah. Both were descended from priestly families, though from rival priestly families. Jeremiah was apparently from the line of Abiathar, which had been forced out of office by Solomon, and Ezekiel was apparently from the line of Zadok. Both men lived and worked at the same time, that is, before and after the fall of Jerusalem, but in different locations. Both men were known for their action prophecies. And both men had similar basic themes: those remaining in Jerusalem were doomed, but the exiles would be protected and blessed by God.

2. Major Themes

Ezekiel As the New Moses

One important insight into the content of this book is that Ezekiel understands himself to be a sort of "new Moses" figure. The first Moses met with God at Sinai, delivered to Israel the laws of the Torah and the design of the Tabernacle and its worship, and led the people in following God on their journey toward the Promised Land of Canaan. Ezekiel had to announce the loss of the Promised Land and the destruction of the Temple and the city of Jerusalem. But when that was fulfilled, Ezekiel had to point ahead to God's continuing plans for the future. Thus the glory of God that appeared to Moses is the same glory that appeared to Ezekiel in Babylon. Ezekiel forecast a return to the Promised Land. Since the Temple built by Solomon had been destroyed, Ezekiel conveyed the heavenly plan for the New Temple, as Moses had conveyed the plans for the Tabernacle. As Moses delivered the instructions for worship using the sacrifice rituals, Ezekiel delivered the new instructions for the new sacrifice ceremonies (Ezek 43—46). These new instructions do not harmonize perfectly with the old instructions from Moses, so many Jewish scholars have been very troubled by them. Judaism has been so rooted in the old covenant brought through Moses that it has been unable to understand how Ezekiel could be speaking of a new age with a new situation, when the old covenant had been replaced by something new. Ezekiel's contemporary Jeremiah speaks of this bluntly as a New Covenant replacing the Sinai Covenant (Jer 31). Ezekiel speaks of this more symbolically in terms of a New Temple and new worship system that is not polluted or affected by the weaknesses of the old system. Christians understand all of this to be fulfilled in Christ Jesus, who both set up the New Covenant and spoke of the new "Temple" of his body (John 2:18–22, Matt 12:5, 1 Cor 3:10–17, Eph 2:19–21, 1 Pet 2:4–5) and the new sacrifice of his body.

Along the way to the new land of Canaan, Moses was used by God to bring water out of a rock. In Ezekiel's vision the River of Life comes out of the new temple (Ezek 47). Christ's body is the New Temple, and Christ is also the solid rock who supplies the water of life to his followers. As for the land, in the first Exodus the actual division of the territory of Canaan among the Twelve Tribes was carried out under the administration of Joshua, but Ezekiel again forecast the new division of the land among the traditional Twelve Tribes in an idealized way that ignores both geography and population differences (Ezek 48).

This sense of Ezekiel as a New Moses can be carried much further. The muteness of Ezekiel may be compared to the complaint of Moses in Exodus 4:10 and 6:30 about his poor speaking ability. Most of the Pentateuch is prose narration and instruction, for example, with only some scattered poetry within it. So the book of Ezekiel the would-be priest is mostly prose, with only a little poetry here and there. In fact, many of the themes used within the book of Ezekiel to complain about the sin of the Israelites can be viewed as an adaptation or expansion of the contents of the Song of Moses contained in Deuteronomy 32.

The Holy Presence of God

A second important theme in the book of Ezekiel is the concept of the presence of God. In the book of Exodus we read that God had come down from heaven to rescue his people Israel and to take them up to Canaan. This special presence of God on earth was displayed in awesome ways on top of Mt. Sinai, in the cloud during the migration, and in the cloud filling the Tabernacle and later filling Solomon's Temple. Indeed, Moses asked in Exodus 33:15–16: "If your Presence does not go with us, do not send us up from here. How will anyone know that you are pleased with me and with your people unless you go with us? What else will distinguish me and your people from all the other people on the face of the earth?" This presence of God is often referred to in the Old Testament as the Glory of the Lord, and it was understood to rest enthroned between the cherubim on top of the Ark of the Covenant inside the Temple, which was the earthly palace of God, the ultimate King. It is this Glory of the Lord that appears to Ezekiel in Babylon (Ezek 1). The point of this visitation is that God is not far away in Jerusalem, but God has come near to Ezekiel and to his fellow exiles in Babylon. God is there to care for them, to watch over them and to prepare to bring them back some day to the land of Israel. In fact, God is no longer residing in the Temple in Jerusalem. The great vision given to Ezekiel in Ezekiel 8—11 dramatizes the departure of God from the Temple. It will fall because he has abandoned it to its fate. He is no longer there. When God brings the exiles back to the land of Israel, and sets up the New Temple as revealed in the great vision of Ezekiel 40—48, God himself will take up residence again there with his people. The end of the book closes with a dramatic play on words concerned with this theme. Ezekiel 48:35 concludes: "And the name of the city from that time on will be: THE LORD IS THERE." Compare the pronunciation of Jerusalem in Hebrew to this name:

ye-ru-sha-laim	Jerusalem (*laim* pronounced like English *lime*)
ya-weh-sham-mah	Yahweh (is) there.

More than this, even the many chapters describing the chastisement that must come to Israel involve this presence of God. It is because God has been close to the Israelites that he must now come near to them to bring them the punishment befitting their wicked behavior. In Ezekiel 14 and 20 God specifically complains that the Israelites try to take advantage of their ability to approach God when they have otherwise disobeyed him and so don't deserve anything from him but wrath.

This concept of the presence of God is very important for Christians. The New Testament teaches that the Glory of God "became flesh" in the incarnation of Christ (John 1), and that the Spirit of Christ now dwells on earth within Christians. St. Paul notes in 1 Corinthians: "Don't you know that you yourselves are God's Temple and that God's Spirit lives in you? If anyone destroys God's Temple, God will destroy him; for God's Temple is sacred, and you are that Temple" (see also Paul's discussion in Rom 8—9). In addition to the fact that the Spirit of Christ now dwells within us, we also have the special worship ceremony called the Lord's Supper, at which we recognize what Lutherans call the Real Presence. Not only is Jesus enthroned with the Father in heaven, he is also physically (though invisibly) present with his people in every congregation when they celebrate Holy Communion. Along with the bread and the wine we receive and physically "handle" this Real Presence of the body of Christ. Compare the warning Paul gives in 1 Corinthians 11:29. Although these encounters with the Presence of God in Ezekiel were very dramatic, the New Testament reveals that contemporary Christians have even greater interaction with the Presence of God than did the people of the Old Testament.

God Is the Judge

The third important theme to note in Ezekiel is that God maintains his role as judge of all the earth. The first two major sections of Ezekiel emphasize this fact: Ezekiel 1—24 reveal that God will judge Israel and Judah for their conduct, and Ezekiel 25—32 reveal that God will judge foreign nations for their conduct. While the third section, Ezekiel 33—48, brings the promise of God to restore and bless Israel, many of the passages within it continue to emphasize that judgment belongs to God. For example, Ezekiel 34 speaks of God's judgment upon the leaders or "shepherds" of Israel, and Ezekiel 38—39 speak of God's judgment upon all the nations of the earth. (See also the paragraphs below on Ezekiel 3 and 33 and Ezekiel 18.)

Let us here take note of the title that is used of Ezekiel in this book. Ezekiel is frequently (93 times) addressed by God as "son of man". In Hebrew this title is "son of Adam," and means something like "human being, member of the human race." Ezekiel is not addressed as "son of Israel" or "son of Judah", or "son of Aaron" or "son of Levi." Ezekiel is not special in any way because he has these particular inherited family lines. What is significant here is that Ezekiel is human, merely human, a representative of all the humans that come from the original Adam. Although God is giving special attention to the community of Israel within this book, the use of this title for the prophet emphasizes that these people are nothing in themselves. They are all merely human. God is acting for the sake of his choices and his promises. But God is the creator of all and the God of all the earth, and before him all humankind is just that, mere humans. The only privilege they have before God is that which God chooses to give to them.

This title, *son of man* is only used of one other simple human individual in the Old Testament. In Daniel 8:17 the man Daniel is addressed by this title. This is quite different from its only other use in the book of Daniel (Dan 7:13), where it applies to the mysterious figure in Daniel's vision who was able to approach God. But this title is used again in the New Testament, for it was the favorite title Jesus used of himself. Scholars are quick to point out that Jesus used this title to link himself to Daniel's vision in Daniel 7:13, and thus identify himself as the Messiah. But true as this may be, we must also recognize a relationship with the use of this title for Ezekiel. In so far as this title emphasizes humanness, Jesus is stressing the fact of his true humanity. He is not only True God, begotten of the Father from eternity, but also True Man, born of the Virgin Mary. Also, by using this title, Jesus, at least to some degree, identifies himself as the new Ezekiel. He is the special human being through whom God speaks to his generation. And since Ezekiel understood himself to be the new Moses figure, so Christ is again a new Moses figure. Ezekiel had to forecast a new age with a replacement for the Temple of Solomon. Jesus is the new prophet who brings all of these things to their fulfillment.

3. Overview of the Book

The book of Ezekiel dates from the end of Ezekiel's ministry, and has an obvious chronological and topical organization to it. There are three major sections, and within each section all but one of the dates mentioned are in chronological order. Ezekiel 1—24 contains the prophecies he delivered from the time of his call until the destruction of Jerusalem. Ezekiel 33—48 contains the prophecies he delivered after the destruction of Jerusalem, up to his fiftieth year, which would have been his retirement year if he had served as a priest. In between these two sections we find the collection of oracles predicting God's judgment upon the neighboring nations. This section is organized by topic: Ezekiel 25 contains four brief oracles condemning Ammon, Moab, Edom, and Philistia, Ezekiel 26—28 contain four oracles condemning the Phoenician cities of Tyre and Sidon, and Ezekiel 29—32 contains seven oracles condemning Egypt. (Note that this totals seven locations.) Only the first oracle against Tyre is dated, and that falls between the dates of Ezekiel 1—24 and 33—48. In the oracles against Egypt we find six dates. They begin after the Tyrian oracle, and continue in chronological order until a few months after the time that Ezekiel 33 resumes its story. However, the second oracle against Egypt interrupts the chronological sequence. This is the oracle dated to 571 BC, two years after the last part of Ezekiel 33—48, and it is the latest dated piece of the entire book. These foreign nation oracles have clearly been grouped together in the middle of the book, and so this last-dated oracle against Egypt has been intentionally placed here for unity of topic despite its late date.

In addition to this clear chronological and topical organization, there is an obvious correlation between the oracles of the first and third parts. Both of these sections begin with similar oracles emphasizing that Ezekiel is appointed by God as a watchman for the people of Israel, with a responsibility to warn them of the judgments God is bringing upon them (Ezek 3 and 33). Both sections contain dramatic visions in which Ezekiel is enabled by the divine Spirit to see the Temple in Jerusalem. In Ezekiel 8—11 the prophet is allowed to see the sinful compromised worship of other gods that is taking place in the Temple of Yahweh, and he is allowed to see the dramatic abandonment of the Temple and city by God. In Ezekiel 40—48 he is provided a view of the New Temple that God will cause to be built in Jerusalem. In this vision God returns, the worship is perfect, the relationship between the Temple and the royal authority is completely proper, and the entire community of the Twelve Tribes exists again in an idealized even division of the land. Ezekiel 6 contains a sermon predicting doom for the mountains of Israel, but Ezekiel 36 contains a sermon promising God's blessing to these mountains. Ezekiel 3:22—Ezekiel 5:17 contain the account of the prophet acting out the doom to come to Jerusalem, during which time the prophet is made mute, and Ezekiel 33:21–33. contains the account of the refugee bringing the news that Jerusalem has fallen, and the account of the end of the prophet's muteness. Guided by these parallel passages, it is possible to note further relationships between other parts of these two sections. Ezekiel 12 forecasts how the prince of Judah will go into exile, while Ezekiel 37:15–28 forecasts the reunion of the two communities of Israel and Judah under one Davidic king. Ezekiel 22 condemns the wicked leaders of Judah, while Ezekiel 34 predicts that God will remove the wicked leaders (pictured as shepherds) and provide his own leadership (fulfilled in Jesus the Good Shepherd). Ezekiel 21 calls for the destruction of Jerusalem, but Ezekiel 35 calls for the destruction of Edom for being a foe of Jerusalem. Ezekiel 23 talks about the wicked behavior of Judah and Israel in terms of sexual infidelity, but Ezekiel 36:16–38 predicts that God will clean up this unfaithfulness and put a new heart into his people to be faithful to him.

The book of Ezekiel is notably different in style from two other Major Prophets—Isaiah and Jeremiah. Unlike these two other books, Ezekiel is all in the first-person autobiographical voice, his sermons are all in chronological order (except for collecting the sermons against Egypt), and the book consists mostly of prose with only a small amount of poetry. The only verses in which someone else talks to the reader about Ezekiel are 1:2–3, which appear to be an editorial insert to let the reader know more about the identity and situation of Ezekiel.

Ezekiel provides more specific dates for his sermons than any other prophetic book (Jeremiah has more dated passages, but Jeremiah often lists only the year, not the specific date). The years are calculated according to the time Ezekiel and King Jehoiachin were taken captive, which are also the years of the "reign" of Jehoiachin. Thanks to modern astronomy and ancient astronomical records recovered by archaeologists, we can translate Ezekiel's dates into our calendar system with a high degree of confidence.

Many of the oracles collected in the chapters are not given specific dates. The simplest conclusion would be that Ezekiel gathered together his material in his old age, and assembled it into the book. He placed the material in chronological order, providing fixed dates where he had recorded them, and placing the other material in the proper relationship to those fixed dates. He varied this chronological order only with the foreign nation oracles in order to group them by nation. At the end of his life he was able to demonstrate the accuracy of his predictions of doom in the early years, and he arranged the book to leave a testimony of hope for the future. Since his predictions of doom for Jerusalem, Tyre and others all came true, his readers should trust that his predictions of God's forgiveness and restoration would also come true.

As noted above, there are three obvious major sections of the book, and there are several correlations between part I and part III. Within part I there is no obvious pattern; the material is probably arranged simply by chronology. But again there are some correlations or repeated themes within this first part. The following outline structures some of these correlated sections in subparts I-C and I-E around Ezekiel 18, which has thematic connections to Ezekiel 3 and 33.

Verse	Year–Month–Day	Modern Date	Event
1:1 1:2 3:16	"30th yr." – 4 – 5 5 – [4] – 5 "seven days" later	July 31, 593 BC Aug. 7, 593	God calls Ezekiel
8:1	6 – 6 – 5 (only 406 days later)	Sept. 17, 592	Vision of doomed Jerusalem
20:1–2	7 – 5 – 10	Aug. 14, 591	Israel's history of rebellion
24:1	9 – 10 – 10	Jan. 15, 588	Siege of Jerusalem begun
26:1	11 – ? – 1	Feb. 13, 586 or Mar. 15, 586	Against Tyre
29:1	10 – 10 – 12	Jan. 7, 587	Against Egypt
29:17	27 – 1 – 1	Apr. 26, 571	Egypt will fall like Tyre
30:20	11 – 1 – 7	Apr. 29, 587	Pharaoh will be broken
31:1	11 – 3 – 1	June 21, 587	Against Pharaoh

32:1	12 – 12 – 1	March 3, 585	Pharaoh will fall
32:17	12 – [12?] – 15	Mar. 17, 585	Egypt will go to the grave
	11 – 4 – 9	July 18, 586	Jerusalem fell
	[11] – 5 – 7	August 14, 586	City & Temple destroyed
33:21	12 – 10 – 5	Jan. 8, 585	News arrives of Jerusalem's fall
40:1	25 – 1 – 10 14th year after Jerusalem fell	Apr. 28, 573	Vision of New Temple

I. Oracles of Doom for Jerusalem and God's People
    A. Inaugural vision of God and ingesting of God's word 1:1—3:15
        1. First warning of responsibility as Israel's watchman 3:16–27
    B. Prophecies of the coming destruction of Jerusalem
        1. Symbolic war against the city 4:1–3
        2. Symbolic experience of siege 4:4–17
        3. Symbolic dissolution of the population 5:1–17
        4. Prophecy against the mountains of Israel 6:1–14
        5. The end is coming to Israel and Jerusalem 7:1–27
        6. Vision of the sin of Jerusalem and the departure of God 8:1—11:25
        7. Symbolic exile of the wicked prince of Judah 12:1–16
    C. Additional prophecies condemning the people and leaders of Israel and Judah
        1. Jerusalem should eat in fear 12:12–20
        2. God's vision is coming soon 12:21–25, 26–28
        3. False Prophets condemned 13:1–23
        4. All false worshippers condemned 14:1–23
            i. Condemnation 14:1–11
            ii. Even men like Noah, Daniel, and Job cannot intercede 14:12–23
        5. Judah is a useless vine 15:1–8 (commentary on Isa 5!)
        6. Two adopted daughters turn to prostitution 16:1–63
        7. The vine Israel is caught between Babylon and Egypt 17:1–24

D. Each person is judged for his own conduct 18:1–32
E. More prophecies condemning the people and leaders of Israel and Judah
    1. The "lions" of Israel and Judah are caught between Babylon and Egypt 19:1–14
    2. False worshippers have no recourse in God 20:1–44
    3. The fire is coming soon, believe it or not 20:45–49
    4. God sends a sword against Jerusalem 21:1–17
    5. Nebuchadnezzar will be led to attack Jerusalem 21:18–32
    6. The wicked leaders of Israel will be purged 22:1–31
    7. Two sisters compete in prostitution 23:1–49
F. The boiling point is reached with the beginning of the siege of Jerusalem 24:1–14
G. Ezekiel is forbidden to mourn his wife as the Jews cannot mourn Jerusalem 24:15–27

II. Oracles of God's wrath on the neighbor nations of Israel for their part in bringing woe to Israel
    A. Ammon, Moab, Edom, Philistia 25:1–17
    B. The Phoenicians Tyre & Sidon 26:1—28:26 (in Ezek 28 the King of Tyre is compared to the fall of Satan)
    C. Egypt 29:1—32:32
III. Oracles of Restoration and Hope for God's People
    A. Second warning of responsibility as Israel's watchman 33:1–20
    B. News of the fall of Jerusalem reaches Ezekiel in Babylon 33:21–33
    C. God condemns the wicked shepherds and declares their replacement 34:1–31
    D. God condemns Edom for its hatred of Israel 35:1–15
    E. Prophecy of blessing for the mountains of Israel 36:1–15
    F. Prophecy of the new heart and cleansing for the people of Israel 36:16–38
    G. Vision of the valley of bones: God will restore life to the nation 37:1–14
    H. Israel & Judah will be reunited under the Messiah 37:15–28
    I. Prophecy of the last battle between God and the forces of evil in this world 38:1—39:29
    J. Vision of the New Temple, the return of the presence of God, the purified leaders, the purified worship, the River of Life, and the idealized division of the land. 40:1—48:35

Daniel

As anyone who has spent a substantial period of time living in a foreign country knows, there are many adjustments that have to be made. One must adapt to different customs, foods, cultural assumptions, weather and perhaps even learn a new language. It may take some time to become accustomed to living and working in such a new and different environment. Similar adjustments had to be made by the people of Judah during the Babylonian captivity. Not only did they face the challenges that anyone faces in a foreign land, they also had the challenge of preserving their faith in the true God in a polytheistic society that did not understand their insistence that the God of Israel was the only God that existed. At times they faced persecution. Moreover, they were not willing inhabitants of the land where they found themselves—they had been resettled in Babylon by force. They may have felt abandoned by God and tempted to adopt the pagan polytheism of their new neighbors. The book of Daniel speaks to their situation to offer comfort and hope despite their existence as aliens in an alien land. In doing this it also speaks to Christians, who are citizens of a better kingdom, an eternal city whose maker is God (Heb 11:16).

1. Authorship and Date— *Did Daniel Write the Book that Bears His Name?*
2. Higher Critical View of Daniel — *Challenges to the Message of Daviel*
3. Themes — *Speaking to People Living in a Hostile Environment*
4. Overview of the Book — *What is Contained in Daniel?*
5. The Messiah in Daniel — *Eternal Hope for a Captive People*

1. Authorship and Date

Perhaps no other Old Testament prophetic book has been dissected and denied as the work of its putative author as Daniel has been. Critical scholars date its various sections much later than the dates given in the book itself, and none of the events in the book is viewed as historical. This critical view has even influenced some more traditionally-oriented Christian scholars, who adopt some form of these critical theories, while attempting to modify the critical view to make it compatible with biblical inspiration. However, many Christian scholars defend the traditional view, which was also held by Luther and the Reformers. This view accepts the book as coming from the pen of Daniel and understands the events related in the book as historically accurate.

Daniel divides neatly into ten major sections. Each of the first nine chapters of Daniel is a distinct story from the Babylonian captivity (Daniel 1—6) or a vision received by Daniel (Daniel 7—9). The tenth section is a vision that spans the final three chapters, Daniel 10—12. The visions all claim to be from the pen of Daniel as the frequent notice "I, Daniel" implies (Dan 7:15, 28; 8:1, 15, 27; 9:2; 10:2, 7; 12:5). Traditionally, both Christians and Jews understood the entire book, including the third person narratives of Daniel 1—6 as coming from Daniel.

The various accounts in Daniel 1—6 contain historical references that enable a reconstruction of the time of the events narrated. Depending on the type of notice given in each account, the time frame may span several years or may be pinpointed to a particular month or day. The narratives of Daniel 1—6 are in chronological order from earliest to latest.

Chapter	Date of Events in the Chapter
1	Summer 605—Spring 604
2	Fall 603 or Winter 603/602
3	January 593
4	Sometime between 573–569
5	October 11, 539
6	Sometime between November 539–March 538

Daniel is the first of the prophets to date all of his visions to the years of the reigning king. The visions, like the narratives, are in chronological order. However, the visions overlap the last narratives so that Daniel received the visions of Daniel 7 and 8 after the events of Daniel 4 but before the events of Daniel 5. The visions of Daniel 9 and 10—12 were received after the events of Daniel 6.

Chapter	Date of the Vision
7	Sometime between April 7, 553—April 25, 552
8	Sometime between April 16, 551—April 4, 550
9	Sometime between March 24, 538—March 11, 537

| 10–12 | April 23, 536 |

Therefore, the visions are chronologically interlocked with the narratives, pointing to a unity of the book despite its two different basic genres of historical narrative and visionary account.

The book itself cannot have existed in its present form before 536 BC, since that is the date of the final vision. Moreover, there are some indications that the entire book was written after that final vision. Daniel 1:21 indicates that Daniel served in the Babylonian court until the first year of Cyrus (538/537 BC), so even the account of the earliest incidents in Daniel was composed after the Persian conquest of Babylon. Therefore, the earliest date for the writing of Daniel is 536 BC. Given the fact that Daniel was probably in his early eighties at this time, it is unlikely that Daniel wrote the book later than about 530 BC. This means that Daniel probably committed his experiences in Babylon to writing during the same time that the construction of the Second Temple was beginning in Jerusalem (Ezra 3:8; 4:24).

2. Higher Critical Views of Daniel

Higher critical scholarship has long challenged the traditional date and authorship of Daniel as well as its unity. The objections that have led to this rejection of the traditional view fall into two broad categories: historical concerns that question the book's authenticity and literary-critical concerns.

Historical concerns about the book date back to Porphyry, a virulent anti-Christian Neo-Platonist philosopher of the late third century, whose writings are no longer extant, but are known only through a number of refutations of his position contained in a commentary on Daniel by Jerome (c. 340–420). Porphyry challenged especially the visions in Daniel 7—12, believing them to have been written after the events they supposedly predict. While conceding that the visions were largely historically accurate, Porphyry presupposed that there was no such thing as genuine divine revelation of the future. Instead, he argued that Daniel was written as if it were predictive prophecy, but was actually written during the first half of second century BC after the supposed events that it prophesied concerning Antiochus IV Epiphanes (175–164 BC). Those prophecies which attempted to prophesy events later in the reign of Antiochus (Dan 11:40–45) were inaccurate (demonstrating that there is no divinely revealed predictive prophecy) and, therefore, betrayed the author's real identity, a Jew in Palestine about the year 165 BC. While Porphyry's views found little support at the time, this same approach to understanding and dating Daniel's visions as pseudo-prophecies that were actually written after the events they supposedly prophesy was revived with the rise of higher critical approaches to the Bible. Modern critics assume that the visions are compositions from the Hellenistic era.

However, objections are also raised with respect to other historical references in the book. For instance, the first historical notice in Daniel, that Nebuchadnezzar besieged and captured Jerusalem in the third year of Jehoiakim (Dan 1:1) is challenged both as to whether such an event actually happened and because it seemingly conflicts with Jeremiah 25:1, which dates the siege to Jehoiakim's fourth year. Both objections are answerable, but critical scholars often dismiss any explanations and often are much more inclined to search for apparent historical anomalies to bolster their theories concerning the late composition of Daniel than to search for explanations of these apparent inaccuracies.

A good example of this is the person of Belshazzar, who is mentioned in Daniel 5, 7 and 8. Until the 1860s no source outside the book of Daniel or those dependent upon Daniel could provide independent confirmation of the existence of Belshazzar. Since he is not mentioned in any of the ancient Greek historians, many nineteenth century critical scholars viewed Daniel 5 as a purely fictional account about a fictional king.

However, beginning in the 1860s Babylonian sources came to light naming Belshazzar as the son of the King Nabonidus and demonstrating that he was made regent over Babylon in the third year of his father's reign. It would seem as if the historical nature of Daniel's account had been vindicated. Since all memory of Belshazzar had been lost to history outside of the Bible and works dependent on it, this seemed to furnish proof positive that the writer of Daniel 5 had to have been a contemporary of the events, since later writers, especially Maccabean era writers, would have had no knowledge of Belshazzar. Despite the clear refutation of their skepticism concerning Belshazzar's existence, critical scholars continue to dismiss the story as largely fictionalized.

Ironically, contemporary critical scholars often take a similar approach to the person of Darius the Mede (Dan 5:31; 6:1, 6, 9, 25, 28; 9:1; 11:1). Since no such person is known from ancient sources, this person is assumed by critics to be a fictional figure invented to explain a Median presence in the conquest of Babylon (see Jer 51:11, 28). However, given the experience with the identity of Belshazzar, some caution is in order concerning the identity of Darius, and several reasonable explanations for his identity are available.

The other line of objections—those arising from literary-critical concerns—has led not only to a denial of the book's authorship by Daniel, but also to challenges to its unity. Until the late nineteenth century both conservative and critical scholars accepted the unity of the book. Critical scholars since that time have tended to view literary features of the book as testifying to it being the work of several authors. The trend among critics has been to view Daniel as a compilation of several Daniel sources. The visions are said to be products of the Maccabean era and were combined with the earlier stories by a Maccabean editor, who also added some editorial touches to the earlier material.

This does not mean that there is widespread agreement as to the composition of the stories in Daniel 1—6. According to some critics, they may have originally been oral tales. Some view them as originating with Jews living in the East, while others argue that they are Palestinian in origin. A number of studies seek to find a social or political setting that gave rise to the tales, looking for clues within the tales themselves. While older critics often viewed the stories as Maccabean in origin, later scholars have tended to view the stories as originating earlier, most often in the third century BC. While there is little consensus, therefore, among critical scholars on the origin of the stories in Daniel 1—6, there is widespread agreement that the composition of visions in Daniel 7—12 as well as the final editing of the book took place in Maccabean times.

While it may at first seem that the main threat posed by critical theories about the date and composition of Daniel concerns the inspiration of the Scriptures, the problem runs much deeper than this. The theology presented in Daniel is intimately tied to the historicity of its events and the reliability of its predictive prophecy. These, in turn, are dependent upon a theme that runs throughout Daniel, both in its early chapters relating events in Babylon and its later chapters that relay Daniel's visions: God is in complete control of human events both in the near term and in the more distant future. The book makes clear that God controls all that happens (Dan 1:2; 2:21–22; 4:35): the fall of Jerusalem to Nebuchadnezzar, the Babylonian king's dreams, the events in the fiery furnace, the fall of Babylon to the Persians, and the future events seen by Daniel. If the book is not historically accurate, then this assertion about God's power is false. Daniel would be nothing more than a collection of documents manufactured by human minds in an attempt to grant (false) hope and confidence to its readers. If the Daniel is not reliable, then God may be in control of human events, but Daniel does not prove that.

The reason that Daniel emphasizes God's control of all things is that it serves one of the major theological themes of the book: the Messianic kingdom. If the critics are correct, then Daniel does not speak of the Messiah and the coming of the kingdom of God in Jesus, and the New Testament appropriation of Daniel in this respect is later Christian ideology based on an understanding of the book not intended by the original author(s) or the final editor. Therefore, those Christian messianic understandings that are based on Daniel are built on a false foundation.

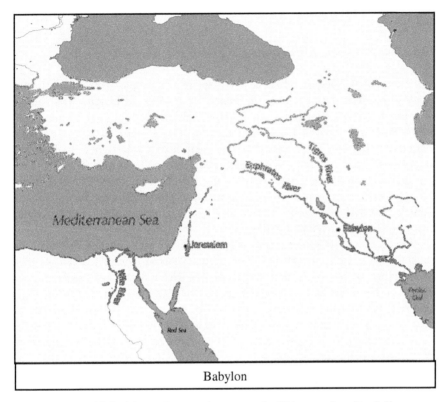

Babylon

Moreover, if God is not in complete control of history, then Daniel's example of maintaining one's faith in the face of persecution and cultural pressure is perhaps quaint and is certainly the result of the strength of the human will against great odds. However, Daniel portrays it as something else—it is the work of God in the lives of his people. Maintaining one's religious integrity through resisting temptations to compromise one's piety and faith would be simply a triumph of the human spirit, if the critics are correct. The critical view relegates God to the sidelines and exalts human capacities and effort, despite the fact that Daniel places human *achievement* far below God's wonderful work of granting his people faith and the integrity to maintain that faith (Dan 2:30).

3. Themes

God as the Protector of His People

Throughout Daniel God is the protector of His people. This has an ironic touch to it, since the beginning of Daniel depicts God as handing His people over to Nebuchadnezzar (Dan 1:1–2). However, this is only an apparent abandonment of the people of Judah. By the end of Daniel 1 it is clear to the reader that God is still with his people. He grants them favor in the sight of their Babylonian overlords (1:9) and gives them intelligence and wisdom (Dan 1:17) so that they can survive and even prosper in a foreign land. Thus, Daniel 1 introduces the two primary means through which God protects His people throughout Daniel: He controls events—present and future—among humans and he grants His people useful gifts and abilities.

God's control of human events is found in every major section in Daniel. In Daniel 2 he controls the events surrounding Nebuchadnezzar's dream so that Daniel alone is able to interpret the dream. The dream itself demonstrates God's control of the future as it prophecies about four kingdoms and God's kingdom. God not only remains in control in Daniel 3, but by rescuing the three young men from the fiery furnace, he demonstrates to Nebuchadnezzar, that He, not the Babylonian king, is in control. Daniel 4 re-emphasizes this to Nebuchadnezzar as the king is humbled because of his arrogance. God revealed this to the king through a dream before it happened, and then he brought it about, leading even Nebuchadnezzar to acknowledge God's power and greatness. The continued arrogance of Babylonian rulers in Daniel 5 provides another occasion to demonstrate God's control of all events as he first pronounces judgment on Belshazzar through the mysterious handwriting on the wall and then sees that this judgment is carried out through the conquest of Babylon by the Persians. The Persians are not exempt from being under the Almighty's control, as is made plain by the rescue of Daniel from the lions' den (Dan 6).

Of course, Daniel's visions (Dan 7—12), all of which prophesy about future events, clearly demonstrate that God will never lose control of human events. Instead, He will always bring about those things He wishes.

This control of events by God is not intended merely to demonstrate God's omnipotence. It is primarily designed to comfort God's people. He is in control of all human history *for their benefit*. While this benefit may be seen in the short term (Daniel rescued from the lions' den or the young men from the fiery furnace), it often is not immediately evident (as in the capture of Jerusalem by Nebuchadnezzar or the prophesied persecution under Antiochus IV Epiphanes in Daniel 8 and 11). Yet Daniel emphasizes that God always has his people's welfare in mind, so that by his mighty hand, often unseen in the course of human events, "all things work together for good for those who are called according to His purpose" (Rom 8:28).

God also protects his people by granting them gifts and abilities. Daniel can interpret dreams (Dan 2 and 4) and mysteries (Dan 5). Shadrach, Meshach and Abednego are given the gift of steadfast loyalty to God in the face of seemingly certain death (Dan 3), while Daniel is moved to worship God even when forbidden by royal decree (Dan 6). Moreover, Daniel is given visions. Once again, all of these gifts are given to Daniel and the young Judeans for the benefit of God's people. At times the benefit may be immediate (rescue from death—Dan 2, 3 and 6). However, the benefit of these gifts may be less obvious and immediate. Certainly, Daniel's ability to receive visions could be at first a frightening experience (Dan 7:28; 8:27). The prophecy of the future persecution of God's people (Dan 8 and 11) could seem to be no blessing at all. However, both of these yield benefits for God's people as they are encouraged by knowing that their God knew their circumstances before they ever faced them, and that he will "refine them, purify them and make them white" (Dan 11:35). Of course, God's control of events is best demonstrated in his Son, whom Daniel prophecies as the Messiah (Dan 9:25–26), God's greatest gift to his people. Daniel's detailed depiction of the coming of the Messiah into human history confirms that God accomplishes His work for His people in "the fullness of time" (Gal 4:4; Eph 1:10).

The Uselessness of the False Gods and the Power of the True God

Almost every reader of Daniel will see Daniel 3, the account of Shadrach, Meshach and Abednego as a confrontation between worship of idols and trust in the true God. This narrative, more than any other, confirms that gods like the one set up by Nebuchadnezzar are powerless, whereas Israel's God is omnipotent. Yet, this theme is not confined to Daniel 3. Already in Daniel 1 the confrontation between God and the pagan gods serves as a subtext for the narrative. Nebuchadnezzar believes that his gods, especially Marduk, the head of the Babylonian pantheon, have shown their superiority to Israel's God in the conquest of Jerusalem. Therefore, he put the vessels from Jerusalem's Temple in the temple of his god (1:2). However, it is the servants of Israel's God that are shown to be wiser and better than the wise men who claim allegiance to the pagan gods (1:20). This continues in Daniel 2 as Daniel, the servant of "the God of gods and Lord of kings" (2:47) can do what no servant of the Babylonian gods can do: tell Nebuchadnezzar his dream and its interpretation. The God of Israel is superior, since he does indeed dwell with humans, unlike the pagan gods (Dan 2:11). This same superiority is demonstrated in Daniel 4 and 5 as Daniel once again is the only wise man in the Babylonian court who can interpret God's revelations. Even in Daniel 6, God is superior to all gods, since he can rescue from the lions, something the Babylonians in the royal court never suspected that a god could or would do. This is reinforced by Daniel's visions, which reveal the power of the true God to accurately predict even the details of future history several centuries in advance, something no diviner dedicated to the gods of the nations could ever do.

Yet the point of emphasizing God's superiority to the gods of the nations is not simply to motivate readers to worship and trust in the true God because of his omnipotence and omniscience. Instead, it is designed to reveal the graciousness of God. The God who created the universe is also the God who has pity on humans, who understands their sins and weaknesses. He is patient with them, as he was with Nebuchadnezzar, granting him the time and opportunity to repent (Dan 4:27; although Nebuchadnezzar did not avail himself of this opportunity). He is the God who, unlike the pagan gods, is not capricious or fickle. Instead, he keeps his promises (as in the fulfilling of Daniel's prophecies), shows mercy through his Messiah and never abandons his people. He is reliable, and his people rely on him. Daniel portrays the God of Israel as a true God. He is never a false god, either by failing to truly exist (like the idols) or by breaking His promises (which are sacred and unbreakable).

Maintaining the Integrity of One's Faith

The third major theme in Daniel is the ability of God's people to maintain their faith with integrity. Throughout Daniel this ability is implied to be from God himself. Thus, Daniel and his friends are able to resist defiling themselves with the king's food because of God's strength that is in them, and that strength becomes evident even in their appearance (Dan 1:15). Shadrach, Meshach and Abednego are able to resist Nebuchadnezzar's order to worship the idol he erected because God is with them, as becomes evident in the fiery furnace (Dan 3:25). Daniel worships God daily without ceasing even under the threat of death (Dan 6:10), a testimony to the work of God's Spirit in his life.

The visions, also, are intended to offer the strength of God to his people who read and believe the promises of God. He will "refine them, purify them and make them white" (Dan 11:35), so that they can maintain their faith with integrity, even in the face of persecution. He will make them insightful enough to avoid compromising their faith (Dan 11:33, 35; 12:3, 10; also see 1:4, 17; 5:10, 12, 14; 9:20), and will also make them shine like the brightness of the sky (Dan 12:3).

This integrity of faith in the face of persecution is not simply the product of belief in a omnipotent God. Instead, it is the product of faith in a merciful God who will keep His promise to send His Messiah and establish God's kingdom. Daniel and his friends can defy an errant and arrogant Babylonian king because they are servants of the eternal king, the Son of Man (Dan 7:13–14) who establishes his eternal covenant (Dan 9:27) with his people.

4. Overview of the Book

The book of Daniel is unique in form among the books of the Old Testament. It is a work in two languages, Dan 1:1—2:4a and Dan 8:1—12:13 in Hebrew, and 2:4b—7:28 in Aramaic. It contains stories of Daniel and his companions in Babylon (Dan 1:1—6:28) and visions seen by Daniel (Dan 7:1—12:13). In the first part of the book Daniel is referred to in the third person, while in the second part he narrates the visions in the first person. Thus, the book divides into two parts—the stories and the visions—but each part contains both Hebrew and Aramaic. These two parts are organized into two interlocking chiasms.

Both chiasms are bilingual. The first has a Hebrew introduction followed by the chiasm proper in Aramaic. The second has an Aramaic introduction followed by the chiasm in Hebrew. The two chiasms, moreover, are interlocked. The first vision serves both as the end of the first chiasm by virtue of its four kingdom parallel to Nebuchadnezzar's dream and its Aramaic language, and as the introduction to the visions by virtue of its visionary style and its chronological placement in the first year of Belshazzar.

Both introductions contain themes developed later in the book. The first introduction presents the captured vessels of the Jerusalem temple (Dan 1:2) which play a pivotal role in Daniel 5, the wisdom of Daniel (Dan 1:4) which plays a role in Daniel 2, 4, and 5, and Daniel's companions Hananiah (Shadrach), Mishael (Meshach), and Azariah (Abednego) who are the heroes of Daniel 3. The second introduction presents the vision style which dominates the second half of the book; it introduces animal imagery used also in Daniel 8; it is the first section of the book to present an angelic interpreter who explains the revelations to Daniel as is done in all the subsequent visions.

Introduction #1: Prologue 1:1–21	NARRATIVE	*Hebrew*
A. Nebuchadnezzar dreams of four kingdoms and God's kingdom 2:1–49	NARRATIVE	*Aramaic*
B. Nebuchadnezzar sees God's servants rescued 3:1–30	NARRATIVE	*Aramaic*
C. Judgment on Nebuchadnezzar 4:1–37	NARRATIVE	*Aramaic*
C'. Judgment on Belshazzar 5:1–31	NARRATIVE	*Aramaic*
B'. Darius sees Daniel rescued 6:1–28	NARRATIVE	*Aramaic*

A'/Introduction #2: Daniel has a vision of four kingdoms and God's kingdom 7:1–28	VISION	*Aramaic*
D. Details on the post-Babylonian kingdoms 8:1–27	VISION	*Hebrew*
E. Jerusalem restored 9:1–27	VISION	*Hebrew*
D'. More details on the post-Babylonian kingdoms 10:1—12:13	VISION	*Hebrew*

This produces two interlocked chiasms: a Hebrew introduction followed by an Aramaic chiasm interlocked with an Aramaic introduction to a Hebrew chiasm. The Hebrew and Aramaic languages of the sections of Daniel were carefully chosen to serve as a way to unite two different genres in one book. Therefore, the dual languages or genres of the book are a result of its careful composition. Moreover, the interlocking of the two parts of Daniel (narrative and vision) through dual language is also achieved by the overlapping chronology of the two parts, since both the narratives and the visions are arranged in chronological order. However, the visions overlap the narratives in time sequence, since the first and second visions take place chronologically before the fifth narrative.

The last part of the first chiasm (7:1–28) also serves as the first part of the second chiasm. This section of Daniel shares the Aramaic language of the first chiasm, but is a vision instead of a narrative, thereby matching the second chiasm. Thus, it rounds out the first chiasm by repeating the four kingdom theme of Daniel 2:1–49 while simultaneously serving as an introduction to the second chiasm by giving readers their first view of Daniel the seer and his visions. Moreover, since Daniel 7 serves as the hinge connecting the two parts of the book, the author has highlighted it as the pivotal chapter of the entire book. It is Daniel 7 that introduces the Son of Man (Dan 7:13), an important messianic concept that is taken up by Jesus himself in the Gospels (Matt 24:30; 26:64; Mark 13:26; 14:62; Luke 21:27). It is Daniel 7 that first discusses the role of the saints in God's eternal kingdom. Therefore, Daniel 7 is the key to understanding several major themes that run throughout the book: God's control of history, the messianic promise and the protection God affords his people even during the darkest hours of persecution. This means that Daniel, like Scripture as a whole, revolves around Christ, His kingdom and His work for His people.

5. The Messiah in Daniel

Since the structure of Daniel was intended to highlight the central, messianic figure called "the Son of Man," (Dan 7:13–14) it should not be surprising that the book contains several other messianic passages. Each messianic passage is part of a section of the book that contains eschatological revelations, that is, revelations relating to the "last things" (from Greek *eschatos*, "last"). These include Daniel 2, 7, 9 and 10—12. This is not remarkable, since from the view of the Old Testament, the end times begin with the Messiah's arrival. In fact, the Scriptures as a whole depict a divine dividing of human history into two great periods by the use of the phrase *latter/last days*, which implies an earlier *former/first days* (Rom 15:4). The latter or last days commence with the coming of the Messiah and his kingdom (Num 24:14; Isa 2:2 = Mic 4:1; also see Jer 48:47; 49:39; Ezek 38:16; Hos 3:5). The reference to the Messianic era as the latter days is also found in Daniel (Dan 2:28; 10:4). The New Testament clarifies this. Both Peter and the writer to the Hebrews understood that the last days began with the coming of Christ and confirm that they and their hearers or readers were already in the last days (Acts 2:17; Heb 1:2). The Apostles' use of the phrase *last days* to describe conditions that were already present as they wrote is further confirmation of this (2 Tim 3:1; James 5:3; 2 Pet 3:3). Therefore, from Daniel's viewpoint even the first coming of Christ is **eschatological**.

This eschatological view first surfaces in Nebuchadnezzar's dream of a large statue (Dan 2). In this dream the statue, represening four kingdoms, is shattered and crushed by a rock from heaven. This stone was hewn "not by hands," a reference to Christ's divine origins (Dan 2:34, 45). The rock not only crushes the kingdoms, but itself grows into a great kingdom. The picture of the Messiah as bringing an end to earthly kingdoms and establishing God's kingdom is always part of Daniel's portrayal of the coming of the Messiah. Therefore, the New Testament connection between the coming of Christ and the nearness of God's kingdom is a continuation of this theme from the Old Testament, including especially Daniel (Matt 3:2; 4:17; 10:7; 12:28; Mark 1:15; 9:1; Luke 9:27; 10:9, 11; 11:20; 17:21; 21:31).

However, the vision of the Son of Man who appears before the Ancient of Days makes this connection explicit in Daniel. This messianic passage not only depicts the Son of Man as divine, thereby showing forth the two natures—divine and human—in Christ, but it also states that he receives "dominion, honor and a kingdom" Dan 7:3–14).

This picture of the Messiah as king is assumed in Daniel 9, when Gabriel reveals Jerusalem's future to Daniel. Here the Messiah is called "a Leader" who confirms a covenant. In the only reference to Christ's crucifixion and atonement in Daniel, the Messiah will be "cut off and have nothing" (Dan 9:26) in order "to end rebellion, to finish sin, and to atone for iniquity" (Dan 9:24).

Finally, there is an oblique reference to the coming of the Messiah in Daniel's final vision. In Daniel 11:30 it is prophesied that ships will come from Kittim. The combination of *ships* and *Kittim* occurs elsewhere in Scripture only at Numbers 24:24, part of Balaam's messianic prophecy of a star that will arise from Jacob. The implication is that during the time prophesied in Daniel 11:30 (168 BC, during the reign of Antiochus IV Epiphanes), the Messiah's coming was near. In comparison with Balaam's day (1407 BC), the time of Antiochus is near to the time of the Messiah. Daniel, therefore, adds detail to Balaam's prediction and thereby renews the hope of the people of Judah in his day and beyond.

While Daniel has perhaps the clearest depiction of resurrection in the Old Testament (Dan 12:2), there is no explicit connection with the Messiah or mention of his resurrection. This would be left to the revelation of God through Christ himself, who would not only speak of his resurrection but become "the firstfruits of those who sleep" (1 Cor 15:20).

In summary, the depiction of the Messiah in Daniel is that of a king who is both divine and human and who brings his people into the kingdom of God. His death and atonement are mentioned in Daniel 9 and are related to the new covenant that God will make with his people. Thus, Jesus is the focus of Daniel. He is both king and suffering Savior, and his work is for the benefit of God's people, "to bring in everlasting righteousness" for them (Dan 9:25).

Other major themes in Daniel find their greatest fulfillment in the Messiah but are often developed in sections of Daniel where the Messiah is not in direct view. Thus, God is depicted as the great protector of his people, a role ultimately fulfilled in the Messiah. God's superiority to all other gods is emphasized several times in Daniel. This is demonstrated most clearly in Christ and His cross. The emphasis on maintaining the integrity of one's faith is found throughout Daniel. This faith is first and foremost sustained through the messianic promise that Daniel's prophecy renews and reinvigorates.

28

Prophecy After the Exile
Haggai, Zechariah and Malachi

Haggai

When is it the right time to take action? Doing the right thing at the wrong time can lead to as many problems as doing the wrong thing. In Haggai's day the people of Jerusalem who had returned from Babylon to live in their ancestral home land claimed that the time was not right to complete the rebuilding of the Temple. Despite the fact that they had returned and begun the Temple's reconstruction some seventeen years earlier, they claimed, "The time has not yet come for Yahweh's house to be rebuilt" (Hag 1:2). God had another idea, however, and he called Haggai to deliver a message of encouragement and hope that would motivate God's people to rebuild the Temple.

> 1. Authorship and Date—*Who Was Haggai and When Did He Prophesy?*
> 2. Theme—*What Is Haggai About?*
> 3. Overview of the Book—*The Contents of Haggai*

1. Authorship and Date

We know little about Haggai apart from his name and the brief references to him in Ezra (Ezra 5:1; 6:14). His ministry to the Jews who had returned from Babylon to live in Jerusalem lasted less than five months in the second year of the Persian king Darius (520 BC). Unlike previous prophets, Haggai carefully dated all of his messages and the events that he recorded:

Prophecy	Hebrew Date	Modern Date
Hag 1:1 Haggai's 1st message	1 Elul	August 29, 520 BC
Hag 1:15 Work on Temple resumed	24 Elul	September 21, 520 BC
Hag 2:1 Haggai's 2nd message	21 Tishri	October 17, 520 BC
Hag 2:10 Haggai's 3rd message	24 Kislev	Dec 18, 520 BC
Hag 2:20 Haggai's 4th message	24 Kislev	Dec 18, 520 BC

Haggai's brief ministry overlapped the beginning of Zechariah's much longer ministry. Both prophets are mentioned in Ezra, and their ministry predated Ezra's activities in Jerusalem by some sixty years.

2. Theme

Haggai's message concerns the rebuilding of the Temple in Jerusalem. When the Judean exiles in Babylon first returned to Jerusalem by permission of Cyrus the great they had begun reconstructing the Temple (Ezra 3; 537 BC), and work continued for seven years until it was stopped by order of Persian officials (Ezra 4:24). Ten years had passed without any further work on the Temple. Though Jerusalem's inhabitants had been inactive during this decade, God had not. He had arranged for the times to change so that it was now time to resume the work on the Temple.

Haggai's message was directed to Jerusalem and its leaders, the governor Zerubbabel and the high priest Joshua. In August of 520 BC Haggai spoke his first message. The people were saying that the time was not right to finish the Temple (Hag 1:2). Yet, the prophet noted that the people had built fine houses for themselves while neglecting God's house. Since they had neglected God's house, Haggai revealed that God had withdrawn his blessing from them. Their harvests were slight, because God had sent drought (Hag 1:5–6; 9–11). God came through the words of the prophet to encourage the people to finish the Temple (Hag 1:7–8).

In contrast to Judah and its leaders before the exile, the people of Jerusalem, led by Zerubbabel and Joshua, listened and obeyed the words of God's prophet. Haggai encouraged them, telling them that God said "I am with you" (Hag 1:13). So less than one month later, the work of the Temple began again.

Haggai's ministry did not end there, however. As the work progressed God sent him with words of encouragement. The small community in Jerusalem would never have the resources that Solomon had when he built the first Temple. The oldest among the inhabitants in Jerusalem could remember the magnificence of that Temple, and there was a danger that the people would be discouraged as they worked on the new Temple, since it could never match the grandeur of Solomon's work. Haggai's third prophecy not only promised that God was with the people of Jerusalem as they worked on the Temple (Hag 2:4), but it also would be a more glorious Temple than the one built by Solomon. Its glory would not be found in the beautiful craftsmanship of its decorations or the gold that once overlaid everything in the first Temple. The glory of this Temple would be that:

> I will shake all nations, so that the desired things of all nations will come, and I will fill this house with glory, says Yahweh of armies. (Hag 2:7)

The nations would come to worship Yahweh. This, of course, is in keeping with what earlier prophets had prophesied about the consequences of the coming of the Messiah. When the Messianic era came, not only Israel, but also all the nations would stream to the house of God (e.g., Mic 4:1; Isa 2:2). This house would have glory because God would grant peace in this place (Hag 2:9)—the peace of the Gospel of forgiveness in Christ Jesus (John 14:27; 16:33; Rom 5:1; Gal 6:16; Eph 2:14–17). Indeed, when Jesus first came to the Temple the prophet Simeon confirmed that God had begun to fulfill Haggai's prophecy not only by bringing light to the nations, but also by bringing the glory of Israel to the Temple (Luke 2:27–32).

Haggai's third prophecy begins with a question for the priests by the prophet about holy and defiled offerings (Hag 2:10–13). God uses their answer to demonstrate that until now the people's offerings had been defiled and worthless (Hag 2:14–19), but now as a result of their obedience God would reverse that and bless them (Hag 2:19).

The prophet's fourth and final message from God is directed at the governor Zerubbabel and records God's promise of a special blessing for him since God had chosen him (Hag 2:20–23).

3. Overview of the Book

Haggai is the second-shortest book in the Old Testament. Its two chapters are most easily viewed as four messages from the prophet.

I. Haggai's first message: It is time to rebuild the Temple (1:1–15)
   A. God has withdrawn his blessing (1:1–11)
   B. The people respond and obey (1:12–15)
II. Haggai's second message: The glory of this Temple will be great (2:1–9)
III. Haggai's third message: God blesses and purifies his defiled people (2:10–19)
IV. Haggai's fourth message: Blessing for Zerubbabel (2:20–23)

Zechariah

Being the first to do something is often seen as an accomplishment that outshines all others who do the same thing later. Haggai was the first prophet to call on the people of Jerusalem to rebuild the Temple. Zechariah was second. However, this does not make Zechariah's prophecy less important, nor is it to be understood as merely derivative of Haggai's work. Instead, Zechariah's prophecy is outstanding in its own right. Among the Minor Prophets he stands out as the one with the most Messianic references and is surpassed in this among the prophets only by Isaiah.

> 1. Authorship and Date—*Who Was Zechariah and When Did He Prophesy?*
> 2. Theme—*What Is Zechariah About?*
> 3. Overview of the Book—*The Contents of Zechariah*

1. Authorship and Date

Zechariah was one of the exiles who returned to Judah under the leadership of Zerubbabel. He was a priest, and he apparently returned to Jerusalem with his father Berekiah and his grandfather Iddo (Zech 1:1). Later, under the high priesthood of Joiakim when his grandfather Iddo died, Zechariah took his place as the head of his clan of priests (Neh 12:10–16). This may imply that Zechariah's father had already died.

Zechariah was a contemporary of Haggai, but his prophetic ministry lasted much longer. Like Haggai, Zechariah dates many of his prophecies, although he did not include dates for the late half of his book (Zech 9—14). From these dates we can see that the beginning of Zechariah's ministry overlapped that of Haggai:

Prophecy	Hebrew Date	Modern Date
Zech 1:1 Preaching (1:1–6)	Bul 520	October/November 520
Zech 1:7 Night visions (1:7—6:15)	24 Shebat 519	February 15, 519
Zech 7:1 Preaching repentance (7:1—8:23)	4 Kislev 518	December 7, 518

From this information we can see that Zechariah's ministry spanned at least two years. However, many scholars believe that it lasted much longer and date Zechariah 9—14 to sometime after 480 BC.

Because Zechariah 9—14 is somewhat different in style and message than Zechariah 1—8, many critical scholars have doubted whether Zechariah wrote this portion of his book. However, if Zechariah 9—14 are part of a prophecy of Zechariah that he preached some forty years later, the difference in style and content is understandable, since the prophet would have been addressing different circumstances in Jerusalem. Therefore, there is no reason to doubt that Zechariah wrote the entire book that bears his name.

2. Theme

Zechariah is about encouragement. He uses several types of prophetic proclamation to lift the spirits of the people of Jerusalem: preaching, description of visions that God gave him, dialog between the people and the prophet and prophetic oracles.

Zechariah begins his prophecy with a call to repentance. He notes that God was angry with the ancestors of the people in Jerusalem (Zech 1:2). He urges the people not to be like their ancestors, but to repent and turn to God (Zech 1:3). The ancestors did not repent when the prophets spoke to them, but the word of God overtook them even though they ignored it (Zech 1:4–6). Only then did some from Judah repent. In this opening address, Zechariah invites Jerusalem to trust in God's promise "Return to me, and I will return to you" (Zech 1:3).

Immediately after this Zechariah reports that he had seen eight symbolic visions on February 15, 519 BC. These eight visions are encouragement to rebuild the Temple in Jerusalem. They cover four basic perspectives on God's work to make the rebuilding possible and are arranged in a **chiasm**:

Universal: The world is at peace so that God can bless Jerusalem (Zech 1:7–17; 6:1–8)

International: God has subdued the nations and removed Judah's sin (Zech 1:18–21; 5:5–11)

Jerusalem and Judah: God has again chosen Judah and Jerusalem, blessed them, and purified them (Zech 2:1–13; 5:1–4)

Temple: God has purified Joshua the high priest and strengthened Zerubbabel the governor to rebuild the Temple so that Joshua can be a symbol of one who is to come: the Branch [i.e., the Messiah, Zech 3:8; see Isa 4:2; Jer 23:5; 33:15] (Zech 3:1–10; 4:1–14)

Following these visions is an additional vision in which the prophet is instructed to make a crown for the high priest Joshua and encourage him to rebuild the Temple, since God promises to be with him (Zech 6:9–15). This encouragement is encapsulated in the words used when the crown is placed on Joshua:

> And say to him [Joshua], "Thus says Yahweh of Armies, 'Behold, the man whose name is the Branch: He will branch out from his place, and he will build the Temple of Yahweh. It is he who will build the Temple of Yahweh and will bear royal honor, and will sit and rule on his throne. And there will be a priest on his throne, and the counsel of peace shall be between them both.'" (Zech 6:12–13)

Joshua the high priest is pictured as a forerunner of the true builder of God's Temple (1 Pet 2:4–6), the Messiah himself—the Branch. He will be a ruler and a priest (see Heb 4:14—10:39). Therefore, Joshua was encouraged to build the Temple from where the Messiah's work would branch out.

Additional encouragement follows in Zechariah 7—8 as the people come to Zechariah with a question about an annual fast they had been observing as they mourned the destruction of Jerusalem and its Temple at the hands of the Babylonians. Should they continue to mourn? (Zech 7:1–3) The prophet tells them that since they were mourning for themselves, and not for God, they should stop mourning (Zech 7:4–7). The people of Judah brought the destruction upon themselves and were mourning over their misery, not over their offense against God. But now God has promised blessing for Jerusalem, and the fasts will become feasts:

> Thus says Yahweh of Armies: "The fast of the fourth month and the fast of the fifth and the fast of the seventh and the fast of the tenth month will be seasons of joy and gladness and cheerful feasts for the house of Judah. Therefore love truth and peace." (Zech 8:19)

Moreover, like Haggai, Zechariah's prophecy promises that the rebuilt Temple will see the coming of the messianic age with the nations streaming to Jerusalem:

> Thus says Yahweh of Armies: Peoples will yet come, even the inhabitants of many cities. The inhabitants of one city will go to another, saying, 'Let us go at once to plead for the favor of the Yahweh and to seek Yahweh of Armies. I myself am going.' Many peoples and strong nations will come to seek Yahweh of Armies in Jerusalem and to plead for the favor of Yahweh. (Zech 8:20-22; see Hag 2:1–9)

Thus, Zechariah's message reinforced Haggai's message and encouraged the people as they worked to rebuild the Temple in Jerusalem (Ezra 5:1; 6:14).

Zechariah's further encouragement for the people of Jerusalem came in the form of two oracles: Zechariah 9—11 and 12—14. Both of these oracles envision the coming of the Messiah. The first speaks of his coming (Zech 9:9–10,

14, see Matt 21:5; John 12:15) but his rejection by God's people (Zech 11:4–13; see Matt 26:15; 27:3, 9). The second tells of the Messiah's arrival and reception by those who repent (13:8–9). In this oracle the Messiah is depicted as God who is pierced by the inhabitants of Jerusalem (12:10–14; see John 19:37) as well as the shepherd who is struck with the result that his sheep are scattered (13:7; see Matt 26:31; Mark 14:27).

These two oracles, probably delivered thirty or more years after Zechariah's first messages, were intended as additional encouragement once the Temple had been completed. The prophet sought to lift the vision of the Jews in Jerusalem to the messianic future that God had promised, to encourage them to look beyond their present troubles to the glorious future that was coming when the Messiah arrived. Therefore, from beginning to end Zechariah's encouragement always involves the promise of the Savior, the confidence that in the Messiah God would establish an everlasting kingdom for his people.

3. Overview of the Book

Zechariah's book divides easily into two main parts: his early ministry encouraging the rebuilding of the Temple and his later ministry encouraging faithfulness once the Temple had been rebuilt.

Part One: Encouragement to Rebuild the Temple
 I.   Superscription (1:1)
 II. A call for repentance (1:2–6)
 III. Eight visions and a vision for Joshua (1:7—6:15)
   A. Horseman among myrtle trees (1:7–17)
   B. Four horns and four craftsmen (1:18–21)
   C. A man with a measuring line (2:1–13)
   D. Clean robes for Joshua (3:1–10)
   E. A gold lampstand and two olive trees (4:1–14)
   F. A flying scroll (5:1–4)
   G. A woman in a basket (5:5–11)
   H. Four chariots (6:1–8)
   I. A crown for Joshua (6:9–15)
 IV. A question on fasting leads to a promise about Jerusalem's glorious future (7:1—8:23)
Part 2: Encouragement after the Temple has been completed
   V. An oracle: The Messiah's coming and his rejection by the people (9:1—11:17)
   VI. An oracle: The Messiah's coming and his reception by those who repent (10:1—14:21)

Malachi

It is always nice to have the last word about something, to place an ending and definitive pronouncement on a subject. Malachi is not only the last book of the Old Testament in Christian Bibles, but he was also the last of the prophets that God inspired to write a book of the Old Testament. His name means "my messenger," and he depicts the final message of God before the coming of the Messiah, the ultimate messenger of God's covenant (Mal 3:1).

1. Authorship and Date—*Who Was Malachi and When Did He Prophesy?*
2. Theme—*What Is Malachi About?*
3. Overview of the Book—*The Contents of Malachi*
4. The Messiah in Malachi—*The Messenger of the Covenant*

1. Authorship and Date

The book claims to be "the word of Yahweh to Israel through Malachi." Since the name Malachi means *my messenger* some scholars have considered this name to be a title, since both priests and prophets could be called God's messengers (Hag 1:13; Mal 2:7). Some would even identify Malachi as Zechariah (compared Mal 3:7 and Zech 1:3). The matter remains unresolved, however, and it is just as likely that Malachi was the author's name.

Unlike Haggai or Zechariah, Malachi does not date his prophecies. However, the sins that Malachi denounced are very similar to those denounced in the book of Nehemiah. This has led many scholars to date Malachi to sometime during Nehemiah's terms as governor, perhaps about 430 BC during Nehemiah's second term as governor.

2. Theme

Malachi reassures the people of Israel that God continued to love them. Although Haggai and Zechariah had given great promises to the people of Jerusalem a generation or two earlier, the people had once again become discouraged and neglectful of their duties in worship. The prophesies of a great and glorious Jerusalem and God's coming to his Temple had not yet been realized, so the people became discouraged and began to view their obligations to God as simple acts to be done without having enthusiasm for following the Law of Moses.

Malachi begins his prophecy by reassuring the people that God loved them even though they questioned his love (Mal 1:2). He told them to compare his love for Jacob to his hatred of Esau. Esau's descendants, the Edomites, were an example of God's hatred, and the prophet foretold their demise (Mal 1:4–5; see Isa 34:5–15; Jer 49:7–22; Ezek 24:12–14; 35:1–15; Obadiah). In contrast to this, God loved the people of Jerusalem and Judah.

However, the people of Jerusalem were not honoring God. Both the people and the priests were guilty. The priests allowed people to bring blemished sacrifices to God and failed to teach God's Law to the people (1:6—2:9). The people began to intermarry with foreigners who worshipped pagan gods and had not honored the marriage vows they had taken. Instead, they divorced their wives, a practice that God hated. They also became cynical about God's justice, since they perceived evil people to be prospering (Mal 2:10–17). In rebuking Israel for its sin, Malachi was demonstrating God's love for Israel. Yahweh corrects those he loves (Prov 3:11–12), just as a father corrects a son he loves (Prov 13:24) or a neighbor corrects his fellow Israelite out of love (Lev 19:17–18).

God had a solution for all of Israel's sin. He was going to send messengers:

"Behold, I will send my messenger and he will prepare the way before me. Then the Lord whom you seek will suddenly come to his Temple. The messenger of the covenant in whom you delight, behold, he is coming," says Yahweh of Armies. (Mal 3:1)

First, God would send a messenger to prepare his way—John the Baptist (Matt 11:10; Mark 1:2; Luke 7:27; see Isa 40:3). Then God himself, the messenger of the covenant, would come (see Isa 42:6). With God's coming would also come the day of the Lord (Mal 3:2) when God would refine his people (Mal 3:3–4) and punish all evildoers (Mal 3:5).

The solution to being discouraged was the same solution offered by Haggai and Zechariah—to look to the Messiah, the messenger of the covenant. Instead of wallowing in problems of the present, Malachi urged Jerusalem to trust in God's loving promise. Those who did not do this would be punished on the day of the messenger's coming, but those who repented and were purified by God would offer acceptable sacrifices to him.

However, the people of Israel were not offering acceptable sacrifices. They were robbing God by not bringing the tithes and offerings demanded in the Law of Moses (Mal 3:6–15). But, like Zechariah before him, Malachi offered God's promise, "Return to me, and I will return to you" (Mal 3:7; see Zech 1:3).

Then those who "feared Yahweh" repented because of Malachi's preaching and made a pledge in writing to honor God (Mal 3:16). For this reason God promised that they would be spared from his punishment and that in the judgment they would see the difference between the righteous and the wicked (Mal 3:17).

Finally, Malachi reassured those who had become cynical about God's justice that the day of the Lord was coming and that the wicked would be judged while the righteous would be delivered. They would escape the condemnation of the wicked:

> But for you who fear my name, the sun of righteousness shall rise with healing in its wings. You will go out leaping like calves from the stall. (Mal 4:2)

Therefore, instead of neglecting the Law of Moses, the people should remember it and live by it (Mal 4:4). Finally, Malachi promised that another messenger like him will come to prepare Israel for the Messiah:

> Behold, I will send you the prophet Elijah before the great and awesome day of Yahweh comes. He will turn the hearts of fathers to their children and the hearts of children to their fathers. Otherwise, I will come and strike the land with a decree of total destruction." (Mal 4:5–6; see Matt 11:14; 17:11–12; Mark 9:12–13; Luke 1:17)

3. Overview of the Book

Malachi's four short chapters are organized around the theme of God's love for Israel.

I.   Superscription (1:1)
II. God loves Jacob but hates Esau (1:2–5)
III. God's love: He rebukes Israel's unfaithfulness (1:6—2:17)
IV. God's love: He will send his messengers before the day of the Lord (3:1—4:6)
    A. The messenger to prepare the way of Yahweh and the messenger of the covenant (3:1–5)
    B. Rebuke for robbing God (3:6–15)
    C. Response of those who feared the Lord (3:16–18)
    D. The day of the Lord (4:1–6)

4. The Messiah in Malachi

Although Malachi begins with God's love for Israel as shown in the contrast between Jacob and Esau, the prophet's ultimate demonstration of God's love is in his prophecies of the Messiah. These primarily revolve around the prophet's name, Malachi—my messenger. Malachi is God's messenger of hope (Mal 1:1). The priests were to be God's messenger (Mal 2:7). God would send a future messenger to prepare for the coming of the Messiah, who would be God's messenger with the spirit and power of Elijah (Mal 3:1; 4:5–6). Thus, when John the Baptist appeared in the wilderness of Judea preaching repentance, God signaled that the Messiah and his kingdom, the kingdom of God, was near (Matt 3:2; Mark 1:15).

However, the greatest messenger was to be the Messiah himself, the messenger of the covenant (Mal 3:1; see Jer 31:31–34; Matt 26:28; Mark 14:24; Luke 22:20; 1 Cor 11:25; Heb 9:15; 12:24). This messenger is the Lord, the Messiah that Israel desired, in whom the kingdom of God has come near (Matt 4:17; 10:7). His message not only is proclaimed, but has the power to accomplish its own message—to purify:

> But who can endure the day of his coming? Who can stand when he appears? For he is like a refiner's fire and like fullers' soap. He will sit as a refiner and purifier of silver, and he will purify the sons of Levi and refine them like gold and silver, and they will bring offerings in righteousness to Yahweh. Then the offering of Judah and Jerusalem will be pleasing to Yahweh as in the days of old and as in former years. (Mal 3:2–4)

This messenger is superior to all other messengers of God that came before him because his message brings forgiveness and life in the new covenant. That is why Malachi also depicts the Messiah as "the sun of righteousness...with healing in its wings" (Mal 4:2).

Preparing the Way for the New Testament

Unlike Jewish Bibles, Christian Bibles place Malachi as the last of the Old Testament books. Part of this arrangement may be that it is only logical that the Minor Prophets follow the Major Prophets and that as the last of the prophets Malachi is last among the Minor Prophets. However, there is no inherent reason why the prophetic books should follow the Poetic and Wisdom books instead of the reverse.

In fact, the arrangement of the prophets at the end of the Old Testament and Malachi at the end of the prophets betrays a conscious decision to tie the Old Testament to the New Testament and especially to the Gospels. As we have seen, the prophets' message in almost every case includes the messianic promise. In many of the prophetic books the Messiah is the central or at least a major concern of the prophecy that God revealed to the prophet. Thus, in Christian Bibles the Old Testament prophecies about the Messiah lead naturally into the Gospels' depiction of Jesus as the Messiah. This is especially true of Malachi. Malachi ends with a prophecy of John the Baptist, the Elijah who is to come (Mal 4:4–6), the messenger who prepares the way for the Lord (Mal 3:1). The reader who continues into the New Testament finds that early in Matthew and Mark one encounters John the Baptist, the fulfillment of Malachi's (and Isaiah's) prophecy (Matt 3:1; Mark 1:2–4).

Therefore, the arrangement of the books of the Old Testament in Christian Bibles is itself a testimony to the ancient faith of the Christian church: Jesus is the Messiah prophesied by Moses and all the prophets (Luke 24:27). The prophetic books from Isaiah to Malachi prepare the way for the New Testament and its witness to Jesus as Savior, Lord and Messiah.

Section 6
Beyond the Old Testament

29

Between the Testaments

Usually if one walks out of a concert hall at the beginning of an intermission, there is little concern about missing something. While the orchestra rests, the people engage in jovial chatter. The interlude seems unimportant. Parts one and two of the beautiful concert are the main events, after all. Let us relate this to reading the Bible. When one has read the Old Testament, one has observed the wonder of creation, the fall into sin, God's patient mercy to Israel during the Exodus and conquest, and the unpredictable age of the kings and prophets. The content of the entire Old Testament centers around the coming Messiah. That is part one. Now one might be tempted to skip the four hundred year interlude (432–435 BC) and proceed immediately to part two, the New Testament. Unlike a concert intermission, this interlude is important for continuity with the Old Testament. In these four centuries many historical events occur, which provide vital background for the New Testament: the Diaspora, Ptolemaic and Seleucid occupations, Maccabean Revolt, and Roman occupation. Religious groups lacking in the Old Testament such as Pharisees, Sadducees, and Zealots suddenly appear in the New Testament. How and when did all this happen? An overview of the Intertestamental period can provide the answers.

Christians would assert that Judaism began to exist during this Intertestamental Period, since the term "Judaism" most properly refers to the legalistic movement which deviated from the Old Testament faith and then rejected Jesus. Therefore, many Christians prefer to call the Old Testament people "Israelites" rather than Jews. This title emphasizes the covenant name given to God's people, the covenant which has its fulfillment in Christ. Paul's letters to the Romans (Rom 9:6–9, 11:26) and Galatians (Gal 3:26–29, 6:16) concur by referring to the early Christians as the new Israel or Abraham's true offspring. Although Judaism was not a monolithic movement during the time of Jesus, the Pharisees and the subsequent rabbinic movement significantly represent Judaism as it opposed Christ and the Messianic hope of the Old Testament.

1. The Late Persian Period

The Old Testament ends with the benevolent Persian Empire in power instead of the brutal Babylonian Empire, which destroyed Jerusalem and exiled many Israelites. Cyrus the Great, first king of Persia, significantly impacted Israelite history when he allowed the exiles to return to Judea and rebuild the Temple in 538 BC (Ezra 1:1–4). Subsequent Persian kings in Biblical times also showed favor to Israel. Darius I (522–486 BC) confirmed the order of Cyrus when challenged and ordered his officials to help the Israelites (Ezra 6:1–12). Xerxes I (486–465) is the king who married Esther and played a role in foiling an attempt to exterminate God's people (esp. Esther 4—9). Artaxerxes I (465–424) had Israelite representation in his court with Ezra and Nehemiah, whom he allowed to return to Judea and assist with the restoration of the nation (Ezra 7—8, Neh 2). The Old Testament biblical record comes to a close during the latter reign of Artaxerxes I.

After the reign of Artaxerxes I, the Persian Empire did not thrive as in previous years. Particularly with Artaxerxes II (404–358), the decline of the entire empire became obvious with successful revolts against Persia. The Libyan Amyrtaus expelled the Persian troops from Egypt and became an independent ruler. Artaxerxes II had to abandon his attempt to reconquer Egypt (401 BC) when his brother, Cyrus, tried to overtake the throne. Although Cyrus died fighting at Cunaxa (400 BC) and lost this battle, his Greek mercenaries showed amazing success against the Persians. Artaxerxes III (358–338 BC) continued to deal with increasing instability through the revolt of Syria and an unsuccessful attempt to retake Egypt (350 BC). Although Darius III (338–330) had initial success in Greece and Egypt, his empire succumbed to Alexander the Great in several battles. The Persian Empire officially ended with the assassination of Darius III.

During the latter Persian Empire, Judea held the status of an independent province under Persia. Jews lived in many other provinces of the empire as well. Little historical data exists about this era in Judea. The Jewish historian Josephus, however, does report an event concerning the high priesthood in Jerusalem, the leading political and religious office. The high priest Johanan murdered his brother who plotted against him. In response Bagoas, the governor of Judea, imposed sanctions on the Jews.

Much more information about Judaism in this era comes from the Elephantine Papyri, discovered in 1903. Elephantine, an island on the Nile River in Egypt, was inhabited by a garrison of Jewish mercenaries stationed there by Persia. These Jews left numerous letters and business documents in the Aramaic language. The documents tell how the Jews enjoyed self-government, carried out professions, practiced a syncretistic Jewish religion, and even built their own temple. Rioters destroyed this temple in 410 BC, whereupon the Jewish soldiers unsuccessfully requested the help of the high priest Johanan. Finally, in 402 BC the Persian provincial governor in Egypt made reconstruction of the temple possible.

2. The Rise of Hellenism

The Coming of Alexander

Alexander the Great was the son of Philip of Macedon, a ruler who brought significant unity to the historically disparate Greek states. Alexander capitalized upon the groundwork of his father. An admirer of Greek culture and student of Aristotle, Alexander led a unified host of 35,000 Greek troops in 334 BC with a view of attacking Persian strongholds but did not stop until he conquered much of the civilized world. He first engaged and defeated Darius III of Persia at the Granicus River in Asia Minor, thereby liberating the Lydians. He continued to take the cities of southern Asia Minor in 334–333 BC. In October of 333 came the great battle at Issus in which Alexander conquered a much larger Persian army and forced Darius III to retreat. Alexander then approached the cities on the eastern Mediterranean coast. Although some voluntarily surrendered, Tyre did not. Its fall to Alexander in 332 BC, which ended the Phoenician Empire, was prophesied by Ezekiel (Ezek 26:4, 5, 12–14).

After conquering Gaza (prophesied by Zech 9:5), Alexander proceeded to Jerusalem in 332 BC. Josephus tells a rather fanciful story of how Alexander paid homage to the high priest and Yahweh. When the high priest showed Alexander how the book of Daniel spoke of him, Alexander became a friend of the

Jews. Although some aspects of the account may be unhistorical, it does accurately demonstrate Alexander's favor to the Jews throughout his reign. For example, when he founded the city of Alexandria, he granted them their own section of the city and allowed them free practice of their religion. Additionally, he did not compel Jewish men to join the military and, thus, be forced to fight on the Sabbath.

After Jerusalem, Alexander invaded Egypt and founded the great intellectual city of Alexandria in 331 BC. He continued his decimation of the Persian Empire when he defeated Darius III at the battle of Gaugamela in Mesopotamia, although Darius' army vastly outnumbered Alexander's. After Alexander liberated Babylonian and Median cities, Darius III was murdered in 330 BC, which ended the Persian Empire. His conquests proceeded even as far as India in 327 BC. With such overwhelming conquests and treasures, Alexander's wearied troops convinced him to return westward. During his years of conquest he attempted to unify his empire by leaving troops in conquered areas to intermarry with local women and by spreading Greek culture and language wherever he went. This phenomenon of spreading Greek culture and language is called **Hellenization**. Alexander returned to Mesopotamia in 324 BC. There he attempted to join East and West by marrying Eastern noble women. Macedonians, however, did not approve of Alexander's polygamy. They also disapproved when he called himself a god and when he killed his own nephew. In the midst of further plans of conquest, however, Alexander at the age of thirty-three died in 323 BC of a fever. He was interred at Alexandria. At such a young age and just in thirteen years of efforts Alexander had conquered more lands than any predecessor.

The Diadochi

The term *Diadochi* is a Greek word which means *successors*. With the death of Alexander the Great in 323 BC, rivalry arose between his assistants regarding succession to Alexander's vast empire. The initial major figures were Antipater, Perdiccas, Eumenes, Craterus, Antigonus I, Ptolemy I, Seleucus I, and Lysimachus. Between 323–315 BC the number of Diadochi decreased, mainly by virtue of attrition from war with each other. The first divisive issue was regency rights over the remaining blood relatives of Alexander, namely, his mentally handicapped brother Philip and his infant son by an Eastern noblewoman, Roxana. Because of this issue and others, four major wars occurred among the rivals as power was consolidated among them. The First War of the Diadochi occurred in 322–320 BC, while the Second War raged in 319–315 BC. By 315 BC the major players were Antigonus, Cassander (son of Antipater), Ptolemy I, Lysimachus, and Seleucus I. The Third War took place in 314–311 BC and the Fourth War in 308–301 BC. Additionally, there was subsequent struggle over Macedon (298–285 BC) as well as war between Lysimachus and Seleucus (285–281 BC). Finally, after nearly fifty years of battles, a shaky settlement was reached among those left. The Ptolemies retained Egypt and Palestine. The Seleucids held Asia Minor, Syria, and eastern portions of Alexander's empire. Macedonia and Greece belonged to the house of Antigonus. This division of Alexander's vast territory continued under the descendents of these houses for a century.

Ptolemaic Dominance of Palestine

From Alexander's death in 323 BC to 319 BC, Palestine changed hands five times between the Ptolemies and Seleucids. Finally, from 319–198 BC Palestine remained under the control of the benevolent Ptolamaic kings of Egypt. During this period, the Jews experienced little interference from Egypt, although skirmishes between Ptolemies and Seleucids took place on their soil. The major concern of the Ptolemies was to receive taxes from peoples under their control. They chose not to enforce Greek culture and religion as the later Seleucids, even though some in Palestine voluntarily embraced Hellenization. With the tribute paid, the Jews could retain their religious and cultural traditions and rule their own internal matters. The high priest continued to have the primary political and religious office as under the Persians. Josephus tells about the struggle between the house of Onias and the pro-Egyptian house of Tobias. When the high priest Onias II refused to render tribute to Ptolemy III (246–221 BC), the situation was resolved by appointing the rival Joseph son of Tobiah as the tax collector for all Palestine in 242 BC. This rivalry of houses previews the larger battle between those for and against Hellenization. Additional information from about 200 BC concerns the existence of the *Gerousia* or council of elders, which held political power with the high priest at its head. At this time the high priest Simon the Just, a Seleucid supporter, gained the right of taxation from the Tobiads. He received oversight to repair the Temple and Jerusalem.

The reign of Ptolemy II Philadelphus (238–246 BC) is significant for Judaism of this period. The *Zenon Papyri*, administrative documents from an Egyptian finance official, enlighten the situation in Palestine during his reign. Garrisons were stationed in Palestine to deal with Seleucid incursions. Accordingly, the Ptolemies established Greek cities in Palestine in which the soldiers settled in the land and intermarried with local women. As in the time of Alexander, such measures spread Hellenization. Palestine also became a trade partner with Egypt, including the export of fruits, meats, cheese, grain, and spices. Additionally, Ptolemy II Philadelphus is noteworthy in Jewish history in his quest for learning and literature. While stocking the great Alexandrian library, he became a benefactor in the production of the **Septuagint**, the Greek translation of the

Hebrew Old Testament, as reported by the *Letter of Aristeas*. Although some parts of the letter are fanciful, the document likely communicates a core of accurate data regarding Ptolemy II and his role with the Jews and Septuagint. This became the first major translation of the ancient world and the Bible of Hellenistic Judaism and the early Christian church. A Greek translation for Judaism of this age became especially important, since Jews inhabited many countries of the civilized world, especially Egypt. As a result, they lost their ability in Hebrew and Aramaic but knew the universal language of Greek.

Seleucid Dominance of Palestine

Antiochus III came to power in the Seleucid Empire in 223 BC. After several unsuccessful attempts to conquer the strategic area of Palestine, his opportunity finally came at the death of Ptolemy IV in 203 BC. The new Egyptian ruler, Ptolemy V (203–181 BC), experienced increasing instability in his empire. Therefore, Antiochus III began his attacks in 202 BC and finally acquired possession of Palestine in 198 BC. The inhabitants of Jerusalem gave the new victor a cordial welcome. Antiochus III graciously granted the Jews the privileges received under the Persians and Ptolemies. They could practice their religion and customs as they wished and manage their own internal affairs. Additionally, Antiochus built new cities and encouraged the Jews to settle there.

Unfortunately, Antiochus III disastrously decided to make war against the Romans. As a result of the final battle at Smyrna in 190 BC, Antiochus lost much of Asia Minor and was required to pay enormous sums of tribute to Rome. To acquire this money, Antiochus began to raid the temples in his territory, places known to house much wealth. His looting included the Jerusalem Temple. Antiochus was killed in the process of raiding another temple in 187 BC. Antiochus' successor, Seleucus IV (187–175 BC), continued to deal with this heavy debt. He tried to rob the Jerusalem Temple but was dissuaded by the great opposition of the Jews.

The Seleucid ruler who most negatively impacted the Jews was Antiochus IV Epiphanes (175–163 BC). He avidly wanted to unify his empire through Hellenization. Although the staunchly traditional high priest Onias III opposed Hellenism, many others gladly welcomed this cosmopolitan movement. Therefore, the Jewish Hellenizers arranged through bribery to Antiochus IV to have Onias' brother Jason take over as high priest in 175 BC. Jason promoted the moderate political and commercial Hellenization of Jerusalem, including a gymnasium (a Greek academy) with nude exercise. Jews were encouraged to adopt of Greek personal names. Since Jason was apparently not Hellenistic enough in the eyes of some, a radical Tobiad Hellenistic group arranged through greater bribery to have Menelaus, not from a priestly line, replace Jason in 171 BC. His radical

Hellenization and illegitimate priesthood enraged the more conservative Jews. When Jason tried to retake the priesthood by force, Antiochus IV invaded and slaughtered many innocent people. Since he viewed Judaism as a hindrance to unification and a source of insurrection, he forbade the practice of Judaism in 168/167 BC. Under penalty of death, Jews could not observe customs such as the Sabbath, circumcision, or dietary laws. Normal sacrifices could not take place in the Temple. Instead, pigs were sacrificed there to desecrate the building. More desecration took place by dedicating the temple to a foreign god and introducing sacred prostitution.

Hellenization as a Cultural and Intellectual Movement

Hellenization was a movement from the time of Alexander the Great in which various ethnic groups adopted Greek culture, including language, ornate architecture, dress, religion, education, thought, and more. First, it was indeed a cultural movement. All these aspects of Greek culture were no longer limited to ethnic Greeks but now accessible to anyone who joined this movement. Additionally, while the Greek city-states formerly embodied Greek culture, now foreign cities and even entire monarchies could be Hellenistic. As it swept through various countries, Hellenization did not remain static. Although primarily Greek, Hellenization became a synthesis of the local culture as well, particularly including a mixture of Eastern traits. Newly founded Hellenistic cities were a primary means for spreading this movement. The new cities experienced a stream of immigration because of exemption from certain taxes and duties, wealth from commerce, increased opportunities for participation in government, and life in the cosmopolitan Greek ethos. An amalgamation of religions occurred in which official Hellenistic city cults incorporated Eastern influences as well. Beginning with Alexander the Great, Hellenistic rulers used Hellenism as a means to unify their territory. Numerous lands gladly embraced this cultural movement, since many Eastern cultures were experiencing stagnation. Thus, an international identity and commonality arose like never before.

Second, Hellenization was indeed an intellectual movement. Hellenistic intellectual centers arose at Alexandria, Pergamum, and Antioch. The great Alexandrian library became legendary. Greek philosophical disputation gained prominence, particularly through Stoic and Epicurean philosophers. Intellectuals of this era studied and preserved the literary and artistic treasures of ancient Greece and passed them on to Rome, which continued the trend. Production of literature and art flourished with an emphasis on the Greek virtue of beauty. Greek thought was characterized by humanism, which viewed mankind as the center of the universe and touted the abilities of the mind. Of course, a highly-prized aspect of Hellenization was education, a commodity increasingly available in cities. Thereby, people learned the Greek language and embraced this intellectual heritage.

3. The Maccabean Revolt and Hasmonean Rule

The Maccabean Revolt

Particularly the books of I & II Maccabees recount this Jewish revolt against superior Seleucid forces in Palestine. In 168/167 BC a Seleucid delegation in the town of Modin came to a public meeting place, set up a pagan altar, and insisted that local Jewish residents make a sacrifice to the god Zeus. The elderly Mattathias of priestly descent viewed an apostate Jew obeying the order to sacrifice. In anger, Mattathias slew that Jew as well a Seleucid official at the scene. Mattathias and his five sons (John, Simon, Judas, Eleazar, and Jonathan) destroyed the altar and sought refuge in the hills. Other Jews joined this family and waged guerrilla warfare against the forces of Antiochus, emphasizing surprise attacks against small groups of Seleucid soldiers in nearby villages.

When Mattathias died in 167 BC, his son Judas the Maccabee ably took over the revolt. After numerous victories by the rebels, Antiochus began to realize the magnitude of this insurrection. Therefore, he sent a large military contingent under the command of General Lysias to destroy Judas and his followers at the battle of Emmaus. However, Judas' army surprised them by night, slaughtered many Seleucid forces, and took huge sums of booty. This victory opened Maccabean passage to Jerusalem. In 165/164 BC Judas and his men cleansed and rededicated the Jerusalem Temple, thus inaugurating the festival of Hanukah. When Lysias returned to siege Jerusalem, a peace treaty resulted. Most approved of this treaty, including the religious group known as the Hasidim (very possibly the early Pharisees). Judas, however, would not accept these terms and left Jerusalem with a small band of followers. When the new high priest Alcimus turned against the Hasidim, many Jews again joined with Judas and renewed the civil war. However, with weakened numbers and Alcimus acquiring Seleucid aid, Judas did not have his previous military strength. He died in battle in 160 BC.

Judas' brother Jonathan ably assumed the leadership role (160–142 BC), followed by Simon (142–134 BC) With many successes over the Syrian Seleucids, Jonathan was able to retake Jerusalem from the pro-Hellenistic party. In a struggle for succession of the Seleucid throne, Jonathan became high priest as well as political ruler in 153 BC, a combination which became contentious for conservative Jews. Because of the weakened Seleucid condition, Jonathan acquired increasingly more territory. He also made a treaty with Rome. Unfortunately, on a mission of friendship to Syria, he was assassinated by the Seleucid general Trypho in 143 BC. Simon, the last living son of Mattathias, took over in 142 BC. Overall, Simon was able to unite the three main parties: Hellenists, Hasidim, and Maccabees. The Hasidim, however, recognized the priestly line of Onias, thus disputing Simon's offices of ruler and priest. Simon additionally acquired full independence from Syria in 142 BC and was able to bring peace and security. Rome declared a treaty with Simon and warned neighboring countries against attacking the Jews. Simon was murdered by a relative in an attempted coup in 134 BC. This marked the end of the original group of rebels.

Later Hasmonean Rulers

The successive rulers experienced many years of political prosperity but slowly strayed from the solid religious foundations of the original rebels. The dynasty is labeled **Hasmonean** in honor of a Maccabean ancestor. John Hyrcanus, son of Simon, took over thereafter (134–104 BC). Although he lost some coastal territory early in his rule, he was able to reconquer it and in addition acquired Transjordan territory, Idumea and Samaria. Thus, his domain approximated that of Solomon. During his reign the parties of the Pharisees, Sadducees, and Essenes are first definitively mentioned. John Hrycanus particularly encountered tensions with the Pharisees, who emphasized religion whereas John Hyrcanus paid greater honor to political matters. Later in life he found himself resonating more so with the Sadducees before he died in 104 BC. Aristobulus I (104–103 BC) succeeded his father, John Hyrcanus. Although in power for only a year, he caused much havoc. While he conquered the additional territories of Iturea and Galilee, he showed much ruthlessness, especially in killing multiple members of his family. Aristobulus, first to call himself "king," also leaned toward Hellenism and promoted Greek culture in his domain.

The height of cruelty, tensions, and separation from original Maccabean underpinnings occurred with Alexander Jannaeus (103–76 B.C). Indeed, he increased Hasmonean territory even more. However, once again a Hellenizer with the offices of priest and king, he enraged the Pharisees. When they revolted against him and invited Seleucid aid, he killed 6000 of his enemies. On another occasion he had 800 Pharisees crucified and their families killed in front of them. On his deathbed, he supposedly encouraged his wife, the future queen Alexandra Salome, to make peace with the Pharisees and show them favor instead of the Sadducees. Alexandra (76–67 BC) indeed favored peace much more than her husband and overall was admired by the people. She did show favor to the Pharisees, whereas the Sadducees decreased in power. The Pharisees, however, used this power in retribution to have some Sadducees put to death. Under Alexandra and leading Pharisees, Jewish ceremonies were restored, Temple upkeep was funded by a tax, and education of children became compulsory. Her son

Hyrcanus II assumed the high priesthood and received the favor of the Pharisees. Her other son Aristobulus II was an able military leader, favored by the Sadducees. Although so many things improved under Alexandra Salome, these differing sons and parties would prove detrimental in the future.

The Decline of the Hasmoneans and the Coming of Rome

The succession dispute between Hyrcanus II and Aristobulus II eventually led to Roman interference and occupation. The process began when Alexandra Salome died and appointed Hyrcanus II to succeed her in 67 BC. Aided by the Sadducees, Aristobulus revolted and removed Hyrcanus II from office. Moved by Antipater, the Idumean governor and father of Herod the Great, Hyrcanus II struck back and imprisoned Aristobulus II. To avoid civil war both brothers appealed to Rome to mediate. Pompey was the ruling Roman official in the region. His representing general Scaurus accepted the greater bribe of Aristobulus II, who then governed from 67–63 BC. In 63 BC Pompey appointed Hyrcanus II in his place. Aristobulus II refused this decision and fled to Jerusalem, which Pompey then sieged. When Pompey conquered the city he killed thousands of Jews and took Aristobulus to Rome in humiliation. Hyrcanus II became a mere figurehead ruler and high priest. This essentially ended the Hasmonean dynasty and commenced Roman rule in Palestine. Since Rome preferred to govern through a loyal local ruler, Antipater received the office of governor of Judea in 63 BC. He ruled under Roman authority until his assassination in 43 BC. The Roman leader Antony appointed the two sons of Antipater, Herod and Phasael, as successors. When Phasael died after the Parthian invasion of Jerusalem, Herod the Great became the sole ruler of Judea by authority of the Roman Senate in 40 BC. At this time much upheaval was occurring in Roman politics. The Roman Republic came to an end, while the Roman Empire was arising under Octavian (later Caesar Augustus). With the battle of Actium against Antony and Cleopatra in 31 BC. Octavian now ruled. For Herod it was beneficial that Octavian confirmed his appointment as governor of Judea. Thus, the rulers were now in place for the birth of Jesus, both Herod as well as Caesar Augustus.

4. Internal Developments in Palestinian Judaism

Jewish Thought

Ben Sira

Ben Sira is one of several titles for an Intertestamental wisdom book written in Hebrew by Jesus ben Sira between 200–175 BC. The book has also been called, "The Wisdom of Jesus Ben Sira," "The Wisdom of Ben Sira," "Sirach," or "Ecclesiasticus." The author was a learned scholar, well versed in the Old Testament, particularly the wisdom books, and very dedicated to Mosaic Law, the priesthood, and the Temple. He traveled much, even in dangerous circumstances. The book most closely resembles Proverbs, although unlike Proverbs Ben Sira is the work of one author. It consists mainly of topically organized maxims of moral advice in situations such as: family relations, behavior of the rich, praise of wisdom, appropriate treatment of the poor, hypocrisy, duty to society and state, duty to God, the glory days of olden times, education, worship, politeness and so forth. Many of these maxims emphasize secular, mundane matters of practical living, asserting care for the poor as the height of religion. Ben Sira equates wisdom with the fear of God as well as the Law of Moses. Although Ben Sira does speak of a Messiah, he denies that the Messiah will come from the house of David because subsequent kings have polluted the Davidic line. Ben Sira does not mention a resurrection of the dead, immortality of the soul, or the Pentateuch's dietary laws (noted often in Judith and Tobit).

Matters of canonicity are pertinent with Ben Sira. First, Judaism and Christianity differ regarding the status of the book; even within Christianity differences exist. Judaism did not include it among the list of canonical Old Testament books, in part because at times it reflects Hellenistic society. Yet, Judaism highly respected the book, as demonstrated by allusions to it in *Tobit, Enoch*, the Midrashim, and the *Talmud*, for example. Christianity embraced the book more so than Judaism. Early works such as the *Didache* and the *Epistle of Barnabus* cite it. Clement of Alexandria, Origen, and Cyprian quote it like Scripture. Roman Catholicism and Greek Orthodoxy accept it as canonical, although the remainder of Christianity does not. Second, the prologue of the Greek translation of Ben Sira touches upon canonicity. The grandson of Jesus ben Sira completed this translation into Greek sometime after 132 BC. He includes a prologue to his translation, in which he tells about himself and his grandfather. The prologue is particularly important, since it mentions what some scholars believe is the threefold division of the Old Testament canon: Law, Prophets, Hagiographa (other books). This would imply a fixation of the canon by this point in time. Additionally, Ben Sira's imitation particularly of Job and Proverbs also contribute to this evidence. Only the Greek and Syriac translations of Ben Sira were known until 1896, when Hebrew manuscripts were discovered in Egypt. Additional Hebrew texts were discovered at the fortress of Masada and among the Qumran texts as well.

Apocalyptic Thought

The English noun *apocalypse* and the adjective *apocalyptic* are derived from the Greek and denote a revealing, uncovering, or disclosure. The term usually describes a body of Jewish or Christian literature which shares certain characteristics. These common characteristics include a first person narrative in which the speaker is privy to the revelation of matters beyond human experience. Such matters might include the levels of heaven, the future of Israel, the story of creation, and the demise of oppressors. The revelation comes in a vision or a dream with an angel as an intermediary. The angel guides, interprets, and explains for the recipient. Apocalyptic literature typically concerns the future and often emphasizes the end of the present age. It also presents this revelation in powerful imagery beyond human experience, including much symbolism. Such imagery and symbolism might include powerful beasts which resemble humans, seven heavens, the Messiah and the Messianic kingdom, fantastic horns, heads, watchers, great supernatural battles, and symbolic numbers.

Apocalyptic literature exists in the Bible as well as outside the Bible. Examples in the Old Testament include portions of Isaiah, Ezekiel, Daniel, Joel and Zechariah, while Revelation is the sole representative in the New Testament. Prominent extra-biblical Jewish examples include Enoch, Baruch, the Testament of the Twelve Patriarchs, 4 Ezra, the Assumption of Moses, the Sibylline Oracles, Jubilees, and the Life of Adam and Eve. Biblical apocalyptic literature correctly distinguishes Law and Gospel and emphasizes the gracious covenant of the Old and New Testaments, which is fulfilled in Christ. While some extra-biblical apocalyptic literature does concern the Messiah, the Messianic age and nature of salvation tends to be more nationalistic. It lacks the divine favor in the forgiveness of sins won on the cross. Much extra-biblical literature can be described as fantastic speculation on a biblically-related theme.

Apocalyptic literature often originated from a historical setting of oppression and difficulty. When all seems hopeless the author wishes to grant assurance in cosmic terms that God indeed will conquer evil, set things straight, and rescue His people. Thus, apocalyptic thought emphasized comfort to the hopeless. The fantastic and powerful imagery illustrated that God will bear all his mighty power upon the enemies of God's people. The indistinct imagery may also have the purpose of avoiding reprisals from any oppressor who might read the literature. Extra-biblical authors often wrote under the name of a biblical figure to gain greater acceptance for their message. Indeed, this type of literature played an important role in its time. Today when one becomes familiar with the historical background of an apocalyptic work and understands the nature of this literary genre, one can see the comfort and encouragement which it brought to its recipients.

Jewish Institutions and Life (Synagogue, Diaspora, Temple, Ritual Baths)

The word *synagogue*, originating from the Greek language, means a congregation of people as well as the building in which Jews of this era gathered for religious meetings. This institution of the synagogue likely arose during the Babylonian Exile. Before the exile, the Temple in Jerusalem served as the center of religious life for all Israelites, especially the sacrifices. Separated from the designated place for sacrifices, they were in a quandary. However, they still could be active in reading and studying Scripture, explaining Hebrew Scripture in their new language, discussion, and public prayer. With these needs, the synagogue arose. Also, it became a place for the instructing children, judging cases, and lodging for visitors. A gathering of ten families could organize a synagogue in a given community. Any Israelite, even a minor, could conduct the public reading of Scripture. The head of a synagogue held an important office, being responsible for matters of the synagogue building. In summary, as Jews were dispersed to Babylon and other countries, the synagogue became the institution for practicing their religion and preserving their heritage.

The term **Diaspora** refers to the dispersion of Jews into countries other than Palestine. This may have occurred through force, such as in the Babylonian Exile, or through some voluntary relocation for political or economic advantage. Regardless of the reason, Jews inhabited many countries in the Intertestamental Period and beyond. A demonstration of this fact occurs in the Pentecost account of Acts (Acts 2:5–12), where Luke tells of multiple Jews from various lands on a pilgrimage visit to Jerusalem. Wherever they settled, Jews faced a dilemma of identity in the new culture. Both the new language and temptations by forces such as Hellenization encouraged syncretism. Therefore, the synagogue indeed played a vital role. Important Jewish communities existed in Egypt in particular. The city of Alexandria contained a large Jewish sector in this period. As mentioned above, Ptolemy II Philadelphus (238–246 BC) respected Jews and their teachings so highly that he supported the translation of the Septuagint. Additionally in Egypt, the papyri from Elephantine also speak of a significant Jewish military population.

When the Babylonians conquered Judea in 587 B.C, they also destroyed the Jerusalem Temple (2 Kgs 25). After the exiles from Babylon returned to Judea, Zerubbabel oversaw the construction of the Second Temple, beginning in 536 BC and completed in 516 (Ezra 1—6). Thus, in addition to the title *Intertestamental Period*, this era also has the designation *Second Temple Period*. This second building was marked by moments of tragedy, such as its desecration by Antiochus IV in 167 BC. Moments of joy also characterized it, such as the reconsecration at Hanukah in 164 BC. Significant renovation and enlargement of the Temple complex took place under Herod the Great, beginning 20/19 BC.

The project was so enormous and elaborate that segments of it continued even after his death in 4 BC. The sacrifices and additional rites of the Temple remained vital in the Jewish religious life of this era. However, influence over the Temple often became a political tool, both with the Hasmonean rulers, their successors placed by the Romans, as well as the Pharisees and Sadducees. The ultimate demise of this beautiful Temple occurred in AD 70 when Romans destroyed it in the midst of a Jewish revolt.

Ritual baths were significant in the Old Testament as well as Intertestamental times. Such bathing emphasized purification from uncleanness. While this practice is not an equivalent to Christian baptism, it does provide a foreshadowing of the sacrament in Christ for the forgiveness of sins. Some examples of this requirement in the Old Testament include: a leper just healed of his leprosy (Lev 14:8–9); someone who comes in contact with an unclean person or articles touched by that person (Lev 15:5–10); the high priest on the Day of Atonement as well as his assistants (Lev 16:24–28); the person who came into contact with a corpse (Num 19:19), women after a menstrual cycle (2 Sam 11:2–4), or one about to approach God (Exod 19:10, 1 Sam 16:5, 2 Chr 29:5). The practice of ritual bath continues into the Intertestamental period as indicated by sources such as the *Sibylline Oracles* (*Sib. Or.* 3:591–593) and *Judith* (Jdt 12:7). Also, the Septuagint translators bathed before translating, according to the *Letter of Aristeas* (*Let. Ar.* 305). Such bathing frequently occurred in the Essene community at Qumran. Rabbinic interpretation prescribes the bath as immersion in a natural fountain or stream or in a *mikveh,* a large basin which holds about 120 gallons of water. Numerous examples of these have been located in archaeological digs throughout Palestine and countries of the Jewish Diaspora.

Jewish Sects

Sadducees

The origin of the title **Sadducee** may come from the Hebrew word for *righteous*. It may also be derived from the name *Zadok*, the priestly line which supplanted Abiathar from the time of Solomon (1 Kgs 1:8–53; 2:26–27). The Sadducees arose during the Hasmonean period (166–63 BC) and wielded significant power, although their numbers were fewer than the Pharisees. They were typically wealthy, aristocratic priests, and moderate Hellenizers. Their outlook often emphasized politics and culture more than religion, thus strongly disagreeing with the Pharisees in most areas, except in their joint opposition to Jesus (e.g., Matt 16:1, 6, 12; 22:23–45; 26:57–67). The Sadducees rejected the oral tradition of the Pharisees and only recognized the written Scripture, specifically the Pentateuch. They rejected the resurrection of the body, future retribution, the existence of angels, demons, and a spiritual world. The Sadducees emphasized Levitical purity and free will as opposed to fate or divine determination. Although they enjoyed great dominance during much of the Hasmonean period, their influence waned under Alexandra Salome (76–67 BC). However, with Aristobulus II (67–63 BC), they again became powerful and dominated the priesthood and temple until its destruction.

Pharisees

The word **Pharisee** means *separated ones*, possibly referring to their separation from influences like Hellenization which corrupt the Law. This group also arose during the Hasmonean period, perhaps to be associated with Hasidim of the Maccabbean Revolt. An early citation about them occurs in the reign of John Hyrcanus (134–104 BC), where a Pharisee opposed his possession of both the political rule and high priesthood. Their influence varied among the Hasmoneans, at times even being persecuted by them. However, they obtained greatest power during the reign of Alexandra Salome (76–67 BC). Whereas the Sadducees' domain was in the Temple, the Pharisees emphasized the synagogue. Whereas the Sadducees mainly consisted of aristocratic wealth and appealed to such a populace, the Pharisees arose from the middle class and appealed to the common people. Their outlook was more religious, specifically ethical, and less political than the Sadducees. They accepted the entire Old Testament as canonical and added the oral traditions as well. Namely, the Pharisees and subsequent rabbis claimed that Moses received both a written and oral revelation from God at Sinai. The oral tradition, which supposedly elaborates upon the written, was not written down but transmitted verbally by memory throughout the centuries. The Pharisees upheld both free will and divine determination, angels, demons, and a spiritual world. They accepted a resurrection, immortality of the soul, and retribution or reward after death. The Synoptic Gospels (Matthew, Mark and Luke) mention the Pharisees frequently. Particularly in Matthew 23 Jesus denounces them as legalistic hypocrites.

Essenes and Others

The Jewish authors Josephus and Philo provide the bulk of information regarding the **Essenes**. Pliny and Dio Chrysostom mention them briefly as well. Most scholars assume that the Essenes described by these sources are the same group whose Dead Sea Scrolls and settlement at Qumran were discovered in 1947 and became likely the greatest archaeological discovery of the twentieth century. Although the title *Dead Sea Scrolls* can refer to a larger corpus of literature, including Bar Kochba texts, the title most commonly designates the great discoveries at the caves of Qumran. This group of monastic, ascetic, and celibate men lived in a remote part of the Judean desert near the Dead Sea, although possibly some contingents of this sect resided in nearby towns and lived family life. This sect arose during the Hasmonean period between 165–155 BC, likely in opposition to the Hasmoneans, and inhabited their settlement until AD 70. Archaeological evidence from coins (numismatic evidence) indicates that the complex flourished from 135 BC through AD 68. Their settlement is distinct from the caves where the wealth of manuscripts was located. Apparently, when Roman destruction appeared inevitable in the great Jewish revolt of AD 66–70, they hid the manuscripts in high caves several kilometers from their settlement. They resorted to this desert haven for the practice of pure Judaism, since they considered other Jews corrupt in their doctrine and practice. The Essenes followed a very stringent observance of the Law, had strict punishment for community lawbreakers, required a long and involved process of initiation, practiced ritual baths regularly, held property in common, emphasized the study of Scripture, regarded themselves as the only true Israel, and interpreted the fulfillment of Scripture occurring only in and for their community.

Another group of this time was the **Zealots**, possibly thus named as zealous successors of the Maccabees who bravely fought for their faith. As such, they sought a violent solution to foreign interference. Josephus claims that they arose in AD 6 when Judas the Galilean revolted against Rome. They refused to pay taxes and considered loyalty to Caesar a sin, since God is the only king. Interestingly, one of Jesus' disciples is called Simon the Zealot (Matt 10:4). Perhaps the Pharisee Gamaliel considered Peter and his associates to be Zealots when he compared them to Judas the Galilean and company (Acts 5:34–39). During the Jewish revolt of AD 66–70, the Zealots played an active role. They made their last stand at Herod's Masada fortress in AD 70, where they eventually committed suicide instead of falling into the hands of the Romans.

The Dead Sea Scrolls and Their Importance

Biblical Scrolls

The discovery of the Dead Sea Scrolls in 1947 brought a treasure trove of ancient manuscripts to light. This is particularly true regarding the Biblical manuscripts uncovered, some dating before Christ. The texts include portions of every Old Testament book except Esther. The complete Isaiah Scroll is the most impressive among the texts and most publicized among the pictures of Biblical texts from the Dead Sea Scrolls. The Biblical manuscripts are vastly important, since they are centuries older than any other Hebrew Old Testament texts in existence. Before the Qumran texts, the oldest complete Hebrew Old Testament, the Aleppo Codex, hailed from the tenth century AD. Otherwise, partial fragments from the Geniza (text storage room) of the Old Cairo synagogue came from the sixth through eighth centuries AD. The concern existed that with such late Hebrew texts as our source for the Bible, perhaps the text had become significantly corrupted over the centuries. Upon comparison with the Biblical manuscripts of the Dead Sea Scrolls, the exactness was amazing. The copyists of the Hebrew text had paid great attention to slavish accuracy in that centuries-long gap.

The Qumran commentaries or *Pesharim* on Old Testament books are valuable as well. In these works, the Essenes would cite the Biblical text and then provide an interpretation. The discoveries included partial commentaries from the books of Nahum, Habakkuk, Micah, Isaiah, Zephaniah, Hosea, and the Psalms, the Habakkuk commentary being the most complete. Their interpretation of the Biblical text betrays a unique *pesher* approach. Namely, the commentaries emphasize the eschatological age with fulfillment of Scripture only in and for the Qumran community. They declare a day of reckoning for all evil-doers, especially those who oppose the views of the Qumran sectarians. Finally, the *Genesis Apocryphon* might also loosely fit into this category of commentary. It contains an imaginative, expanded account of Genesis.

Extra-Biblical Texts

Although apocryphal books are also among the discoveries at Qumran, the unique sectarian documents have received more attention. Below are some of the most familiar texts. Two works called *Damascus Document* and the *Rule of the Community* recount the origin of the sect, the detailed manner of initiation into the sect, and their rules of living. The group originated during a time of confusion after which a messianic figure called the Teacher of Righteousness established the community to practice true Judaism in the desert haven. They encountered difficulty, however, through a figure called the Wicked Priest. The documents describe the highly regimented stages of initiation with testing by leaders of the group to determine one's fitness for membership. The final step involved contributing one's property for common possession. The entire initiation process took at least two years. The rules of their regimented life become particularly apparent with annual evaluations at which the leaders assess one's progress. Habitual disregard for rules resulted in expulsion. *The Scroll of the War of the Sons of Light against the Sons of Darkness* tells of an eschatological war where the Qumran members, called the Sons of Light, and the angels battle the forces of evil. Besides the Sons of Darkness, another name for the enemy is the *Kittim*, likely a reference to the Romans. *The Temple Scroll* details the ideal Temple in Jerusalem and the ideal practice of Judaism therein. *The Thanksgiving Psalms* are original hymns for the worship life of the sect, written with a very similar vocabulary and style to Old Testament psalms.

5. Important Sources on Intertestamental Judaism

Philo

Philo Judaeus (20 BC–AD 50), a contemporary of Jesus and Paul, is one of the most influential Jewish writers and thinkers of the ancient world. He grew up in Alexandria and spent most of his life in this intellectual center of the world. Hailing from a wealthy and prominent family, he had significant political connections. For example, one of his nephews was married to of King Agrippa's daughter. Another nephew was Tiberius Julius Alexander, procurator of Judea. Philo himself held a place of honor in the Jewish community of Alexandria. In AD 38/39 Philo was sent to represent the Alexandrian Jews before the emperor Caligula regarding riots against the Jews. He details these riots in his work *Against Flaccus* and his delegation to the emperor in *On the Embassy to Gaius*. Although this meeting with Caligula proved unsuccessful, Philo did return to Rome a second time in AD 50 for the sake of his people.

Politics, however, consumed relatively little of his time and energy in comparison to his passion to meld the Old Testament and Judaism with Greek Platonic philosophy. This syncretism comprises most of his writings and made him especially noteworthy in Jewish and early Christian thought. A thorough education prepared him for this task, having attained much background in Judaism as well as Hellenistic areas such as grammar, philosophy, and rhetoric. A driving force behind this melding of two worlds was the desire to make Judaism palatable to Hellenists, since the material and anthropomorphic aspects of the Old Testament would be offensive to them. He used the tool called **allegory** to reinterpret the Bible in this fashion. Allegory involves a non-literal, highly symbolic reinterpretation of the text to make it say whatever the interpreter wishes. The allegorical method was not new. For example, Stoic philosophers employed it to make the works of Homer more acceptable to the contemporary intellectual world. However, Philo did not ignore the literal words of the Old Testament either. He asserted the value of both the literal and allegorical, the historical and philosophical. Both the literal and symbolic are appropriate levels of understanding the text, according to Philo. For example, in his work *Life of Moses*, he presents Moses as an archetypal lawgiver and virtuous hero in a Hellenistic fashion. In *On the Decalogue* he recasts the law and Jewish practice in philosophical fashion. In *Allegorical Interpretation* Philo asserts that the first seventeen chapters of Genesis actually concern Greek philosophical issues. With the works *On the Eternality of the World* and *On Providence* he provides philosophical treatises, apart from a pure exposition of the Biblical text. Early Christian church fathers appreciated Philo, because they also employed allegorical method and because of their mutual emphasis of the "logos," the word and wisdom of the deity. Philo finds in this concept a meeting point for the God of the Old Testament and the Greek view of a supreme being. Christian Church fathers emphasized the "logos," since the Gospel of John refers to Jesus with this term (John 1:1–14).

Josephus

Flavius Josephus (AD 37/38–100), a younger contemporary of the apostles and Philo, has provided voluminous and invaluable historical resources for the two thousand years previous to his death. Hailing from a priestly family, his parents had him study to become a priest. In his studies, Josephus received an excellent education in both Judaism and Hellenistic culture. He became acquainted with the various Jewish groups (Pharisees, Sadducees, Essenes) by attending their meetings and eventually became a Pharisee at age nineteen. Josephus traveled to Rome in AD 64 to plead for the release of certain priests accused of agitation against the Romans. As he succeeded in this mission, he became particularly impressed with Roman culture and convinced of Rome's power. When Josephus returned to Palestine, the Jews had become even more militant against Roman rule until war broke out in AD 66. Although personally viewing the war as a futile endeavor, Josephus was made commander of the Jewish forces in Gailiee and governor of the same region. When Josephus and his troops fled from the Romans in AD 67, Josephus surrendered to them. After his surrender, Josephus acted as an intermediary between the Romans and Jews during this great revolt, a role which naturally invited the label of traitor among many Jews as well as suspicion from the Romans whenever the Jews won a battle. During this time, he became friendly with the Roman general Vespasian, who later became emperor. Vespasian brought him along to Rome and granted him Roman citizenship, a residence, a regular stipend, and land in Judea. The same emperor also engaged Josephus to write about the Roman victory over the Jews. He spent much of his thirty years in Rome, writing historical works about various time periods. In his works, he was obligated to present the Romans in a positive light. But he also wished to defend the Jews and Judaism. It should also be noted that Josephus heavily leaned upon quotations from other sources to write his books. Relatively speaking, he did not compose much original material.

The Writings of Josephus

The Jewish War: Written especially to place the Romans in a favorable light, this book mainly recounts the Jewish revolt against Rome from AD 66–70 but also presents previous conflicts and events in Palestine as far back as 175 BC. Josephus had exceptionally vivid information available to him for this work, since he served as Galilean commander and since he had access to the Romans. He indeed avoids offending the Romans in this work. Yet, he also minimizes the Jewish role in the revolt by blaming the events on a limited number of rebels. He mollifies his own role in the war as well. Additionally, he wishes to convince Jews to accept Roman domination, since they thankfully grant freedom of religious expression.

Jewish Antiquities: Since the Romans grant legitimacy to a people group based on its established antiquity, Josephus wishes to show the long, rich history of Judaism since ancient times. Therefore, he records Jewish history from creation to the Jewish revolt, emphasizing their great cultural and military achievements. He uses the books of Genesis to Daniel for the period of Biblical history and various sources beyond that.

The Treatise Against Apion: In this work Josephus uses refined literary and rhetorical skill to refute accusations against Judaism by Apion and other first century critics. As part of the defense he presents Mosaic Law as the archetype of ethics.

The Life of Josephus: In this autobiographical work Josephus answers the attacks of the historian Justus and others concerning his conduct in the Jewish revolt.

CPSIA information can be obtained
at www.ICGtesting.com
Printed in the USA
LVHW012048310821
696580LV00013B/1192

9 781498 229081